DATE DUE

SAMUEL ADAMS

SAMUEL ADAMS

The Life of an
American Revolutionary

JOHN K. ALEXANDER

ROWMAN & LITTLEFIELD PUBLISHERS, INC.
Lanham • Boulder • New York • Toronto • Plymouth, UK

Published by Rowman & Littlefield Publishers, Inc.
A wholly owned subsidary of The Rowman & Littlefield Publishing Group, Inc.
4501 Forbes Boulevard, Suite 200, Lanham, Maryland 20706
http://www.rowmanlittlefield.com

Estover Road, Plymouth PL6 7PY, United Kingdom

Distributed by the National Book Network

British Library Cataloguing in Publication Information Available

Library of Congress Cataloging-in-Publication Data

The hardback edition of this book was previously cataloged by the Library of
Congress as follows:

Alexander, John K.
  Samuel Adams : the life of an American revolutionary / John K. Alexander.
    p. cm.
  Includes bibliographical references and index.
  1. Adams, Samuel, 1722–1803. 2. Politicians—United States—Biography.
3. United States. Declaration of Independence—Signers—Biography. 4. United
States—History—Revolution, 1775–1783—Biography. 5. United States—
Politics and government—1775–1783. I. Title.
  E302.6.A2A543 2011
  973.3092—dc22
  [B]   2010045582

ISBN: 978-0-7425-7033-7 (cloth : alk. paper)
ISBN: 978-0-7425-7034-4 (pbk. : alk. paper)
ISBN: 978-0-7425-7035-1 (electronic)

♾™ The paper used in this publication meets the minimum requirements of
American National Standard for Information Sciences—Permanence of Paper
for Printed Library Materials, ANSI/NISO Z39.48-1992.

Printed in the United States of America

For my favorite historian,
June Granatir Alexander

CONTENTS

PREFACE

Samuel Adams was a titan of America's greatest generation—the generation that achieved independence and crafted written constitutions that made the ideal of republican government a living reality in the new nation. Samuel's contemporaries, both friend and foe, understood his importance. In the fall of 1770, Stephen Sayre, an American born in New York but living in England, famously called Samuel Adams "the Father of America." In July 1773, George Clymer, a future signer of the Declaration of Independence, met Adams in Boston. Upon returning home to Philadelphia, Clymer, having been awed by Adams's "integrity and abilities," gushed that "all good Americans should erect a statue to him in their hearts." Time and again as the colonists moved ever closer to the break with Great Britain, advocates of defending American rights singled out Samuel Adams for the influence he exerted. In 1780, James Warren, a fellow Massachusetts revolutionary, even extolled Samuel as "the Man who had the greatest hand in the greatest Revolution in the world."[1]

George III's supporters ruefully agreed that Samuel Adams played a pivotal role in the coming of the American War for Independence, only they usually voiced it with hatred, malice, and loathing. When the prominent Massachusetts loyalist Peter Oliver penned a lengthy description of Adams as a vile rebel, the opening lines set the tone. Oliver expressed agreement with a painter who said that, if he wanted to draw a picture of the devil, he would have Samuel Adams sit for the portrait. In the late spring of 1774, an anonymous advocate of England produced a list of evil men supposedly leading the people of Massachusetts to their ruin; Adams's name headed the list. In January 1775, the London *Gazetteer* published a letter from Boston whose author called Adams "the planner of all the measures of the rebels." In July, the London *Morning Post* offered its readers an extract of a letter from Rhode Island. Belittling Adams as "having nothing to lose" and hoping to gain "every thing," the author styled him "a man properly calculated to become a consequential leader in times of anarchy."[2]

Given his fame, or infamy, it is hardly surprising that, upon meeting Samuel Adams in December 1780, a French general casually observed that "everybody in Europe knows that he was one of the prime movers of the present revolution." As important as Adams was in the coming of the revolution, it would be a mistake to focus narrowly on the years through 1776. As Samuel himself emphasized, the American Revolution involved much more than proclaiming independence and forcing Great Britain to acknowledge it. As he steadfastly asserted and worked diligently to ensure, the British had to yield the territory and rights to natural resources necessary for the new nation to prosper. For its part, the revolutionary generation had to craft governments and strive to mold societies that would make independence worth having. Samuel Adams had an important hand in those endeavors. He helped shape the influential Massachusetts constitution of 1780, and, although he was not one of the framers or even an ardent proponent of the United States Constitution of 1787, he played a central role in its adoption. Then, in the 1790s, especially as the governor of Massachusetts, he took an active part in the contentious struggle over interpreting and implementing the new national constitution. In addition, from the start of the American War for Independence onward, Adams also devoted considerable thought and effort to creating what he termed a virtuous society.

Samuel's cousin and fellow revolutionary John Adams knew of his cousin's expansive and pivotal role in the revolutionary era when he proclaimed that "without the true character of Samuel Adams, the true history of the American Revolution can never be written." James Sullivan, Samuel's old friend and oftentimes political ally, expressed a similar thought when he wrote a lengthy obituary upon Adams's death. Saying he had produced "but a gazette sketch" of Samuel Adams, Sullivan asserted that "to give his history at length, would be to give an history of the American revolution."[3]

Despite their boldness, there is much truth in the judgments John Adams and James Sullivan offered. Certainly the story of Samuel Adams, American revolutionary, compels us to think about why and how the revolution occurred; it also forces us to confront the ideas and assess the actions of those Americans who opposed the revolutionary movement. In addition, Adams's life story reveals a great deal about how the American Revolution played out and how it influenced politics and society in late eighteenth-century America and beyond.

Notwithstanding his central role during the era of the American Revolution, scholarly interest in Samuel Adams has fluctuated dramatically, and so too have the assessments of him. In the nineteenth century, Adams was typically praised as one of the greatest heroes of the revolution; by the mid-twentieth century, he was often denigrated as a mob-leading demagogue. An occasional biography of Samuel Adams appeared in the decades that followed. But it has only been in the last few years, amid renewed interest in the era of the American Revolution—and especially interest in those typically called "the founding fathers"—that Samuel Adams has once again drawn significant attention.[4]

However they interpret him, those who study Samuel Adams must contend with the fact that eighteenth-century American English looks strange to the modern reader. In addition to British English and obsolete spellings (such as *colour*, *defence*, and *centinel*), one encounters added letters (such as *republick*), peculiar omissions (such as *observ'd*), or seemingly missing letters (such as *pressd* for *pressed*). And while writers of that era often sprinkled their prose with capital letters, the word *negro* was rarely capitalized. Still, what looks odd to the modern eye was not necessarily wrong in the eighteenth century. Accordingly, I have followed this rule: quotations are given without alteration and without any attempt to indicate "errors" through the use of *[sic]*. In the very few cases where it seemed necessary to add material for clarity's sake, it has been inserted in brackets. These points merit special comment because in crafting this biography I have striven to allow Adams and the people who lived in his time ample opportunity to express themselves in their own words.

Long ago a wise fellow historian—my wife, June—reminded me that history is not like detective stories. There is no reason to "hide" the ending. As I hope the following pages reveal, James Sullivan was not far off the mark when he said that exploring Samuel Adams's life at length would provide something of a history of the American Revolution. Adams was, above all else, a political being. He was a practicing and extraordinarily skillful politician. Even more important, the evidence reveals that his political life was built on a principled defense of liberty and an abiding concern for ensuring that future generations of Americans would live in a society that protected their liberties and promoted equality. As we shall see, this American revolutionary had his faults, but his life provides an example of commendable patriotism worth remembering and emulating.

This volume has its roots in my earlier biography of Samuel Adams. But while my general interpretation of Adams has not altered, this study is fundamentally different from the previous one, which had to adhere to severe limitations on the length of the work. For this volume, I have been able to explore many topics in greater depth and delve into important aspects of Adams's life that could be only lightly touched on in the earlier book. And this publication, as any such work ideally should, contains notes. They do more than point readers to the sources on which the analysis is built. Some issues that are tangential, yet still important to the life of this American revolutionary, are discussed in the notes. In addition, a few factual errors discovered in the original work have been corrected.

Many individuals provided important encouragement and assistance as I fashioned this biography. Niels Aaboe, executive editor for political science, American history, and communication at Rowman & Littlefield, merits special thanks for actively supporting the idea of bringing out this full-life biography of Samuel Adams. As the process of transforming the manuscript into a book moved forward, the editorial and production staffs at Rowman & Littlefield provided skillful assistance in a friendly manner. They have my sincere thanks. My historian wife, June, offered sage advice and proved yet again that she is the best first reader a historian could hope for. Offering her but one page in a volume seems rather skimpy recompense. But, then, I have long believed that the most precious gift an author has to bestow is a dedication page. And it is June's now and always.

JKA
Cincinnati

1

THE FAILURE OF PROMISE

Samuel Adams was born to a life of promise. Although his merchant father lacked a gentleman's education, he had a knack for making money. In 1712, when only twenty-three years old, Samuel Adams Sr. could afford to buy a substantial parcel of land in Boston, the largest city in British America. His property extended from Belcher's Lane, which later became Purchase Street, down to the harbor. He quickly set about having an impressive dwelling erected on his land. The house, which offered an unobstructed view of the harbor and had a rooftop observatory accessible by its own stairs, stood out in what was then a semirural setting. On April 21, 1713, the senior Adams wed Mary Fifield, and they moved into the new house. As the newlyweds turned a house into a home, the property soon boasted a garden and an orchard.[1]

Religion played a central role in the couple's lives. Mary Adams devoutly followed the Puritan faith, and her husband answered to the title Deacon Adams because of his lengthy service with the Old South Congregational Church. In 1715 he helped lead a successful petition effort asking the Boston Town Meeting for a parcel of land on which to erect a church. The New South Church, located just a few blocks from the Adams home, opened its doors in January 1717. Samuel Adams was baptized there on Sunday, September 16, 1722, the day of his birth.[2]

One can only catch glimpses of the personal side of the Adams family. What Samuel thought about his pious mother has not been preserved, but he remembered his father as "a wise man and a good man." Young Samuel's relationships with his siblings—and perhaps to a degree with his parents and especially his mother—could not help reflecting a grim demographic fact. Mary Fifield Adams bore a dozen children between 1716 and April 1740, but only three lived past their third birthday. In addition to Samuel,

1

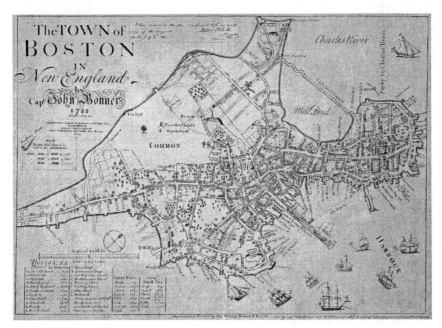

"[Map of] The Town of Boston in New England by John Bonner 1722" as reprinted by George G. Smith (Boston, 1835). Courtesy of The Massachusetts Historical Society.

Mary (born in 1717) and Joseph (born in 1728) survived to adulthood. So the rigors of pregnancy and the sadness of death regularly visited the Adams home as Samuel grew up. The frightening child mortality that afflicted the family made Samuel the eldest Adams son from the day of his birth. By Samuel's own account, his sister Mary, who possessed her mother's fervent religiosity and was five years his senior, exerted an important influence on him. As a mature man, he observed that it "is a happy young man who has had an elder sister upon whom he could rely for advice and counsel in youth."[3]

Samuel also had reason to be happy because he grew up in an increasingly prosperous and politically influential family. The senior Adams improved the quality of his mercantile operations by acquiring a wharf, and he also owned a malt house. Through the 1720s and 1730s he purchased additional lands and houses, presumably to lease.[4] Continuing a process begun before young Samuel's birth, the elder Adams's role in Boston's political affairs also kept expanding. In 1710 the town meeting elected him a tithingman, a post that centered on enforcing laws concerning public houses. He moved up the political ladder when he served as a constable in

1718. At that time, a constable's duties included collecting fines and taxes, responsibilities that made the post so burdensome many paid a fine to avoid the job. But Adams accepted the position. In the 1720s, the elder Adams ascended the political ladder. The town meeting routinely elected him a tax assessor, and in March 1729 he became a selectman. This executive position made him one of the leaders of the town meeting.[5]

The political rise of Samuel Adams Sr. did not happen by chance. The eighteenth-century historian Reverend William Gordon asserted that by 1724 Adams and about twenty others met in caucus and formulated strategies to get their candidates into positions of power. This organization, later called the Boston Caucus, gained political favor by championing economic issues that mattered to common folk. Because hard money was in chronically short supply, the caucus advocated the emission of paper currency. The group supported tax officials, often caucus members, who typically overlooked delinquent taxpayers suffering hard times. The caucus also strove to protect the political rights of citizens. It fought to ensure the integrity of Boston's town-meeting government, a system that gave the citizens a direct say in determining how their city functioned. The system's democratic features came at a price, though. The town meeting, which relied on elected committees rather than a few officials to set policy, often proved less than efficient, and that prompted calls for incorporating Boston as a city. Under the leadership of the caucus, the town meeting thwarted various incorporation schemes during the 1730s that would have significantly diluted the voters' power by eliminating the elected committee system.[6] To further protect the citizens' political clout, the Boston Caucus also ardently supported the legislature's successful efforts to deny the royal governor a guaranteed salary.[7] By the mid-1730s, as a result of being appointed a justice of the peace, the senior Adams had become Samuel Adams, Esquire.[8]

The senior Adams wanted his son to have advantages that he had not enjoyed. He and Mary, therefore, made sure young Samuel received a gentleman's education. In 1729, Samuel entered the Boston Latin School and embarked on a seven-year course of study designed to make him proficient in Latin as well as introduce him to the intricacies of Greek. During their first three years, Boston Latin students spent considerable time with the writings of Marcus Porcius Cato, the Roman statesman famous for promoting the moral integrity and simplicity of manners associated with the early Roman Republic. Aesop's *Fables*, the brief moral tales involving anthropomorphic creatures or entities such as those found in the story of "The Tortoise and the Hare," also figured prominently in the curriculum.

In the fourth year, or sooner if they showed real ability, the pupils began with Erasmus's *Colloquies*, a collection of writings of the noted Dutch scholar, theologian, and satirist. By the end of the year, they were reading the acclaimed poet Ovid's elegies about his banishment from Rome and subsequent sufferings. Ovid's *Metamorphoses* was added the following year, as was Cicero's *Epistles to Atticus*. In his last two years, Samuel would have devoted much time to studying Cicero's orations and discussions of moral duties. Lucius Florus's history of the Roman Republic was also required reading. In addition, Samuel was introduced to the work of Virgil, Homer, Horace, and Isocrates as well as Justin Martyr's writings on the Old Testament.[9]

Samuel was a receptive pupil. While still at Boston Latin, he adorned one of his school books with his own youthful comments on learning being more important than wealth. And almost half a century later, Samuel still referred to lessons learned from Aesop's *Fables*. Adams also continued to demonstrate a deep interest in both the writings and history of ancient Greece and Rome. In 1780, a French visitor to Boston remarked that Adams was known, and often criticized, for "consulting his library" and supposedly "always proceeding by way of the Greeks and Romans."[10]

Upon graduating from the Boston Latin School, Samuel was admitted to Harvard College in 1736. In those days a Harvard undergraduate's class ranking reflected his father's attainments, not the student's performance or even his academic promise. So it is hardly surprising that this son of a wealthy justice of the peace was placed sixth in a class of twenty-three. Even that high ranking was, in fact, artificially low. Had the normal system been followed, young Samuel would have been second—not sixth—in his class. The reason for the demotion is revealing. The president of Harvard, Benjamin Wadsworth, apparently disliked the idea that the top two positions in the class would go to the sons of men who, although justices of the peace, possessed neither a gentleman's education nor other special distinctions; so Wadsworth arbitrarily decided to rank the sons of clergymen ahead of the sons of justices of the peace. Nothing in the sparse records that have survived from Samuel's youth suggests he or his parents knew about this snub. Still, the ranking process and the snub are important. They illustrate how elite members of Massachusetts society endeavored to keep social distinctions sharp. The slight in ranking Samuel reveals that wealth and even important political standing could not, in the eyes of some, transform his father into a gentleman. Deacon Adams, it seemed, lacked the proper education that marked a true Massachusetts gentleman. Attending Harvard would give young Samuel the education his father prized and also prepare him for the ministry, the profession his parents expected him to follow. So, at the age of fourteen, which was not that uncommon for the time, Samuel began his college career.[11]

The Harvard that young Samuel entered was as committed to producing learned gentlemen as it was to replenishing the colony's supply of clergy. The college's increasingly secular thrust is illustrated by the fact that only five of the twenty-three members of Samuel's class made the ministry their life's work.[12] And by the mid-1730s the moral fiber of the students seemed to have deteriorated. The faculty bemoaned that in recent years the undergraduates had increasingly engaged in "drinking frolicks," cursing, swearing, "shamefull scandalous Routs and Noises for sundry nights"—and worse. As a consequence, new college rules adopted shortly before Samuel enrolled stipulated that any student found guilty of such offenses could be fined and publicly admonished. Samuel never faced a fine for such shenanigans. He was, however, admonished once for sleeping late and missing morning prayers; on another occasion he was fined for "drinking prohibited Liquors."[13]

If Samuel took course work in theology to prepare for the ministry, he would have been taught by Harvard's sole professor of divinity, Edward Wigglesworth. This learned man opposed religious enthusiasm and advocated toleration rather than religious orthodoxy.[14] In any case, it soon became clear that Samuel did not fancy becoming a clergyman. The ancient Greek and Latin authors and the modern political philosophers proved more appealing than theology. Perhaps it was his growing interest in politics that prompted Adams to arrange a general debate among classmates on the topic of "Liberty."[15]

Samuel received his bachelor's degree on schedule in 1740 and returned home to a promising, if uncertain, future.[16] Having decided against the ministry, he had to choose a new career. As Adams family descendants later recounted, Samuel, urged on by his father, eagerly began studying the law; but for some unrecorded reason his mother came to oppose this course. A new plan emerged: Samuel would become a businessman. He soon found himself in a countinghouse under the tutelage of Thomas Cushing, a leading Boston merchant. Cushing quickly decided that the recent Harvard graduate was not merchant material. As Cushing reportedly saw it, young Samuel worked hard and was intelligent, but he lacked business sense, in part because politics dominated his thoughts. In an effort to jump-start his son's business career, the senior Adams loaned him £1,000, a huge sum for the time. The effort fizzled. Young Samuel loaned a friend half his start-up fund, and the friend never repaid the money. The other

£500 soon disappeared as well. In 1743, perhaps realizing the accuracy of Cushing's judgment about his son's lack of business talent, the senior Adams effectively became young Samuel's employer by making him a partner in one of the family's enterprises, a malt-house business.[17]

While it hardly explains the younger Adams's false career starts and failures as a fledgling businessman, Thomas Cushing may have voiced the fundamental point when he spoke of young Samuel being distracted, almost consumed, by politics. Such a preoccupation would have been natural because the political intrigues of the early 1740s were of immediate, pressing concern to all the Adamses. In fact, the Adams family found itself sucked into a political firestorm that threatened to incinerate its prosperity. To understand the formative years of Samuel Adams and why he became an American revolutionary, one must examine what was called the *land-bank controversy*.

The political turmoil sprang from a chronic problem faced by Massachusetts and the other British colonies in North America: the lack of a medium of exchange, literally an absence of money in circulation. As New England's economy grew, its money supply needed to expand. Since hard money—gold and silver—was always scarce, colonies wanted to issue paper money. However, to protect merchants who routinely advanced credit to colonial merchants, the British opposed the issuance of legal-tender paper money because of the likelihood of depreciation. Still, on occasion, chiefly during wartime, England reluctantly allowed some colonies to print currency. Massachusetts began issuing paper money in 1690, and it circulated throughout New England. Under orders from the British government, however, the many issues of Massachusetts currency, which depreciated rapidly in the 1730s, were being withdrawn from circulation. So the Massachusetts currency could not meet the region's money-supply needs.

At this juncture, Rhode Island entered the picture. Because that self-governing corporate colony was not as tightly regulated as the royal colony of Massachusetts, Rhode Island found it easier to issue paper money and in the late 1730s flooded New England with its currency. In 1738 and again the next year the Boston Town Meeting sounded the alarm in instructions sent to its representatives in the colonial assembly. The town meeting maintained that Rhode Islanders were stealing Massachusetts's trade because the Bay colony lacked a medium of exchange. The situation worsened a year later when the British government decreed that all Massachusetts paper money must be retired from circulation by 1741. Faced with what it perceived to be imminent economic ruin, the Boston Town Meeting, in instructions Deacon Adams helped draft, renewed its call for legislative action. The Massachusetts House of Representatives responded in June 1739 with an almost plaintive cry for help. Agreeing that Massachusetts desperately needed some form of currency, the representatives established a committee to receive proposals from anyone willing to suggest how a medium of trade might be created.[18]

Samuel Adams Sr. did more than help write instructions for the Boston representatives. Realizing that England's prohibition against Massachusetts issuing paper currency did not extend to *private* ventures, he and other leaders of the Boston Caucus proposed creating a land bank. It issued currency and loaned it to individuals who secured the loans by mortgaging their land. The land bank was also called the *manufactory scheme* because it accepted payments in marketable items such as hemp, flax, cordage, and bar or cast iron. The land bank benefited the colony in important ways. It provided a desperately needed money supply. It was designed to promote manufacturing ventures, and that, in turn, would provide more jobs. Adams Sr. and other caucus leaders became directors of the land bank.[19]

Eventually over a thousand people became land-bank subscribers. The plan enjoyed widespread support, in part because virtually all landowners could subscribe and by subscribing obtain what amounted to a loan. Thus men on the rise could use the land bank to improve their economic opportunities. If Thomas Hutchinson, a prominent member of the long-established, politically powerful, and conservative merchant family, was right, the economically vulnerable found the land bank appealing. Hutchinson, who considered the idea of a land bank repugnant, claimed that "the needy part of the province in general favored the scheme." Those who actually subscribed to the land bank were, Hutchinson sniffed, not much better off. The subscribers were "generally of low condition . . . and of small estate, and many of them perhaps insolvent." Still, Hutchinson conceded that a few men "of rank and good estate" backed the endeavor. Samuel Adams Sr. would certainly belong in that more esteemed group.[20]

Many other leading Boston merchants joined Hutchinson in recoiling at the thought that a medium of exchange would be based on something other than gold or silver. Ten merchants, headed by Edward Hutchinson, a cousin of Thomas, quickly established a bank that issued currency based on silver holdings. These merchants openly proclaimed their opposition to the land bank by announcing that no silver-bank subscriber would accept land-bank notes.

The political battle lines formed quickly. The backers of the land bank typically came from what was, over time, labeled the *popular* or *country party*. The leading Massachusetts supporters of the royal governors, often aristocrats such as the Hutchinsons, became known as the *court party*. Each faction dominated a branch of the colony's legislature, the General Court. The popular forces held the lower house, the House of Representatives. The House, which contained several land-bank directors, supported the idea of private ventures like the land bank. The court party controlled the Governor's Council, the upper house of the legislature, and several silver-bank directors were councilors. The Council and the royal governor, Jonathan Belcher, worked to destroy the land bank. Using the veto powers granted by the Massachusetts Charter of 1691, Governor Belcher played rough. Having rejected the Massachusetts House's selection for speaker because the man chosen was a director of the land bank, Belcher then vetoed appointments that would have placed land-bank men on his Council. The governor pressed the attack by dismissing justices of the peace and militia officers who were prominent supporters of the land bank. Samuel Adams Sr., who in addition to being a justice of the peace was a captain of the Boston militia, thus lost two significant and prestigious offices. But the worst was yet to come.

Responding to lobbying by Governor Belcher, the Council, and leading Boston merchants, the British government, which on principle opposed anything like the land-bank or the silver-bank schemes, took action. In late March 1741 reports reached Massachusetts that the House of Commons had enacted a bill to dissolve the private banks and ensure that no such ventures could be launched in the future. Weeks later, Belcher confided to Thomas Hutchinson that unnamed champions of the land bank had supposedly declared they would defy any anti-land-bank act Parliament passed. These people, said Belcher, had grown so brassy and bold that they planned to rebel. No rebellion occurred, but Belcher rightly sensed the deepening anger festering among many Massachusetts citizens.

The text of Parliament's antibank bill reached Massachusetts in July 1741. Parliament made it obvious that its chief target was the land bank, not the silver bank. This extraordinary legislation was demonstrably unfair. Moreover, although the British constitution was an unwritten entity built on traditions, laws, and precedents, the law was also demonstrably unconstitutional. Adopting a flagrantly ex post facto (after the fact) position, Parliament determined that a 1720 law that would have made the land bank illegal in Great Britain also applied to the American colonies. Despite Parliament's assertion, the 1720 law clearly did not apply to the colonies. Parliament took special aim at the leaders of the land bank by stipulating that anyone who possessed its currency could demand that any partner or director immediately remit the value of the notes plus the applicable interest. If the partner or director refused to pay, he became liable for triple damages. Thomas Hutchinson reported that some land-bank supporters wanted to fight Parliament's actions but the directors—and that would include the senior Adams—argued to end the scheme. The directors did that, Hutchinson pointed out, because they faced economic ruin if they continued the venture.

By employing draconian methods embedded in unconstitutional legislation, Parliament successfully crushed a popular program designed to help Massachusetts and its ordinary citizens. Writing years after the fact, Samuel's second cousin John Adams, who was only six years old in 1741, maintained that the fight over the land bank raised "a greater ferment" in Massachusetts than the Stamp Act did. Considering the turmoil the Stamp Act unleashed, John's pronouncement seems hyperbolic; however, the land-bank controversy undoubtedly created long-lasting bitterness. Certainly the Samuel Adams family had more reason than most to dislike Parliament and Massachusetts's anti-land-bank forces. Although the senior Adams cooperated in the dissolution of the scheme, the legacy of the land-bank controversy inflicted pain on his family for decades because Parliament's 1741 law proved an open invitation for anyone who disliked them to harass the senior Adams or his son. Indeed, efforts to seize the family's property continued even after the elder Adams died. So the danger the Adams family faced, to say nothing of the suffering and anger, did not fade when the land bank was dissolved.[21] It burned itself into Samuel's consciousness. Indeed, John Adams asserted that Samuel had steadfastly and unflinchingly championed the cause of Massachusetts liberties from 1741 onward.[22]

Samuel Adams thus grew up in a politicized atmosphere. He watched his father assume a leading role in the Boston Caucus and witnessed its efforts to defend the common people against abuses of power by both the British Crown and the local gentry. The political firefight over the land bank not only threatened to destroy his family's economic security but also exposed the danger posed by the rich merchants of the court party, who seemed more concerned with self-advancement by wedding themselves to British power than with supporting their native colony. And parliamentary power exercised in an arbitrary way to crush the needs—to savage the very rights—of the people formed the core of the problem. It is not surprising that Samuel later said that "I was led to believe in early Life, that Jealousy is a political Virtue." For those of his era, jealousy in this context meant protecting the people's interests and political rights, as Adams phrased it, by "the People keep[ing] a watchful Eye over the Conduct of their Rulers."[23] This was the political world in which young Adams came of age in the early 1740s

Much had happened between his graduation in 1740 and when he briefly returned to Harvard to receive his M.A. in 1743. At that time, although those seeking to join the clergy were urged to remain in residence, candidates for the M.A. at Harvard were neither required nor expected to spend time studying at the college. But M.A. candidates were required to put forward a question linked to any aspect of their college work, to propose to support the negative or positive of the question, and to be prepared to defend their position. Reflecting the importance and influence of John Locke, the great English political theorist, one of Adams's classmates argued the affirmative of the question "Does Civil Government originate from Compact?" Samuel was more audacious than his classmate. Having experienced the searing trauma of the land-bank fight, Samuel proposed to argue the affirmative of the position "Whether it be lawful to resist the Supreme Magistrate if the Commonwealth cannot be otherwise preserved." Adams's choice, which was also rooted in Locke, revealed his increasing concern about defending basic rights.[24]

Samuel began his own career as an officeholder shortly after receiving his M.A. In March 1746 the Boston Town Meeting selected him as one of its clerks of market and then kept him in that post through March 1749.[25] In the wake of explosive riots against impressment—the practice whereby the British navy forcibly rounded up men to serve on its ships—that rocked Boston later in 1747, Samuel and some of his friends created a club for discussing public issues. Although it is not clear whether they provided financial support for the venture, Samuel and his friends did supply the political essays that became the chief fare of the *Independent Advertiser*, a weekly newspaper that first appeared in January 1748 and continued to offer political commentary until it ceased publication in December 1749.[26]

Two *Independent Advertiser* essays attributed to the younger Adams are extraordinarily important.[27] They show that issues Samuel stressed as a college student—the questions of "liberty" and a citizen's right to resist the government's "unlawful" actions—became deeply embedded in his thinking. Commenting on "*Loyalty* and *Sedition*," he asserted that "True Loyalty . . . is founded in the Love and Possession of Liberty." For Adams, "the true Object of Loyalty is a good *Legal Constitution*" that allowed a citizen to protest when grievances occur. The people must know how their constitution works, and they must display "a becoming Jealousy of our Immunities, and a steadfast Resolution to maintain them." Anyone who tried to subvert the constitution, or even to weaken it, was disloyal. Slashing at the aristocrats who formed the backbone of the court party, Adams also denounced anyone who "despises his Neighbours' Happiness because he wears a *worsted*

Cap or a Leathern Apron" or who "*struts* immeasurably above the *lower* Size of People, and pretends to adjust the Rights of Men by Distinctions of Fortune."[28] Adams returned to that theme in an essay on "Liberty" that praised the Massachusetts Charter for protecting the people's rights. He opined that "it is not infrequent, to hear Men declaim loudly upon Liberty, who if we may judge by the whole Tenor of their Actions, mean nothing else by it, but *their own* Liberty—to oppress without Controul, or the Restraint of Laws, All who are poorer and weaker than themselves."[29]

Adams's *Independent Advertiser* essays reflected his reading in political philosophy and more particularly his study of John Locke. In fact, sections of Adams's second essay read like extracts from Locke's influential *Second Treatise of Government*. Samuel's commentary also suggests that the traumatic land-bank struggle may have helped convince him that haughty aristocrats, such as the Hutchinsons of the court party, were especially prone to trample on the people and their rights. Even more important, these essays outlined the fundamental political ideals Adams steadfastly followed throughout his long political career. He believed the people deserved a constitution that protected their rights and that gave them a legal way to redress grievances. Once such a constitution had been established, the people must vigilantly, jealously guard it against attack from any source. And while a threat to the people's fundamental rights could come from any direction, the people must be particularly wary of the aristocracy.

As Samuel staked out his philosophical niche in the political world, his father, long known as a leader of the popular party, continued as a role model. In the aftermath of the land-bank dispute, Samuel Adams Sr. again consented to serve as a selectman. He held that post from March 1743 until June 1746, when the town meeting elected him to represent Boston in the House of Representatives. He was an especially active House member and would have joined the prestigious Governor's Council had not Governor Belcher quashed the appointment. Deacon Adams also continued, as he had for years, to provide Samuel with something more than a political role model. When the *Independent Advertiser* began publication in January 1748, Samuel still depended on his father for employment and still owed him £1,000.[30]

Samuel's supportive father died on March 8, 1748. The *Independent Advertiser*, in words his son might have written, proclaimed Deacon Adams "one who well understood and rightly pursued the Civil and Religious Interests of this People [of Boston]—A true *New-England* Man—An honest Patriot." Even in death, the elder Adams extended special help to his namesake. The estate passed to Mary Fifield Adams and upon her death would ultimately be divided equally among the three Adams children. However, noting Samuel's position as the eldest son, his father's will stipulated that the £1,000 loan should be stricken from the accounts so Samuel could receive his full share of the estate.[31]

With the passing of his father, Samuel assumed control of the family's financial affairs. Shortly thereafter, he took a major personal step. In October 1749 he married Elizabeth Checkley, the daughter of the Reverend Samuel Checkley, a friend of the family and the pastor of the New South Church.[32] Over the next seven years, the couple had six children. Only two—Samuel, born in 1751, and Hannah, born in 1756—survived to adulthood. The other children died in infancy, and the last was stillborn on July 6, 1757. Adding to Samuel's grief, Elizabeth died less than three weeks later, almost surely owing to complications from that stillbirth. Assessing her life, Samuel gloried that Elizabeth had "run her Christian race with a remarkable steadiness and finished in triumph." "To her husband," he added, "she was as sincere a Friend as she was a faithful Wife." Perhaps all too aware of his own meager financial skills, he boasted that those who knew Elizabeth admired "her exact economy" in all capacities. Now in his mid-thirties, Samuel Adams suddenly faced the daunting task of raising two small children without their mother and his loving and frugal wife. The future seemed anything but bright.[33]

Fortunately for Samuel, he had recently acquired a political position that could support his family. In March 1756 the Boston Town Meeting made him one of its four tax collectors and, as usual with such posts, reelected him the next year. For their service, tax collectors received 5 percent of what they garnered, provided the collection of the taxes occurred within a specified period. The town soon lowered the potential compensation; from mid-1758 until he stopped serving as a tax collector, the maximum Adams could have earned for his efforts would have been 9 pence on the 1£ or 3.75 percent of the total amount he garnered.[34] Still, Adams's economic fortunes stood on a firmer footing even as his personal life crumbled. But as Adams knew all too well, as long as the land-bank accounts remained unsettled, his family's economic foundation could deteriorate quickly.

Samuel's contemporaries often stressed that he was not materialistic—far from it. But the lingering effects of the land-bank controversy meant that as the 1750s unfolded he had special reason to fret about his family's economic security. With bothersome regularity throughout the 1750s Adams had to fight to keep his father's estate from being sold at public auction to settle land-bank accounts. The efforts to force a sale of the Adams property began in 1751. On two separate occasions in that year Samuel had to defend his father's estate against commissioners the Massachusetts General Court had authorized to settle the land bank's financial affairs. In mounting his defenses against the attempts to deprive him of his father's estate, Samuel used tactics and voiced arguments he would draw on again in the movement toward revolution.[35]

Adams employed a lengthy 1756 newspaper essay to recount his travails and link them to a denial of basic English rights. He groused that, although Massachusetts had created a commissioner system in 1743 to settle the land bank's finances speedily and equitably, the accounts remained unsettled thirteen years later! Worse yet, in 1748, after a fire destroyed most of the commissioners' land-bank records, the General Court passed legislation that pitted land-bank directors, such as Adams's father, against others in the land-bank scheme in a way that "touch'd the New-England Constitution in its tenderest parts." According to Adams, the land-bank commissioners had adjusted his financial statements and, without giving him a full hearing, somehow turned a balance into a debt. "Would any Man of Virtue and Candor say," he asked, "that a due Regard was had to Property, or even to natural Justice?" Surely natural justice required the commissioners to hold a full hearing, yet they did not. Adams said he next tried petitioning the legislature, but it refused to act. None of this should have happened, since, according to Samuel, the commissioners had admitted that their assessment of the Adams account "was grounded on Mistakes." The commissioners' persistent hounding thus constituted "an Injury to the innocent." Proclaiming his determination to keep fighting against the possible seizure and sale of the Adams estate, Samuel closed by trumpeting more than his own injured innocence. He carefully linked his struggles to the idea of defending basic rights by asserting that "In the whole of these Affairs, I have never ask'd *Favor*, nor taken *undue Methods* to obtain it.—I have ask'd for *Justice*, and God be thanked, in an *English* Government we have a Right to expect it."[36]

Adams's rhetoric may have forestalled action in 1756, but the land-bank nightmare recurred the summer after Elizabeth died. On August 10, 1758, Sheriff Stephen Greenleaf, acting on a warrant from the land-bank commissioners, advertised in the *Boston News-Letter* that segments of the late Samuel Adams's estate would be sold at public auction on August 25. All the buildings and lands as well as the wharf and dock would be offered for sale. On the very day that announcement appeared, Samuel penned a response. Observing that the estate had been put up for sale four times since 1751, Samuel asserted that each time it happened the persons attending the sale had become persuaded of "the inequity and illegality" of the whole proceeding. As Adams pointedly added, once the potential bidders realized the risk to themselves, no one ventured a bid. He again emphasized, as he did in 1756, that the commissioners had supposedly admitted their claim against the Adams estate rested on mistaken calculations. That fact, according to Adams, justified his resistance to the whole process. Again donning the mantle of an injured innocent, he proclaimed that he could not understand why the commissioners continued to hound him "*so contrary to their own Apprehension of Justice.*" The truth was, Samuel stressed, the commissioners knew he always stood ready to submit the case to arbitration or to the ordinary courts of justice. With a flourish, he asserted, "this I have a Right to contend for as an English Freeholder." He closed with an appeal that made any further action by Sheriff Greenleaf appear both unfair and a threat to fundamental rights. "I shall only," he remarked, "beg Leave to caution the Sheriff against taking such Steps as will have a Tendency to weaken the Security of English Property."[37]

To strengthen his position, Adams authored another essay. Following the standard practice of adopting pen names, he signed it "A Freeholder," a signature that invited all landowners to consider how the problems associated with settling the land-bank accounts might touch themselves. Observing that the commissioners received compensation for their work, Adams suggested that they kept dragging their feet as a way of milking their lucrative posts. He described how the commissioners' actions might reduce "many good and loyal Subjects" to a pitiable uncertainty "with Respect to our Rights and Estates." Adams implied that that uncertainty hung over anyone associated with the land-bank company. Obviously the commissioners were acting "contrary to all Reason, and the Spirit of the common Law, by which British Subjects are secured in the quiet Possession of their Property." Having invited all landowners to share his fears about an outrageous attack on property rights, Adams further disparaged the commissioners by asking, "I would be glad to know whether these Commissioners are accountable *in this life* for their Conduct?" Adams's complaints produced tangible results. The commissioners were fired. That pleasing outcome surely helped Adams realize the value of political mudslinging and of emphasizing how political opponents allegedly threatened everyone's basic rights.[38]

But Adams's forceful missives, which appeared in the *Boston Gazette*, could not stop Sheriff Greenleaf. On August 17, 1758, Greenleaf again announced the upcoming auction of the senior Adams's estate. Adams responded by moving beyond rhetoric. He threatened legal retaliation against anyone who participated in the sale. Probably timing its appearance to achieve maximum deterrence, on August 24, the day before the scheduled public auction at the Exchange Tavern, Samuel bypassed the *Boston Gazette* and had a statement inserted in the *Boston News-Letter* right below Greenleaf's final advertisement that the sale would occur at noon on the following day. Adams maintained that former Sheriff Benjamin Pollard had not tried to force such a sale. Why? Because he and Adams had been advised by lawyers that the sale would be "illegal and unwarrantable." Realizing his own estate might be endangered if he took illegal action, Pollard, according to Adams, "very *prudently*" declined to proceed. As for Sheriff Greenleaf, almost menacingly Adams pondered, "how far your Determination may lead you, you know better than I." Lest Greenleaf, or any potential bidder, miss the point, Samuel warned, "I would only beg leave, with Freedom, to assure you, that I am advis'd and determined to prosecute in the Law any person whomsoever who shall trespass upon that Estate."[39]

Although it is not clear why, the scheduled sale did not occur. In a published notice of September 21, Sheriff Greenleaf, without any explanation, announced that the auction scheduled for September 22 was being further adjourned until September 29. On September 28, Greenleaf again published a notice of the sale scheduled for the following day at the Royal Exchange Tavern from noon to one o'clock.[40] This time, Adams did not place a counterannouncement in the press, quite possibly because he took more direct action. Thomas Hutchinson's recollections reveal that somewhere in the process of repeatedly thwarting the sale of his father's estate Samuel moved beyond publishing threats. Recounting an unnamed sheriff's efforts to sell the estate, Hutchinson proclaimed that Adams "first made himself conspicuous on this occasion. He attended the sale, threatened the sheriff to bring action against him, and menaced all who should attempt to enter upon the estate, under pretense of a purchase; and, by intimidating both the sheriff and those persons who intended to purchase, he prevented the sale, [and] kept the estate in his possession."[41]

In the process of thwarting what he considered the land-bank commissioners' unwarranted actions, Samuel Adams learned the value of carefully escalating efforts and of putting opponents on the wrong side of a basic rights issue. When his offer to adjudicate the matter fell on deaf ears, Samuel sought legal advice. Once armed with a favorable legal opinion, he broadcast that opinion in word and print. He maligned his opponents, depicted the issues as involving basic rights, and invited people to see the attacks on him as potential future assaults on themselves. Adams already understood what in later years he repeatedly declared to be a good maxim:

"to put & keep the Enemy in the wrong."[42] When physical intimidation seemed necessary to prevent what he considered an assault on basic
rights, he accepted the challenge and personally stopped the public auction. Samuel's bold efforts saved the day more than once in the 1750s.
Thus, the land-bank controversy, in all its complexity, helped Samuel to
understand the importance of blending philosophy and action in ongoing
political struggles. It also demonstrated the value of using the press to respond quickly to important developments. Moreover, the continuing threat
of attacks on the family's property served as a constant personal reminder
that Britain's power over the colonies could be exercised in arbitrary and
destructive ways.[43]

If John Adams remembered it accurately, Samuel's fear of British
power had fully matured by 1758 when he tangled with the commissioners and Sheriff Greenleaf. Samuel's cousin asserted that, based on his own
personal knowledge, he could testify that from 1758 to 1775 Samuel diligently sought out and courted the friendship of bright young men with political talent (including, eventually, John Adams himself). More important,
Samuel worked with each man "to cultivate his natural feelings in favor of
his native country, to warn him against the hostile designs of Great Britain,
and to fix his affections and reflections on the side of his native country."
Writing to a friend in 1771, Samuel himself said that for over a decade the
Crown had acted to weaken the Massachusetts House, "the Democratical
part of this Government."[44] Samuel had ample reason to stand watch and
be ready to sound the alarm if the Parliament, aided by the court party,
challenged the rights of the colonists.

Adams did not stand watch alone. As the 1750s unfolded, Samuel, like
his father, became an increasingly influential leader of the Boston Caucus,
a vital component of the Massachusetts popular party. As it had in the
days when Samuel's father helped make it run, the caucus continued to
champion the economic and political rights of ordinary citizens. In 1760,
a committee of tradesmen, claiming efforts were afoot to destroy Boston's
form of government, publicly called for the members of "the old and true
Corcas" to make sure that did not happen. The committee described the
"Corcas" members as having "*from Time immemorial been zealously affected to
our ancient Establishments in Church and State.*" The caucus's opponents
offered a different interpretation then and later.[45] In 1763, court party
members derisively called the caucus "the Junto," denounced its members
for supposedly adopting an antigovernment position, and accused them of
having selfish motives.[46]

John Adams, then a Braintree country lawyer, received a report of how the Boston Caucus, or at least the South End segment, worked in early 1763. The members met in the home of Thomas Dawes in Purchase Street near Samuel's own residence and deliberated in a large, smoke-filled room. Copying town-meeting procedures, the caucus selected a moderator, who ran the meeting. The members then voted for nominees to offices ranging from the House of Representatives and selectmen, to tax assessors and collectors, to wardens and firewards. Having chosen their candidates, the caucus sent committees to meet with the Merchants Club and, if possible, secure its backing for the men and measures the caucus put forward. As its name indicates, the Merchants Club, which by 1763 had been functioning for about fifteen years, considered itself the voice of the merchants. For its part, the caucus perceived itself more as the champion of the artisans and mechanics of the city, the people who manufactured various goods. The image of the caucus as what in the modern day might be labeled a political machine sharpens when one considers what James Cunningham, a glazier and militia captain, confided to John. Cunningham said that caucus members had often invited him to attend their meetings and "they have assured him Benefit in his Business, &c." John asserted that the caucus system worked so well that its members, rather than the town meeting, actually selected Boston's officials.[47]

John Adams's description of the caucus as it functioned in 1763 can be compared to the analysis offered in that same year by "E. J.," a newspaper essayist. Although he admitted that he now opposed the caucus, this penman claimed he had once been a member and thus knew how the organization functioned. According to E. J., the heads of the caucus met weeks before the town meeting and decided on candidates. Their choices got forwarded to a petty caucus, which debated them and settled points. Finally, the grand caucus convened just before the town meeting and formally approved what had already been decided. E. J. derisively portrayed the caucus leaders beguiling the ordinary people with meaningless rhetoric about freedom and English liberty. As for those common people, he depicted them as merely hunting for political offices and favors.[48]

Although they voiced decidedly different views on the worth of the caucus, John Adams and E. J. agreed that the caucus of 1763, possibly using a tiered system, worked to control the major actions of the town meeting. The few existing minutes of a caucus, which cover a brief period in the early 1770s, confirm that depiction. By 1772, it had three branches, the North, Middle, and South Boston Caucus. Each branch chose nominees, formulated positions on important issues, and then sent representatives to the other caucus branches to reach a consensus on candidates and issues.[49]

As he helped direct the caucus and went about recruiting potential luminaries to defend the people's rights, Samuel Adams cultivated the friendship of ordinary Bostonians. His daughter Hannah remembered him being so admired that he frequently served as an arbitrator when his neighbors became embroiled in disputes. Possessing a good singing voice and a mastery of vocal music, Adams founded singing societies of mechanics.[50] Adams's popularity with common people can also be traced to the caucus's long-established lax approach to collecting taxes. Indeed, while Boston tax collectors were justifiably famous—or notorious—for less than vigorous collection of taxes, Samuel was the champion noncollector.[51] In May 1763 a town-meeting committee appointed to assess the situation reported that just over £4,000 of the 1761 tax had not yet been collected. Significantly, of the three tax collectors whose 1761 books remained open Samuel stood responsible for almost £2,200; the other two collectors owed less than £1,000 each. Many Bostonians probably appreciated the way Samuel went about garnering taxes, and that likely enhanced his popularity. Adams, the caucus, and Boston could not, however, put off a reckoning forever. By the early 1760s, Boston faced a financial crisis that caused the town meeting to search for ways to reduce the colony tax levied against Bostonians, to speed up collection of taxes, and to cut the costs of government.[52] In such a world, Adams's seemingly casual attitude toward gathering taxes could suddenly look less appealing.

Samuel Adams's lack of diligence extended to his personal finances. His cousin John, who admired Samuel immensely, remarked in late 1765 that Samuel's only real flaw was probably that "he is too attentive to the Public and not enough so, to himself and his family."[53] Samuel received only a small income from his tax-collector post and minor positions he may have held, such as possibly serving as a clerk for land developers.[54] So Samuel had little in the way of material wealth to offer in December 1764 when he married Elizabeth Wells, the twenty-eight-year-old daughter of Francis Wells, a merchant. In fact, by all accounts, Samuel gained material advantages from the marriage because Elizabeth Wells, like Samuel's first wife, could manage a home effectively and run it on a limited income. In addition, she was an educated woman who shared or came to share Samuel's commitment to politics.[55] Elizabeth's friends might have questioned the wisdom of her marrying Samuel, but Samuel's friends could reasonably judge it a brilliant match for him. If Elizabeth's acquaintances fretted about her prospects for happiness as Mrs. Samuel Adams, events proved

Samuel Adams as depicted in a Alonzo Chappel painting from an engraving published by Johnson, Fry, and Company (New York, 1862).

their worries unfounded. In July 1766, Abigail Adams, John's wife, noted that Elizabeth and Samuel had visited for a few days and she found them "a charming pair." Indeed, "in them is to be seen the tenderest affection towards each other, without any fulsome fondness, and the greatest Complasance, delicacy and good breeding that you can imagine, yet separate from any affectation."[56]

The Samuel Adams who wed Elizabeth Wells was a man of average height, with a muscular build and light-blue eyes. His cousin John described him as having engaging manners. But to an outsider and even to many Bostonians the Samuel Adams of 1764 probably cut a less than impressive figure. This Harvard-educated son of one of Boston's most popular and wealthy politicians had never shown skill as a businessman. He was just scraping by financially. And because of his slipshod way of collecting taxes, by 1764 he faced possible economic ruin. Even his popularity might have been dismissed as a mere reflection of his failure to collect taxes rigorously. For all the promise of his birth, for all the advantages given by generous parents, Samuel Adams appeared to represent the failure of promise. In fact, it would not have been unreasonable to judge Adams as little more than a political hack destined, at best, for an obscure future as a minor Boston politician.[57]

Appearances can, of course, be deceiving. Although the scent of failure hung over him, Samuel Adams was a dedicated and skilled politician. He had long devoted himself to learning what contemporaries would have called the art and mystery of his craft, the craft of being a politician.[58] He had also developed a clear political philosophy that, as he said time and again in word and deed, was deeply influenced by John Locke's treatises on government. But Adams fashioned his political philosophy from more than abstract theory; it also grew out of his own experience, especially his family's struggles in the land-bank affair. Adams firmly believed that once the people had a good constitution or constitutions, such as the British constitution and the Massachusetts Charter of 1691, they must jealously guard their constitutional rights. Steady vigilance was required lest the imperial government, quite probably aided by local elites, trample the people's rights. If defending their rights required it, the people must be willing to take decisive action. On the basis of his own experience, Adams distrusted both the British and the aristocrats of the court party. The motives of the Hutchinsons—especially Thomas, who kept accumulating more and more political posts—appeared particularly suspect.[59]

Adams's unequaled political contacts and activities in the Boston Caucus gave him the potential to assume leadership in any effort to defend the people's rights. No one else, it seems, belonged to as many political clubs as Adams did. No other caucus leader rubbed shoulders with ordinary Bostonians to the extent Samuel did. He had also cast himself as a champion of those who wore "a *worsted Cap* or a *Leathern Apron*" and of those numbered among the "poorer and weaker" segments of society. His cousin John realized the importance of Samuel's ties to the less powerful members of society. Writing in early 1765, John declared that Samuel understood "the Temper and Character of the People" better than did any of Boston's other popular political leaders. Staunch supporters of the monarchy, including Thomas Hutchinson and Peter Oliver, ruefully came to agree that Samuel was a consummate politician who possessed a special ability to reach those in the lower ranks of society.[60]

While Samuel Adams was transforming his personal life by courting and marrying Elizabeth Wells, the British Empire was also undergoing profound changes. In 1763 the people of the British Empire, Bostonians included, basked in the glory of having finally defeated France and her allies in the titanic Seven Years' War. It began in North America, and eventually much of Europe was drawn into the expanding conflict. Winning the war made Great Britain the most powerful nation on earth and greatly expanded the boundaries of the empire, which stretched from the Americas to India and now included more than two dozen colonies in the Western Hemisphere alone. Imperial victory did not come cheaply. Despite heavy taxation at home, the British national debt almost doubled during the Seven Years' War. With the British people groaning under an oppressive weight of taxes, the newly installed prime minister, George Grenville, cast his eyes on the Americas as a possible source of income.

As he looked westward, Grenville saw colonies that occupied a well-established economic niche in the empire. Everyone, colonists included, understood that colonies existed for the benefit of the mother country. The mother country had the right, which England had long exercised, of regulating the colonial trade for its own benefit. The colonists, who were expected to, and did, buy Britain's manufactured goods, were prohibited from manufacturing or growing products that might compete with Britain's home economy. Of course, the colonists had to prosper too, and the British imperial system offered the colonists many benefits. For example, the British had long required that the empire's goods be carried in ships built within the empire, and that regulation had helped New England develop a profitable shipbuilding industry.

Politically, the colonists, like the inhabitants of the British Isles, were subjects of the British Crown and owed the monarchy unwavering loyalty. In fact, many North American colonists were more directly linked to the monarch than the people who lived in Great Britain. Over the years, Parliament had chipped away at the monarch's powers in the realm while leaving the monarch a freer hand in the colonies. That was especially true of royal colonies, whose governors the monarch appointed. And in 1763 most of Britain's American colonies, including Massachusetts, were royal colonies. In addition to pledging loyalty to the Crown, Americans routinely acknowledged the supremacy of the British Parliament. Only a fool would have challenged Parliament's right to pass the navigation acts that regulated aspects of the colony economy for the benefit of the mother country.[61]

Despite holding a subordinate position within the empire, Britain's North American colonists were, as a noted English politician later phrased it, England's sons, not her bastards.[62] Economically that meant the colonists could engage in any commerce and manufacturing not prohibited by Britain. Politically it meant the colonists were British subjects. In practical terms, it meant that all the colonies had been allowed to develop their own legislatures, which the colonists saw as miniature parliaments. Of course, the colonial legislatures could not enact laws that violated the British constitution or laws, and colonial laws could be disallowed in Britain. Moreover, in royal colonies such as Massachusetts the governor appointed by the Crown had an absolute veto over colonial legislation. Although the colonies were seen as subordinate—as political children—none of the limitations placed on them aimed to, nor could they, obscure the fact that the protections of the British constitution covered the colonists as fully as they covered people living in the realm. English politicians as well as Americans gloried in the fact that, as British subjects, the colonists had all the rights of Englishmen. But constitutions and phrases like "all the rights of Englishmen" are always open to interpretation. That was especially true of the unwritten British constitution. Because it was built on traditions, laws, and precedents, it served as an open invitation for a family squabble over exactly what rights the colonists did have.[63]

George Grenville and his political advisers understood the status of the colonists in the empire. And despite a surprising dearth of specific knowledge about the American colonies, the Grenville administration also knew that the colonists often evaded Britain's trade laws. Furthermore, the prime minister realized that the colonists had avoided heavy taxes. By the time he became prime minister in April 1763, Grenville had already decided the empire must undergo reform. He quickly ordered more vigorous enforcement of existing trade regulations. Then in March 1764 the prime minister proposed revising colonial trade duties, particularly those based on the colonists' extensive and profitable trade with the French sugar islands of the West Indies. What made this legislation, enacted in April and commonly called the Sugar Act, so significant was the precedent it set. Until that time, trade duties had been used to regulate trade, not to raise revenue. However, the preamble to the Sugar Act openly stated that its goal was to raise revenue, in effect to tax the colonists.

When he introduced the Sugar Act, Grenville indicated that in approximately a year he would propose a stamp act that, modeled on the long-established British Stamp Act, would force colonists to pay an internal tax on most printed materials. Grenville knew many persons considered this direct taxation innovative. To blunt any future criticism, he made a bold offer to the MPs, as members of Parliament were called. Grenville announced that if *any* MP doubted the constitutionality of a colonial stamp act he would establish a committee to determine its legality. No MP voiced a doubt.[64] In the colonies, however, people like Samuel Adams had a very different response. As Adams saw it, Grenville's program of imperial reform directly challenged the constitutional rights of every American colonist and must, therefore, be resisted with all the skill he could muster. When Samuel Adams turned his attention toward defending the people's rights, the image of the failure of promise soon gave way to a recognition that he had a genius for politics and an unshakable commitment to preserving constitutional rights.

2

THE PEOPLE SHALL BE HEARD

Samuel Adams's standing in the Boston Caucus, and consequently the town meeting, grew in the early 1760s. Each year the town meeting reelected him a tax collector, and he often served on committees that drafted documents for the meeting's consideration. In 1760 he helped create instructions for Boston's four members of the Massachusetts House of Representatives. Although addressed to the representatives, the instructions amounted to a political platform that informed the entire colony of the Boston Town Meeting's position on important issues. The 1760 directives urged the House to hire a colonial agent based in London. Reflecting Adams's concern for protecting basic rights, the agent should have "natural Attachments to our Religious as well as Civil Rights."[1] Those instructions helped produce results. In April 1762 the House appointed Jasper Mauduit, a religious dissenter from the Church of England, as the colony's agent in London.[2] In May 1764, reacting to Prime Minister Grenville's tax plans, the town meeting again placed Adams on the instructions committee. He authored the directives, and the town meeting approved them with only minor changes. Those instructions, the first response crafted in America to Grenville's imperial reform program, systematically attacked the logic and constitutionality of Parliament taxing the colonists. As the author of the town's instructions, Adams soon emerged as a prominent spokesman for the colony's popular party.[3]

Adams opened with a sketch of the citizens' rights and the duty representatives had to protect them. Representatives, he stressed, must constantly support "the invaluable Rights & Privileges of the Province." They had an obligation to safeguard the rights the colonists possessed "as free born Subjects" of Great Britain. Representatives must also remember their obligation to protect the rights set forth in the Massachusetts Charter of 1691.[4]

Adams appealed to Britain's economic self-interest. Asserting that Massachusetts languished in debt because of its patriotic exertions in the late war, he argued that taxing the colony's profitable branches of trade would ruin Boston and consequently injure Britain. Knowing most Englishmen would nod in agreement, Samuel observed that it was the colonies' trade that made them worthwhile to Britain. The commerce of Massachusetts had, he maintained, always been centered in the mother country. By paying cash for manufactured goods, the colonies provided the British with more income than parliamentary taxation might reap. As Adams depicted it, Massachusetts colonists already furnished the mother country with large amounts of revenue and were themselves just scraping along. In fact, if Parliament disrupted the colony's commerce, Bostonians would scarcely be able to earn their bread, much less buy the mother country's manufactured goods.[5]

Adams also challenged Grenville's revenue plan on constitutional grounds. The issue was not money; it was the precedent such a levy would establish. "For if our Trade may be taxed why not our lands? Why not the Produce of our Lands & every thing we possess or make use of?" Adams sliced to the core of the matter by asserting that parliamentary taxation "annihilates our Charter Right to govern & tax Ourselves." By undercutting the powers of the legislature and the colonists' right to manage their own affairs, parliamentary taxation attacked the fundamental rights that citizens held as British subjects and as citizens of Massachusetts. Grenville's unjust policy must, Adams insisted, be reversed. For, "if Taxes are laid upon us in any shape without our having a legal Representation where they are laid, are we not reduced from the Character of free Subjects to the miserable State of tributary Slaves?" This argument clearly implied that parliamentary taxation was unconstitutional, but Adams did not use the term. Although he phrased his constitutional challenge gingerly, Adams just as carefully refrained from speaking of a subordination to Parliament. He merely acknowledged a dependence on, and subordination to, Great Britain. By doing that, Adams could later argue that an act of Parliament was unconstitutional and not be inconsistent.

To keep his challenge to Parliament's power from being labeled disloyal radicalism, Adams informed the representatives that they should have their agent emphasize Boston's unshaken loyalty and unrivaled exertions in support of the king's government. Through a clever linkage of protecting the Crown's prerogatives and protecting the people's freedoms, he spoke of how the Massachusetts representatives had championed the king's rights in the colony. The British could also, Adams asserted, count on Massachusetts merchants to follow "all just & necessary Regulations of Trade." Such properly deferential comments did not negate Adams's assertion that *any* parliamentary taxation of the colonists violated their liberties and was therefore unjust.

Adams also skillfully emphasized other fundamental rights. He observed that the people always had "the constitutional Right of expressing their mind & giving fresh Instruction" to their representatives. But Massachusetts could not instruct its MPs because, like the other colonies, it did not directly elect members of Parliament. Adams's words also implied that the colonists could never effectively be represented in Parliament. How could the citizens offer fresh instructions to representatives meeting an ocean away?[6]

As future events demonstrated, Adams showed real foresight by also commenting on the issue of compensating judges. Although the British monarch appointed the colony's judges, the Massachusetts Charter made the colonial assembly responsible for paying them. By stressing that the judges depended on "the free Grants of the General Assembly" for their salaries, Adams underscored a cardinal tenet of the British constitution: taxes were voluntary gifts authorized by representatives elected by the people. Taxes levied by Parliament, in which the colonists were not represented, could not meet that constitutional test. Adams's reference to judicial compensation also silently, but forcefully, underscored an important political reality; the Massachusetts legislature had, over the years, used its control over judges' salaries to keep the judiciary focused on the colony's, not the Crown's, interests. Adams's discussion thus touched on basic constitutional rights and also reminded the representatives of the need to retain their power of the purse.[7]

The directives also offered a plan of action. After pressing the colony's legislators to show Parliament the folly of its new colonial policy, Adams suggested that Massachusetts work toward formulating a unified colonial stance. A united approach made sense, he suggested, because Britain's new colonial initiatives threatened all Americans. If the other colonies joined Massachusetts in resisting, "by the united Applications of all who are aggrievd, All may happily obtain Redress."[8]

When the Boston Town Meeting approved the Adams instructions on May 24, 1764, it became the first political body in America to go on record stating that Parliament could not constitutionally tax the colonists. The directives also contained the first official recommendation that the colonies present a unified defense of their rights. Even with the acknowledgment of subordination to Great Britain, Adams had staked out what became the colonists' bedrock political position: any form of taxation without representation was unjust.[9]

The instructions Adams drafted helped link him with James Otis Jr., one of Boston's four members of the House of Representatives. Otis had become famous in 1761 when he opposed writs of assistance—general warrants that allowed officials great latitude in searching for smuggled goods. Otis argued that writs of assistance violated "the fundamental principles of law." And, because "an act against the constitution is void," the writs were unconstitutional. His arguments did not sway a Thomas Hutchinson–dominated court, but they propelled Otis into the House and made him the acknowledged leader of Massachusetts's defenders of American liberties.[10] In response to the Adams instructions of 1764, the House of Representatives approved a memorial, written by Otis, that was forwarded to the colony's agent. The House enclosed a copy of Otis's pamphlet, *The Rights of the British Colonies Asserted and Proved*, which had been published in July and included an appendix containing the Boston Town Meeting instructions Adams had crafted. Since Otis and Adams were considered a team by 1765, it is important to understand how their ideas and relationship developed.[11]

In both his *Rights* pamphlet and the House memorial Otis took a bolder stance than Adams had in his town-meeting instructions. Although he raised the kinds of economic arguments Adams advanced, Otis pushed them harder and further. He warned the imperial authorities that the colonies might start smuggling on a wide scale and engage in the commercial production of wool if Parliament's offensive acts remained in place. Since smuggling was illegal, and since Britain had decreed that colonists could not produce wool for export, Otis's threats would naturally infuriate British authorities.[12] Adams, on the other hand, displayed a lighter, more skillful touch. He merely suggested that parliamentary taxation would, by impoverishing the colonists, render them unable to buy Britain's manufactured goods. And he made it sound as if he rued the possibility. Thus Adams's appeals to British self-interest were less offensive and, as events proved, more likely to obtain revisions in British policies.[13]

On the issue of political rights, Otis was again more aggressive than Adams. He opened *The Rights* with a summary of what John Locke had said about the conditions under which a people might legitimately rebel against their government. Otis did not, however, link Locke's analysis with the colonies' situation. Like Adams, Otis drew on the Massachusetts Charter and the British constitution, but he also emphasized natural rights as he argued that the power of Parliament was limited. Parliament could not, for example, justifiably tax the colonists, since the colonists were not represented in Parliament. Otis, speaking as the voice of the Massachusetts House, bluntly held that acts of Parliament that went against "natural equity" or the fundamental principles of the British constitution "are void."[14] Otis's bold—some would say reckless—pronouncements lost their potency when he tried to reconcile them with his acceptance of Parliament's supremacy. In fact, Otis maintained that the colonists could do nothing about Parliament's unconstitutional legislation. So while they might be justified in refusing to pay the taxes, the colonists "must and ought to yield obedience to an act of Parliament . . . till repealed."[15] Although Adams's language was less likely to raise hackles, he actually took a stronger constitutional stance against Parliament. Adams could not be challenged, as Otis came to be, for conceding too much to claims of parliamentary supremacy.[16]

The differences between the approaches of Otis and Adams illustrate why John Adams, writing in late 1765, observed that Samuel was "always for Softness and Delicacy, and Prudence where they will do." John added the vital qualification that, while Samuel artfully employed a soft approach when possible, he was "stanch and stiff and strict and rigid and inflexible" in the cause of protecting American rights. Thomas Hutchinson, who believed that Samuel Adams sought colonial independence from the beginning, offered a similar analysis. He claimed that Adams's public pronouncements were based on what he thought would help achieve independence. Thus Adams might sound moderate in public, but he was at heart a devious radical. The arch-loyalist Peter Oliver concurred and added a twist of nastiness. Samuel Adams was, Oliver thought, "a *Machiavilian*" who "was all serpentine Cunning."[17]

Whether they praised or damned him, public figures from opposite ends of the political spectrum agreed on Samuel Adams's importance both as a political writer and ardent defender of American rights. Commenting approximately a year after Samuel composed the town-meeting instructions of 1764, John Adams praised Samuel's "artful Pen." John added that none of Boston's defenders of America possessed Samuel's "thorough Understanding of Liberty"; none of them could match his "habitual, radical Love" of liberty. Discussing the same 1764–1765 period, Hutchinson, the ultimate loyalist, declared that Samuel "had for several years been an active man in the town of Boston, always on the side of liberty," and had authored many of the publications championing colonial liberties. Hutchinson added a measured assessment. He described Samuel's earliest political writings as the work of an indifferent scribbler. But, with grudging admiration, Hutchinson remarked that practice had subsequently allowed Adams "to arrive at great perfection." He had, alas, developed "a talent of artfully and fallaciously insinuating into the minds of his readers a prejudice against the characters . . . he attacked, beyond any other man I ever knew."[18]

Adams labored hard to produce effective political writing. He was famous for working deep into the night in his second-floor study. Joseph Pierce, whose business took him by the Adams house in the early morning hours, remarked that he usually observed light in Samuel's study. That indicated to him that Samuel "was hard at work writing against the Tories."[19] (This British term referred to those who favored the royal authority of the monarch; those who championed parliamentary authority were labeled Whigs. In the American colonies, *Tory* came to mean those who supported British authority, while *Whig* signified those who championed the rights of the Americans.) As he wrote into the night, Samuel perfected a technique he had utilized in the lengthy land-bank controversy. He put his political opponents on the defensive and hammered them. In modern parlance, as a political writer Adams believed the best defense was a good offense. Equally important, both John Adams, the Whig and future rebel, and Hutchinson, the future loyalist, concurred: Samuel Adams was unwaveringly committed to safeguarding American liberty. They did not, they could not, say the same about Otis.[20]

Despite their philosophical differences, James Otis and Samuel Adams both wanted to protect American rights, and they harmonized on many points. They certainly agreed that the colonies should work in unison to safeguard their interests. It was Otis who influenced the Massachusetts House to implement Adams's call for crafting "united Applications" from all the colonies so they "All may happily obtain Redress." The House agreeably informed the other colonial governments of its activities, including its efforts to get the Sugar Act repealed and to thwart passage of a stamp act. The representatives invited the other colonial assemblies to take similar action.[21]

Merchants in Boston and elsewhere in the colonies added economic measures to the growing political resistance. In August 1764, fifty Boston merchants pledged to quit buying some British luxuries, including those associated with showy, often ostentatious, funerals. The public responded so positively that newspaper writers spoke of burials "according to the new mode." And, following the lead of New Yorkers, groups in various areas, including Boston, promoted colonial manufacturing, especially the production of cloth. In these tentative and small-scale but symbolic ways, people worked to undermine British support for Grenville's policy.[22]

In June 1765, after receiving word Parliament had actually passed a colonial stamp act scheduled to take effect on November 1, the Massachusetts representatives, under Otis's leadership, carried Adams's call for unified colonial action to new heights. Emphasizing that they had unanimously agreed, the representatives issued a circular letter inviting the other colonies to send delegations to a congress that would meet in New York City in October. Reflecting the tone of Adams's earlier instructions, the invitation said the congress would strive to produce "a general and united, dutifull, loyal and humble Representation of their Condition to his Majesty, and the Parliament, to implore Relief."[23]

At the same time that the House proposed an all-colony congress, the Virginia House of Burgesses, led by Patrick Henry, approved resolutions that advanced arguments resembling those Adams had composed a year earlier. The burgesses declared that the rights of Englishmen guaranteed in Virginia's royal charters stipulated that Virginians could only be taxed by legislators they elected. An additional resolution the burgesses adopted but quickly rescinded was also widely reported in newspapers, which declared that the colonists were not bound to accept any tax unless it was levied by their representatives. Because it implied that colonists should disregard a law passed by Parliament, the statement flirted with treason.[24]

The constitutional arguments advanced in the colonial petitions mattered. As Adams continually stressed, if Americans acquiesced in even one of Parliament's taxes, they would give the MPs a precedent to tax *any* of the colonists' possessions. In building their case against taxation, colonial assemblies often argued, as Adams did, that the restrictions on colonial trade would undermine Great Britain's economic welfare. However, although they staked out bold positions, by limiting themselves to petitioning, the colonial assemblymen advocated passive resistance. The legislators seemed to believe Parliament would eventually realize that its new colonial program harmed Britain's overall economic situation. Of course, one could hardly have expected more. The colonial assemblymen were in many instances fundamentally conservative planters and merchants, and they had been brought up in a political world steeped in the principle of petitioning for redress. Regular, orderly, and legal methods must, they believed, be followed. Adams shared that view and in the summer of 1765 supported the tactic of passive resistance. Although Adams and the colonial legislators did not exert immediate, intense pressure on Parliament to rescind the Stamp Act, others did.[25]

By mid-1765, colonial merchants contemplated waging economic warfare by boycotting British goods until Parliament repealed its taxes. This approach would also foster an increase in colonial manufacturing, another form of economic coercion. Based on his belief that trade made the colonies valuable to Britain and also on the fact that a boycott was legal, Adams approved this course of action. Well-organized economic resistance could, he reasoned, turn prophecies about the Stamp Act producing economic hardships for Britain into reality. If British merchants and manufacturers could be enlisted against the Stamp Act, Parliament would be pressured to change its policy. But the boycott strategy, even if successful, would take time, and it could not stop the Stamp Act from taking effect.

Many Bostonians and radicals elsewhere wanted more active resistance. They took to the streets to neutralize the Stamp Act before it could be implemented. The first colonial crowd action against the Stamp Act occurred in Boston on August 14, 1765, and it targeted Andrew Oliver, the stamp distributor for Massachusetts, who was also the secretary of the colony. The plan originated with the Loyal Nine, middle-class Bostonians who came primarily from the artisan and shopkeeper ranks and who formed the nucleus of what became the city's Sons of Liberty. Although the Loyal Nine considered Adams a friend, he was not a member of the group; moreover, there is no clear evidence he worked directly with them on their August 14 ventures.[26] Having first arranged for usually antagonistic working-class groups from the city's northern and southern sections to unite against the Stamp Act, the Loyal Nine created effigies, potent symbols often used when people took to the streets. When daylight came on that Wednesday, it revealed an effigy of Oliver along with one of the devil peeping out of a boot. The effigies dangled from the Liberty Tree, a large old elm located in South End near the Boston Common and about one-half mile from Faneuil Hall, which became a staging area for anti-British activities. The effigy of Oliver carried the verse "A goodlier sight who e'er did see? / A Stamp-Man hanging on a tree!" Thousands viewed the display.[27]

Throughout the day members of the Northside group, led by Henry Swift, stood guard so the effigies could not be removed. In the evening, a large contingent, headed by Ebenezer Mackintosh of the Southside group, took charge and paraded the effigies through the city. The crowd, which at times perhaps numbered three thousand, came upon the small building that reportedly would serve as Oliver's stamp-distribution office. The crowd demolished it. The throng then marched in an orderly fashion to Fort Hill for a celebration, which included beheading the Oliver effigy and burning all the effigies. Boards ripped from Oliver's stamp distribution building fueled the fire. The Loyal Nine soon left the celebration. After they departed, members of the throng, apparently under no one's direction, traveled the short distance to Oliver's home and attempted to burn his coach. In the process, they smashed windows, destroyed garden furniture, and consumed some of Oliver's wine. Nothing, however, was stolen.[28]

Daniel N. Chdowiecki 1784 engraving "Die Americaner wiedersetzen sich der Stempel-Acte, und verbrennen das aus England nach America gesandte Stempel-Papier zu Boston, im August 1764 [i.e., 1765]." Courtesy of the Library of Congress.

Andrew Oliver resigned his stamp distributorship the next day. His resignation satisfied the Loyal Nine; they saw no reason for further action. Nevertheless, on August 26, crowds not led by the Loyal Nine or other middle–class persons sought out a variety of targets, including three men associated with enforcing Britain's customs regulations. As the evening deepened, a large multitude, by all accounts made up primarily of members of the lower orders, went after their main target: Thomas Hutchinson, the colony's wealthy lieutenant governor. He evaded those he labeled "the Ruffians" by fleeing to a neighbor's home. But Hutchinson's mansion and possessions could not run. People spent most of the night and early morning ransacking and then demolishing large sections of the house. As Hutchinson recounted the event, when "the hellish crew" finished at about four in the morning, "one of the best furnished houses in the Province had nothing remaining but the bare walls and floors." Members of the crowd also stole many valuable items. That is significant. Traditionally, British and American crowds might purloin food from hoarding merchants, but they did not make off with personal property such as money or clothing. The theft of personal property and the lower-class character of the crowd suggest Hutchinson was targeted in part because he was a rich aristocrat. Governor Francis Bernard thought so. Reflecting on the events of August 26, he voiced the fear that Boston would soon experience a war waged for the purpose of "taking away the Distinction of rich and poor."[29]

The actions of August as well as Boston's other revolutionary-crowd actions have been attributed to Samuel Adams. He has inaccurately been depicted as the man, the propagandist, the dictator who controlled "the Boston mob."[30] That interpretation originated with Governor Bernard and loyalists, who, in addition to hating Adams, assumed ordinary people could not act for their own logical reasons. Loyalists reasoned that since Adams was closely associated with the lower orders, and since the lower orders must have been manipulated to act, Adams must have been the chief manipulator. Bernard talked of the government needing to be rescued from "a trained mob." Hutchinson sneered that the "mob . . . might be let loose, or kept up" depending on what its "keepers," the leaders of "the liberty party," wanted. Loyalist Peter Oliver, the stamp distributor's wealthy brother, put it more emphatically. In 1781, referring to his fellow Americans and the coming of the Revolution, he asserted that, "As for the People in general, they were like the Mobility of all Countries, perfect Machines, wound up by any Hand who first might take the Winch." Oliver considered Samuel Adams particularly good at cranking the winch. His "Power over weak Minds was truly surprizing"; Adams "could turn the minds of the great Vulgar as well as small" to whatever course he chose. Indeed, said Oliver, "perhaps he was a singular Instance of this kind." Thomas Hutchinson voiced a similar slur when he labeled Adams "the master of the puppets."[31] Hutchinson and Oliver could not see that ordinary people might have their own reasons for taking action. Unfortunately that myopic view was perpetuated by many latter-day scholars who repeated the partisan claims that people joined crowds because they were manipulated by propaganda and by Samuel Adams.[32]

Ordinary colonists did not need to be goaded into opposing British policies. Dire circumstances and their own sense of justice animated them. Many Bostonians, and others throughout the colonies, could not passively wait for Parliament to change its mind about taxing the colonists. Boston was already facing hard times, and British imperial reform exacerbated the city's difficulties. The close of the Seven Years' War in 1763 ended what little benefit Boston had experienced due to wartime spending. And while all major American cities suffered from a postwar recession, Boston hurt the most. In 1764, smallpox ravaged the city. In January 1765, in the midst of a bitterly cold winter, several leading business firms failed. John Rowe, a wealthy merchant, observed that the repeated bankruptcies caused general consternation. Businessmen moaned about bad times and dull trade. In June a Bostonian maintained that the West Indies trade had plummeted 80 percent within the past year and that a person rarely saw cash circulating in Boston. He blamed these developments on the Sugar Act.[33]

All this happened at a time when the city's government, the town meeting, teetered on the brink of bankruptcy. Samuel Adams's changed attitude toward tax collecting offers a useful illustration of the problems Bostonians faced. A town meeting report of May 1765 revealed that five tax collectors had not yet gathered back taxes totaling slightly more than £18,000. Adams, who perhaps not coincidentally had declined another term as a tax collector in March 1765, accounted for just over £8,000 of that deficit. By July 1765, under increasing pressure to obtain these back taxes, Adams abandoned his easygoing ways. In an effort to collect unpaid taxes, some on his books since 1759, Adams sued delinquent taxpayers, including two shoemakers, two house carpenters, and "Jack a free Negro."[34]

In such difficult times Bostonians, like other urbanites, who had little or no economic reserve, stared poverty in the face. Ordinary Bostonians, therefore, had special reason for wanting to abolish or at least neutralize the Stamp Act. That was doubly true for the city's seafarers, who confronted the additional threat of literally losing their liberty by being impressed into the British navy. It was the common people who most knew and hated the British press gangs. It was the commonality who could not afford to wait for passive measures—petitions and possible economic boycotts—to overturn Parliament's new taxing laws. Ordinary people, on whom rich aristocrats often heaped contempt, had to work or starve. They reasoned that, if they could stop the implementation of the Stamp Act, they could continue to work, to survive. These people did not have to be controlled by Samuel Adams or anyone else. They did not have to be propagandized. They had their own good reasons for taking immediate and aggressive action, for transforming the Adams-Otis rhetoric into political action.[35]

Samuel Adams applauded the accomplishments of Boston's first anti–Stamp Act crowd. He later proclaimed that August 14 should be remembered forever in America. It was the day "the People shouted; and their shout was heard to the distant end of this Continent." Adams and other Whig leaders, however, had no hand in the crowd actions of August 26; moreover, Adams was horrified by their "truly *mobbish* Nature," which included stealing money. Boston's noted defenders of American liberties,

Adams among them, thus treated the two major August crowd actions very differently. The town meeting ignored the events of August 14 but responded to the August 26 assaults by holding an emergency meeting the next day. After expressing revulsion at the extraordinary and violent activities, the meeting urged the city's officials and citizens to do their utmost to prevent recurrences. The vote was unanimous. The *Boston Gazette*, the most radical newspaper in the colony, punctuated the sharp distinctions that persons like the Loyal Nine and Adams made between what happened on the 14th and the 26th of August. The publishers, one a member of the Loyal Nine, claimed that virtually all Bostonians wore smiles after the events of August 14. But the violence that occurred a dozen days later elicited gloom. Although they knew that Mackintosh took a leading role in the August 26 events, the *Gazette* editors ignored that fact as they denounced the perpetrators of the "horrid Scenes of Villainy" as behaving "like Devils let loose." And the editors stressed that Bostonians intervened to counter and stop the villainy.

Adams also tried to distance the Whigs and the city from the outrages of August 26. Writing to a well-connected correspondent in London, Adams echoed the analysis presented in the *Boston Gazette*. He bemoaned the events of August 26 but stressed that any honest person would see that Boston was not to blame. He claimed that "an universal Consternation" appeared in the faces of everyone the next morning, and, just hours later, the largest town meeting ever known unanimously declared its "detestation" of the August 26 events. Samuel added that "I voted to assist the Majistrate to their utmost in preventing or suppressing any further Disorder." By early November, a newspaper writer carried the argument about Boston's innocence to an almost predictable conclusion by asserting that the "horrid Violences" of August 26 were "only the lawless Ravages of Some Foreign Villians" and "a very few people" of Boston.[36]

Adams and other popular leaders distinguished between the two crowd actions for both philosophical and practical reasons. They believed, first of all, in the rule of law. Writing for the Massachusetts House later in 1765, Adams put it this way: "when our sacred rights are infringed, we feel the grievance, but we understand the nature of our happy constitution too well, and entertain too high an opinion of virtue and justice . . . to encourage any means of redressing it, but what are justifiable by the constitution." Although he heaped contempt on the events of August 26, Adams offered a revealing defense of the earlier crowd action. Writing to an Englishman, he recounted the events of August 14 and maintained that Americans believed the Stamp Act endangered their essential, unalienable rights. He then speculated on what the English might do in the same situation. "After taking all *legal* Steps to obtain redress *to no Purpose*, the *whole People of England* would have taken the same Steps [the Bostonians took] & *justified themselves*." Adams did not have to add that the process he described met the standard set by John Locke for how an aggrieved people might justly respond to perceived tyranny. But neither Adams nor anyone else who followed Locke could sanction the August 26 violence. All legal means of redress had not been exhausted; the August 26 crowd's violent actions smacked of class warfare.[37]

Practical considerations also made "truly *mobbish*" crowds unacceptable. Adams wanted to travel the constitutional high road, and he hoped to elicit British sympathy for the supposedly beleaguered, debt-ridden colonists. The attacks on private property, especially the wholesale destruction and looting of property belonging to royal officials, would outrage British politicians. Their anger would in turn stiffen opposition to repealing Parliament's noxious laws. Thus, for pragmatic as well as philosophical reasons, Adams and other leaders of the popular party strove to ensure that nothing resembling the crowd actions of August 26 would occur again. They succeeded, but not because they controlled the crowd or bribed crowd leaders, as some have thought. They succeeded because the lower classes themselves saw where their interests merged with those of the middle and upper classes in defending American liberties. Moreover, the success of collective action in Boston and elsewhere reduced the need for yet more crowd actions.[38]

The leaders of the popular movement in Massachusetts, and in other colonies as well, clearly did not head a unified group. Supporters of the popular colonial position agreed on the ends: parliamentary taxation must be resisted. They did not necessarily agree on the means. Adams and fellow Whig leaders, like their counterparts in other colonies, wanted to pursue only legal, constitutional avenues of opposition. They had ready answers to basic questions about methods. Should one petition for redress of grievances? Of course. Support persons bringing economic pressure to bear by boycotting British goods and by increasing colonial manufacturing? Excellent. Should one organize—or at least applaud—large nonviolent demonstrations, particularly those involving symbolic acts such as hanging stamp distributors in effigy? Yes. The leaders could argue that these activities proved that the commonality, not just elected officials, opposed Parliament's schemes. Moreover, even if they did not organize them, leading Whigs realized that some crowd actions achieved desirable results. If they prevented the Stamp Act from taking effect, that might make it easier to get the act repealed. But Whig leaders like Adams found nothing beneficial in what happened in Boston on August 26. They believed that such violent outbursts tinged with hints of class warfare must be squelched.[39]

The popular forces soon had reason to hope the Stamp Act would disappear. In early September, Bostonians received the news that the Grenville administration had been dismissed in July. Better yet, General Henry Seymour Conway, one of the few MPs who vigorously opposed the Stamp Act, had become secretary of state for the Southern Department in the new ministry. Conway now had the principal administrative responsibility for the colonies. Apparently at Adams's urging, the town meeting acted quickly to take advantage of the change in administrations. On September 18 the meeting selected a committee that included Adams. The committee was to contact General Conway and Colonel Isaac Barré, another MP who had denounced the Stamp Act. Barré had electrified Parliament by calling the Americans "Sons of Liberty" and by describing them as a people jealous of their liberties. Americans would, Barré predicted, vindicate their rights if they were ever violated. The committee's recommendations, which Adams wrote, called for sending Conway and Barré formal addresses thanking each for his noble speech defending the colonies' rights. In addition, copies of these speeches should be obtained and placed "among our most precious Archives." And, as soon as possible, paintings of the two great men should be acquired and placed in Faneuil Hall "as a standing Monument to all Posterity, of the Virtue and Justice of our Benefactors, and a lasting Proof of our Gratitude."[40] Ever the thinking politician, Adams understood the value of cultivating allies, and here he worked the art of political flattery with impressive thoroughness.

With powerful allies across the Atlantic, Adams increased the pressure. When he again prepared the town meeting's instructions for its representatives, Adams reiterated the basic themes of his May 1764 instructions, but with less delicacy. In the instructions approved on September 18, 1765, he flatly declared the Stamp Act "unconstitutional." Only representatives chosen by the people could levy taxes, and "it is certain that we were in no sense represented in the Parliament" when the Stamp Act was enacted. Adams proclaimed that the representatives should not join in any public measures that countenanced or assisted in executing the Stamp Act. Certainly no tax funds should help put the Stamp Act into operation. By inviting the representatives to find a way to subvert an act of Parliament, Adams danced close to the line separating legal protest from treason. But his position likely pleased the bulk of the Bostonians who had joined in the recent crowd actions.[41]

It turned out—and given how the Boston Caucus operated, Samuel may have known it—that Adams was crafting his own instructions. The death of Oxenbridge Thatcher had opened a seat in the Massachusetts House, and on September 27 the Boston Town Meeting selected Adams as one of its four representatives. Wasting no time, Adams was sworn in that day.[42] This election, obviously a personal milestone for Adams, signaled a change in leadership for Massachusetts and, in time, for the colonies as a whole. James Otis Jr. and Adams were soon working together so closely that court-party leaders often mentioned them in the same breath. But, as their 1764 writings indicated, the two men had important philosophical as well as personality differences that, over time, would cause the breakup of their partnership. Otis, a magnificent and fiery orator, could be disturbingly inconsistent on the issue of whether Parliament could constitutionally tax the colonies. In 1765 Otis escaped being branded as a turncoat only because he published items anonymously. By 1766 he seemed to have flip-flopped once more as he argued that America's rights were being trampled.

Adams, who was no orator, balanced Otis's fire with a noted reserve. Adams also possessed a deft political sense Otis lacked.[43] Most important, Adams never wavered in his defense of colonial rights, and his presence in the House made the representatives much less likely to defer to court-party elites. Once Adams entered the House, it never again compromised with the Council as it had under Otis's leadership in late 1764 when drafting a petition against parliamentary taxation. Thomas Hutchinson, who had embarrassed Otis and the House by his skillful maneuvering to water down that petition, witnessed the profound change. Admitting that the "liberty party" had made a "great advance" during Samuel Adams's first session in the House, Hutchinson attributed that movement to Adams's "influence." Governor Bernard also recognized and lamented the difference Adams made. Offering a backhanded compliment on Adams's organizational skills, Bernard moaned in 1765 that when placed on a legislative committee Adams typically "pulled out a set of resolves, ready cut & dryed." And in February 1767 Bernard complained that, after Adams entered the House, its addresses to him had "the Air of a Manifesto."[44]

Adams demonstrated his influence quickly. It was evident in the way the House responded to the governor's September 25 address on the opening of the legislative session. While saying he disliked the Stamp Act, Governor Bernard defended Parliament's right to pass it. Then, alluding to the August crowd actions, he rebuked Boston for being a lawless city where the people supported mobs. Two days later, on the day Adams assumed his seat, Bernard recessed the House until October 23 on the pretense that many members had not yet reached Boston. Shutting the House down for a month proved a mistake. It gave the popular party extra time to craft an effective response. Because Otis spent much of October attending the Stamp Act Congress in New York, the task of formulating a response fell mainly to Adams.[45] From that time forward, Adams became the principal author of the House replies, petitions, and circular letters. And, as both friend and foe attested, impressive political prose flowed from his pen. Even when others drafted documents, Adams was routinely called on to add his own editorial flourish.[46]

The response to the governor's address, issued the day after the House reconvened, mocked Bernard by reminding him that he had fled the city when the August 26 crowd actions erupted. Far from being lawless, when Bernard's flight left them to their own devices Bostonians had "raised a spirit" among all classes that prevented any further violence. Indeed, Bostonians endeavored to use only "legal and regular" methods to defend their liberties. This helped demonstrate, as Adams put it, that Bostonians were "a people ever remarkable for their loyalty and good order; tho' at present uneasy and discontented." The problem was, of course, the Stamp Act. That pernicious legislation violated both the Massachusetts Charter and the basic rights of Englishmen.

Embracing positions advanced in other colonies, Adams underscored two additional points. First, the colonists were not represented in Parliament, and, moreover, such representation would be "impracticable." Although Adams did not elaborate, the clear implication was that, since the colonists could not be represented in Parliament, they could never be taxed by Parliament. The second point flowed from the fact that colonists accused of violating the Stamp Act could be hauled into vice-admiralty courts, which did not use the jury system. Invoking England's most sacred guarantee of liberties, Adams contended that adjudicating these cases without a jury violated Magna Carta. Pushing even harder, Adams warned that if the king's Massachusetts subjects were not governed "according to the known stated rules of the constitution," they might, horror of horrors, "become disaffected." So, if any thoughts of independence eventually crept into American minds, the blame would rest solely on British politicians who had acted unconstitutionally. Once again Adams was putting his opponents in the wrong.[47]

Illustrating the kind of cross-colony fertilization that occurred time and again as the resistance movement progressed, the arguments Adams employed matched well with positions the Stamp Act Congress enunciated in late October 1765. In a statement of essential principles, the congress highlighted the colonists' loyalty to the Crown and acknowledged "all due Subordination" to Parliament. However, the delegates held that the colonists possessed all the rights of Englishmen, and that included being taxed only by their own representatives. Since Americans were not, and from their local circumstances could not be, represented in the House of Commons, Parliament could not tax them. Moreover, extending the powers of the vice-admiralty courts undermined the people's "inherent and invaluable Right" to trial by jury. Just as Adams had done, the Congress warned that restrictions on colonial trade would inhibit American purchases of British-manufactured goods. Thus, for both constitutional and pragmatic reasons, Parliament should repeal the Stamp Act and other recent laws restricting American commerce.[48]

Shortly after the Stamp Act Congress adjourned, the Massachusetts House prepared a similar statement. The House approved fourteen resolves that, as Hutchinson indicated, Samuel Adams composed. Although the resolves generally covered the same ground the Stamp Act Congress traversed, on two substantive issues Adams was more radical. While the Stamp Act Congress explicitly admitted Parliament's supremacy, Adams merely stated that Massachusetts had the greatest veneration for Parliament. Hutchinson noted the difference, which he found both galling and alarming. The failure to acknowledge the supremacy of Parliament did not happen accidentally. The instructions Adams crafted in May 1764 had not mentioned Parliament's supremacy. Adams also outdistanced the Stamp Act Congress by asserting that "certain essential Rights" were "founded in the Law of God and Nature, and are the common Rights of Mankind." Well ahead of many other popular leaders, Adams here enunciated the proposition that the colonists' rights rested on more than the colonial charters and the British constitution. Thus, there was good reason for Stephen Hopkins, a radical Rhode Islander, to call Adams's resolves "the best" America had yet produced.[49]

Having done what he could with official political pronouncements, Adams joined other prominent Boston Whigs as they worked with the Loyal Nine and with established crowd leaders to keep opposition to the Stamp Act within legal bounds. By the fall of 1765 the members of the Loyal Nine had dramatically expanded their membership and, along with popular leaders in other colonies, embraced the name Sons of Liberty. In an effort to ensure that nothing untoward happened in future crowd actions, popular party leaders and the Sons of Liberty worked closely with Ebenezer Mackintosh, the leader of the South Boston crowd, and with Henry Swift, the leader of the Northsiders. On November 1, as church bells pealed, normal business ground to a halt and anti–Stamp Act effigies were hung on the Liberty Tree. At two o'clock, the figures were cut down, carried through the streets to the public gallows, strung up, taken down, and then ripped apart and cast to the winds. A crowd of about three thousand, accompanied by columns of men on horseback led by Mackintosh, witnessed the spectacle. This huge, orderly crowd included many inhabitants from the surrounding countryside. Crowd actions, and the threat of them, worked in Boston and throughout America. All the stamp distributors in the mainland colonies resigned their posts or promised not to distribute stamps. So on November 1, 1765, when the Stamp Act officially went into effect, no one implemented it. Since no stamps or stamped paper were available, colonists could argue for carrying on business as usual, except of course for any boycotts against British goods.

The events of November 5, "Pope's Day," a day noted for anti-Catholic activities and violence, also pleased Adams and other leaders of the popular party. The Northside and Southside groups skipped their usual end-of-the-day combat. Instead, Mackintosh and Swift, resplendently attired in uniforms and carrying speaking trumpets supplied by the Sons of Liberty, led their effigy-carrying forces in a united protest against the Stamp Act. Under the leadership of Mackintosh and Swift, the normally antagonistic North and South Boston factions first met in King Street and then marched harmoniously to the Liberty Tree and then to Copp's Hill, where they jointly burned their effigies. Even Hutchinson had to admit that the demonstration seemed remarkable for the peaceful, orderly behavior of those who paraded through the streets. Adams and other proponents of peaceful protest had succeeded, at least for now, because the members of the crowd were not inherently prone to violence and because they shared the goal of defeating Parliament's new colonial policy.[50]

The money needed to supply Mackintosh and Swift with impressive uniforms and speaking trumpets came in part from the pockets of John Hancock, a young merchant who had inherited between £70,000 and £100,000 in late 1764. From that time forward, Adams befriended Hancock and assiduously drew him into anti-British activity. As Adams is reported to have put it, he wanted to make the young man's fortune work for the benefit of Boston.[51]

The economic war against Britain intensified in the fall of 1765. New York City merchants led the way. On October 31, about two hundred of them pledged to stop buying British merchandise until Parliament repealed the Stamp Act. Within a week, Philadelphia merchants followed suit. Boston did not produce a formal agreement until December 9, but 250 merchants and traders signed it. Nonimportation might help force the British to retreat, but the program raised the specter of crowd violence since it meant less shipping and less shipping meant less work. It would take time for that potentially explosive mix to develop because many Boston merchants planned ahead. They obtained shipping papers before November 1 for vessels not scheduled to leave port for weeks. But by early December, as the supply of prepurchased shipping papers dwindled, merchants and the lower orders clamored for relief. The popular forces, the Whigs, needed to find a way to do what the crowds in Boston and other colonial cities advocated: carry on business as if the Stamp Act did not exist.[52]

Boston's leading Whigs began pursuing that goal shortly after the city's merchants formally embraced nonimportation. On December 17, in the presence of a large crowd gathered at the Liberty Tree, Andrew Oliver reiterated his earlier abdication of the post of stamp distributor. He was compelled to swear on his oath, before a justice of the peace, that he had never functioned as a stamp distributor and would never attempt to do so. The Sons of Liberty, who arranged all this, obviously worked to give the proceedings a legal cast. Later that afternoon, the customhouse reopened and began conducting business without stamped papers. Except as limited by the nonimportation effort, commerce could proceed as usual. That evening, the Sons of Liberty, with Samuel Adams as one of their invited guests, celebrated this achievement. Sailors, dockworkers, and others who depended on shipping for their livelihoods had even more reason to rejoice.[53]

Having reduced the threat of crowd action by ensuring that shipping could move without stamped papers, popular leaders turned their attention to reopening the civil courts, which had shut down because no stamped paper was available. On December 18 the Boston Town Meeting unanimously selected a committee headed by Samuel Adams to present a memorial to the governor and his Council. Wrapping itself in a law-and-order cloak, the meeting bemoaned the closing of the civil courts because they could not obtain stamped paper. With studied disingenuousness, the Bostonians said they could find no just and legal reason for the closures. Proclaiming that "the Law is the great rule of Right, the Security of our Lives and Propertys, and the best Birth right of Englishmen," they called upon Governor Bernard to reopen the civil courts. Adams, continuing his practice of promoting the careers of talented young supporters of America, saw to it that cousin John was one of the lawyers selected to argue Boston's case before Bernard and his Council. His Braintree resolutions in defense of American liberties had already enhanced John's reputation, and Samuel wanted him to become active in Boston.[54]

Everyone knew the civil courts lacked stamped paper because of crowd violence and the threat of yet more violence. So Bernard and most of his Council, headed by Hutchinson, considered the Boston memorial hypocritical nonsense. Still, they agreed that the civil courts must function. To avoid responsibility for violating the Stamp Act, Bernard and his councilors finessed the situation. Their response, produced on December 21 and considered by the town meeting the same day, called the question of reopening the courts a legal one. Accordingly, the judges must decide if their courts could operate without stamped paper. By unanimous vote, the town meeting proclaimed this an unsatisfactory answer. Although the popular party and the court party continued skirmishing over the issue, the minor courts quickly resumed operations, and by the spring of 1766 all of the courts in Massachusetts functioned without stamped papers. Massachusetts had eviscerated the Stamp Act.[55]

The story varied slightly from colony to colony, but the results duplicated what happened in Massachusetts: the Stamp Act was effectively nullified. One aspect of the general colonial effort is especially important for illustrating Samuel Adams's ongoing efforts to achieve a unified defense of American rights. Sons of Liberty in various colonies, not just in Massachusetts, helped spearhead anti–Stamp Act activities in 1765 and 1766. To coordinate their efforts, they established committees to correspond with one another. Samuel urged that this network of committees be maintained even after the Stamp Act had been repealed. As he envisioned it, a union of correspondents could help defeat any designing men who might again assail American rights. His suggestion did not produce results in 1766, but the idea of achieving a unified colonial approach by maintaining committees of correspondence was not a passing one. Samuel kept returning to it until it bore fruit.[56]

The colonists' triumph on the home front did not guarantee the Stamp Act would be repealed. The ultimate victory had to be won in Britain. So Adams used his role as an author of Massachusetts House pronouncements to promote repeal. In November and December of 1765, while working to gut the Stamp Act in the colonies, Adams wrote to the Massachusetts colonial agent and to British "friends" of America to supply them with arguments. The central themes were those Samuel had been trumpeting since May 1764: trade made the colonies valuable to Britain, and Parliament could not constitutionally tax the colonists. Britain's general control of colonial trade, when coupled with the American purchase of Britain's manufactured goods, already amounted to "at least an indirect Tax."[57]

When he turned to constitutional arguments, Adams took the offensive. Again drawing on political theory popularized by John Locke, Adams stressed that the British constitution "is founded in the Principles of Nature and Reason." It followed that the constitution endowed the government with no more power than "was originally designed for the Preservation of the unalienable Rights of Nature." By again emphasizing a natural-rights position, Adams ensured that the colonists could challenge parliamentary taxation even if arguments rooted in the British constitution or the Massachusetts Charter got swept aside. At the same time, Adams continued to highlight the protections and rights grounded in the charter. In terms drawn from Locke, Adams described the charter, granted by the monarchy in 1691, as a compact. Violating the compact, or contract, would break it. So if the British broke the compact, the people would be justified in forming a new government. Natural rights, the British constitution, and the Massachusetts Charter formed a powerful triumvirate to protect American rights.[58]

Adams also urged his correspondents to challenge the claim that the colonists were represented in Parliament. This was a crucial issue because even the supporters of the Stamp Act acknowledged both that the colonists did not directly elect any MPs and that Parliament could not tax the colonists if they were unrepresented. British politicians dealt with the issue by asserting that the colonists had virtual representation. In theory, MPs represented the whole empire, and, therefore, all the people of the empire were represented. The idea of virtual representation, widely accepted in Britain, reflected the fact that MPs were not required to live in the area they represented. Adams savaged the virtual-representation argument by pointing out that every county in England elected MPs even if individual towns did not; thus, every inch of England was actually, not virtually, represented in Parliament.[59]

Because he understood the potential danger in actual representation, Adams was not content with merely demolishing the virtual-representation theory. He realized that Parliament might let the Americans elect a few MPs and then heap taxes on the colonists. This possibility forced Adams to spell out what made colonial representation impractical. He considered geography a crucial factor. The tremendous distance between America and England, which Adams constantly stressed was three thousand miles, made actual representation impossible. The situation in the colonies was, he argued, so often and continually varying that even a knowledgeable colonial MP would soon be woefully out of touch. It was also a question of power. As Adams admitted, "we think the Colonies cannot be equally and fully represented; and if not equally then in Effect not at all." That was the key. Adams and most other colonists did not want to elect any MPs because the British would not allow the colonists enough MPs—enough actual political power—to block legislation the colonists opposed. So, as 1765 came to an end, Adams endeavored to do more than help overturn a specific tax act; he became increasingly concerned with ensuring that Parliament could *never* tax the colonists.[60]

Parliament was not interested in colonial arguments about its right to tax. The MPs even refused to consider petitions that questioned Parliament's taxing authority. And many in Britain wanted to punish America for its violent response to the Stamp Act. But Americans were not the only ones concerned about pocketbook issues. When large numbers of British merchants and manufacturers, pinched by colonial nonimportation, began clamoring for relief, the MPs listened. Rumors that Parliament would repeal the hated Stamp Act circulated in Boston by early January 1766. Soon thereafter, the Sons of Liberty started planning for a gala repeal celebration. By early spring, the colonists knew British merchants and manufacturing interests had urged repeal of the Stamp Act. In late April the Boston Town Meeting issued instructions designed to keep the repeal celebration orderly.[61]

On May 16 the brigantine *Harrison* sailed into Boston harbor carrying copies of the repeal act. A huge, orderly celebration took place three days later. Special lights flickered in the city's windows; fireworks lit the night. A large decorated and transparent obelisk, prepared by the Sons of Liberty, told the story of how Americans, aided by their British friends, had protected their basic liberties and defeated the vile Stamp Act. Boston staged more elaborate festivities than most localities did, but outpourings of joy occurred throughout the colonies.[62] The colonists' exuberance should perhaps have been muted. On March 18, the same day it repealed the Stamp Act, Parliament adopted the Declaratory Act. Without actually mentioning the power to tax, the Declaratory Act proclaimed that Parliament had the right to pass legislation "to bind the colonies and people of *America* . . . in all cases whatsoever."[63] True, the renowned British politician William Pitt had advanced the novel thesis that the legislative power did not include the power to tax. He held that Parliament had every power over the colonies except the power "of taking their money out of their pockets without their consent." Pitt's position, however, was generally ridiculed in Britain

Paul Revere engraving "A View of the Obelisk" (1766). Courtesy of the American Antiquarian Society.

and had few adherents.[64] The colonists might also have been lulled into a
false sense of security because the Massachusetts colonial agent, knowing
a declaratory act of some kind would be enacted, had expressed his belief
that the act would not apply to taxation. Colonists might therefore have
assumed, and many did, that Parliament had conceded that it could not tax
them.[65] Still, given the Declaratory Act, it remained unclear whether the
Americans had defeated parliamentary taxation or merely won a battle in
an ongoing political war.

Looking toward the annual May election of 1766, Samuel Adams
and other leading Whigs had already begun to consolidate their legislative
forces in anticipation of future battles. The residents of Massachusetts's
rural townships despised the Stamp Act as much as Bostonians did. To
help translate that resentment into votes in the House, Adams and Otis resorted to the press. They produced various items attacking representatives
willing to back Governor Bernard and his court party. Adams and Otis
skewered thirty-two representatives, more than one-fourth of the House,
for their alleged pro–Stamp Act, pro-British position. The results delighted Samuel. Nineteen of the thirty-two targeted House members lost
their seats. The popular forces also retained their strength in Boston. At
the May 6 town meeting, Adams nominated John Hancock, his wealthy
protégé, for a place on the four-member Boston House delegation. The
meeting voted Hancock onto the delegation and reelected Adams, Otis,
and Thomas Cushing, another champion of America's rights and the son
of the merchant who had long ago realized Adams was not destined to be
a businessman.[66]

The popular party soon flexed its new political muscle. On May 28
the representatives selected James Otis as speaker of the House. Rejecting
the sage advice of prominent court-party politicians, Governor Bernard
exercised his charter-given right to negate the House's choice for speaker.
That was not a smart move. The governor's veto merely bolstered Otis's
popularity, and the members of the House named Thomas Cushing speaker.

Bernard's ill-conceived action made it easier for the popular party to
eliminate Bernard's staunchest Council supporters. The Council had traditionally been made up of rich, powerful, and generally conservative men
inclined to support Britain's policies. In the early days of agitation against
the new imperial policies, the Council tried, at times effectively, to check
the House's aggressiveness in defending America. Nevertheless, the representatives, who together with the old Council members annually elected
the new Council, had deferentially continued to help keep the individuals
Bernard wanted on his Council. But in May 1766, perhaps not coinciden-

tally the first time Adams participated in the process, the House stopped deferring to the governor. Following Bernard's veto of the House's choice for speaker, the popular party used its small but workable majority to compile a list of councilors notable for the names it did not contain. The list did not include the following: Thomas Hutchinson, the lieutenant governor who served as chairman of the Council's committees and was also chief justice of the superior court; Andrew Oliver, the unlucky would-be stamp distributor and royally appointed secretary of Massachusetts; Peter Oliver, Andrew's brother and a superior court justice; or Edmund Trowbridge, the king's attorney general in Massachusetts.

Samuel Adams was particularly pleased when these royally appointed officials got tossed off the Council, and his pleasure did not stem merely from seeing the court party weakened. Adams had long argued for the separation of powers. He considered it dangerous to let a person hold offices in different governmental branches, and he was particularly adamant about judges not serving in the legislature. All four excluded councilors served in more than one branch of government. Two excluded councilors served on the superior court. And Thomas Hutchinson held so many and varied posts that he was simultaneously serving in Massachusetts's legislative, executive, and judicial branches of government! Anyone who believed, as Adams did, in a separation of powers had a strong philosophical justification for expelling Hutchinson, Trowbridge, and the two Olivers from the Council.

A livid Governor Bernard did not see it that way. He denounced the House for not reelecting the "best and most able Servants, whose only Crime is their Fidelity to the Crown." In retaliation, he resorted to his charter-given power to veto anyone selected to serve on the Council. He refused to accept six councilors he considered too friendly to the American cause. Nothing in the charter, however, required the House to replace the persons the governor rejected; therefore, when the House balked at choosing others, Bernard had to make do with twenty-two councilors.[67]

Bernard and Hutchinson searched for innovative ways that would allow Hutchinson to function as a member of the Council, but the House parried these maneuvers. Months later, when Hutchinson boldly took a seat in the Council Chamber to listen to the governor's address to the General Court, the members of the House seethed. Writing for the representatives, Adams proclaimed that Hutchinson's effrontery provided "a new and additional instance of ambition and a lust of power." While Adams's own conflicts with Hutchinson stretched back to the land-bank controversy, Samuel clearly voiced a widely held view. Many in the popular party believed that the aristocratic Hutchinson—an advocate for bowing to

Britain's supremacy and the acknowledged leader of the court party—ruthlessly grasped at power in Massachusetts. They were right.[68]

Keeping Hutchinson off the Council made a real difference. James Bowdoin, a Boston merchant numbered among the supporters of American liberties, replaced him as chairman of the Council's committees. Hutchinson himself conceded that "from this time the council, in matters which concerned the controversy between the parliament and the colonies, in scarce any instance, disagreed with the house." The court party had lost a vital power base.[69]

In addition to purging the Council, the representatives elected Adams clerk of the lower house, and Governor Bernard could not negate that selection. In the late colonial era the clerkship carried a modest annual stipend of £90, which was only raised to £100 in 1774. Still, that salary formed an important part of the Adams family income and hence attested to the fact that Samuel made his living as a politician. Being House clerk reinforced Adams's role as a principal author of House documents and gave him the power to release them when he considered it politically advantageous to do so. Adams's election as clerk did not produce the immediate shock waves that accompanied the Council purge. In time, however, it helped unleash far more powerful quakes.[70]

Samuel Adams's political status evolved dramatically in the two years from May 1764 through May 1766. When the period began, he was a leader of the Boston Caucus and a tax collector who was not very good at the job. Then, drawing heavily on philosophical ideals and political techniques he had used during the land-bank controversy, he produced the precocious Boston Town Meeting instructions of May 1764. They forcefully delineated the case against Parliament imposing taxes on the Americans and pointed the way to a unified colonial opposition to that taxation. Elevated to membership in the Massachusetts House in September 1765, he quickly assumed a leadership role, especially as the author of documents that championed American liberties. By May 1766, with the House clerkship in hand, Adams was, all agreed, a major force in the popular party. More than that, friend and foe alike considered him the popular party's most skillful politician. He lacked oratorical skills, but he wrote with power and clarity. His determination to safeguard the colonists' constitutional liberties was unmatched. And while he opposed what he called "*mobbish*" crowds, he did not disdain those in the lower ranks of society. He mingled with them and was especially sensitive to their concerns. His opponents might mockingly refer to him as "Samuel the Publican," but he understood that more than leaders were involved in politics and that it was the ordinary people he mingled with who "shouted."[71]

Parliament's efforts to tax the colonists helped catapult Samuel Adams to political importance in Massachusetts, not just in Boston. In the spring of 1766 it was not at all clear whether Parliament, having gotten a bloody nose from its Stamp Act, would renew its effort to tax the colonies. But if Parliament, supported by the Massachusetts court party, did try again, Samuel Adams and the popular party of Massachusetts were better positioned than ever before to resist any assault on American rights.

3

THE LURKING SERPENT

Massachusetts court-party leaders often groused about Whigs seeking power for selfish ends. Envy, especially of Thomas Hutchinson, and yearning for political office supposedly drove the leading Whigs. Boston's popular party leaders, and many of their colleagues from outside the city, did despise Hutchinson. And, although he corralled an amazing number of political posts for himself, some of the antagonism he sparked arose at least in part from jealousy or a thirst for prominence. James Otis Jr. and his father had been politically conservative before 1761, and both became bitter when Thomas Hutchinson, rather than the senior Otis, was appointed chief justice of Massachusetts in late 1760. Moreover, even after he became a leader of the popular party, James Otis Jr. seemed willing, at times, to support the royal government in exchange for political preference. Jealousy undeniably tinged the animus John Adams expressed toward Hutchinson.[1]

Although some leading Whigs envied Hutchinson, court-party analysts should have acknowledged points Hutchinson himself admitted: ordinary people also hated him, and their hatred stretched back decades. As he recounted his opposition to paper-money schemes such as the land bank, Hutchinson boasted he pushed a hard-money bill through the House in 1749. He also observed that his victory against paper money cost him more than a seat in the House; it made many Bostonians furious with him. As Hutchinson confided to his diary, "more than once [I] was threatened with destruction." Adopting an imperial persona, he added that, when his house accidentally caught fire in May 1749, "some of the lower class cursed him, and cried 'Let it burn.'" People of all ranks justifiably thought that the court party headed by Hutchinson composed an arrogant aristocracy. The great majority of Bostonians had ample reason to think members of the court party habitually sacrificed the people's interests and rights for their own advancement. If one believed in protecting basic freedoms, if one believed in anything remotely approaching the ideal of social equality, one logically distrusted Hutchinson and his aristocratic crew. Samuel Adams did. From the time he published his first political analysis, Adams did more than stand ready to oppose British threats to the people's fundamental rights. He also stood against the local aristocratic nabobs who did the royal governor's bidding and who viewed the poorer people with contempt.[2]

The aggressive political moves, such as purging the Governor's Council, that the popular party undertook beginning in May of 1766 thus were not rooted in petty jealousy or lust for political office. The Whigs' actions reflected the lingering fear that Britain, aided by its court-party allies, might again try to subvert American liberties. Assessing the situation in late 1766, Adams acknowledged that the British government did not pose an imminent danger to American freedoms. Nevertheless he told a prominent South Carolina Son of Liberty that every colony should be awake and ready to counter a surreptitious assault on the people's rights. Having likened the threat of the Stamp Act to something as obvious as sailors confronting a giant sea monster, Samuel warned against the less visible threat of "the lurking Serpent" that, lying concealed and unnoticed by the unwary passerby, suddenly "darts its fatal Venom."[3]

In June 1766, after ousting Governor Bernard's favorites from the Council, the Massachusetts House implemented further measures to guard against the lurking serpent. Urged on by Adams, the representatives authorized a physical change that was both symbolic and useful to the popular party. The members of the House, the acknowledged people's branch of the General Court, approved building a gallery so citizens could observe their representatives' deliberations. Until that time, roll calls were not routinely taken, and, therefore, constituents might not know how their representatives voted. Now they would. From Adams's perspective, a gallery offered other benefits. If large numbers of Sons of Liberty and other Whigs packed the gallery, they might influence the House votes. One newspaper commentator astutely observed that the House of Commons had always allowed for visitors to hear the debates. Thomas Hutchinson saw the addition of the gallery in a different light. He considered it yet another example of Adams making the Massachusetts House of representatives resemble, and yet be clearly separate from, the House of Commons.[4]

The representatives took another significant step in December 1766 when they dismissed Richard Jackson, the MP who had succeeded Jasper Mauduit as the colony's agent. Otis and Adams distrusted Jackson; he seemed too friendly with Bernard and Hutchinson. So Adams and Otis convinced the representatives that Dennys De Berdt, who had served the House as its own special agent for over a year, should replace Jackson. After De Berdt became the colony's agent, Adams used his position as House clerk to change the lines of communication. He ended the practice of letting the Council examine letters sent to an agent. The new procedure kept sensitive political information out of court-party hands and allowed Adams freer rein to issue instructions to De Berdt when the House was not in session.[5]

Again exploiting his role as House clerk, a position that made him responsible for all House papers and for the official journal of House actions, Adams introduced another change that increased his and the popular party's power. Until Adams became clerk, addresses the House sent to the governor appeared in the press shortly after he received them. Petitions and other documents sent to Parliament, British government officials, or the monarch, however, were withheld from publication until they could reach England. Adams abandoned that tradition. If he thought it would benefit the colony's position, Samuel released items for publication as soon as the representatives approved them. He knew that once the petition or letter appeared in Massachusetts papers, it might be reprinted throughout the colonies. When challenged for rushing such items into print, he reportedly snapped back, "I am Clerk of this House & I shall make what use of the Papers which I please." The House clerkship was not a bully pulpit, but, through innovation, Adams came close to making it one.[6] In these as with so many of the other innovations he developed and exploited, Adams moved toward the modern political system of drawing the people into the political process while simultaneously developing methods, especially the use of the available media, to spread his political message.

Adams steadfastly emphasized a continental approach as he labored to protect American freedoms. From the start of the time of troubles with Britain, he stressed the importance of the colonies working in unison. He broached the idea yet again in a December 1766 letter to Christopher Gadsden, a leader of South Carolina's Sons of Liberty. Samuel said he wished merchants from all the colonies would organize and communicate with each other. That kind of "Union" might help alert the people to subtle efforts to tax them. To illustrate the danger, Adams offered the example of Parliament's 1765 Quartering Act, which ordered the colonists to pay some of the costs of maintaining British troops posted to their colony. This legislation, he argued, taxed the colonies as effectively as the Stamp Act. Samuel then raised an issue to which he returned with increasing intensity over time. Observing that some British politicians contemplated stationing troops in America's populated areas, he spoke of the danger of a standing army, especially in peacetime. It constituted more than a disturbance; it was "in every respect dangerous to civil Community." Writing to De Berdt, Adams proclaimed, as he habitually did, that standing armies were always dangerous to liberty.[7]

Adams could not shake the fear that the British might again pursue measures "calculated to enslave" America.[8] Over time, many Americans, including Adams, made the theme of Britain turning the American colonists into some form of slaves a central part of their rhetoric. But that powerful imagery ran afoul of a bothersome fact: full-blown chattel slavery where thralldom was passed on to one's children was legal in every British colony in America. So, while the language of being reduced to slavery had long been used in the context of losing basic political rights and liberties, colonists who moaned about being reduced to political or tributary slavery opened themselves to the charge of hypocrisy.[9] Samuel Adams could not be numbered among them. One of his relatives recounted how Samuel responded in the mid-1760s when his wife received a young black female slave named Surry as a present. He said that no slave could live in his house; if Surry came, she must be free. Although nothing in the records indicates what Elizabeth Adams thought about the situation, it seems likely she agreed with Samuel. In any case, Surry entered the Adams home as a free woman, and, as another Adams relative testified, she lived as a servant in the Adams family for decades.[10]

Samuel, who strove for political consistency, did more than ensure that his own family avoided the taint of slavery. He endeavored to see that Massachusetts could not be accused of inconsistency on the question of liberty and slavery. In May 1766, under the caucus system Adams helped mold, the Boston Town Meeting openly confronted the issue of American freedom and slavery. Immediately after informing its representatives that they must "be very watchful over our Just rights, liberties and privileges," the meeting instructed the representatives to seek a ban on the importation and sale of slaves and to push for the abolition of slavery in the colony. The next month, the House put Boston's representatives on a committee to prepare a bill outlawing the importation of slaves and directed the committee to present that bill at the next session. Boston's representatives followed the directives of the town meeting rather than adhering to the House's more limited agenda. On March 13, 1767, the House began consideration of a bill "*for preventing the unnatural and unwarrantable Custom of enslaving Mankind in this Province, and the importation of Slaves into the same.*" Despite efforts to delay consideration, its supporters pushed the bill through to a third reading on March 16. Early that same day, the Boston Town Meeting reaffirmed its directive to its representatives that called not only for the abolition of the slave trade but "for the total abolishing of Slavery among us." Despite this carefully timed support, the House refused to follow Boston's lead. After debate, the House voted to let "the Matter subside" and created a new committee charged with drafting a bill to levy a duty on slaves imported into the province. Significantly, none of the Boston members of the House were appointed to this committee, and even its modest recommendations died amid House and Council wrangling. With a majority of the House having blocked the antislavery efforts led by Boston and its representatives, the General Court did not finally pass even an anti-importation law until 1771. The governor, however, vetoed the bill and also thwarted a similar attempt in 1774.[11]

Although Boston's antislavery stance did not convince the House to embrace the abolition of slavery, Samuel Adams was one of the American Whigs who realized the inconsistency of denouncing the British for allegedly trying to reduce the Americans to tributary slavery while chattel slavery flourished in America. A group of local blacks illustrated how they perceived Adams's thrusts against slavery when they petitioned Massachusetts for their freedom in 1773. As their request languished, they pressed the petition in early 1774 and asked Adams to intercede on their behalf. He did.[12]

Despite Adams's suspicions about British intentions, a relative political calm settled over Massachusetts once the initial fireworks set off by the Council purge of May 1766 subsided. Major differences persisted, but the governor and House attempted to formulate reasonable compromises as they worked through a thorny political agenda. One vexing and potentially explosive problem concerned compensating victims of the Stamp Act crowds. In June, operating under directions from the home government, Governor Bernard began pressuring the House to pay compensation. Because crowd actions had erupted in various parts of Massachusetts, many people would receive help, but the detested Hutchinson would benefit the most. And while the British government had merely recommended that the colonial legislatures fund recompense, Bernard created an additional difficulty by labeling compensation a "requisition." If the representatives accepted that language, they would concede that the colonists could be taxed by order of the British government. The fact that individuals still languished in jails for participating in the crowd actions further complicated matters. These intertwining issues produced festering disagreements until Joseph Hawley, a bright lawyer from Northhampton who shared Adams's political views and friendship, devised a compromise. Rejecting the term *requisition*, the House declared it would, of its own volition, support a compensation measure in a bill that would offer a full pardon and amnesty to crowd members for "all Riots, Routs, and unlawful Assemblies . . . and all Burglaries, Felonies, and Breaches of the Peace whatsoever, committed in, by, or during such Riots, Routs, and unlawful Assemblies" from August 1765 through May 1, 1766. Both the governor and the General Court knew that legally only the monarch could issue such a pardon, but both sides wanted the matter settled. So Bernard accepted the compromise and signed the legislation in early December. The governor, no doubt, expected that the Privy Council would disallow the bill once it reached England. That is what happened, but by then Hutchinson and the other victims of the crowds had been compensated and the imprisoned "rioters" freed.[13]

As the compromise linking amnesty with compensation was being hammered out in late 1766, Adams discovered an ingenious way to subvert the Quartering Act that he had described as taxation in disguise. Adams and the House attacked the legislation indirectly; they did it by helping the British army. When severe weather forced ships into Boston harbor in December, about seventy British soldiers suddenly needed temporary maintenance. The Quartering Act obliged Massachusetts to aid the soldiers. Since the House was not in session when this occurred, the governor and his Council authorized using public funds to maintain the troops. After re-convening, the House ultimately approved spending the money to assist the soldiers, but it did so without mentioning the Quartering Act. As Adams, who was a member of the drafting committee, put it, a sense of humanity coupled with the people's strong regard for their king had prompted the representatives to provide aid "of their own free accord." Using that expla-nation, Adams and the House underscored a fundamental principle: only the citizens' elected representatives could determine how the public money would be spent. It was their freely given gift. It could not be requisitioned; it could not be wrenched from the people by an act of Parliament; it could only be given by the duly elected representatives.[14]

In the year following the repeal of the Stamp Act, none of these is-sues generated anything like the conflict the Stamp Act had produced. Reflecting on this period, members of the House and Governor Bernard proclaimed it a relatively tranquil time brought on, in part, by a mutual desire to work together as harmoniously as possible. These efforts calmed the churning political waters, but the calm proved deceptive. As 1766 gave way to 1767, both the popular and court parties became increasingly con-vinced that the other party pursued a horrific agenda. The popular party suspected that the British, aided and abetted by arrogant Massachusetts aristocrats, would attack America's liberties. That concern deepened when Bernard invited Thomas Hutchinson to attend the speech the governor gave in January opening the meeting of the General Court. For its part, the court party feared that their enemies wanted independence and would manipulate lower-class rowdies to achieve it. Because each side believed it must control the legislature to thwart the other side's evil schemes, each faction considered the May 1767 election crucial.[15]

The changes Adams and the popular party had introduced into the House—installing a gallery and Samuel's policy of quickly releasing House documents—were designed to help the popular party win elections. To increase its chances for victory, the party also initiated the practice of commemorating events associated with the recent defense of American freedoms. The anniversary of the repeal of the Stamp Act fell conveniently close to the annual May election, and Boston Whigs took advantage of the opportunity. On the afternoon of March 18, large numbers of people gathered at Faneuil Hall, which was lit up to signal the occasion's importance. There at the home of the Boston Town Meeting, people drank a variety of pro-American toasts. The Liberty Tree was also illuminated, as were the residences of various Whigs. John Rowe, who participated in the festivities, wrote in his diary that "I never saw more Joy than on this occasion." Celebrating March 18 became an instant tradition, and so did August 14 festivities that commemorated the first Boston crowd action against the Stamp Act.

While the celebrations inaugurated in 1767 became more elaborate over time, the assessment John Adams offered of the August 14, 1769, event probably applies to the earlier 1767 activities as well. John credited the duo of Samuel Adams and James Otis with political shrewdness in promoting such festivals. John said the gatherings touched the minds of the people and "impregnate[d] them with the sentiments of Liberty." He also frankly admitted that the events were designed to serve the more immediate goal of making the people fonder of their leaders "in the Cause" and more "averse and bitter" toward all who opposed the cause. John might have overestimated the impact of political festivals, but he accurately described what Samuel and other Whig leaders hoped to accomplish. The celebrations added yet another weapon to the Whig arsenal.[16]

Although he did not mention him by name, at least one Whig made a special effort to support Samuel Adams's reelection to the House in 1767. On April 27, the *Boston Gazette* carried a lengthy essay by "Freeborn American." Building on the premise that a representative must defend the

people's constitutional rights, the author reviewed "the necessary qualities" a representative should possess. In addition to a general knowledge of
the Massachusetts constitution, these included wisdom, ability, integrity,
prudence, fortitude, and an independent spirit. Having established these
criteria, Freeborn American explored the issue of a person's wealth. The
author asserted that a rich man who lacked even one of the qualities necessary for being a representative was "not a suitable person to obtain your
confidence and be entrusted with the guardianship of your liberties." Why?
Because history demonstrated that the wealthy were as likely as the poor,
and perhaps more so, to be "seduced from their duty to their constituents."
So poverty need not disqualify a potential representative. "On the contrary
tho' he is intimately acquainted with poverty, yet if he is in all respects otherwise qualified, his poverty should be no obstacle to his choice, *especially if
he has been proved and found faithful*: because his virtues will more surely keep
him out of reach of temptation than the riches of the other." Harbottle
Dorr, an ardent Whig and political junkie who routinely annotated copies
of Boston newspapers, had no trouble discerning who Freeborn American
was referring to. Highlighting the whole "On the contrary" sentence,
Dorr wrote in the margin: "a true Character of Samuel Adams, one of the
Representatives of ye Town, who has always Proved himself a Steady, wise
Patriot, in the Worst of Times."[17]

Governor Bernard, who desperately wanted his firmest supporters
returned to the Council, also poured extra effort into winning the May
1767 election. He placed his hopes mainly on preferment, the dispensing
of political posts and favors. By linking a person's self-interest to the government, preferment gave the beneficiary a powerful motive to support
the government. Political considerations traditionally played some part in
appointments, but Bernard used patronage in such a partisan way that his
brazenness embarrassed some of his supporters. Judge John Cushing, a court
party man, lamented how Bernard went about gathering votes. In exchange
for supporting his candidates, Bernard was putting "Scandalous and unfit
persons" into office, throwing commissions at people, and "promising almost Everybody" some kind of preferment.

Bernard's tactics failed. The May 1767 election did not alter the balance of power. The popular party kept control of the House, and the
representatives again refused to vote for Hutchinson and other court-party
politicians Bernard wanted on his Council. Adams retained his post as clerk
of the House. Samuel was delighted with these victories, but pleasure soon
gave way to anxiety when Parliament took steps that revealed the lurking
serpent had indeed begun darting "its fatal Venom."[18]

In the summer of 1767, Charles Townshend, one of the most brilliant debaters in Parliament, pushed the MPs to make the Americans acknowledge the supremacy of Parliament. As chancellor of the exchequer, the chief financial minister in the British government, Townshend developed a plan ostensibly to raise revenue from the American colonies. He believed, and Adams agreed, that any program designed to garner revenue constituted a tax. However, during the Stamp Act troubles Benjamin Franklin, a colonial spokesman then in England, had suggested that the colonists distinguished between internal and external taxes. According to this view, the colonists would oppose any direct internal taxes, such as the Stamp Act; external taxes might, however, be acceptable. Although Townshend considered this reasoning absurd, he seized on the alleged distinction between internal and external taxes. In formulating his plan, he even avoided the word "tax." Townshend proposed that Parliament levy duties on tea, glass, paper, and printing materials (red and white lead and painters' colors) shipped to America. These "external" duties would be collected in the colonies.

Townshend's complex proposals revealed the aptness of Samuel's imagery of the lurking serpent and the unwary passerby. Although labeled a revenue measure, the Townshend plan imposed relatively low duties and would only raise about £37,000 per year. When combined with related changes in trade regulations, the British government's annual income would actually *drop* by about £23,000. Townshend obviously was not after immediate revenue. He was stealthily pursuing constitutional leverage. He wanted to establish a solid precedent for future and much higher levels of taxation. As Adams had warned, if the colonists once paid even small duties, they could, in time, be compelled to carry a heavy tax burden. Townshend also struck at the power of the purse that colonial legislatures utilized to hamstring royal governors and undermine judicial enforcement of the trade laws. His plan earmarked the new duties to pay the salaries of royally appointed government officials, including colonial judges. Townshend had good reason to believe he could inflict his venomous thrusts on unwary colonists. John Huske, one of the few American-born MPs, praised the Townshend plan. Even more important, the colonial agents, a group that had challenged passage of the Stamp Act, did not voice complaints about what were quickly dubbed *the Townshend duties*.[19]

The chancellor of the exchequer also aimed to make the colonists obey Britain's trade laws. To achieve that goal, Townshend introduced legislation creating the American Board of Custom Commissioners. He anticipated that stationing this board in America would produce better enforcement of the existing trade regulations. Tighter control would diminish, if not eradicate, American smuggling. British officials considered locating the new board in Philadelphia, New York City, or Boston. Although the reason for the final choice was not recorded, it is hardly surprising that the British decided to put the board in Boston. In 1767 Boston was a major smuggling port. Probably more significant, the English already deemed Boston the center of colonial opposition. Indeed, the city was well on the way to earning the title Peter Oliver gave it: "the Metropolis of Sedition."

Parliament passed the Townshend duties in June 1767. At the same time, it authorized the American Board of Custom Commissioners, which began functioning in November. By enacting the Townshend duties, Parliament created a constitutional gauntlet for all the colonies to run. And by placing the board of custom commissioners in Boston, the British signaled their intention to punish the city for its role as a smuggling center and as a breeding ground of opposition to Britain's new imperial policies.[20]

The colonial legislatures were not in session when news of the Townshend duties reached America. In Massachusetts, Adams and the other Boston representatives, all members of the popular party, urged Governor Bernard to convene the General Court. Bernard refused, but Adams and his fellow Whigs had another forum at their disposal. The Boston Town Meeting swung into action on October 28. It also pressed the governor to call the legislature into session and, without once directly mentioning them, declared war on the Townshend duties. Proclaiming that Massachusetts faced poverty and economic ruin, the meeting laid out a plan to promote industry, economy, and manufacturing. The town meeting challenged the Townshend duties by agreeing to do its utmost to encourage the domestic manufacture of glass and paper.

Even more important, adopting the language of Britain's navigation acts, the meeting compiled an extensive list of over fifty enumerated items that would not be imported after December 31. The town meeting asked Bostonians to sign an agreement supporting nonimportation and also sent copies of the document to all Massachusetts towns as well as to major cities and towns throughout the continent. Boston was trying to resurrect the nonimportation weapon that had played the crucial role in destroying the Stamp Act.[21]

Boston's actions outraged the British. Writing from London in late December, Benjamin Franklin reported that Boston's resolutions "make a great noise here" and that "the newspapers are in full cry against America." He added that, while attending a political function, he had been told that he "could not conceive how much the friends of America were run upon and hurt by them." On January 9, Franklin described Boston's resolutions as having unleashed "a prodigious clamour." His comments may well have been influenced in part by a commentary that appeared in the London *Gazetteer* four days earlier. The piece certainly suggests that many Britons had come to despise Bostonians. The author mused on the fact that Barlow Trecothick, a Boston-born MP, was up for reelection. "I think we might now, with equal propriety," the author sarcastically opined, "seek a representative from among the French or Spaniards, as from Boston, for neither of these countries have, as yet, outdone the Bostonians in malicious combinations against our existence."[22]

By February of 1768 many towns in Massachusetts, Rhode Island, and Connecticut had embraced Boston's nonimportation plan, but Philadelphia and New York had not. Then in March about one hundred Boston merchants pledged to stop importing virtually all European goods for a year or until Parliament repealed the Townshend duties. As Adams had urged, committees of correspondence kept merchants in the individual colonies informed of these developments. Thomas Hutchinson accounted for such developments in part by saying that Adams and Otis had started meeting with the merchants and the two men "had great influence among them." New York City finally agreed to the Boston proposal, but Philadelphia's merchants held back. Without Philadelphia, colonial nonimportation could not succeed. So, despite the efforts of the Boston Town Meeting and many Boston merchants, the colonists still had not created an effective boycott by the spring of 1768.[23]

America's less than solid support for nonimportation could not be blamed on a failure to grasp the significance of the Townshend duties. Beginning in early December 1767 and continuing through mid-February of 1768 John Dickinson's extraordinarily popular *Letters from a Farmer in Pennsylvania* forcefully laid out the issues. While conceding that Parliament could regulate both the colonial trade and manufacturing, Dickinson insisted that any bill enacted by Parliament solely for the purpose of raising revenue was unconstitutional. Therefore, he said, even small taxes, such as the Townshend duties, set a dangerous precedent. As Dickinson phrased it, if Parliament could levy a tax of one penny, it could levy a tax of millions.[24] Adams, of course, had made all these points before but not in widely reprinted essays. Well aware that the Pennsylvania legislature would not vigorously challenge the Townshend duties, Dickinson sought help from Massachusetts. Writing to James Otis, he said that he expected Massachusetts would again take the lead in "the Cause of American Freedom." "The Farmer," as Dickinson came to be known, was not disappointed.[25]

What evolved into Samuel Adams's and the Massachusetts House's thoroughgoing assault on the Townshend duties, and any similar revenue laws, began on December 30, 1767. The House placed Adams on a committee to assess and report on "the State of the Province." Adams soon drafted a lengthy letter that the committee recommended sending to agent De Berdt. After discussing the document for several days, the House approved it on January 13, 1768. The letter, which took up almost ten pages of the House's official *Journal*, amounted to a brief history of the time of troubles between Great Britain and the colonies since 1763. Maintaining that "the security of right and property is the great end of government," Adams asserted that the recent British policies threatened both liberty and property. He reiterated the core arguments that, since the colonists were not and could not be represented in Parliament, they could not constitutionally be taxed by Parliament. He again pointed out the danger of the monarch both appointing and paying the salaries of colonial officials including judges. Bemoaning the fact that some in England wanted to establish "a Protestant Episcopate in America," Adams branded that an effort to undermine the people's religious liberty. The horrors of a standing army and rapacious custom commissioners were revisited, as was the argument that the colonists already contributed mightily to England's economic well-being by consuming her manufactured goods. Samuel even alleged that Great Britain's manufacturers had an "advantage" that amounted to 20 percent of the value of what they produced, which, as he had said before, "is in reality a tax, tho' not a direct one." As he had been doing since 1764, Adams thus piled reason upon reason to support the case that Great Britain's post-1763 colonial policies were unconstitutional *and* harmful to the mother country's own economic interests.[26]

Powerful as it was, Adams's De Berdt letter was merely a prelude to more consequential action. On January 20, 1768, the Massachusetts House approved what it called a humble petition to the king. The petition, which Adams had a major hand in crafting, endorsed many of Dickinson's arguments and incorporated language Adams had earlier employed. After expressing loyalty to the king, the representatives recounted how their ancestors had invested their own money to create and develop the colony. Massachusetts, according to the legislators, had cost the mother country little, and yet Britain reaped enormous profits from the colony's trade and from supplying Massachusetts with manufactured goods. Then came the essential philosophical arguments. First, based on "the fundamental rights of nature and the constitution," the people of Massachusetts could be taxed only by their own elected representatives. Second, local circumstances made it "utterly impracticable" for the people of Massachusetts to be represented in Parliament. The petitioners' logic suggested that anything Parliament did solely to raise revenue in the colonies constituted a tax and was therefore unconstitutional. Adams championed that position. He could not, however, convince a majority of the representatives to state it. The petition merely lamented that the people would not truly be free subjects if the revenue acts remained in force. The representatives closed by imploring the king to help his loyal but beleaguered Massachusetts subjects.[27]

Two days after the House approved the petition to the king, Adams and others of what Bernard contemptuously called "the factious Party of the House" tried to up the stakes considerably. They forcefully urged the House to consider asking the other North American colonies to join the Massachusetts House in petitioning the king. When the vote on this recommendation occurred, probably on January 28, the motion lost. Indeed, if Bernard's report is accurate, the Adams and Otis–led forces got trounced by a two-to-one majority.[28] The matter might have ended with this defeat. But Bernard's determination to get key supporters, especially Thomas Hutchinson, back onto his Council kept it alive. On February 3 Bernard ordered the members of the House to listen to Andrew Oliver, the ill-fated stamp distributor who was the secretary of province, read a letter the governor had received from William Petty, the Earl of Shelburne. As Britain's southern secretary, he was responsible for dealings with the colonies. Responding to information supplied by Bernard, Petty chastised the House for refusing to elect the principal government officers, such as Lieutenant Governor Hutchinson, to the Council. The Right Honorable Earl seemed to sneer at what he called the House members' "mistaken zeal" and "private resentments (and I shall be sorry to ascribe to them motives still more blamable)." He insisted that the Council members had every right to let Hutchinson attend their sessions—provided he was not given voting privileges. In a final jab, Petty implied that the members of the House did not understand their true interests. As "men of real property" they should, he warned, realize that their actions endangered "the peace and Safety of the State."[29]

The dressing-down of the House orchestrated by Bernard occurred on February 3. On February 4, as Adams phrased it, a large majority of the House agreed to reconsider the proposal to call upon the other colonies to join in petitioning against the Townshend duties. The House not only approved the motion and selected a committee of leading radicals to draft the circular letter but also directed that the initial vote against the motion to send a circular letter "be erased." Just one week later, on February 11, the House approved the circular letter crafted by Samuel Adams.[30] It emphasized the ideal of unified colonial action. When faced with issues vital to all the colonies, their individual assemblies "should harmonize with each other." If the other assemblies agreed, they too would petition the king. The circular letter summarized many points included in the petition; but, using language he had employed before, Adams expanded on crucial issues. As he composed the circular letter, Adams was well aware that the House petition had waffled on the question of the constitutionality of the Townshend duties. Moreover, the petition rested the representatives' claims on the charter and the rights of Englishmen without asserting, as Adams had, that Parliament's taxation also violated the colonists' natural rights. So Samuel knew he had to devise wording that would gain the approval of less radical representatives while also building a more thoroughgoing case that Parliament's taxation of the colonists was unconstitutional.

Adams placated the House moderates and conservatives by first accepting the fact that Parliament exercised "the supreme legislative power over the whole empire." He then immediately gutted that seemingly vital concession. Adams began the gutting by observing that "in all free States the constitution is fixed; and as the supreme legislature derives its power and authority from the constitution, it cannot overlap the bounds of it without destroying its own foundation." Since "the constitution ascertains and limits both sovereignty and allegiance," it followed that "his Majesty's American subjects . . . have an equitable claim, to the full enjoyment of the fundamental rights of the British constitution." Moreover, "it is an essential unalterable right in nature, ingrafted into the British constitution, as a fundamental law, and ever held sacred and irrevocable by the subjects within the realm [of England], that what a man hath honestly acquired is absolutely his own, which he may freely give, but cannot be taken from him without his consent." Therefore, since the colonists were not represented in Parliament, it followed that any acts of Parliament designed solely for raising revenue in the colonies were "infringements" on the people's "natural and constitutional rights." Having yet again drawn on Locke, Adams carefully reiterated that it would never be possible for the colonists to have representatives in Parliament, in part because the colonists would not be equally represented.

The circular letter also addressed issues that the House's petition to the king had ignored. After taking brief swipes at the Quartering Act and the American Board of Customs Commissioners, Adams directly challenged how the Townshend duties would be spent. He stressed that the colonists' "happiness and security" could be subverted if the Crown both appointed the governor and forced the colonists to pay him whatever amount the monarch might determine. Because American judges were appointed and dismissed at the monarch's pleasure, the integrity of the American judicial system could be undermined if judges also received their pay from the British. If that happened, the judges would become totally independent of the colonial legislatures. Such developments would have "a tendency to subvert the principles of equity, and endanger the happiness and security" of the king's American subjects. Adams thus maintained that the Townshend duties endangered many essential freedoms.[31] As Adams might have phrased it, he and his supporters had improved on the situation. They used Bernard's bullheadedness to convince the House to support a far more powerful assault on British policies than the one advanced in the original petition to the king. And, in the process, they also promoted intercolonial cooperation.

In the petition to the king, the circular letter, and messages to their London agent, the representatives carefully stressed their loyalty to king and country. They emphasized that, contrary to what some malicious people said, the colonists did not want independence. Adams, speaking for the House, told colonial agent De Berdt that the colonists did not harbor even a distant thought of independence. He insisted that, if offered independence, the colonists would refuse it. Such protestations of loyalty only sugarcoated the message: the Townshend duties must go. When these and related House documents were published in London in 1768 as part of *The True Sentiments of America,* English readers typically credited Samuel Adams with having authored them, an attribution that fueled his growing repute in the mother country.[32]

By early 1768 the popularity of Dickinson's *Letters* and the Massachusetts attack on the Townshend duties suggested that most colonists agreed with what Townshend had uttered privately: a tax was a tax. Maintaining that an internal tax differed from an external tax was absurd. Calling a tax a duty or a requisition could not disguise the truth. Equally important, most colonial leaders contended that those taxes were unconstitutional because they were levied on an unrepresented people. Still, as the differences between the Massachusetts petition to the king and the Massachusetts circular letter demonstrated, translating philosophical ideals into effective political action proved difficult. At a crucial juncture, the petition to the king backed away from a frontal assault on the Townshend duties. It took Bernard's blundering, two attempts, and political maneuvering by Adams and Otis to win approval for Adams's hard-hitting circular letter—a document that marked a significant milestone on the road to revolution.

Having gotten the circular letter approved, forces led by Adams and Otis intensified the pressure on Bernard. On February 13, the House, claiming its actions stemmed from a desire "to cultivate an Harmony between the several branches of this Government," decided to send a delegation to the governor. The members were to inform Bernard that the House would supply him with the text of the circular letter as soon as a copy could be produced. And, if he wished, the House would also provide the governor with "all of the Proceedings of this House relative to said Affair." That offer served as a pretext for the House's committee to ask Bernard to give the House a copy of the Earl of Shelburne's letter *and* copies of Bernard's communications mentioned by the Earl. That request, which Adams championed, constituted a clever political ploy. If Bernard refused to supply his letters, which he naturally did, derogatory charges leveled against him would gain credence. Had the governor supplied his letters, Adams and others could use them as bludgeons against him. While the House could not pry letters out of Bernard, it managed to make Lord Shelburne's letter public. The House quoted portions of it in a February 18 message to Bernard, and Adams, as clerk, sent a copy of that message to the press. In response, Bernard allowed the House to enter Shelburne's letter into its records, and soon the full letter appeared in the *Boston Gazette*, with the editors adding the snide notation that it was being published "in Consequence of the Governor's Permission."[33]

The colony-wide May election arrived before Massachusetts learned how the British would respond to the House's petition and its circular letter. In the run-up to the election, the now-annual March 18 celebrations of the repeal of the Stamp Act produced toasts to the defenders of American rights both at home and in England. Adams entered the 1768 election campaign by taking up his favorite weapon, the pen. He wrote a series of three letters, signed "A Puritan," which appeared in the *Boston Gazette* in April. While ostensibly assessing the degree of "popery" that existed in various Massachusetts towns, Adams actually commented on the extent to which certain individuals and geographic areas did or did not support American liberties. As Harbottle Dorr remarked, "by Popery" Adams "means the Representatives of some Towns, who he supposed were the Governors Tools." In this way, Samuel promoted the idea that only committed advocates of American rights, only Whigs, should be elected.[34]

As the elections drew near, Adams's continuing problem with uncollected taxes gave the court party a special opportunity to attack him. In 1767, Boston's deepening economic woes had led to legal action that eventually resulted in a judgment of £1,463 against Adams for taxes he failed to collect. He had to pay that huge sum by March 1768 or face possible imprisonment. Samuel began making payments but still owed what he described as "a large balance" when the deadline arrived. He petitioned the town meeting for a six-month delay so he could garner the long-overdue taxes. Adams explained how, in the early 1760s, hard times had made collecting taxes so difficult that he used the tax moneys obtained in one year to pay the previous year's requisition. The meeting approved his request, but his irregular methods opened him to a charge of gross mismanagement bordering on criminality.

Members of the court party refused to let the matter rest. They demanded and got another town meeting to vote on reconsidering Adams's petition. A lengthy, heated debate erupted at that second meeting. Although they could make Adams squirm and perhaps even humiliate him, the court-party people lost. The meeting overwhelmingly reaffirmed its decision to give Adams a six-month extension. Nevertheless, a six-month reprieve could not have saved Samuel; it took a subscription of over £1,000 raised by friends to keep him from immediate financial ruin. He managed to escape further responsibility in 1769 when, in response to yet another petition from him, the town meeting transferred the task of gathering the remaining taxes to another collector. In 1772, with more than £1,100 of those taxes still outstanding, the town meeting finally ended Samuel's agony by acknowledging that the taxes would most likely never be collected and by deciding that nothing more could be done.[35]

Bostonians, and not just members of the court party, grumbled about Adams being treated so leniently. Still, the tax-collection issue, embarrassing as it was, did not diminish his popularity. In the May 1768 election the town meeting once again reelected him, along with Otis, Cushing, and Hancock, to the House. The returns from the rest of Massachusetts indicated that a majority of the House would once again support the popular party. As they had done the two previous years, the representatives refused to seat Hutchinson and other favorites of Governor Bernard on the Council. But this time the contest was close. Bernard complained, and probably justifiably so, that Hutchinson suffered defeat only because Adams and Otis, the men Bernard described as the "chief heads" of the opposition, ambushed Hutchinson on the second round of voting. They did it by announcing that the British government had granted Hutchinson a pension of £200 a year. They also pointed out that, because of the Townshend duties, the colonists would pay that pension. Making those points did the job. Hutchinson's support withered, and he lost any chance of again sitting on the Council. Nevertheless, the closeness of this election gave the court party hope that it might regain the ascendancy.[36] Much would depend on how the British responded to the House's challenge to the Townshend duties.

Writing home in March 1768, General Thomas Gage, the commander in chief of the British forces in North America who was headquartered in New York City, gave a hint of how the British government would likely view the actions of the Massachusetts House and any colonial efforts to promote local manufacturing. Advancing a conspiratorial interpretation, Gage decried how the colonists had and would escalate their resistance. "From the denying the Right of internal taxations, they next deny the Right of duties on Imports, and thus they mean to go on step by Step, 'till they throw off all subjections to your laws." Gage predicted that, once they had cast off Britain's laws, the colonists "will acknowledge the King of Great Britain to be their King, but soon deny the prerogatives of the Crown, and acknowledge their King no longer than it shall be convenient for them to do so." In sum, the colonists "will struggle for independency," and the British must face that fact and proceed accordingly.

A copy of the Massachusetts circular letter reached England in April 1768. Parliament was not in session, but the king and his ministers acted quickly. Fearing that the circular letter might produce another colonial congress—this one aimed at the Townshend duties—Lord Hillsborough, the recently installed secretary of state for the colonies, took immediate action. He wrote to Governor Bernard and instructed him to tell the Massachusetts House that its circular letter must be rescinded. Bernard presented the demand to the House on June 21. Two days later, the representatives revisited ground they had traversed in mid-February. Accusing Bernard of misrepresenting their actions to the Crown, the representatives renewed and expanded their earlier request that the governor give them copies of his correspondence with the home government. Responding the next day, Bernard said his correspondence would be made public only when he chose to do so and then only for his own reasons. He also warned the representatives that he would dissolve the House unless it revoked the offending document. Moreover, he would not again call a House into session until the king authorized it. Bernard increased the pressure on June 28 by informing the representatives that, if they delayed much longer, he would consider it a refusal to rescind. The representatives asked for a recess so they could consult with their constituents and receive instructions. Bernard refused. The House now had but two options: it could fight and be dissolved, or it could surrender.[37]

On Tuesday, June 30, the representatives met to determine their action. They began by having the House gallery cleared and taking measures to ensure that they would not be interrupted and that no member could leave before a decision had been reached. Faced with the expressed displeasure of the king and with Bernard's bullying threats, the members chose to fight. By a roll-call vote of ninety-two to seventeen, they refused to rescind; agreeing to revoke would, they argued, "have left us but a vain Semblance of Liberty." They then sent Bernard a lengthy address authored mainly by Adams. It justified their former deeds as reasonable endeavors rooted in the right to petition. Moreover, the representatives' efforts had actually helped foster "Ease and Quiet" among the people, who now peacefully awaited the king's response to their humble petition. Once again employing classic Lockean phraseology, the representatives described themselves as "preserving Life, Liberty, and Property."[38]

Immediately after refusing to rescind, the House appointed a committee, headed by Adams, to formulate a petition asking the king to remove Governor Bernard. It seems likely that Samuel had already drafted the petition or portions of it because he presented it to the House later that day. This quick action lends weight to Governor Bernard's exasperated 1765 claim that, when Adams was placed on a committee, he usually had a set of fully drafted resolves ready for the committee to adopt. Samuel's lengthy pronouncement resembled a bill of indictment more than an ordinary petition. It charged Governor Bernard with having "an arbitrary Disposition" and spelled out the particulars in fourteen paragraphs. Most were short, and most opened with "He has" followed by a recounting of Bernard's supposed failings and evil deeds. The savagery of parts of the attack probably gave some representatives pause. The House deferred action, ostensibly so the committee could supply evidence to support all the charges leveled against the governor. The committee did not get the chance. Bernard prorogued the House that day and dissolved it the next. The House was not convened again until after the next general election.[39]

Samuel Adams played a central role in the battles that erupted over the Massachusetts circular letter. He served on every important committee the House appointed to compose petitions or other position statements. But, while other leading members of the popular party, including James Otis, were placed on various delegations that carried messages to Governor Bernard, Samuel never once served on one. At first glance that seems odd. Samuel had a penchant for being moderate when moderation might help achieve his goal. And everyone agreed he could be charming, even if Peter

Oliver depicted him as having chameleon-like charm. The reason Samuel was always omitted from these delegations can perhaps be traced to this illuminating fact: the representatives knew that Bernard detested Adams more than any other member of the popular party. In time, Bernard came to consider him, and rightly so, as more intractable, more dangerous than Otis. Otis swung back and forth on the question of Parliament's authority to enact whatever legislation it chose regarding the colonies. Adams, who insisted that Parliament's power had boundaries and that Parliament could not overrun them, held fast to the ideas he had enunciated as early as the 1740s. The people must know their constitutional rights and steadfastly, jealously guard them. Others might waver; Samuel Adams would not.[40]

When confronted with challenges to the new colonial policies, British politicians employed a divide-and-conquer strategy. They aimed to isolate a troublesome colony, or even a city like Boston, and by punishing its inhabitants intimidate colonists elsewhere. Dissolving the Massachusetts House of Representatives would, the theory went, bring the Americans to heel. Just the opposite happened. When other colonies learned that the Massachusetts House had been dissolved, expressions of sympathy and support for the glorious ninety-two who voted against rescinding streamed into the Bay colony. As Thomas Hutchinson ruefully observed, "the number 92 was auspicious, and 17 of ill omen, for many months after, not only in Massachusetts Bay, but in most of the colonies on the continent."[41]

As the increasingly acrimonious struggle against the Townshend duties unfolded, Massachusetts and especially Boston also had to deal with the American Board of Custom Commissioners, the second half of Townshend's program to bring the colonists under tighter control. By chance, three of the five members of the board arrived in Boston on November 5, the day antipope crowds took over the streets. When the three men landed in 1767, they encountered a crowd of perhaps a thousand carrying twenty effigies bearing the labels "Liberty & Property & no Commissioners." The nonviolent crowd did no more than escort the customs commissioners to their quarters. Although they landed without violence, it took little time for the commissioners, as Adams observed, to "alarm the People." Most merchants and seafarers disliked the British navigation acts, but the customs commissioners did more than enforce trade regulations. The board created its own coast-guard patrol, and the crews often got their pay from their seizures. Worse yet, customs commissioners developed a system that the historian Oliver M. Dickerson dubbed "customs racketeering." By altering how they applied rules or by enforcing obscure regulations, customs officials could confiscate property even if the owners had tried to comply with the law. Aggrieved colonists could do little about the injustices. Because the trade laws protected them, commissioners or their agents could practice customs racketeering with virtual impunity. Under the laws, if an official could show probable cause for seizing goods, a person found innocent of the alleged violation still had to pay the court costs. And to the chagrin of its innocent victims, the admiralty courts that tried the cases typically decided that probable cause had existed.

Customs racketeers preferred targeting less powerful merchants or owners of small vessels who could not afford the costs of mounting a legal defense. Even common seamen fell victim to customs racketeering. Long-established tradition allowed sailors to carry small amounts of trade goods in their sea chests. But using the technicality that no such items could be transported without proper papers, by 1768 customs agents were confiscating sea chests containing trade goods. Not surprisingly, anticommissioner hostility intensified. The customs commissioners responded by repeatedly asking for military protection. Writing to colonial agent De Berdt on May 14, Adams summed up how most Bostonians had come to view the customs board. The people, he said, generally hated the commissioners as much as they had hated the Stamp Act distributors.[42] If Samuel had known what would happen three days later, he would have been even harsher in his condemnation.

The commissioners' repeated calls for military support eventually worked. HMS *Romney*, a fifty-gun warship, dropped anchor in Boston harbor on May 17, 1768. This display of military force—the first aimed directly at Boston—made the situation more volatile, and that volatility was heightened because the *Romney* arrived shorthanded. To remedy his manpower shortage, Captain John Corner had men from inbound vessels pressed into service aboard the *Romney*. Boston crowds had often challenged impressment, and they did so again. The anti-impressment crowds of 1768, like those before them, were composed primarily of the kinds of individuals most likely to be impressed: seafarers and young men from the lower classes. No one needed to inform them of the immediate threat to their freedom. It was not necessary for Samuel Adams, or anyone else, to instruct them. And there is no evidence Adams tried to direct their actions.

The common people's anger came to a head on June 10 when commissioners used a customs-racketeering technicality to seize John Hancock's merchant ship, the *Liberty*. Although he possessed a well-deserved reputation for smuggling, for political reasons Hancock had curtailed his illegal activities. The commissioners did not, however, target him for his notorious smuggling operations; rather, they seized the *Liberty* because Hancock had spoken contemptuously of customs commissioners and because he was a highly visible member of the popular party. Numerous Bostonians supported Hancock. He was, after all, a well-liked leader who employed many people in his extensive business activities. But more than support for Hancock was involved. Customs racketeering and impressment were at the root of popular enmity. Indeed, on June 9 before the commissioners confiscated the *Liberty* a crowd armed with stones forced the release of a man who had just been pressed. Impressment was, in fact, a central issue in the *Liberty* incident. When British sailors and marines came to tow the *Liberty* to the *Romney*, they were confronted by what the *Boston News-Letter* called an ever-increasing crowd that included many sailors and vagrants, just the kind of individuals press gangs typically seized. The crowd showered the British with stones until they rowed out of rock-throwing range. Elements of the crowd also assaulted and bloodied the two commissioners who had ordered the seizure of the *Liberty*. Later the crowd snatched a pleasure boat belonging to a commissioner, dragged it onto a commons area, and torched it. Belying the image the term *mob* now conjures up, after holding a discussion on what to do next the participants voted to disperse and did so without further incident. Within the next two days, fearing for their lives, four of the five customs commissioners together with their families and various customs personnel—a total of sixty-seven people—fled to the *Romney* for protection. It is significant that commissioner John Temple, who often disagreed with the policies his fellow board members pursued, saw no need to flee and was not molested.

In an effort to dampen the people's anger, the commissioners, relying on a negotiator, acquiesced to Hancock's suggestion that he post a bond and have his ship returned pending the outcome of a trial. However, Adams, Otis, and others convinced Hancock to cancel the arrangement. That meant the *Liberty* incident would remain a newsworthy example of British oppression as long as the court case lasted, and that could likely be a long time.[43]

In the months that followed, Adams and the popular party adopted the old tactic of downplaying the level of violence that had accompanied crowd actions in Boston. As in the case of the Stamp Act crowds, spokesmen wanted to convey the impression that Bostonians embraced only legal and reasonable means of resisting oppression. Although violent crowds were anathema to Whig leaders like Adams, they firmly believed that large, peaceful demonstrations helped support the cause. They were delighted when the town meeting of June 14 that met as a consequence of the *Liberty* incident resembled a huge, peaceful demonstration. Faneuil Hall, which could hold between twelve hundred and thirteen hundred, proved much too small to accommodate the meeting, so it adjourned to the Old South Church, which had room for several thousand. Claiming that the critical state of affairs forced it to act, the town meeting petitioned Governor Bernard. It offered a toughly worded defense of Massachusetts's opposition to the Townshend duties and also denounced the actions of both the customs commissioners and the navy. The fact was Boston found itself "invaded with an armed force, Seizing, impressing . . . our fellow Subjects contrary to express Acts of Parliament." Demanding redress, the meeting called on the governor to ensure that the customs commissioners never resumed their posts. In addition, he should order the *Romney* out of the harbor—at least until the king and government officials in Great Britain had time to respond to the people's pleas for relief.[44]

The Boston Town Meeting also appointed a committee to prepare a formal statement on the evils of introducing an armed force into the city. As usual, Adams exerted a strong influence. He served on the committee along with Dr. Joseph Warren and Dr. Benjamin Church, young men Adams had cultivated and put forward as talented defenders of American liberties. The three produced resolves that the town meeting transferred to a larger committee, headed by Dr. Warren, to be used as it saw fit in drafting instructions for the Boston representatives. Those instructions, adopted on June 17, reviewed the people's many grievances, including the claim of being overrun by swarms of government officials. The threat of military occupation merited particularly sharp criticism; in addition, a lengthy section denounced impressment and offered evidence that it was illegal. The Boston representatives should, the instructions directed, consider asking the House to pass a resolution branding anyone who called for stationing troops in Boston an enemy to both the city and the colony. The town meeting's actions did not spark a major confrontation, most probably because they were soon overshadowed by the question of rescinding the Massachusetts circular letter.[45]

Governor Bernard understood the explosiveness of impressment, and he tried to defuse the issue. After reminding the town meeting that he could not order the *Romney* out of the harbor, the governor promised to do his best to halt impressment. At Bernard's urging, Captain Corner publicly said he would not impress any Massachusetts seamen. The governor believed his actions "have given me a little popularity," but he also glumly prophesied it would not last a week.[46] He was right. On June 21, Bernard asked the representatives to comply with the king's demand that they rescind the Massachusetts circular letter. The ensuing fight turned his momentary popularity into a call for his dismissal.

By voting against rescinding the circular letter, the Massachusetts representatives signaled their determination to keep up the fight against the Townshend duties. Boston merchants soon sent a similar signal by escalating resistance to the duties. According to Hutchinson, Adams and Otis helped influence the merchants to stiffen their nonimportation resolve even though other cities, especially Philadelphia, had refused to join the effort. On August 1, the great majority of Boston merchants entered into a formal agreement to stop virtually all importation from Great Britain for one year commencing in January. And they would boycott all items subject to the Townshend duties until Parliament abolished them. The merchants' committee of correspondence, a technique Adams promoted, would keep their counterparts throughout America informed about Boston's determined stance.[47]

By the summer of 1768, in the aftermath of the *Liberty* incident and the fight over rescinding the circular letter, Governor Bernard and Samuel Adams agreed on one thing: to restore political peace in Massachusetts, Bernard must be replaced. Adams ventured that argument in a letter to agent De Berdt that, as usual, gave the colony's agent talking points to further Massachusetts's cause in England. Bernard advanced the idea as part of a campaign to secure a transfer to a more agreeable, more profitable locale. In July he sent the British government letter after letter recounting his heroic defense of the king's government against an increasingly formidable opposition. Bernard argued that only a show of force could save the day against the demagogues who aimed to overthrow the British Empire and who for three years had used "a trained mob" to pursue their goal. Of course, Bostonians did not want soldiers sent to their city. Indeed, as Bernard sadly observed, antisoldier sentiment ran so deep that even his own Council had unanimously opposed requesting troops. The distressing fact was, he moaned, "we are not without a Government, only it is in the Hands of the People of the Town, and not of those deputed by the King or under his Authority." Bernard bluntly asserted that Britain had only two choices: allow the situation to continue, in which case the king's government would be totally impotent, or use military force to stop the demagogues and their minions. Bernard recommended sending troops. The customs commissioners, who had shifted their residence from the *Romney* to Castle William, a fort on an island in Boston harbor, also claimed that only regular troops could restore law and order to Boston.[48]

The home government, having heard the same refrain for months, did not need this additional badgering. On June 8, even before the *Liberty* incident happened, Lord Hillsborough sent a secret and confidential message to General Thomas Gage. To "strengthen the Hands of Government" in Massachusetts and "enforce due Obedience to the Laws," Gage was directed to move a regiment, or whatever force he considered necessary, to Boston. It would take many weeks for the British troops to arrive. Still, the wailings of Bernard and the customs commissioners following the *Liberty* incident, which included the governor's plea for a force "sufficient to awe the Town," produced some immediate results. Britain beefed up its naval presence in Boston in the early summer of 1768. And, in late July, Hillsborough convinced the king to order an additional two regiments to Boston.[49]

By August rumors circulated that regular army troops would be coming. Adams discussed the possibility in an essay published on August 8. He began by trying to discredit the view that the people of Massachusetts were a mobbish lot. To prove this, he claimed the *Liberty* crowd did no more than break a few panes of glass before being convinced to disperse peacefully. Following his traditional pattern, this defense turned into an attack. Having downplayed the level of violence in an obviously misleading way, Adams accentuated the many grievances that had generated even this supposedly limited violence in peace-loving Boston. The unjustified confiscation of the *Liberty* had been achieved "by aid of military power, a power ever dreaded by all lovers of the peace and good order." Who could blame the people for boldly asserting their freedoms when their rights were infringed, when their property was endangered, when a naval force executed unconstitutional acts before their eyes, and when they were daily threatened with military occupation? Worse yet, all of this happened while their legislature was dissolved. Such grievances justified popular protest. Indeed, if the people did not complain, and loudly, they would be "fitted to be made the slaves of dirty tools of arbitrary power." As his pen name— "Determinatus"—suggested, an aggrieved people must defend their rights with determination or lose them.[50]

Confronted with the threat that British regulars might soon arrive, the popular party worked to bolster local resolve and morale. One tactic involved making the August 14 celebration—what John Rowe called "the Anniversary Day of the Sons of Liberty"—more elaborate than ever before. The *Boston Gazette* offered a lengthy report on "the extraordinary Festivity." The 1768 event, promoted by Adams and Otis, began at dawn at the Liberty Tree and featured the firing of fourteen cannons. At eleven o'clock, the leaders of the town, naturally including Adams, met "under the venerable Elm." Musical performances commenced at noon and concluded with the singing of "the *American* Song of Liberty" and yet more firing of cannons. According to the *Gazette*, shouts of joy arose from a huge audience "fraught with a noble Ardor in the cause of Freedom." As they stood at the windows in the neighboring houses, "the fair Daughters of Liberty . . . testified their Approbation by Smiles of Satisfaction." Then fourteen toasts, including one to "The glorious Ninety-two, who defended the Rights of AMERICA," filled the air. After French horns sounded, the cannon roared again—"completing the Number Ninety-Two"—and then the "Gentlemen" who had led the festivities climbed into carriages to attend "a *frugal* and *elegant* Entertainment" at the Greyhound Tavern in nearby Roxbury. The crowd that remained offered additional toasts often punctuated by celebratory cannon fire. Throughout these festivities, and throughout the struggle against British efforts to tax them, the supporters of American liberty often linked their struggles to others famed for defending the people's rights. Thus, the second round of toasts totaled forty-five in recognition of the famous publication by John Wilkes, the dissident British MP renowned at home and in America as a fighter for freedom who suffered imprisonment for his beliefs. The Bostonians also saluted Pascal Paoli, the Corsican who led his people's fight for freedom first from the Genoese and later from the French.[51]

All this pageantry with its symbolism of resolutely defending freedom could not obscure a bald reality. The colonial resistance to the Townshend duties did not come close to equaling the resistance the Stamp Act had unleashed. The Massachusetts circular letter did not propose convening another intercolonial conference equivalent to the Stamp Act Congress. The many crowd actions that prevented the implementation of the Stamp Act were not repeated against the Townshend duties. And even after most of the customs commissioners retreated to Castle William, Bostonians continued paying the required shipping duties. Despite the efforts of Adams and Otis, the Boston Town Meeting, and many Boston merchants, the economic warfare waged against the Townshend duties in 1768 hardly resembled that conducted against the Stamp Act. The colonists had organized a massive and general nonimportation effort against the Stamp Act. Unified action against the Townshend duties failed to materialize. By late summer 1768 many areas, including the vital city of Philadelphia, eschewed nonimportation. As a consequence, the kind of massive pressure British merchants and manufacturers quickly exerted against the Stamp Act simply was not exerted against the Townshend duties.[52]

Although the colonies as a whole did not challenge the Townshend duties as forcefully as they had the Stamp Act, letters dispatched to England by royally appointed politicians and officials made it appear as if the people of Massachusetts, or at least of Boston, stood perilously close to outright rebellion. That was a wild exaggeration, as Adams and other Whigs had striven to prove. But it was too late. Each side had come to believe that the very essence of the British constitution was at issue. And the British government had had enough of Boston's sedition. In addition to dispatching troops to Boston, it ordered that investigations be undertaken to determine whether the leaders of the popular party could be indicted for treason. Affidavits were obtained against Samuel Adams and others, including his protégés Dr. Warren and Dr. Church.[53] Although no formal charges were filed, the threat of them remained, and the Whigs soon had to confront the harsh reality that the British government had ordered four infantry regiments and a fleet to Boston.

By September 8, based on information supplied by a reluctant Governor Bernard, Bostonians learned that soldiers were indeed coming to Massachusetts. A petition to hold a town meeting quickly circulated, and on September 10 Adams, Otis, and Warren reportedly prepared resolves for adoption. When the citizens convened on September 12, they sent a committee to Bernard to discover the source of his information and to request that he call the House of Representatives back into session. The meeting also created a large committee charged with assessing the situation and recommending a course of action. The committee naturally included all of Boston's representatives as well as many other noted Whigs.[54]

When the town meeting reconvened the next day, the citizens learned Bernard's response. His expectation that troops would soon arrive came, he said, from private information; he had not received official word. As for reconvening the House, he could not do that because the king had that issue under consideration. The town meeting responded by unanimously adopting a "Declaration and Resolves." While pledging unwavering loyalty and support for the king, the meeting said that only the Massachusetts legislators could authorize spending the citizens' money. Any attempt to tax the people or to station an army in peacetime without the people's approval constituted "an infringement of their natural, constitutional and Charter Rights." Employing the army to enforce laws passed without the people's consent would compound the offense.

The town meeting then undertook a series of defiant and symbolic actions. To promote opposition to the Townshend duties, it praised New York City merchants for adopting a strong nonimportation stance. Hiding behind the obviously spurious claim that war might soon break out with France, the meeting ordered strict compliance with a law that required all householders to keep a musket and ammunition handy. Having hinted that they might fight, the citizens invoked God's protection.

The selectmen were instructed to visit the ministers and arrange for a day of fasting and prayer. More important, given Governor Bernard's refusal to call the assembly into session, the meeting attempted to come as close as possible to issuing that call itself. By express messengers, it invited all Massachusetts towns and districts to send representatives to a convention scheduled to begin on September 22 at Faneuil Hall. Boston selected its House delegation—Samuel Adams, James Otis Jr., Thomas Cushing, and John Hancock—to represent the city at this convention. Since a similar kind of convention had helped transform England's government during the Glorious Revolution of 1688–1689, the town meeting's actions were provocative. Underscoring the importance of all it had done, the meeting ordered that its votes and proceedings be published in all the newspapers. This, in effect, meant that the news of its actions would be reprinted and spread throughout America.[55]

The town meeting's effort to re-create something like the Massachusetts House proved impressively successful. Ninety-eight towns and eight districts dispatched representatives to the convention. Thomas Cushing, the speaker of the House, was elected moderator; Adams, the House clerk, became the clerk. For some unexplained reason, Otis missed the first half of the brief convention. The delegates began by petitioning Governor Bernard. They reiterated the request, already articulated by Boston's representatives and the town meeting, that the legislature be reconvened. The governor, who considered the convention an illegal gathering, refused to receive the petition. He did, however, return a threatening message demanding that the delegates disperse instantly. The delegates did not comply, nor did they stop imitating the House in yet another way. Just as the House might do, the convention authorized sending a letter to De Berdt, the House's agent in London. To publicize the convention in America, this lengthy letter was published in the *Boston Gazette*. The letter repeated arguments advanced by the Massachusetts House, by the Boston Town Meeting, and, of course, by Adams. For example, the letter stressed that, despite the malicious comments articulated by "interested and designing men," the people of Massachusetts, who contributed so much to Britain's wealth, were not given to mobbish violence. Instead, they protested reasonably, legally, and respectfully against Parliament's recent acts and against the prospect that a standing army, which threatened their natural rights as well as their charter and constitutional rights, would soon be stationed in their midst.

Although the delegates defied Bernard by continuing to meet, the convention, much to Adams's chagrin, did not produce radical results. The delegates had good reason to stress, as they repeatedly did, that they had assembled to promote peace and good order, not to usurp governmental powers. The delegates did little more than reaffirm support for the petition the House had sent to the king. Bernard gloated that his threatening message had sapped the delegates' courage. As he recounted it, his challenge to the legitimacy of the convention rendered the late-arriving Otis "perfectly tame" and explained why the more radical Samuel Adams failed in his attempts to cajole the delegates into adopting the harsh language often used by the House.[56]

Bernard may have puffed up his role in blocking more radical action, but he was right about a difference between Otis and Adams. There was a growing rift between the two popular party leaders. Otis headed the conservative wing of the party, which had a hard time even imagining the colonies might become independent; Adams led the more radical wing, which did not shrink from doing whatever was required to protect American rights. Adams's political philosophy—the people must know their rights and ardently defend them against any assailant—had been formed long before the troubles with Britain began. And while Adams the pragmatic politician would adjust to the realities of the current political scene, he refused to betray his political principles.

By the time the convention broke up on September 29, British transports carrying more than two regiments of soldiers rode at anchor in Boston harbor amid eight warships and four armed schooners.[57] For Samuel Adams this military presence constituted much more than another in a growing list of grievances against Britain. Since the time of troubles with Britain began he had repeatedly expressed the hope that the mother country would abandon her new and unconstitutional imperial policies. And, as a pragmatic politician, he counted on more than arguments about natural, charter, and constitutional rights to convince the British. He had constantly reminded the British of how the mother country profited from controlling American trade and from selling British manufactured goods in the colonies. He seemed to believe that the British would eventually realize that jettisoning their new imperial policies would serve their own self-interest. However, by the fall of 1768 it appeared the British could no longer be reasoned with. The mother country had forsaken reason in favor of naked military power. The serpent was darting its fatal venom.

Long before the relationship between Britain and its colonies turned sour in the 1760s, Samuel Adams had asserted that a free people must know their constitutional rights and guard them jealously. And well before soldiers marched into Boston, Adams had often warned about the special dangers a standing army posed for a free people. So the thought of British regiments descending on Boston horrified him. Indeed, if the reports of his contemporaries are correct, the arrival of a British army of occupation marked a transforming moment for Samuel Adams and, in time, for the British Empire.

4

THE POLITICS OF PRINCIPLE

On Friday, October 1, 1768, British warships crowded Boston harbor. Sailors stood ready to fire broadsides into the city. Shortly after noon, British regulars, smartly attired in bright scarlet coats, began landing on the Long Wharf. Once ashore, the Fourteenth and Twenty-ninth Regiments, along with elements of the Fifty-ninth Regiment, paraded through the heart of the town and onto Boston Common. The soldiers, more than seven hundred strong, marched to the beat of drums and the sound of fifes. Each man had been issued sixteen rounds of powder and ball. Their muskets were charged, their bayonets fixed. None of Boston's sixteen thousand inhabitants challenged them. At about two o'clock, the accompanying artillery unit armed with two cannons joined the soldiers on the common. In an afternoon, Boston had become an occupied city. The occupying force grew quickly. Two more regiments, the Sixty-fourth and the Sixty-fifth, began arriving in November.[1]

For Samuel Adams, any hope of reconciliation with the mother country apparently evaporated once British regulars transformed Boston into a garrisoned city. Claiming his information originated with James Warren, a close friend of Samuel, Peter Oliver asserted that the question of American independence "was settled in *Boston*, in 1768, by *Adams* & his Junto." The Reverend William Gordon, who was in Boston as the revolutionary movement unfolded and who knew Adams well, reported that as late as 1774 few in the colony sought independence but "at the head of these we must place Mr. *Samuel Adams*, who has long since said in small confidential companies—'The country shall be independent, and we will be satisfied with nothing short of it.'" Years after serving with him in the Continental Congress, Dr. Benjamin Rush reported that Samuel told him about the importance of 1768. Samuel remarked that "independence . . . had been the

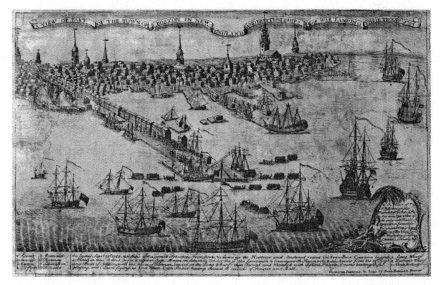

*Paul Revere engraving, "A View of . . . Brittish Ships of War: Landing Their Troops!
1768" (1770). Courtesy of the American Antiquarian Society.*

first wish of his heart seven years before the war." Responding to Rush's
comment, John Adams supposed it was about the time of the British occupation of Boston that Samuel decided America must become independent.
It seems that the arrival of troops in 1768 did convince Samuel that Britain
had left Americans no middle ground between tamely abandoning their
rights and pursuing independence.

Whether or not Adams committed himself irrevocably to independence in 1768 or sometime later, his contemporaries typically emphasized
that he was the first major leader who publically proclaimed that America
must be independent. And it is clear that, faced with the choice of surrendering constitutional rights or following the path of resistance to a revolution for independence, Samuel would tread the revolutionary path.[2] He
knew, however, that it would take time and effort for his radical position
to gain acceptance. And enunciating a belief few notables of the day shared,
he maintained that the thoughts of ordinary people mattered. He argued, in
fact, that the only way to expect success in momentous political struggles
was by supporting what the citizenry—the ordinary people—considered a
just cause.[3] That is why Samuel had labored so diligently to convince his
fellow colonists of the dangers inherent in Britain's new imperial policies.
When the arrival of troops posed a new threat to American liberties, Adams

wrote prodigiously, especially for newspapers, encouraging opposition to the military occupation. By using newspapers instead of pamphlets, Adams responded quickly to the changing political scene while also promoting his cardinal political ideals in a widely circulated medium.

From October 1768 through early 1769, Adams presented a multifaceted attack against standing armies. It made no sense, he reasoned, to garrison Boston since the orderly and pacific inhabitants were enjoying what he repeatedly called a period of "profound peace." Moreover, putting troops in Boston, or any American town, in peacetime violated England's own Bill of Rights. Using military power to enforce unconstitutional laws compounded the perniciousness. Britain's decision to place a standing army in Boston was, therefore, unjust and unconstitutional; worse yet, it could annihilate the people's rights. Alluding to Governor Bernard and his supporters, while conjuring up images of an evil future monarch, Adams warned of wicked men scheming to use military force "to awe the civil authority" and establish "arbitrary and despotic power" over Americans. The danger ran even deeper because the "military power is forever *dangerous* to civil rights." Although the British constitution had established the principle of military subordination to civilian control, soldiers thought differently than civilians. Because soldiers obeyed all orders, even unlawful ones, they might "sooner or later begin to look upon themselves as the lords and not the servants of the people." Soldiers might make their own laws "and enforce them by the *power of the sword*!"[4]

Adams and his radical colleagues employed various tactics to discomfort both the soldiers and the authorities who pleaded for them to be sent. Ironically, one again involved the Quartering Act, which required colonial governments to provide accommodations for soldiers only if they could not be placed in existing barracks. Castle William, located on an island in Boston about two and a half miles from the Long Wharf where they landed, could house the soldiers. Of course, billeting the troops there would hinder their ability to control the city and, as General Gage admitted, thus undermine the very reason for stationing troops in Boston. Therefore, Governor Bernard and Lieutenant Colonel William Dalrymple, the temporary British commander, pressed the Council to provide troop accommodations in Boston proper. Noting that Castle William had abundant room for the troops, the councilors refused with the smug observation that they could not even contemplate violating a law passed by Parliament. One colony-owned building large enough to serve as a barracks was the Manufactory House, and so the British might try to pressure local authorities into allowing troops to be housed there. According to Governor Bernard, "the Sons of Liberty" had anticipated that possibility and were determined to prevent it. He reported that, since word of the possible arrival of troops first surfaced weeks before, "all kinds of people were thrust into this Building." On October 1, Dalrymple, desperate to secure quarters in the city, ordered the occupants of the Manufactory House to vacate in two hours. The tenants, having already barred the doors and windows, sat tight.

The beleaguered Dalrymple next tried to intimidate Boston's selectmen into supplying quarters for his men. Repeating the Council's arguments, the selectmen refused. Dalrymple finally backed down. He had the Twenty-ninth pitch tents on the common and asked that the other troops, who lacked tents, be temporarily housed in the courthouse and in Faneuil Hall. The city officials agreed because they realized that approving these temporary arrangements made them appear generous and compassionate even as they opposed the standing army. While officers secured their own accommodation, John Montresor, the British barrack–master general for America, began renting buildings in various parts of the city to serve as quarters for troops. But housing the troops remained a problem because, as Adams emphasized, the law gave the civilian authority real leverage when it came to providing barracks. And, as General Gage lamented, "Every Art and Evasion has been tried . . . to force the Troops to quit the Town for want of Quarters." By late October, after further complications, including unsuccessful attempts to dislodge the occupants of the manufacturing house by force, enough buildings had been found to allow the soldiers housed in Faneuil Hall finally to move to barracks.[5]

As Adams had predicted, the soldiers caused more difficulties and "tumults" than they stopped. Dalrymple himself quickly faced a special problem. His troops deserted at an alarming rate. In just two weeks, desertions cut the British troop strength by a shocking 10 percent. To shut off this loss of men, Dalrymple placed guards throughout the town. The sentries followed the established military practice of challenging—that is, demanding acknowledgment from passersby. Those challenged, civilians as well as soldiers, were expected to respond with the shout "Friend." Bostonians justifiably resented this practice. In addition, soldiers typically ignored the city's tradition of respecting the Sabbath. The presence of troops also significantly increased the number of prostitutes in the city. And, to keep rent costs down, Dalrymple housed many of his soldiers near the homes and workplaces of less affluent Bostonians. That proximity increased the friction between the lower orders and the British regulars.[6]

The presence of soldiers and the many problems they caused provided Adams and his fellow Whigs with ample material to formulate propaganda.

They did it by creating a kind of news service that provided a day-by-day description and commentary on the effect of the regulars in Boston. The first installment appeared in the October 13 *New-York Journal* and covered the period from September 28 through October 2. At the end of this chronicle, the authors claimed what they had reported was *"strictly fact,"* and they urged all newspaper publishers to reprint it *"for the general satisfaction."* This statement, and commentary interspersed within the chronicle, appeared in italics to distinguish analysis from the reporting of events. Each week for more than a year, the *New-York Journal* carried an installment of this "Journal of Occurrences," or "Journal of the Times" as it was called in Boston. This was an innovation in an era when publishers filled their newspapers with government pronouncements along with material gleaned from other newspapers and items, especially letters and essays, supplied by private individuals. Publishers did not function as reporters, nor did they employ what today would be called reporters. So no one in America had ever published day-by-day reports of events, much less combined them with editorial comment set off in special type. Given its news value and innovative style, the "Journal" was reprinted not merely in Boston but also in other American cities and even in England.[7] Having concocted this powerful public-relations tool, Adams and the other "Journal" authors used it to illustrate a theme Samuel emphasized in other essays and indeed throughout his political life: standing armies threatened a people's basic liberties.[8]

The "Journal of the Times" focused on the many grievances that grew out of the military presence in Boston and, by implication, in any colonial town. While stressing that soldiers—the very troops then in Boston—were actually needed in frontier areas, stationing them in a peaceful urban area amounted to a colossal waste of money. Moreover, this provocative act created a volatile situation because the soldiers, officers and enlisted men alike, abused people and subverted the civil authority. Many soldiers lacked morals; many were criminals. The theme of criminality, buttressed by examples drawn from New York City as well as Boston, highlighted the soldiers' supposed depravity. Accounts of women being harassed and of rapes or attempted rapes appeared with regularity. British officers stationed in Boston were even charged with "tending to excite insurrection." The officers reportedly did that by urging some blacks to "ill-treat and abuse their masters, assuring them that the soldiers were come to procure their freedoms, and that with their help and assistance they should be able to drive all the Liberty Boys to the devil."[9]

In March of 1769, the authors of the "Journal" commented on a new threat aimed directly at Boston's leading Whigs. In December of 1768,

Lord Hillsborough had urged Parliament to pass resolves that, among other things, directed Governor Bernard to secure information concerning treasonous actions that took place in Massachusetts in 1768. In addition to other charges, the resolutions suggested that the petition to the king of February 1768, which denied the authority of Parliament, and the holding of the September 1768 convention might well be treasonous. If sufficient evidence of treason could be unearthed, the governor was to send it to England. Then a special commission would determine whether the ancient treason statute might be used to bring the accused to England for trial. After lengthy and spirited debate, the resolutions were finally approved in February of 1769 but only after the administration said it had no plans to put the treason act into effect. Nevertheless, from that time forward leading Whigs, and especially the ardent Samuel Adams, lived with the threat of possibly being whisked off to England to be tried for treason.

When news of this new menace reached America, the "Journal" authors responded by underscoring a theme Adams and his friends had already been hammering: Governor Bernard and the customs commissioners were yet again charged with conducting "a dark cabal" to mislead the British government into using military power to crush the people's rights. Why? Bernard, who supposedly had a "strange dislike" of the colony's charter, wanted military muscle to subvert the charter so he and his toddies could exert more control over the colony. And why did the commissioners want the soldiers? So they and their ever-increasing herds of unscrupulous officials could manipulate the revenue laws to enrich themselves. The "Journal" also contained numerous entries claiming that the "dark cabal" had caused British warships to descend on the peaceful, innocent people of Boston. And, of course, once warships arrived, the people faced yet another threat to American liberty directly linked to England's use of its military power; they might be pressed into the navy.[10]

Even before the troops arrived, Adams had depicted the customs commissioners as greedy weasels.[11] Reinforcing the "Journal of the Times" exposés, he again savaged the commissioners in numerous newspaper essays, especially a series signed "Candidus," published from late 1768 through mid-February 1769. Adams conceded that the commissioners employed a few honorable, honest men. He later also stressed that his critique did not apply to the one customs board member, obviously John Temple, who had attempted to thwart the other commissioners' nefarious plans. Having shown at least a modicum of fairness and balance, Adams ripped into the offending commissioners. They had, he charged, been biased against Boston even before they reached America. They treated the people insolently. They spent their time in politics and cabals, not in the king's service. They created swarms of officeholders. They maliciously misrepresented the peaceful and lawful conduct of Boston so troops would be stationed in the city. And they did all this in a venal quest for plunder. As he built his case against the commissioners, Adams carefully refrained from suggesting that the British government supported such villainy. Rather, he accused the British of lacking adequate knowledge, and he blamed that lack of knowledge on the great distance between America and England. The extreme distance, Samuel remarked, made it difficult for the administration to understand men or measures. Without openly saying it, Adams was providing a concrete illustration of why the colonies could not be represented in Parliament.[12]

As he assailed the commissioners and the new, intolerable horror caused by a standing army, Adams never lost sight of the fundamental grievance. In his view, the evils he catalogued ultimately sprang from Britain's unconstitutional effort to raise revenue from an unrepresented people. That meant that the Townshend duties had to be defeated. Given how effectively economic warfare had worked against the Stamp Act, it seemed logical to employ the same tactic against the Townshend duties. By refusing to import British goods, the British merchants, manufacturers, and their employees could, it seemed, be pressured into lobbying Parliament to repeal the duties. On the basis of this theory, Adams and Otis had helped Boston take the lead in developing nonimportation against the Townshend duties, and New York City merchants had responded by adopting an even stronger form of nonimportation. By March 1769 when Philadelphia's mercantile community finally joined the movement, all of America's important commercial centers were closed to British imports.[13]

Because it had been dissolved in June 1768, the Massachusetts House could not even applaud the increasingly vigorous economic war being conducted against parliamentary taxation, much less actively oppose the introduction of a standing army. The Massachusetts Charter, however, required that representatives be elected each May. So, as May 1769 approached, the popular and court parties renewed their election battles. Part of the campaign Adams and his colleagues waged involved linking Governor Bernard to the military occupation of Boston. That strategy received an unintended boost from Bernard himself. William Bollan, the Council's agent in England, managed to obtain letters the governor had written to the home government. They depicted Boston as the habitat of lawless anti-British zealots. Learning about the letters in April, the town meeting, adopting a technique Adams and the House had used, petitioned the king and requested that the governor's official correspondence be made public. At the meeting's direction, Adams composed a letter to be sent to Isaac Barré along with the petition and a request that he personally present the petition to the king. After claiming that some of the king's principal appointees had misrepresented the situation in Boston, Adams developed a new line of argument in support of obtaining Bernard's letters. He linked their release to the established right to know the evidence presented by one's accuser, and he added that releasing the letters was even more imperative when, as in this case, the accuser was not a disinterested person.[14]

Two weeks later, Adams used Bernard's alleged misrepresentations of Boston both to question criticism voiced by General Gage and to undermine the court party's credibility. Writing as "A Bostonian," Adams suggested that Gage's negative attitude toward Boston probably stemmed from biased information supplied by Governor Bernard "and his *few adherents* in the province." Once again emphasizing a fundamental right, Adams pointed out that Boston had to be considered innocent until evidence proved otherwise.[15]

While rumors of it had circulated for months, in April Bostonians learned that Bernard would indeed be made a baronet and would probably soon be replaced as governor. That combination made him an especially inviting target for political invective. Just before the annual 1769 election, Adams penned a classic bit of sarcasm that turned the honor of becoming a baronet against Bernard. Writing as "A Tory," Adams mockingly congratulated Bernard for having troops sent to Boston and for quartering them in the town. These achievements, the imaginary Tory opined, showed how much the governor loved the people's rights. Of course, it was a pity the worthy governor did not have a pension to support his new title. However, a well-chosen assembly could remedy the problem. And if that did not happen, why, a tax on the improved lands of the colonies would do the job of supporting Bernard and his friends. "A Tory" closed by calling himself "the most *servile* of all *your* Tools." Although he did not use these words, Samuel's venture into fiction almost shouted, To protect your rights, to protect your property, vote the popular party, vote Whig! Samuel's "A Tory" did double duty; after appearing in the *Boston Gazette* on May 1, it was incorporated into the "Journal of the Times."[16]

Whig leaders also asserted that the standing army threatened the integrity of the election process. Boston's selectmen called on the British commander, General Alexander Mackay, and told him the town had a constitutional right to have the troops moved out of the city when elections occurred. General Mackay, who had just arrived and who hoped to reduce the friction between soldiers and civilians, replied that he could not comply with the request. He did, however, pledge that he would order the soldiers confined to their barracks on election day. When the Town Meeting convened on May 5, it adopted a "Declaration of their Rights & the Freedom of their Elections," which Adams had prepared before the gathering occurred. It was issued in support of Boston's claim of "the full Right of British Freeholders & Subjects . . . founded in the Principles of the British Constitution." Adams cleverly seized on General Mackay's promise to confine the soldiers to their barracks as a concession that Boston's demands in support of free elections were justified. But it was, said Adams, not enough. The people's rights demanded that the troops should be removed from the city, not just restricted to their barracks. It followed that the citizens "cannot proceed to the Election, without declaring their clear & full Sense, that the residence of an armed force in the Town, during an Election of so great Importance, is a gross Infringement of their constitutional Rights." The election would occur, but only "from necessity." Reflecting Adams's emphasis on the importance of precedent, the "Declaration" proclaimed that holding the election could not be considered as a precedent or as a voluntary movement away from "the incontestable rights of British Subjects & freeholders."[17]

After approving the "Declaration," Boston's voters resoundingly reelected Adams, Otis, Cushing, and Hancock. Each received more than 98 percent of the votes cast. Whigs did well throughout the colony, so a political replay occurred when the legislature met on May 31, 1769. Once again Cushing became speaker of the House. Adams continued as clerk. Once again the name of Thomas Hutchinson did not appear on the list of Council members. Governor Bernard vented his anger by negating eleven of the twenty-eight names submitted for membership on the Council. Responding in its now-typical way, the House refused to name replacements for the vetoed councilors.[18]

The acrimony between the representatives and the governor never diminished. In missives drafted mainly by Adams, the representatives peppered Bernard with strident defenses of the people's rights. In addition to denouncing the military occupation in general, the legislators expressed righteous indignation over the fact that a military guard stood by their door and British cannons were pointed at the statehouse. Calling this an insult to the legislature's right to function freely, the representatives exhorted the governor to order both the sea and land forces out of Boston for the duration of the legislative session. When Bernard replied, as he always did, that he lacked the power to remove military forces, the representatives responded with evidence that he did have the authority. Echoing one of Adams's choice themes, the House also retorted that if the governor could not order the removal of the troops, then the military power, always dangerous to civil liberties, had become an absolute power. Although the representatives declared they would remain in session because the charter required it, they announced that they would not conduct normal legislative business until the pernicious assaults on the dignity and rights of the legislature stopped.[19]

Bernard fought back. On June 13, after labeling the representatives' nonactivity a waste of the people's money, he said he would remedy the House's aversion to troops by ordering the representatives to meet in Cambridge across the Charles River. Bernard's tactics opened him to a searing counterattack. The representatives, having been forced to reconvene in Cambridge, escalated their rhetoric. Placing a standing army in the province during peacetime unchecked by civilian authority constituted "a dangerous innovation"; planting soldiers with cannons in front of the statehouse while the assembly met constituted "the most pointed insult ever offered a free people, and its whole Legislature." The fact that the cannons were hauled away the day after the legislature moved to Cambridge heightened the insult. The legislators had, they proclaimed, refused to follow the normal routine because doing so would undermine the dignity and freedom of the legislature. And while Bernard might consider those things unimportant, the representatives believed otherwise. Their time had been well spent, and their constituents would agree since "no time can better be employed, than in the preservation of the rights derived from the British constitution. . . . No treasure can be better expended, than in securing that true old English liberty." The representatives also reiterated that, since they continued to meet out of necessity, their actions could not be construed as a surrender of the people's and the legislature's "constitutional rights, liberties, and privileges."[20]

Governor Bernard, who said that every dip of Adams's pen "stung like an horned Snake," clearly was losing the word battle with Adams and the rest of the Massachusetts House.[21] And although it was well known that Bernard would soon travel to England and probably never return, the representatives took no chances. On June 27, they petitioned the king to remove Bernard from the governorship *forever*. The petition was based on the document the House had considered just before being dissolved a year earlier and used some of that first petition's language. With the new grievance of military occupation, the harsh tone of the June 1768 indictment gave way in June 1769 to undisguised, sarcastic viciousness. The fate of the two petitions, both of which Adams probably composed, indicated how far Bernard's position had eroded. When presented with the June 1768 petition, the House had deferred action. Now a year later, in a very full House of 109 members, the more acerbic anti-Bernard petition received unanimous approval.[22]

Right after petitioning for Bernard's ouster, the House adopted a lengthy set of resolves prepared by a large committee that, as usual, included Adams. The representatives stressed that they were defending the people's most basic natural and constitutional rights against intolerable attacks. The resolves offered an extensive list of grievances that Massachusetts, and the colonies in general, had against Britain's imperial policies. The evils of the customs commissioners and their multiplying minions, of a standing army, of taxation without representation, of extending the power of the admiralty courts, and of threatening to take people out of Massachusetts to face trial were all recounted. Bernard merited special condemnation for supposedly misrepresenting Boston and Massachusetts as being riot torn and virtually ungovernable. He was also lambasted for suggesting, as he did in the private letters agent Bollan had obtained, that the Massachusetts Charter should be revised so the Council would be appointed, not elected.[23]

By early July 1769, the members of the House and Bernard found it virtually impossible to maintain even a pretense of civility. The arrival of news from Virginia exacerbated the situation. In mid-May, in part to support Massachusetts and Boston, the Virginia House of Burgesses had adopted strongly worded resolves defending the American Whig positions on taxation, the right to petition for redress, and the right to be tried where an alleged crime occurred. Virginia's resolves took on great significance because the burgesses sent copies to all the colonial assemblies and asked for their concurrence. The Massachusetts House responded on July 7 and, reflecting the ideal of the colonies working in unison, adopted resolves incorporating the essence, and often the wording, of the Virginia resolves. The legislators added many other sections that repeated their earlier, especially their anti-Bernard, pronouncements.[24]

Bernard did not shrink from the challenge. He escalated the conflict by telling the representatives that Parliament required them to underwrite the maintenance of the troops stationed in Boston. He might have guessed the response. On July 15 the House declared that supplying the funds would obliterate the legislature's and the people's rights. Because of the obligations they owed their constituents, the representatives could never comply with the governor's request. Bernard had had enough of Adams, Otis, and the rest of the popular party. Proclaiming that the House's actions constituted an "invasion of the rights of the imperial sovereignty," Bernard suspended the General Court and postponed a further meeting until early 1770.[25]

While the legislature and governor engaged in increasingly acrimonious confrontation, the civilians and soldiers coexisted uneasily. To discredit the idea that troops were needed, Bostonians strove to maintain tranquility. The British generals in command from November 1768 through mid–August 1769 matched the civilian effort at self-control. Recognizing the explosive, no-win nature of the situation, the British commanders requested transfers for themselves and endeavored to keep things quiet until those transfers arrived. In addition, for all the problems the soldiers created, their presence pumped money into Boston's economy.

The relative quiet that existed in the city made it easier for the British government to implement a plan to reduce tensions by withdrawing troops from Boston. In addition, the British needed more soldiers in Ireland. The decision of how many, if any, regulars should stay in Boston fell to General Gage. He quickly arranged for the removal of two regiments. By July 25, most of the Sixty-fourth had shipped out; the Sixty-fifth and the artillery soon followed.

As July gave way to August, Boston's Whigs had good reason to rejoice. Bernard sailed on August 1, never to return. Perhaps because Bostonians thought the remaining soldiers would soon vanish, the last entry in the "Journal of the Times," which offered a withering critique of Bernard, was for August 1, 1769. The day he sailed, Bostonians celebrated. As John Rowe phrased it, Bernard's leaving brought "Great Joy to the People," and Thomas Hutchinson admitted that "there were many marks of public joy in the town of Boston." Flags covered several buildings as well as the Liberty Tree; bells rang; guns were fired from John Hancock's wharf; huge bonfires lit up Fort Hill and areas adjacent to Boston. The editors of the *Boston Gazette*, who called Bernard "a Scourge to this Province, a Curse to North-America, and a Plague to the whole Empire," proudly observed that amid all the celebrations upon Bernard's departure "there was not the least disorder committed."

On August 3, the Reverend Samuel Cooper, a leading Boston Whig, remarked that the greater part of the military had departed, "and it is said the remainder will not tarry long among us." Nevertheless, two regiments remained, and, as Adams realized, so did the difficult task of defeating any parliamentary taxation. Partial victories were just that—partial. So Adams and Otis continued their tradition of using anniversaries to champion colonial resistance. The 1769 anniversary of the people's Stamp Act resistance of August 14 featured massive celebrations designed to cultivate what John

Adams described as the sensations of freedom. As they had the year before, the celebrants offered praise for John Wilkes and Pascal Paoli. Special attention was also given to a range of people in England viewed as supporters of American rights. Additional toasts hailed the Massachusetts House of Representatives, and especially "The Glorious Ninety-Two." "That *firm* and *intrepid* Band of *Patriots* the *Burgesses* of Virginia" and John Dickinson, "The Farmer of Pennsylvania," were also singled out for cheers. At times, cannon fire accompanied the cheering.[26]

The emphasis the festivities placed on supporting America helped produce a significant change in the meaning of a potent term, *patriot*. Now when the leaders of the popular forces talked of *patriots* and of *patriotism*, they were speaking of loyalty to America, not to Great Britain or to the British Empire. Being a patriot had come to mean supporting American rights. Although Samuel Adams did not single-handedly cause this shift, his efforts to bring it about illustrates that he understood the power of individual words and strove to make iconic terminology support the defense of American rights.

The impressive August 14 celebration and the pro-Whig alterations in political language could not obscure a worrisome fact. As the summer of 1769 drew to a close, support for nonimportation was waning. In late August, writing as "Populus" in the *Boston Gazette*, Adams tried to halt the slide. Asserting that America's "Salvation" was at stake, Adams implored merchants to continue backing nonimportation. And, following his usual strategy, he went on the offensive. Drawing on the dislike of Bernard, Adams observed that the governor knew nonimportation could scuttle the taxes that would provide him with a pension. As Adams presented it, that fact helped explain the actions of John Mein, a merchant and the publisher of the *Boston Chronicle*, the newspaper voice of the court party. Mein had been printing shipping records that purportedly revealed how various Boston Whig merchants violated the nonimportation agreement. After challenging some of Mein's evidence and implying the publisher was doing the bidding of Bernard and his cronies, Adams warned Mein about putting himself in opposition to "an awakened, an enlightened and a Determined Continent." In a parting shot, Adams chastised Thomas Hutchinson's two merchant sons for not supporting nonimportation.[27]

Everyone considered nonimportation crucial. It was the only effective weapon the colonists had devised to fight parliamentary taxation. And, as Adams knew all too well, pumping up support for the existing nonimportation effort was merely a stopgap measure. The nonimportation agreement only obligated America's merchants through January 1, 1770.

Equally important from Adams's perspective, because it only targeted the Townshend duties, the agreement was too limited. Believing the colonists must be consistent in defending their basic rights, Adams and Otis wanted nonimportation sustained until Parliament rescinded every law that taxed Americans. That meant waging economic war until Parliament repealed the Sugar Act as well as the Townshend duties. But the Sugar Act duties on imported molasses, which were neither highly visible nor particularly burdensome, had recently been lowered from 3 pence to a paltry 1 pence. As a result, concerns about consistently defending principle melted away; few Americans seemed willing to suffer the hardships of nonimportation to attack the Sugar Act.

The British government hoped to take advantage of the fact that most Americans, like most people in Great Britain, developed a convenient amnesia about constitutional principles when those principles bumped against immediate economic self-interest. In May 1769 the government sent a circular letter to the colonial governors that, while reiterating the British view of the supremacy of Parliament, indicated the administration had no plans to levy further taxes on Americans. Moreover, when Parliament next convened, the administration expected to eliminate the Townshend duties on glass, paper, and painting materials as being "contrary to the true principles of commerce." The circular letter, which Bernard made public just before leaving Massachusetts, was designed to weaken an already less-than-strong nonimportation effort. But Lieutenant Governor Hutchinson, who would exercise Bernard's powers until a replacement was appointed, had to admit that publication of the circular letter initially strengthened the nonimportation campaign. Realizing that the British aimed to undermine nonimportation, Adams and Otis exhorted Boston's merchants to press for total victory before the British acted. On September 2, 1769, the merchants' correspondence committee sent a letter to Philadelphia's merchants that urged them to continue nonimportation until Parliament repealed all its revenue acts, including the Sugar Act. The inclusion of the Sugar Act harmonized with Adams's call to oppose all of Parliament's revenue statutes as a matter of principle. The merchants were, in effect, embracing Adams's position that it was necessary to deny the British any precedent for taxing the colonists.[28]

As Boston's merchant committee waited for a response, James Otis was effectively removed from the political scene. Angered by a report that customs commissioners had labeled him an enemy of the king, Otis, accompanied by Adams, met with the commissioners on September 1. The participants kept the reason for the meeting secret, but, if it was designed to produce a compromise, it failed. Then, on September 4, Otis published an extraordinary essay under his own name. Denouncing John Robinson and three other commissioners, Otis explained he had asked for personal satisfaction but had not received a proper answer. In short, he had demanded a gentleman's satisfaction—a duel. When Otis strolled into the British Coffee House the next evening, he and Robinson fought. The press carried conflicting versions of what happened. Adams entered the fray as "An Impartialist" and was anything but impartial. In a lengthy, detailed analysis of what happened, Samuel insinuated that Robinson had participated in a prearranged plan to assassinate Otis. And no one could deny that Otis received a vicious blow on the head that probably hastened his already discernible descent into mental instability. After the fight, Otis oscillated between periods of lucidity and bouts of irrational behavior.

Even before the coffeehouse brawl, Otis's popularity had been declining. Samuel Adams had, in fact, supplanted him as the leading Whig in Massachusetts. But Otis's efforts would be sorely missed in the nonimportation effort. As acting governor Hutchinson attested, the team of Adams and Otis had been instrumental in convincing Boston's merchants to support nonimportation. Now, Otis could no longer play his usual animating role.[29] Undaunted, Adams pressed on. A town meeting was scheduled for October 4 to examine the issues of nonimportation and its natural twin, support for American manufacturing. Two days before the meeting, Adams published a lengthy essay under the pen name "Alfred." Building on the idea that Americans would have been reduced to absolute slavery if they had not fought the Stamp Act, Adams proclaimed that the people were more united than ever before, that their opposition was prudent and legal, and that they should continue their opposition until "every American grievance is redressed."[30]

The town meeting did just what Adams outlined in his Alfred essay. The citizens endorsed a statement describing nonimportation as a legal, peaceful strategy that also had the best chance of successfully defending American rights. The merchants of Boston and the whole continent drew praise for "having nobly preferred the publick Good to their own private Emolument." Indeed, posterity would venerate them for their noble and public-spirited actions. The meeting then contemplated the few who were undermining nonimportation. It expressed astonishment and indignation "that any of its Citizens could be so lost to the feelings of Patriotism, and the common Interest" as to keep buying British goods. Seven offending merchants were listed by name and thus held up to ridicule. The list included the three men Adams had openly denounced in his Populus essay:

John Mein, Elisha Hutchinson, and Thomas Hutchinson Jr. And why had
the offending merchants deserted their country in its struggle to protect its
constitutional rights? Because they "preferred their little private advantage
to the common Interest of all the Colonies." To enrich themselves, they
had basely taken advantage "of the generous self denial of their Fellow Citizens for the Common Good." So the statement, which Adams undoubtedly helped craft, praised virtually the whole business community, the city's
people, and even the rest of the continent for standing up for American
rights. How could anyone openly vote against that? The pronouncement
passed unanimously. By thus very publicly attacking the seven miscreants
with loaded words, the town meeting's polemic reminded potential nonimportation slackers that public opprobrium might be visited upon them
as well. To give added punch to its message, the meeting directed that its
votes be published in the town's newspapers.[31]

Adams had to be gratified when the October 4, 1769, town meeting prodded everyone to support nonimportation. Less than two weeks
later, he had even better reason to smile. On October 17, the day before
the town meeting was next scheduled to meet, the merchant committee
did what Adams had advocated. Without waiting to learn whether other
cities had embraced Boston's position, the merchants altered their own
agreement. It now called for continuing nonimportation until Parliament
repealed all the taxes. Then, when the town meeting convened the next
day, the citizens approved a lengthy commentary written chiefly by Adams. The work's title revealed the basic goal: "An Appeal to the World;
or a Vindication of the Town of Boston, from Many False and Malicious
Aspersions" contained in the writing of Governor Bernard and others. The
"Vindication" paraded the old themes of a profoundly peaceful Boston being overrun with soldiers because of the venality of Bernard, his cronies,
and the customs commissioners. And, as he had been doing with increasing
regularity, Adams also used "An Appeal" to urge Americans to defend their
fundamental rights on a thoroughly consistent, not a piecemeal, basis. With
simple clarity and thus with real force, Adams maintained that the colonists'
grievances could never be truly redressed "till *every Act*, pass'd by the British
Parliament for the express Purpose of raising a Revenue upon us without
our Consent, is Repeal'd; till the American Board of Commissions of the
Customs is dissolv'd; the Troops recall'd." As with *The True Sentiments of
America* published the year before, politicos in England came to associate
"An Appeal" with Samuel Adams, and so his reputation as a significant
political personage continued to grow in the mother country.[32]

The public indignation expressed during the town meeting reflected the tension mounting in Boston from midsummer into the fall of 1769. It could be traced to much more than the physical attack on Otis. The anticipated evacuation of the last two regiments of redcoats had not materialized. In addition, Colonel Dalrymple, who resumed command of the British regulars in mid-August 1769, was not interested in placating Bostonians. As a result, repeated violence flared. On the evening of October 23, citizens exchanged insults with soldiers stationed at the guard post on Boston Neck at the outskirts of the city. The next day, a crowd assailed soldiers returning to their barracks. Although several troopers suffered injuries, none of the assailants was arrested. Colonel Dalrymple speculated that this incident presaged something more consequential. Merchants who dared to keep importing British goods also experienced the people's wrath. Nathaniel Rogers, a nephew of Thomas Hutchinson, complained that his house had twice been "besmeared, the last time with the Vilest filth of the Vilest Vault." On October 28, John Mein, a man Adams had savaged in print and the town meeting had denounced, had to scamper behind British sentries to escape an angry crowd. That night a crowd seized George Gailer, a man reviled as a customs-official lackey. Gailer was tarred and feathered, hauled around Boston in a cart, and then forced to repent publicly for his offenses. Along the way, the crowd taunted a British sentry and threatened to pitch him into the cart.[33]

Samuel Adams, always laboring to further the patriot cause, used the increased tension between soldiers and townspeople to press even harder for removing the troops. In late December 1769, about three weeks before the General Court was scheduled to reconvene, Thomas Hutchinson reported that "Adams has declared the troops must move to the Castle, and it must be the first business of [the General] Court to remove them out of the town." The British ministry in London, probably responding to the challenge made by Adams's "Appeal," had already sent orders that precluded that possibility. Acting on the home government's instructions, on January 4 Hutchinson decreed that the legislature would not meet until March.[34] Adams fought back in a newspaper essay published four days later. He held that no person located three thousand miles away could understand when convening the legislature might be essential. And if the assembly could not meet, the people would be deprived of their basic right of having their representatives petition for redress of grievances. Adams asserted that, under the charter, the acting governor could, and should, exercise his own independent judgment and call the legislature into session. Hutchinson naturally ignored Adams's pleadings. The General Court would not meet again until March.[35]

Although the Whigs did not need the General Court to keep non-importation going, Adams, who had proclaimed himself an auxiliary to the merchants and who served on at least one merchant committee, knew that nonimportation faced mounting problems. His hopes for an energized and principled effort had been dashed because merchants in other cities refused to extend nonimportation until Parliament repealed all the revenue laws. They would not commit themselves to any more than continuing nonimportation until the Townshend duties were abolished. Left with little choice, Boston's business community accepted that plan. Some of the city's merchants, including Hutchinson's merchant sons, balked at doing that much. They considered themselves bound only by the original agreement. So, when it expired on January 1, 1770, those merchants began selling imported goods, especially tea, which fetched a high price.[36] Adams rushed into print once again as "Determinatus." He tried to shame the slackers into continuing nonimportation until it succeeded. Reiterating that nothing worked as well as nonimportation, Adams accused those who sold imported goods of selfishly ignoring their obligation to society. Proclaiming that "the fate of *Unborn Millions*" of Americans hung in the balance, Adams urged the whole city to support the patriotic nonimportation effort. Everyone, not just the merchants, must insist on nonimportation "being *Strictly* adhered to."[37]

Members of the merchant committee, with Adams and other Whig leaders joining them, did their part. On January 16 they issued a broadside urging all merchants and anyone connected to commerce to come together the following day to hear a report on the individuals who resisted the nonimportation efforts. Once they heard that report, the group, led by a committee of five that included Adams, moved en mass to harangue six slackers. Thomas Hutchinson's two sons backed down, but four merchants still refused to stop importing. Two days later a large group of merchants and other inhabitants met at Faneuil Hall to hear the merchants' Committee of Inspection report concerning the three or four "perfidious" merchants who still refused to support nonimportation. That meeting adjourned until January 23.

When the meeting reconvened, the acting governor sent a message by way of Sheriff Greenleaf and, as the *Boston Gazette* reported it, "*directed*" the moderator to read it. Alluding to the recent efforts to coerce merchants into continuing nonimportation and implying that the meeting would do more of the same, Hutchinson asserted that the going from house to house "must strike the People with Terror from your great Numbers, (even if it be admitted that it is not done in a tumultuous Manner) and is of very dangerous Tendency." Showing a bit of aristocratic tone deafness, he called upon "such of you as are Persons of Character, Reputation and Property" not to "expose yourselves to the Consequences of the irregular Actions of any of your Numbers." Proclaiming that the gathering "cannot be justified by any Authority or Colour of Law," Hutchinson, stressing that he represented "his Majesty, who is the Father of the People," declared, "I must enjoin and require you without Delay, to seperate and disperse, and to forbear all such unlawful Assemblies for the future." According to the *Boston Gazette*, the 1,300 to 1,400 people at the meeting, having listened to Hutchinson's message, "calmly considered" the issue of continuing their meeting. The vote to proceed was unanimous. Sheriff Greenleaf was then given a statement in which the meeting, again unanimously, informed the acting governor "that this Meeting is warranted by Law." Sheriff Greenleaf scurried away with that missive after making it clear that he wanted it understood he was merely a courier.

Having rebuffed Hutchinson's efforts to break it up, the gathering, styling itself "this Body," publicly castigated four Bostonian merchants—William Jackson, Theophilius Lillie, John Taylor, and Nathaniel Rogers—as "obstinate and inveterate Enemies to their Country, and Subverters of the Rights and Liberties of this Continent." The offenders would "for ever hereafter" be boycotted and treated as nonpersons. Six others, described as mostly being strangers to Boston, were denounced for importing goods in violation of "*the known Sentiments of the Merchants, Freeholders, and Inhabitants in every Colony.*" The meeting also made tea a special symbol by agreeing to abstain from drinking it.[38] On January 31, a group of women drafted a pledge to do the same, except in the case of sickness. The women, "the Mistresses of their respective families," explained that they wanted to help "save this abused Country from Ruin and Slavery." By early February more than three hundred married women had agreed to the pledge. On February 12, young women entered into an "Agreement of the young Ladies of this Town, against drinking foreign TEA." They hoped their abstinence would "frustrate a Plan that tends to deprive a whole Community of their *all* that is valuable in Life." Within a week, 126 had signed the agreement. By February 19, over one hundred additional married women had subscribed to the antitea pledge; this meant that more than five hundred Boston women had publicly endorsed the tea boycott.[39]

As Adams prophesied, and probably hoped, the recalcitrant merchants suffered almost constant harassment. One favorite tactic involved simply identifying someone as an "importer." As the *Boston Gazette* reported on February 19, children had recently done just that without untoward results. Then, on the morning of February 22, young boys set up a sign outside the shop of Theophilus Lillie that identified him as an importer. Ebenezer Richardson, already despised as a customs informer, tried to destroy the sign. After exchanging insults with some adults, he retired to his nearby home. The boys, as they told the story, also had words with Richardson and his wife. Before long, the boys began tossing various kinds of rubbish, and Mrs. Richardson pitched it back at them. During this great garbage fight, or soon thereafter, windows in the Richardson home were broken. After cursing at the crowd and demanding that the people disperse, Richardson appeared at a window with a gun at the ready. The boys responded by pelting the house with whatever they could lay their hands on. Then, to everyone's amazement, Richardson fired. Young Sammy Gore fell wounded, but survived. Christopher Snider, who came from a poor German family, was not so fortunate. Several large pellets tore into him; he

Woodcut depiction of the confrontation that led to the killing of Christopher Snider from "The Life, and Humble Confession, of Richardson, the Informer" (Boston? 1772?; Evans 42373). Courtesy of The Historical Society of Pennsylvania.

died that night. Snider, who was described as an innocent passerby, was only about eleven years old. Even Peter Oliver conceded that Richardson—who was subsequently tried, found guilty of murder, but ultimately pardoned—had "fired at Random & killed an innocent Boy."[40]

Samuel Adams helped turn young Snider's death into a public event filled with powerful symbolism. Notices appeared in the press requesting that "the Friends of Liberty" attend Snider's funeral on Monday, February 26. The funeral procession began in the late afternoon at the Liberty Tree. On it, Sons of Liberty placed a sign that included the pious observation that "The memory of the Just is *Blessed*." Each side of the casket contained a message, in Latin, rendered in silvered letters. The inscription at the head of the casket translated into the lament "*Innocence itself* is *no where safe!*" Newspaper accounts indicated that between four hundred and five hundred boys marched in front of the little casket. Six youths chosen by the boy's parents served as pallbearers. A cortege of more than thirteen hundred men and women walked behind the casket. About thirty horse-drawn coaches closed the procession. John Rowe also estimated that about two thousand people attended the funeral, and John Adams confided to his diary that "my Eyes never beheld such a funeral. The Procession extended further than can be well imagined." A sizable and bereft crowd watched this huge funeral procession. The *Boston Gazette* carried the observation that, "young as he was, he died in his Country's Cause." "A Mourner" hailed "this little Hero and first Martyr to the noble Cause." The publishers of the *Gazette* assured their readers that a monument would be erected to perpetuate the memory of the young martyr. Patriotic gentlemen had, reportedly, already launched a subscription to achieve that goal.

Hutchinson understood the motives of Adams and other Whig leaders. He claimed that Snider's funeral, like other huge public funerals staged for political purposes, was designed to raise the people's passions in support of the cause the leaders espoused.[41] Given how the press functioned, one could anticipate that America's newspapers would spread the news of the tragic death and magnificently patriotic funeral throughout the colonies. The Snider incident clearly had the potential of evolving into a significant landmark in the dispute between the colonies and Great Britain; however, it was soon overshadowed by an even deadlier confrontation.

Many of the city's inhabitants, no matter what their political views, considered a bloody clash between Bostonians and the soldiers inevitable. All Bostonians, even Tories, disliked the way many redcoats behaved, but ordinary Bostonians had special and increasing reason to find their continuing presence offensive. Soldiers standing guard often treated the lower orders with disrespect, even threatening them. In addition, redcoats posed an immediate economic challenge. Because the British allowed off-duty troops to work, the people who typically formed the bulk of the city's crowds now often found themselves competing with soldiers for casual-labor jobs. That economic threat seemed even more menacing in early 1770. Nonimportation had caused the value of Boston's imports to drop by half, and this naturally reduced the number of jobs available in the city. To make matters worse, by late January 1770 ice clogged Boston's harbor, thus curtailing shipping and employment opportunities even more.[42]

The combination of economic difficulties and mutual contempt bred by more than seventeen months of military occupation sparked a number of altercations. Fights on March 2 provided the immediate background of the catastrophe known as the Boston Massacre. As Patrick Walker, an off-duty soldier, strolled by John Gray's ropewalk in quest of work, a rope maker asked him if he wanted a job. When Walker replied affirmatively, the rope maker said, "Then go and clean my shithouse." A fight followed. Getting the worst of it, Walker rounded up eight or nine other soldiers and came back for a rematch. But, when several rope makers joined forces, the redcoats again lost the scuffle. Undaunted, Walker and the other soldiers regrouped and returned about forty strong. Anticipating the soldiers' action, the rope makers had obtained their own reinforcements. In the ensuing melee, the two sides went at each other with clubs and other weapons. Once again, the soldiers were routed. Over the next two days, rope makers and other civilians tussled with individual soldiers, and one, Private John Rodgers, had both his arm and skull fractured. Bostonians remembered soldiers saying they would have their revenge. Commenting on the escalating clashes between the soldiers and townspeople, James Murray, who became a loyalist, talked of "the Turbulent Town of Boston" and how "ill-humour thus worked up on both sides."[43]

On Monday night, March 5, 1770, different groups of civilians and soldiers went looking for trouble. Private Hugh White, standing sentry duty near the customhouse in King Street, suddenly found himself being bombarded with snowballs and chunks of ice. He shouted for help, and soldiers from the Twenty-ninth Regiment, led by Captain Thomas Preston, rushed to White's defense. Estimates of the size of the crowd that gathered in front of the soldiers vary wildly from fewer than a hundred to well over a thousand. But there is no question that people in the crowd hurled snowballs, ice, sticks, and other objects as they pressed close to the soldiers. Knowing the soldiers, clad in their scarlet coats, could not legally fire their weapons unless authorized by a civilian magistrate, members of the crowd taunted them mercilessly: "You cowardly rascals. You bloody backs. Fire, and be damned. Fire, fire, damn you, fire, fire, you lobsters, fire, you dare not fire. We know you dare not fire." As the thunderous crowd pushed ever closer, one of the soldiers was knocked down. Then the soldiers did dare; they fired. They killed three civilians outright and wounded eight more, two of whom later died. Further carnage was avoided when acting governor Hutchinson courageously visited the scene and assured the people that the legal system would deal with the incident. Local authorities then arrested Captain Preston and his soldiers and held them for trial on murder

Paul Revere engraving, "The Bloody Massacre" (1770). Courtesy of the American Antiquarian Society.

charges. The Boston Town Meeting called the event a "Massacre"; the label stuck.[44]

The Boston Massacre again illustrates why it is wrong to depict Samuel Adams as the keeper of a trained mob. Adams did not create the friction that produced repeated clashes between the soldiers and civilians, especially ordinary working people. Adams did not direct the members of the crowd who ventured into King Street that night. Equally important, the crowd was made up of individuals who had the most immediate and personal reasons to challenge the soldiers. John Adams probably exaggerated when he claimed that the crowd was "most probably a motley rabble of saucy boys, negroes and mulattoes, Irish teagues and outlandish jack tarrs." His description is suspect in part because it implies that the members of the crowd came from the margins of society and were, in many cases, perhaps not even Bostonians. That depiction suited John's needs since he, like Samuel, wanted to downplay the image of a lawless, mobbish Boston. Nevertheless, even allowing for exaggeration, John's description seems generally accurate, and it is clear that the persons who pushed into King Street on that snowy night came primarily from the economically and socially less powerful segment of the populace. The five killed in the so-called massacre were Samuel Gray, a rope maker; Samuel Maverick, a seventeen-year-old apprentice; Patrick Carr, an Irish immigrant who worked for a leather-breeches maker; Crispus Attucks, a mulatto seaman; and James Caldwell, described variously as a young mariner, a sailor, and a mate—a rank, which, if accurate, would place his standing above an ordinary sailor.[45] The lower orders opposed Britain's imperial policies and especially the military presence because those policies and those troops directly threatened their rights and their livelihoods. They took to the streets for their own reasons.

Although Samuel Adams did not control the crowd that formed in King Street, he certainly used the massacre to pry the remaining British troops out of Boston. On the morning of March 6, with blood still visible in the streets, the selectmen and other local officials visited the acting governor and demanded that he order the troops out of Boston. Although Hutchinson had the authority to issue such a directive, he claimed that he lacked the power to make the military redeploy. The town meeting convened in an emergency session at eleven o'clock and established a committee of fifteen, which included Adams and other leading Whigs, to tell Hutchinson that only the immediate removal of the soldiers could "prevent blood and Carnage." The governor responded in a written statement. Expressing sorrow over the events of March 5 and promising that an inquiry and appropriate legal action would occur, Hutchinson reiterated his disingenuous claim that he could not command the troops to evacuate. Still, noting that the Council had asked that the troops be removed to Castle William and considering the role of the Twenty-ninth Regiment in the events of March 5, Hutchinson reported that Colonel Dalrymple, who was awaiting orders from General Gage in New York, had stated that the Twenty-ninth would be shifted to the castle. In addition, the main guard would be withdrawn from Boston and the activities of the Fourteenth Regiment curtailed to prevent further bloodshed.[46]

When the town meeting reconvened that afternoon, Faneuil Hall overflowed with people, and so the gathering moved to the Old South Church. Adams took the lead. He publicly read Hutchinson's letter and pronounced it inadequate. With one dissenting vote, the huge meeting concurred. The citizens then selected a seven-member committee to inform the acting governor of the vote and to renew the demand for the immediate removal of troops. When the delegation met with Hutchinson and his Council, Adams, serving as spokesman, conveyed the meeting's decisions. Hutchinson, with Colonel Dalrymple standing at his side, again claimed that he could not dictate troop movements. Adams responded in a cold, clear voice and in a manner Hutchinson himself remembered as showing "a strong expression of that determined spirit which animated all future measures." "If you have power to remove one regiment," Adams reasoned, "you have power to remove both. It is at your peril if you do not. The meeting is composed of three thousand people. They are become very impatient. A thousand men are already arrived from the neighborhood, and the country is in general motion. Night is approaching; an immediate answer is expected."[47] Dalrymple was later quoted as saying that Adams "made me tremble exceedingly." Well might Hutchinson recount, as he did, that "Mr. Adams, their prolocutor, [was] pressing the matter with great vehemence, and intimating, that in the case of a refusal, the rage of the people would vent itself against the lieutenant-governor in particular." Adams recalled how Hutchinson reacted. "I observ'd his Knees to tremble. I thought I saw his face grow pale (and I enjoyd the Sight) at the Appearance of the determined Citizens peremptorily demanding Redress of Grievances."

Having first refused to act, Hutchinson asked the Council for advice. After once again unanimously recommending that all troops be sent to Castle William, the councilors pointedly warned the acting governor that he would bear the responsibility if he failed to act and something horrible happened. Hutchinson and Dalrymple surrendered. All the troops would be relocated to the castle. The accounts that British prime minister Lord

North received of these events reportedly caused him thereafter to refer to the troops then stationed in Boston as "Sam Adams's Two Regiments."[48]

The Adams committee returned to the town meeting in triumph. Speaking for the committee, Adams reported that Colonel Dalrymple had promised, on his honor, that both regiments would be moved to Castle William as quickly as possible. The redeployment would begin the next morning. After expressing great satisfaction with this news, the meeting decided a citizen night watch should be established until the troops actually departed. Adams and the other committee members who had wrung the concessions out of Hutchinson and Dalrymple volunteered to stand guard that night. The meeting agreed and authorized them to increase the size of the force and appoint a watch for the succeeding nights. Adams and John Hancock, William Mollinux, William Phillips, Joshua Henshaw, Samuel Pemberton, and Dr. Joseph Warren had, in effect, become temporary police commissioners of Boston. Since the last soldiers were not transferred to the castle until March 16, the citizen night patrols continued for almost two weeks.[49]

The town meeting was extraordinarily active during the three weeks after the massacre. In addition to its emergency meetings of March 6, the town meeting convened on five separate days from March 12 through March 26.[50] Adams, as usual, helped direct its activities. In the midst of re-peatedly telling Colonel Dalrymple that he must quickly remove all the soldiers from Boston proper, the meeting arranged to publish its own history of "The horrid Massacre in Boston." And soon after ten thousand to twelve thousand people had attended the public funeral of four persons slain in the massacre, the town meeting decided the legislature should consider erect-ing a monument "as a Memento to Posterity of that horred Massacre, and the destructive Consequences of Military Troops, being quartered in a well regulated City."[51]

With Adams again spearheading efforts, the town meeting also tried to ensure that the trials of Captain Preston and the British troops would neither be delayed nor tarnish the image of a peaceful Boston victimized by a standing army. Right after the massacre the judges who would hear the cases considered postponing them. Speaking for a town-meeting com-mittee, Adams personally confronted the judges and demanded that the trials get underway forthwith. He wanted them held while the memory of the carnage of March 5 remained fresh. Intimidated by Samuel's threats, the judges agreed to start the trials expeditiously. However, owing to what Hutchinson called "a number of accidental occurrences," the trials did not take place until late fall.[52]

Adams fared better when it came to ensuring that Boston would be portrayed in the best possible light during the trials. Desperate to get any lawyer to defend him, Captain Preston applied to Josiah Quincy, an ardent young Whig. Quincy accepted the case only after Samuel Adams and others convinced him he should take it and after John Adams agreed to work with him. The soldiers followed their officer's lead by having these lawyers defend them as well. Samuel worked to get Quincy and his cousin John to serve as defense counsel because he knew they would not denigrate the city in order to defend the British soldiers. He was also instrumental in getting Robert Treat Paine, another Whig, installed as a prosecutor. Moreover, at least once during the trials, Samuel provided Paine with commentary on the evidence and also made suggestions about courtroom techniques. There is no doubt Samuel labored hard to keep the trials from besmirching Boston's image.[53]

In addition to dealing with issues rooted in the massacre, the town meeting also used its numerous March 1770 sessions to champion nonimportation. On March 13 the citizens pondered what more they could do to strengthen the nonimportation agreement, discourage the consumption of tea "and other Articles of Foreign Luxury," and provide employment for the poor by encouraging local manufacturing. To make nonconsumption of tea a prime symbol of support for nonimportation, the meeting created a committee to convince shopkeepers to stop selling tea until Parliament repealed the revenue acts. Three days later, the town meeting passed a resolution proclaiming that almost all American merchants embraced nonimportation and thus "nobly preferred the publick Good" to their own private benefit. Adopting Adams's line that nothing defended America's rights as effectively as nonimportation, the meeting excoriated the few merchants who did not back the effort. The gathering expressed astonishment and indignation that any Bostonian could "be so lost to the feelings of Patriotism and the common Interest, and so thoroughly and infamously selfish." These few miscreants suffered what Adams considered the ultimate public humiliation: their names and villainy were recorded in the official town records for posterity. In all, thirteen merchants, two of them women, landed on the roster of shame. Given this kind of leverage, the committee charged with persuading shopkeepers to stop marketing tea did very well. It reported that in less than two weeks of solicitations 212 shopkeepers had signed the agreement.[54]

As Adams and other Whigs had long emphasized, support for American manufacturing went hand in hand with nonimportation. So it made sense for the March 13 session of the town meeting to search for ways to increase the colony's manufacturing. There was another significant reason for promoting manufacturing, and that was, the meeting said, to provide work for "the Poor." The committee assigned to accomplish that goal reported back on March 26 and made it clear that it aimed to arrange employment for tradesmen as well as for poor people. The committee understood that more than the poor faced hard times due to the business constrictions created by nonimportation. If the people in general could not find jobs, support for nonimportation might weaken, and the potential for violence would increase. Fortunately for the Whig forces, the committee succeeded. Asserting that shipbuilding constituted the best and most natural way to create employment, the committee joyfully reported that it had arranged for the construction of three ships.[55]

The popular forces accomplished a great deal in the immediate aftermath of the Boston Massacre. By March 17, all British troops had been shifted to an island in the harbor. By the end of the month, the town meeting had taken strong measures to shore up nonimportation. Manufacturing had been bolstered and, at the same time, work provided for artisans as well as for the poor. If the rest of America acted with equal vigor, the British government might retreat from its latest effort to raise revenue through parliamentary taxation.

The reconvening of the General Court offered Adams and the popular party new ammunition against the imperial government and acting governor Hutchinson. The House was scheduled to resume its work in Boston on March 14, but, on the basis of instructions sent from Britain, Hutchinson ordered the representatives to assemble in Cambridge. They had complained when Bernard temporarily moved them from Boston to Cambridge, and Hutchinson's explanation of yet another forced removal played right into the radicals' hands. After hearing the acting governor's explanation, the House appointed a committee of seven to draft a response. The committee, which included Adams and the other Boston representatives, reported back that afternoon and asserted that, according to the charter, the House must meet in "its ancient Place, the Court House in *Boston*." While giving a number of practical reasons for returning to Boston, the committee stressed that moving the legislature because of instructions from Britain constituted "an Infraction of our essential Rights, as Men and Citizens, as well as those derived to us by the British Constitution and the Charter of this Colony." Hutchinson, who considered these arguments a challenge to the king's prerogative, retorted that he was obliged to follow the king's instructions. In quick order, the House established three committees to enlist the Council's support, to respond to another message from

Hutchinson, and to prepare an analysis of the situation in the province. The House staffing of those committees demonstrates the importance the members placed on Adams's leadership. He was the only leading Whig who served on each committee. The only other representative appointed to all the committees was Daniel Leonard, a new member from Taunton who was noted for his ardent Whig views.[56]

In addition to persuading the Council to join in demanding that the General Court be returned to Boston, the House members resorted to one of Adams's favorite ploys. They asked Hutchinson to produce a copy of his instructions. The acting governor refused on the grounds that the king had forbidden sharing letters of instruction with colonial legislators. Although this was true, the governor was made to appear stubborn, secretive, and uncooperative. The House turned to its regular business only after stressing that doing so could not be construed as acceding to its unconstitutional removal from Boston.[57]

As the lengthy fight over the relocation of the General Court unfolded, Hutchinson inadvertently gave the representatives a new opportunity to lambaste him. On April 7 he informed the House that a horrible riot in the town of Gloucester demonstrated that the "executive Powers of Government" might well need to be strengthened. The House appointed a committee to consider the issue, and, as usual, Adams was on it. The committee report submitted on April 23 illustrates why Hutchinson, when reviewing the events of this period, complained that Adams possessed an extraordinary "talent" for vilifying an opponent. Indeed, Hutchinson, who noted that Adams penned "most" of the House's pronouncements, maintained that Adams "made more converts to his cause by calumniating governors, and other servants of the crown, than by strength of reasoning."[58]

Samuel Adams's reasoning had greater strength than the acting governor cared to admit, but Hutchinson was right about Adams being a master political mudslinger. The mud almost oozed from the April 23 report. Hutchinson's suggestion about strengthening the executive's power was scornfully dismissed as both unnecessary and possibly "dangerous to the Rights and Liberties of the People." Adams openly defended crowd actions and, in doing so, hinted that an increase in the executive's power might generate more violence. "It may justly be said of the People of this Province," he intoned, "that they seldom if ever have assembled in a tumultuous Manner, unless they have been oppressed." The report chastised Hutchinson for bemoaning the Gloucester riot without even mentioning the horrible Boston Massacre. Piling accusation upon accusation, the report implied that, in his capacity as chief justice, Hutchinson had illegally aided the British soldiers when they attempted to muscle the residents out of the manufacturing building in Boston. The committee finished off its attack by again asserting that compelling the General Court to meet in Cambridge violated the legislature's constitutional rights.[59]

An infuriated acting governor responded three days later. He complained that the House committee had used his message as an excuse to fabricate a political harangue. Having clearly been put on the defensive, Hutchinson embarked on a lengthy account of the effort to evict civilians from the manufacturing house. He claimed he had nothing to do with the incident and was not even in the city when it happened. He tried to explain away his silence on the tragic events of March 5 by asserting that the facts were well known and legal proceedings were under way. With respect to forcing the General Court to meet in Cambridge, Hutchinson reiterated that he was following the king's orders. The acting governor then decreed that the legislature be dissolved immediately. Although Hutchinson had the last word, the exchange was a public-relations disaster. He felt compelled to produce his lengthy defense because Adams, utilizing his powers as the House clerk, had already had the House's report published in the press. Hutchinson, like Bernard before him, understood that many of the House messages Adams drafted were intended for the people, not some government official. Samuel Adams was again using the clerkship as a bully pulpit; and, as Hutchinson lamented, because he did it so ardently and skillfully he was the most dangerous of the Whigs.[60]

The exchange between the House and the acting governor became the opening shot of the annual colony-wide election contest. The 1770 election gave the popular party yet more power. In Boston, the voters reelected Samuel Adams, John Hancock, and Thomas Cushing, all well-known Whigs. Due to his increasing medical difficulties, James Otis was replaced by James Bowdoin, a solid Whig and longtime councilor whom Governor Bernard had negated off the Council in 1769. When Bowdoin regained a Council seat in early June, John Adams assumed Bowdoin's place in the House. Bowdoin's return to the Council caused Hutchinson even more headaches. The acting governor complained that "the good understanding and reciprocal communications" between Bowdoin and Samuel Adams meant that "the messages of council and house harmonized." From Hutchinson's point of view, the sad fact was that if the acting governor now encountered opposition from one branch of the General Court, he would also meet it from the other.[61]

Hutchinson considered Samuel Adams his chief adversary because Adams was, as the acting governor said, "the most active member in the house." Adams's ardor "in the cause of liberty" made the difference. Indeed, his "constant application" to that cause "distinguished" him "from all the rest of the province." By the late summer, Hutchinson had become so fixated on Samuel Adams that he routinely described his opposition as being "Adams, &c." or "Adams and the Bostoneers." Hutchinson, like the members of the House who constantly called upon Adams's services in the cause of defending liberty, increasingly saw Samuel Adams as the indispensable Whig politician. In time, their judgment became history's judgment.[62]

When the new legislature convened on May 30, the issue of forcing the General Court to meet in Cambridge quickly surfaced. After the acting governor asserted that the General Court need not convene in Boston and, moreover, that he was merely following the monarch's directives in having the legislature assemble in Cambridge, it took the new House less than a week to escalate the fight into a full-blown constitutional crisis. On June 6, 1770, acting on a report from a committee that naturally included Samuel Adams, the representatives did more than restate their case against being compelled to gather in Cambridge. Employing an argument Josiah Quincy had written into the Boston Town Meeting's instructions, the House maintained that the monarch's prerogative could be used only "for the Good of the Subject." If an exercise of the prerogative power injured the people, it must be opposed lest it "overthrow the Constitution itself." Boldly proclaiming that "it is become our indispensable Duty, as the Guardians of the People's Rights, *now* to make a Constitutional Stand," the representatives announced that they would not conduct any "Business" until the House was returned to Boston. To signal the importance of the issue, the members took a roll-call vote and entered it in the permanent record. The militants carried the day, ninety-six to six. With neither side willing to compromise, on June 25 Hutchinson suspended the legislature for a month. That only intensified the House's resolve. When the representatives reconvened, they unanimously refused to proceed until they were returned to Boston.[63]

Thomas Hutchinson believed that the conflict took an especially dangerous turn when Samuel Adams drafted yet another of his lengthy statements for the House. This commentary, unanimously approved on July 31, was provocative. Adams asserted that the people faced real threats to their most valuable liberties, and he quoted extensively from "the Great Mr. Locke" on an aggrieved people's right to rebel. Although Samuel carefully said that the Americans had not yet been driven to that extreme, he also advanced the stunning claim that the members of the Massachusetts House had the right to oppose any prerogative—even a legal and constitutional one— if it was "abusive." Indeed, if complying with the monarch's instructions would injure the people, those instructions "cease to be binding." And who would determine if that was the case? The people's representatives would decide. Hutchinson called this lengthy missive Adams's "treatise" and denounced it as a criminal and seditious production that hinted at revolution. The acting governor again suspended the House and dictated that it would not again meet until September.[64]

Hutchinson could shut the House down, but he could not silence Samuel Adams. Understanding the value of using the media as well as any modern-day politician, Adams kept the controversy fresh in people's minds by carrying the fight into the press. Adopting the pen name "A Chatterer," in August he produced three essays that reviewed the whole controversy over forcing the General Court to meet outside Boston. In the process, Adams accused various unnamed colonial governors of having acted "like *Verres* . . . to oppress and plague the people they were bound to protect." Most readers of the *Boston Gazette* probably knew of Verres, a Roman governor of Sicily who had plundered the island and its people. Verres's crimes became so infamous that he was tried and eventually exiled.[65] Hutchinson had good reason to rue Adams's skill at besmirching an executive's image.

When the legislature reconvened on September 26, 1770, it faced a new constitutional crisis. Again following instructions from the British government, Hutchinson had relinquished Castle William to the British army on September 10. According to the charter, the governor controlled the castle, a military facility built and maintained by the province. Hutchinson had rather ably defended himself against the charge of having violated the charter when he forced the legislature to meet outside Boston. That issue was not clear-cut. But, by complying with the British instructions to surrender Castle William, Hutchinson compromised the charter, and he knew it. He relinquished control surreptitiously and endeavored to make it appear that he had not subverted the charter. Not surprisingly, as Hutchinson admitted, many people responded to the transfer with "rage." "Adams, in particular," he said, "was inflaming the minds of the people, declaring that I had broken the charter by giving up the Castle."[66]

Faced with this new and more threatening challenge to the charter, the House blinked. Rather than having Samuel Adams fire off yet another thunderbolt, the representatives used the transfer of Castle William as an excuse to resume normal business. A resolve offered to the House on October 9 put the best possible gloss on the retreat. It posed the question, Faced with this new grievance that requires immediate redress, should the House return to conducting business while also, of course, continuing to protest the illegal removal of the legislature from Boston? That resolve passed on a roll-call vote of fifty-nine to twenty-nine with the most committed and prominent Whigs—including Adams, Hancock, and Joseph Hawley—voting no. They opposed the resolution because they feared the assemblymen would begin carrying on all regular business. That is exactly what happened. Adams, who had insisted the colonists must act on principle, was mortified. The British and Hutchinson had worn the representatives down. Too many were no longer willing to endure the hardships caused by pursuing what Adams would call a principled resistance in defense of America's liberties.[67]

Although a majority of the House retreated, it was not a rout. The representatives continued to claim that, on the basis of the charter, the General Court must be returned to Boston. And for the rest of the fall legislative session, especially in pronouncements Adams drafted, the assemblymen kept sniping at the acting governor on a range of issues. Above all, they relentlessly attacked Hutchinson for having complied with the instructions to surrender control of Castle William. The representatives and the acting governor dueled with pronouncements and counterpronouncements right through November 20, 1770, the last day of the session. On that final day, the representatives charged that, by relinquishing control of Castle William, Hutchinson had discarded "a Power of governing, which by the Charter is vested in you for the Safety of the People." Proclaiming that giving up such a power "is a Precedent of the most dangerous Tendency," the legislators urged the acting governor, "in Tenderness to the Rights of this People," to redress this "very great Grievance." The unrelenting assault on Hutchinson led him, when he closed the session, to complain that the representatives had, "by every Way in your Power," sought "to impeach my Conduct."[68]

The representatives did even more to undermine Hutchinson. Because their London agent, Dennys De Berdt, had died, the representatives needed to choose a new agent. Having selected Benjamin Franklin, the House took an important additional step. On November 7, 1770, it created a committee of correspondence to communicate with Franklin and others in Great Britain. The committee, made up of Adams and four other noted Whigs, could function even when the General Court was not in session. Equally important, the committee was authorized to communicate with the speakers of other colonial assemblies or with correspondence committees the assemblies had or might appoint. Although the Massachusetts House did not actually call on the other colonial legislatures to create their own committees of correspondence, the representatives' action reflected an ideal that Adams and some other leading American Whigs had long advocated:

establish intercolonial communication systems to link the defenders of American liberties.[69]

Adams and other radical Whigs could take solace in the fact that the House still attempted to defend American liberties even though it had abandoned the position that it would not function until returned to Boston. Fervent Whigs could not, however, take any comfort in what was happening to the nonimportation effort. By the time the Massachusetts House retreated on the contentious issue of its meeting place, nonimportation was disintegrating.

In April 1770 Great Britain repealed all the Townshend duties except the one on tea. Bostonians and the rest of the American colonists then faced a crucial decision. Should America keep up nonimportation until the British abolished the tea duty? Or should the colonists accept a partial victory by ending or severely curtailing nonimportation? For Samuel Adams the choice was obvious. Time and again he had stressed that nonimportation should be continued until Parliament rescinded *all* unconstitutional acts. The current agreement fell short of that, but it did say nonimportation would last until all the Townshend duties were abolished. If the colonists ended nonimportation merely because most Townshend duties had been repealed, it would not be a partial victory; it would be a defeat. For Adams, the question was precedent; the question was what it had always been—the true nature of the British constitution. Believing that one must uphold fundamental principles, Adams had urged sacrifice, and the Boston Town Meeting had vigorously supported nonimportation. But by repealing all the duties except one, the British government made it tempting for Americans to follow their immediate economic interests and, in so doing, hand Britain a constitutional victory. Over time, the temptation proved too alluring.[70]

As Adams attested with a measure of pride, Boston's merchants held remarkably firm for nonimportation. Unfortunately, the rest of America's business communities did not. Despite the efforts of Massachusetts Whigs, New York City effectively abandoned nonimportation in July 1770. Philadelphia's merchants did the same in late September. Faced with economic ruin if they persisted alone, on October 12 Boston's merchants agreed that the general nonimportation would end; henceforth, only tea and any other articles subject to revenue duties would be boycotted. Since most American merchants said they would not import dutied tea, they could claim they had not abandoned the cause of liberty. But in truth the British had defeated nonimportation. The majority of American merchants had lost the will to carry on the fight against a cleverly scaled-back but determined British insistence on the right to tax the colonists.

Writing in November, Adams claimed he always feared the non-importation effort would "fall short of our Wishes." In fact, he said, the merchants had actually supported it "much longer than I ever thought they would or could. It was a grand Tryal which pressd hard upon their private Interest."[71] Faced with that reality, Adams increasingly came to emphasize that only the masses could be expected to oppose Britain's evil policies, and even more resolutely he extolled the possibilities of American manufacturing. In language clearly intended for English eyes and ears, Adams wrote to Franklin about what might befall the mother country if she kept treating the colonists "as bastards and not Sons" and tried to make them "vassals and slaves." "The body of the people will vigorously endeavor to become independent of the mother-country for supplies, and sooner than she may be aware of it, will manufacture for themselves."[72] If that happened, one of the major benefits the British derived from the American colonies would vanish. Adams worked to turn his predictions into reality by drafting, or helping draft, a House pronouncement calling on the people of Massachusetts to promote and support "our own Manufactures." To achieve that goal, on November 16 the House created a committee to formulate a "Plan for the Encouragement of Arts, Agriculture, Manufactures and Commerce." The committee, on which Adams served, was to have its report ready for the next legislative session.[73]

As he so often did, Adams moved quickly—indeed, that very day—to use the House's actions to try to convince British politicians they must reverse course. He sent a lengthy missive, the kind designed to circulate or be slipped into a newspaper, to Stephen Sayre, an American emigrant living in England. As a part of a political circle that had first formed around Massachusetts agent De Berdt, Sayre had been working with Adams to defend American rights by exchanging information with him. In this letter, Samuel stressed that the colonists would continue to defend their rights and that, if the British continued to oppress the colonists, the mother country might well lose their "Affections." He maintained that, if the British restored Americans to their former status, "Great Britain can lose Nothing which she ought to retain." And, if that restoration occurred, Americans would be satisfied. Emphasizing, as he routinely did, that British assaults on American rights endangered the mother country's own material interests, Samuel warned, "while the Struggle continues Manufactures will still increase in America in spite of all Efforts to prevent it." He then pointedly urged those living on the other side of the Atlantic to contemplate the injury that would do to Britain.[74]

The day after the legislature completed its work, Adams summarized its accomplishments in a letter to a South Carolina Son of Liberty. Once again his letter was clearly designed to be widely circulated. For Adams, the vital achievement was the creation of a committee "to correspond with our friends in the other Colonies." He added that "AMERICAN MANUFACTURES" should be "the constant Theme" of the committee's writings. Adams closed with a bold one-sentence paragraph: "Our young men seem of late very ambitious of making themselves masters of the art military."[75]

Samuel's defiant pronouncements and increasing emphasis on the power of "the Body of the people" could not obscure the fact that the American resistance movement was in disarray in the late fall of 1770.[76] Only a year before, the patriot efforts had been so strident that, according to Hutchinson's later report, Adams revealed his true feelings at an October 1769 town meeting by boldly proclaiming, "Independent we are, and independent we will be."[77] The progress toward a uniform and stalwart defense of American rights was going so well in early November 1769 that Samuel boasted to agent De Berdt that "Britain may fall sooner than she is aware; while her Colonies who are struggling for Liberty may survive her fate & tell the Story to their Childrens Children."[78] By late 1770 the situation had unquestionably changed. Skillful political maneuvering by the British government and acting governor Hutchinson had effectively blunted the American resistance movement. A majority of the Massachusetts House, anxious to get back to regular business, had retreated from their principled stand against being forced to convene outside Boston. More important, although Americans said they would continue to boycott dutied tea, nonimportation was dead. These unwelcome developments presented Samuel Adams with a formidable challenge. He had to find ways to keep the flame of liberty alive when most Americans had abandoned the ideal of consistently adhering to political, philosophical, and constitutional principle.

5

THE GREAT INCENDIARY
CONFRONTS THE QUIET PERIOD

America's Whigs had been thrown on the defensive even before the increasingly timid Massachusetts General Court ended its 1770 fall session. The collapse of nonimportation demonstrated that many Americans placed economic self-interest above patriotism. Although saddened by the dampening of patriotic ardor, Samuel Adams believed, as he later put it, that a politician could not "create Events." The best the Whigs could do, he counseled, was "to be ready *for all Events*, that we may make the *best Improvement* of them."[1] Samuel diligently kept looking for ways to "improve"—to exploit and capitalize on—British mistakes. But for more than two years, he found little he could effectively improve upon. British-American relations became so tranquil that scholars refer to "the quiet period" stretching from mid-1770 into 1773. Although others shied away from confrontation, Adams could not become passive. Driven by his belief that a political leader must sound the alarm when the people's fundamental liberties were threatened, he strove to keep the flame of resistance alive. Equally important, he played the central role in developing an innovative committee-of-correspondence system that could take advantage of whatever missteps the British might eventually make. His unrelenting efforts reinforce Stephen Sayre's 1770 assertion that Samuel Adams was "the Father of America." Sayre and others in the English Society of the Supporters of the Bill of Rights, a group dedicated to backing John Wilkes and democratizing British politics that also supported the American cause, showed their appreciation of Adams by electing him a member of their society. Arthur Lee, a Virginian and fervent champion of American rights living in London at the time, saluted Adams's election to the society. Lee proclaimed that Adams "will do our society honour."[2]

Throughout his arduous and often lonely struggles to rouse his fellow colonists from their lethargy during the quiet period, Adams could draw comfort from two interrelated and fundamental facts. Even when they stopped actively resisting British policies, Americans still overwhelmingly rejected the claim that Parliament could bind them in all cases whatsoever. For its part, the British government remained determined to make the colonists acknowledge the supremacy of Parliament. The British thus seemed destined to provide an issue that, with proper Adams improvement, might rekindle the flame of liberty. But in the fall of 1770 that flame barely flickered.[3]

As soon as the Massachusetts legislature adjourned in November 1770, Adams set about improving on events by penning two essays for the *Boston Gazette*. These missives summarized the legislature's squabbles with acting governor Hutchinson. Although he reviewed long-simmering disputes, Adams focused on new dangers and, as usual, portrayed his adversary as standing on the wrong side of basic-rights issues. Pointedly observing that the British military used instructions from England to seize control of Castle William, Adams described that as the introduction of government by instructions. He warned that this innovation—a development Hutchinson supposedly did not oppose—would destroy the Massachusetts Charter. Having put a Whig spin on the legislative session, Adams confronted the discouraging results of the Boston Massacre trials. A provincial jury acquitted Captain Preston on October 30, 1770. And when the trial of the eight soldiers who fired into the crowd ended on December 5, the jury merely convicted two soldiers of manslaughter, not murder. Such verdicts seemed unimaginable only a few months earlier.[4] Now, when coupled with the collapse of nonimportation, the juries' decisions made it even more difficult for Adams to sustain patriotic ardor. In ten essays published between December 10, 1770, and January 28, 1771, the American revolutionary labored to improve on the disheartening events. Writing once again as "Vindex," Adams dissected the massacre and the subsequent trials to convince the public the verdicts were unjust.[5] He intimated that the judges favored the soldiers. Moreover, the jurymen were not Bostonians and therefore could not assess the veracity of eyewitnesses who presented conflicting testimony. Adams offered his assessments, though, and in one instance played upon anti-Catholic prejudice to discredit a key witness's testimony.[6] Emphasizing that his analysis incorporated material not presented in court, Adams painstakingly reconstructed the massacre. In Samuel's hands, the evidence revealed that "insolent" and "blood-thirsty" soldiers executed a prearranged plan "to assassinate" Bostonians.[7] Describing the events, including a soldier reportedly stabbing his bayonet five inches into the head of a victim who had already been shot, Adams depicted the assassins murdering innocent civilians with "Savage barbarity." The grisly outrages of March 5 once again proved "how fatal are the effects . . . of posting a standing army among a free people!"[8]

Thomas Hutchinson conceded that Adams's writings as Vindex influenced popular attitudes. The essays made "a great part of the people" believe that the acquittals were "unjust and illegal, and contrary to evidence." As a consequence, "the killing of the men was declared to be a horrid massacre, with the same freedom as if the jury had found those concerned in it guilty of murder." Despite Adams's propaganda victory, the Whigs kept losing ground. Hutchinson sensed the changing mood. He remarked that, beginning in late 1770, "four or five months passed away in Massachusetts Bay, more quietly than any other space of time for seven years preceding." Indeed, "it is certain that at the close of the year 1770, the people of the Province seemed to be tired of controversy, and in general, to wish to see an end to it." In a move calculated to perpetuate that mood, the acting governor decided against reconvening the General Court for its normal winter session. As the political calm stretched into the spring, Hutchinson had special reason to rejoice. On March 14, 1771, he was officially installed as the royal governor of Massachusetts.[9]

The decline of American patriotic ardor forced Adams to reassess the situation. As his Boston Massacre essays showed, he still had faith in the common people. Praising the ability of ordinary persons to "judge, as well as their betters, when there is danger of *slavery*," he maintained, as he had before, that "the people in general seldom complain, without some good reason." Equally important, Adams advanced a democratic, and for the time radical, theory that government officials were the people's agents and that governments should serve the people, "the multitude." "The *multitude* I am speaking of," Adams explained, "is *the body of the people* . . . for whose sake government is instituted; or rather, who have themselves erected it solely for *their own* good—to whom even kings and all in subordination to them, are strictly speaking servants and not masters." Samuel Adams was not spewing empty rhetoric; he truly considered himself "the Servant of all" the people.[10]

Although he expressed a faith in the masses that few politicians of his day shared, Adams also believed political leadership played a crucial role in protecting the people's rights. He reasoned that most individuals would ordinarily have to focus on their material concerns, not politics. Political leaders therefore had a special duty to sound the alarm when the threat of tyranny arose. Indeed, "the *true patriot*," upon detecting miscreants poised to subvert the constitution and enslave the people, "will stir up the people" and "will, as far as he is able, keep the attention of his fellow citizens awake to their grievances; and not suffer them to be at rest, till the causes of their just complaints are removed." The leaders' role was so crucial that "the Man who nobly vindicates the Rights of his Country & Mankind shall stand foremost in the List of fame."[11]

Adams blamed the Whig leadership for the people's apathy. In March 1771, writing to James Warren, the staunch Plymouth patriot, Adams chastised Whig leaders for letting the people be temporarily "hushd into Silence." Opining that the leaders' "*mistaken* Prudence" "springs from Indolence or Cowardice or Hypocricy or I know not what," Samuel contemptuously observed that, "for the sake of their own Ease or their own Safety, they preach the People into paltry Ideas of Moderation." Seeking to buck up Warren, and perhaps himself, Adams asserted, "it is no Dishonor to be in the minority in the Cause of Liberty and Virtue." And while he admitted that Massachusetts's patriots faced many difficulties, Samuel maintained he was fretful rather than desperate. Building on this somewhat positive note—and looking as he habitually did to the judgment of "posterity"—Adams proclaimed that "our Sons, if they deserve it, will enjoy the happy Fruits of their Fathers Struggles."[12]

To counter the "paltry Ideas of Moderation," Adams and other Whigs again resorted to the technique of turning anniversaries into public commemorations. On March 5, 1771, Bostonians heard the bells of the Congregational meeting houses ring from noon to one o'clock. In the evening, spectators viewed three panels displayed in the windows of Paul Revere's house. One panel depicted the ghost of young Snider "with one of his Fingers in the Wound, endeavoring to stop the Blood"; the next panel graphically portrayed the bloody massacre of a year before; the third showed a woman representing America holding a staff topped with a liberty cap. According to the *Boston Gazette* report, she had one foot "on the head of a Grenadier lying prostate grasping a Serpent.—Her Finger pointing to the Tragedy." Edes and Gill, the editors, described this "very striking Exhibition" as being so powerful that the "many Thousand" spectators who viewed it "were struck with solemn Silence, and their Countenances covered with a melancholy Gloom." When the exhibition was withdrawn at nine o'clock, "the People" returned to their homes as the church bells tolled "a doleful Peal" until ten o'clock.[13]

A week later, the town meeting selected Adams and other notable Whigs to determine how best to perpetuate the memory of "The horrid

Massacre." They recommended having an oration delivered "to impress upon our minds the ruinous tendency of standing Armies in Free Cities" and to remind the citizens of the need to emulate the glorious resistance the Bostonians of 1770 had mounted to thwart "the designs of the Conspirators against the public Liberty." The first in what became a series of annual Boston Massacre orations was delivered on April 2; to enhance its influence, the town meeting had the speech printed and adorned with mourning borders on the title page. Governor Hutchinson admitted that such commemorations dampened "the spirits of all who were hoping for peace and quietness."[14]

The governor's concern probably intensified because the General Court was scheduled to reconvene on April 3. Whigs would undoubtedly attempt to have the legislators stoke the fires of resistance. Adams tried but could not get the House to take a hard line on the old "grievance" of being forced to meet outside Boston. After maintaining that they should be returned to Boston, the representatives conducted normal legislative business. However, Adams soon uncovered a potentially explosive constitutional issue: who would pay the governor and other royal officials? On the basis of the charter of 1691, the General Court had supplied those salaries for eighty years. Following the established practice, the House passed legislation to pay Hutchinson. When he vetoed it without comment, it seemed obvious that the British government was compensating him and perhaps others as well. As Samuel emphasized in his bold 1764 instructions to Boston's representatives, this was no minor issue. The charter clearly granted the legislature the right to pay such salaries, and, equally important, the representatives had long used their power of the purse as a political weapon. So, for both constitutional and pragmatic reasons, Whigs considered the new salary arrangements a threat to American liberties. Indeed, Adams saw it as a vital part of a "Design," launched even before Bernard became governor, "to render ineffectual the Democratical part of this Government." Adams considered Thomas Hutchinson one of the key "Conspirators" pushing this malevolent plan.[15]

Although Hutchinson vetoed the salary legislation, he offered no indication that the British aimed to gut the legislature's power of the purse. Hutchinson's adroit political maneuvering made Adams yearn for the days when Bernard was governor. "Happy indeed it was for the Province that such a Man was at the Head of it, for it occasioned such a Jealousy & Watchfulness in the people as prevented their immediate & total Ruin." The clever Hutchinson would, Adams forecast, find a way of "artfully concealing his Independency" of the legislature. Prodded by Adams, the

House tried to pin down the governor on this potentially explosive matter. However, Hutchinson skillfully evaded those efforts throughout the rest of the legislative session. So the issue of the governor's salary remained clouded as Whigs and the government party prepared for the annual election of representatives in May 1771.[16]

The race for Suffolk County registrar of deeds, voted on in April, offered an early test of strength. It pitted Samuel Adams against Ezekiel Goldthwait, the longtime registrar known for his conservative views. Adams faced a difficult challenge. Suffolk County included much more than Boston; the taint of his tax-collecting failures still marked him; voters traditionally did not reject officeholders who had served for a lengthy period; and, finally, increasing numbers of citizens were losing interest in challenging Britain's imperial policies. Not surprisingly, Goldthwait won handily, 1,123 to 467. Although Goldthwait's victory could hardly be considered a clear bellwether, Tories grew bolder. John Adams—who had recently moved back to Braintree, said "Farewell Politics," and accordingly decided not to stand for reelection to the House—described the marked change. He noticed that, following Goldthwaits's victory, elated Tories stopped disguising their hatred for Whigs. In early May, John outlined the personal "Insults" he had endured for putting forth a "very small and feeble Exertion" for his cousin in the registrar's race. John sounded thoroughly discouraged. Ruminating on his loss of income while toiling to defend the people's freedoms, he moaned, "now I reap nothing but Insult, Ridicule, and Contempt for it, from many of the People themselves." Proclaiming he had "learn'd Wisdom by Experience," John pledged to himself, "I shall certainly become more retired, and cautious. I shall certainly mind my own Farm, and my [law] Office." John meant it.[17]

The withdrawal of John Adams from politics in the spring of 1771 illustrated the loss of leadership vigor that Samuel decried. John's retirement did not diminish the Whigs' chances of carrying the May election in Boston, but it boded ill for the province as a whole. As Samuel struggled against the political indifference that might swing power to the government party, he naturally attempted to turn the governor's conduct and salary into campaign issues. Focusing on "the black art of Adams," Hutchinson alleged that "our sons of sedition are afraid of a change of members in many towns, and make a strong effort in the newspapers to prevent it."[18]

The annual election did not significantly alter the balance of power in Massachusetts, but it quickly became apparent that the government party had reason to celebrate. James Otis, having been judged well enough to reclaim his House seat, began acting like a Tory. He opposed Adams's motion that the representatives refuse to conduct normal legislative business unless they were returned to Boston. Worse yet, by arguing that the governor could make the legislature assemble anywhere in the colony, Otis undermined a constitutional issue Adams had laboriously developed as a weapon against the governor. Hutchinson believed Otis's actions sprang from a desire to squelch "any design for a general revolt" and from his dissatisfaction "with the great influence which Mr. Adams had obtained." The representatives still petitioned for a return to Boston, but, following Otis's lead, they dropped the charge that forcing them to convene outside Boston violated the charter. Bostonians soon began referring to Otis's "Conversion to Toryism," and Hutchinson expressed hope that Otis might be "serviceable" in keeping radical Whigs in check. That hope soon evaporated when Otis's mental instability returned, but Hutchinson could take comfort in the fact that Otis was not the only Boston representative whose patriotic ardor had cooled. John Hancock and Thomas Cushing, philosophically moderate Whigs, were also willing to capitulate on the question of the governor's right to make the General Court meet outside Boston.[19]

John Hancock's backsliding was particularly important. No one considered him a significant political thinker, but he possessed great popularity and immense wealth. Arch-Tory Peter Oliver derisively said that Adams siphoned that wealth to fund the radicals, and all observers agreed that Hancock's riches helped support the patriot cause. But from the early spring to the fall of 1771 Hancock seemed preoccupied with courting his future wife and shoring up his business interests, not politics. He also worried that Adams was pushing the governor too hard. As a consequence, after supporting Otis on the issue of where the legislature should meet, Hancock essentially joined John Adams on the political sidelines. In addition, perhaps because his fiancée came from a venerable and conservative family, Hancock began hobnobbing with conservatives while, as Hutchinson described it, suddenly ending his friendship with Samuel Adams.[20]

The House's bickering over how to challenge its banishment from Boston revealed that Samuel Adams was the only Boston representative still actively pursuing a radical Whig agenda. Unfortunately for him, the one established issue he had to work with in May 1771 had been tainted by Otis's arguments. Samuel nevertheless managed to raise the stakes—managed to improve on events—by making the issue more complex. On June 10, writing as "Candidus" in the *Boston Gazette*, he skewered the governor for making British "Instructions the rule of his governing," which give them "*the force of laws*" and thus undermined the Massachusetts Charter. At Adams's urging, nine days later the House issued a "Protest" that incorporated arguments and even language from Adams's newspaper attacks on Hutchinson. The House's "Protest," which not surprisingly had Adams on its drafting committee, decried the horror of the legislature being moved to Cambridge "merely by Force of Instructions." Giving British instructions "the Force of Law" was "directly subversive of the Constitution." The "Protest" also broached the potentially inflammatory salary issue Adams had been pushing in newspaper missives. It declared that the Massachusetts Charter made the legislature responsible for paying government officials. Adams rushed the "Protest" to the local press. These propaganda efforts engineered by Adams fizzled. The people refused to be stirred up. Given the backsliding of every member of the Boston delegation except Samuel Adams and given the public's political apathy, it seemed that what Hutchinson called this calm interval might go on and on.[21]

Considering his personal situation and the public's apparent indifference to politics, Samuel Adams might have been tempted to emulate his cousin John and John Hancock by shifting his focus to business and personal concerns. When the General Court adjourned in early July 1771, Samuel was forty-eight and already exhibiting the trembling effects of palsy. And while he was notoriously unconcerned about acquiring wealth, he had a family to maintain. The family's only regular income apparently was the £90 a year he received as clerk of the House. The Adamses had a substantial home only because Samuel inherited it and other valuable property. Because their union did not produce children, Samuel and Elizabeth did not have the economic burden—or the joy—of raising young children on their middle-class but hardly lavish income. However, the children from Samuel's first marriage, Samuel Jr. and Hannah, had to be supported. In young Samuel's case, that included the cost of sending him to Boston Latin School and then to Harvard, where he graduated with the class of 1770. Fortunately, his prospects seemed bright. In 1771, he secured a medical apprenticeship with Dr. Joseph Warren, who was a noted physician as well as one of Samuel's political protégés. And, like his father, the younger Samuel later returned to Harvard to receive his M.A. What the future might hold for Hannah, who turned fifteen in 1771, remained unclear.[22]

Although personal and financial concerns prompted some leading Whigs to curtail their political activities, the idea of stepping back from politics apparently never crossed Samuel's mind. Governor Hutchinson's actions certainly support that view. He dismissed every suggestion that Adams might be bribed to cease his opposition to British policies. Given Adams's precarious financial situation, he seemed a prime candidate for preferment—the well-established practice of offering politicians special favors to entice them into supporting the government's position. Hutchinson would have gladly exchanged preferment for Adams's silence; but, as the governor ruefully observed, Adams "could not be made dependent and taken off by some appointment to a civil office." Hutchinson believed that, on the question of seeking American independence, Adams had "a most inflexible natural temper." Adams's longtime adversary knew Samuel cared about political ideals, not self-aggrandizement.[23]

As the political calm stretched into the summer of 1771 and others pursued fortune rather than politics and, in some cases, cozied up to members of the government party, Samuel ventured into print. He labored diligently to awaken his fellow citizens to Britain's continuing attacks on their constitutional rights, and he emphasized that Governor Hutchinson aided and abetted the assaults. In July Hutchinson, who stressed that no one matched Adams's unwavering advocacy of the radical Whig position, said of him, "I doubt whether there is a greater incendiary than he in the King's dominions." Adams proved Hutchinson right by launching a propaganda campaign under his "Candidus" pen name on August 19 and then intensifying his efforts even after he became extremely ill. From September 9 through mid-October of 1771, each issue of the *Boston Gazette* carried another of Adams's "Candidus" essays. Turning history into a weapon, Samuel built each essay on historical analysis. Although he also drew on ancient history, in the main Adams highlighted the meaning and significance of recent events, including the Stamp Act controversy, the fight against the Townshend duties, the Massachusetts circular letter imbroglio, the horrors a standing army unleashed on Boston, and the legislature's continuing fights with Hutchinson. And, of course, while he emphasized history, Samuel did not neglect to draft political theorists, especially John Locke, into service. That almost seemed to be a requirement, for, as Samuel observed, "Mr. Locke has often been quoted in the present dispute between Britain and her colonies, and very much to our purpose. His reasoning is so forceful, that no one has even attempted to refute it." Calling him "one of the greatest men who ever wrote," Samuel quoted Locke's assertion that the "using of force upon the people without authority, and contrary to the trust reposed in him that does so, is *a state of war* with the people." It followed that political theory as well as history justified the colonists' resistance. Adams developed two interlocking themes in his Candidus series: the British government, aided by evil Americans lusting after power and wealth, conspired to smash America's constitutional liberties. As a consequence, the colonists must actively resist the conspiracy or be reduced to slavery.[24]

As he marshaled his case against Britain and her colonial toadies, Adams constantly reminded the people that the British would use unconstitutional taxes to reduce the colonial legislatures to ciphers. He noted, for example, that the British had started paying Hutchinson an annual salary of £2,000 collected "from the Earnings and Industry of the honest *Yeomen, Merchants* and *Tradesmen,* of this continent, against their Consent." A governor who became financially independent of the legislature would, Adams warned, likely become "a tyrant." Samuel then raised the more ominous specter of the American judicial system being corrupted: "We are told that the Justices of the Superior Court are also to receive fixed salaries out of this American revenue!"[25]

Building on the idea that colonial opposition was justified by Locke's arguments on defending basic rights against arbitrary power, Adams repeatedly urged the people to resist Britain's tax policies and the assaults on the colonial legislatures. Knowing Tories had floated the argument that the colonists had nothing to fear "as long as we continue quiet," Adams urged Americans to "beware of these *soothing* arts." They were, he insisted, part of a conspiracy against liberty. Indeed, since America's constitutional grievances had not been redressed, "what can be intended by all the *fair promises* made to us by tools and sycophants, but to lull us into that *quietude* and *sleep* by which *slavery* is always preceded." To prevent this from happening, "let us adhere to first principles."[26]

As he developed this analysis, Adams warmly embraced continentalism. He argued that, where the colonies' liberty was concerned, "*the cause of one is the cause of all.*" It followed that "an attempt to subdue one province" should "be considered as an attempt to enslave the whole." Therefore each of the American colonies must "be upon their guard" and be attentive "*to the interests of each other.*" If the colonies were inattentive, "the grand cause of American Liberty" could "fall a prey to the merciless hand of tyranny." Adams did more than delineate evils; he offered remedies to defeat the conspiracy. "It is by *united* councils, a steady zeal, and a manly fortitude, that this continent must expect to recover its violated rights and liberties." Adams thus continued to stress the importance of intercolonial councils, an idea he and other Whigs had championed since the time of troubles with England began. He reiterated that "I have often thought that in this time of common distress, it would be the wisdom of the colonists, more frequently to correspond with, and to be more attentive to the particular circumstances of each other."[27]

Spurred perhaps by the growing political apathy, Adams's imagery became more graphic, his language shriller. In his October 7, 1771, essay, the next to last in the series, Adams sounded exasperated. Appealing to "the common sense of mankind," he pleaded, "To what state of misery and infamy must a people be reduced" before they resisted? A week later, he thundered that "no people ever yet groaned under the heavy yoke of slavery, but when they deserv'd it." Truly, if a people did not have "*virtue enough to maintain their liberty against a presumptuous invader, they deserve no pity, and are to be treated with contempt and ignominy.*" Pressing for action, Adams warned that "A Tyranny seems to be at the very door." "The Tragedy of American Freedom," he lamented, appeared "nearly completed." Looking as he habitually did to "posterity"—to "*millions yet unborn*"—Adams insisted that the people had more than a right to resist when their fundamental liberties were assaulted. They had an "*indispensable duty to God and their Country*" to resist "*by all rational means in their power.*" There could be no compromise, no halfhearted measures. "The liberties of our Country, the freedom of our civil constitution are worth defending at all hazards: And it is our duty to defend them against all attacks." Moreover, a stout defense would succeed because "the truth is, All might be free if they valued freedom and defended it as they ought."[28]

Samuel's acerbic pronouncements flowed from the soul of his political beliefs, and his thrusts *were* incendiary. By October, when his Candidus mentioned Hutchinson, the word "tyrant" or "tyranny" appeared close by. On October 17, after enduring nearly two months of Adams's increasingly inflammatory manifestos, Hutchinson assessed the political scene. Hancock "is quiet at present, and so are most of the [Whig] party. All of them, except Adams, abate of their virulence." Adams was *the* troublemaker. He "would push the Colonies into a rebellion to-morrow, if it was in his power."[29]

Less than two weeks later, Adams gave the governor yet more evidence of his virulence when he ventured into print in the *Boston Gazette* as "Valerius Poplicola," a friend of the people. Accurately quoting the governor's *History of the Province of Massachusetts-Bay*, Adams challenged Hutchinson's assertions about supposed differences in the attitudes of the people of Massachusetts. Hutchinson maintained their ancestors had been "wrong" when they asserted in the 1660s that, because they were not represented in Parliament, they could only be bound by laws passed by the Massachusetts legislature. He coupled that with the assertion that the people of the 1760s "are sensible that they are Colonists, and therefore subject to the controul of the parent state."[30] Although Adams incorporated the arguments of an impressive range of political thinkers, as usual he gave prominence to Locke and his *Second Treatise of Government*. Openly drawing on what he called "the sentiments of this great man," Adams stressed that

"Every man was born naturally free; nothing can make a man subject of any commonwealth, but his actually entering into it by positive agreement, and express promise & contract." Repeatedly referring to the "compact," or the "contract," and the people's freely given "consent," Adams built the case that the citizens of the colony had *never* given their explicit consent to be bound by whatever laws Parliament might choose to enact.[31] Samuel clearly intended "Valerius Poplicola" to be the first in a series of essays rooted in political philosophy. But he delayed the next installment because Governor Hutchinson presented him with an opportunity to improve on events, and Samuel pounced.

In late October, as tradition required, Governor Hutchinson issued a proclamation calling for "A Day of Public Thanksgiving" to occur throughout Massachusetts on November 21. Although Hutchinson later claimed, erroneously, that this proclamation was no different than earlier proclamations, he overreached himself by saying the people should give thanks for the *continuance* of their civil and religious liberties and for the marked improvement in the province's trade. Adams turned Hutchinson's own words against him. Using examples drawn from religious history, Adams, who claimed that the proclamation outraged the people, penned an essay branding Hutchinson's message a threat to religious liberty. He then joined in coordinating a campaign that resulted in virtually all of Boston's ministers refusing to read the proclamation to their congregations. Depicting this affair as "an effort . . . to raise a commotion from a very trivial and innocent cause," Hutchinson nonetheless admitted it had "some effect." In the outlying areas of the province many ministers also refused to read the proclamation, and others "declared in the pulpit, that if the continuance of *all* our liberties was intended, they could not join in giving thanks." Hutchinson believed that the opposition, in his view lacking any real grievance, could not have employed "a more artful method of exciting the general attention of the people." Struggling as he was to gain the people's attention, Adams would have considered that a compliment.[32]

Perhaps with renewed hope that the people would pay attention to his warnings of an approaching tyranny, in late November Adams resumed writing his series of newspaper essays. When completed in late January 1772, the series totaled eight publications.[33] Pursuing the same goals enunciated in his earlier historically oriented pieces, Adams vigorously reiterated that the colonists must steadfastly resist "the plan to enslave us." But in these essays, several of which countered publications by a court-party writer, Adams highlighted political theory. Drawing on numerous political theorists but above all emphasizing "the reasoning of the immortal Locke,"

Adams analyzed Massachusetts's constitutional relationship with Great Britain. He once again repeatedly described the Massachusetts Charter as a "compact," as a "contract," between the British Crown and the people. And that charter—the people's "constitution"—granted the citizens of Massachusetts, not the British Crown, the right to pay the governor. That essential right must be safeguarded, said Adams, since having the power of the purse had been consciously designed to keep *"imperious* governors" from subverting the people's liberties.[34]

As he explored the constitutional relationship between America and the mother country, Adams even raised the possibility that Parliament might not have *any* right to pass legislation binding the colonists. A livid Governor Hutchinson called Adams "the Chief Incendiary of the House" and warned that the radicals aimed to make "further advances until they have rejected every act of Parliament which controls the Colonies." Events proved Hutchinson right, but Adams did not go that far in these essays. He contented himself with the Whigs' cardinal arguments: Parliament had no right to tax the colonists, and Parliament's insistence on taxing Americans constituted a sinister attack on the people's basic liberties. Maintaining that those liberties "are originally from God and nature, recognized in the Charter, and entail'd to us and our posterity," Adams reiterated his fundamental argument that "it is our duty therefore to contend for them whenever attempts are made to violate them." He again tried to spur denunciations of Britain's evil plans by warning his "countrymen" that their silence would be construed as acquiescence in the assault on their liberties.[35]

From the close of the legislative session in July 1771 through early 1772, the great incendiary probably spent a good deal on quills, ink, and paper. But, while Adams's impressive propagandistic endeavors helped keep the flickering flame of resistance alive, he could not burn off the political calm. By late January 1772 he seemed to sense that; he did not craft another newspaper essay until the annual election season arrived.[36] Although he turned away from newspaper warfare, Adams kept looking for ways to revitalize opposition fervor. He again participated in arranging what had become, owing in no small part to his efforts, the annual Boston Massacre oration. Starting in 1772, when an estimated four thousand attended, it occurred on the anniversary date. Because the town meeting continued its tradition of publishing the oration, the Whigs again managed to remind citizens of the horrors of British policies. And, as they had done the year before, the Whigs also staged a powerful exhibition on the evening of March 5. The *Boston Gazette* reported that "some Thousands" viewed the massacre exhibition presented from the balcony of Mrs. Clapham's King

Street home. Gazing up at what the *Gazette* described as transparent paintings illuminated by a lantern, the people saw vivid images that included a monument inscribed with the names of those "*who were barbarously murdered.*" This impressive presentation was withdrawn at 9:15, and muffled bells tolled until ten o'clock. From Adams's perspective, these reminders of the need to defend American rights had the added benefit of coming shortly before the annual legislative elections.[37]

When Hutchinson finally reconvened the General Court in April of 1772, Adams soon discovered he could not use the session to rekindle patriotic ardor. Knowing Hutchinson had intimated that the legislators could return to Boston if they spoke of inconvenience rather than constitutional rights, John Hancock urged the House to adopt that argument. Adams opposed Hancock's motion by again emphasizing the danger of according the status of law to British instructions. A scant majority backed Adams, but the open split with Hancock seemed ominous for the Whig cause. Once the legislators turned to their regular business, Hutchinson continued his practice of avoiding political fights. The session ended quickly and quietly. On April 28, shortly after dissolving the assembly and well into the second year of what he had described as the political calm, Hutchinson voiced confidence. Assessing his opponents, the governor remarked, "I think we have so divided the [Whig] faction that it must be something very unfortunate which can unite them again."[38]

Although angered by Hancock's apparent duplicity, Adams put the best face on the situation and continued his efforts to awaken the people as well as lethargic Whig leaders. In late April, as he regularly did, Adams turned to the press in hopes of influencing the annual election. He presented a lengthy list of grievances linked to the threat of "the alteration of our free and mutually dependent constitution, into a dependent ministerial despotism."[39] Some Tories, confident that the people had rejected Adams's brand of radicalism, struck back boldly. For years Boston's Tories had not even contested the election of Whigs, but in 1772 they tried to get the town meeting to jettison the House of Representatives' chief incendiary. The odious scent of his tax-collecting failures had not dissipated, and Adams's brand of fervent American patriotism had fallen out of favor. Still, although he received only 505 of a possible 723 votes, Adams, who like the other winning candidates was backed by the Boston Caucus, easily gained the final spot on the delegation. Although Tories had merely reduced Adams's victory margin, Andrew Oliver, the lieutenant governor, bragged about the sharp decline in popularity of the man "who has been so long the idol of the populace."[40]

Although they failed to unseat Adams, Tories had reasons to gloat. The Whig leadership had fractured, perhaps irrevocably. And the quiet period was about to enter its third year. This state of affairs, which made Tories optimistic and frustrated Adams, can be traced to a complex set of factors. Intriguingly, Adams and Thomas Hutchinson, who not only occupied opposite ends of the political spectrum but who also truly hated each other, offered similar explanations for this period of calm.

Adams believed a politician could not spur the people to action unless the masses believed their rights were being trampled. And even before the Boston Massacre the British government and Hutchinson had made it harder for radicals such as Adams to capitalize, to improve, on events. From early 1770 on, the British cultivated a moderate policy and image. Parliament lowered the duties it imposed and eliminated every Townshend duty except the one on tea. The British ministry also waged its own propaganda campaign by suggesting that *all* taxes might be repealed—if the colonists continued to behave. The specter of a standing army had been diminished by withdrawing the troops from Boston proper. And when the British began paying the salaries of colonial officials, they did it surreptitiously. For his part, Hutchinson so dexterously evaded admitting the truth about his salary that Adams referred to the "*silent*" attack on constitutional rights. Additionally, in all his dealings with the General Court, Hutchinson endeavored to deny Whigs any flashpoint issues. Thus, the quiet period stemmed in part from Britain's policy of moderation and from the skillful way the British and their American friends implemented that policy.[41]

Brightening economic conditions aided the British strategy. Even though he expressed faith in the people, Adams believed most individuals would usually be politically inattentive because they were "necessarily engaged" in earning a living. This assessment reflected the way events in Massachusetts had unfolded. People formed anti-British crowds when their livelihoods or freedom seemed in *imminent* danger from the Stamp Act or from impressment. And, while the economy was sour when the Stamp Act controversy erupted, by the early 1770s the economy hummed and the threat of impressment had dissipated. Because they were experiencing a sense of well-being, the people had become less active politically and political crowds were much less likely to form. Hutchinson understood the importance of economic considerations. Speaking of developments from roughly 1770 into 1772, he gushed that "commerce never was in a more flourishing state" and, economically, Massachusetts was "the envy of all the other colonies." As both Adams and Hutchinson emphasized, events demonstrated that the people seemed more politically apathetic in good times.[42]

The quiet period also stemmed from the fact that most Americans found Whig extremists like Samuel Adams too radical. The British government and their American allies believed that the vast majority of colonists—including notable Whigs like Otis, Hancock, and Cushing—did not want independence. They were right. Virtually all colonists merely sought a return to the imperial relationship that existed before 1763. And while the majority of colonists rejected Adams's zealous patriotism, many of his fellow Whigs considered his ideas on government dangerous. When Adams argued that power flowed from the people and that government officials were the servants of the people, he voiced a democratic ideal anathema to many who later became revolutionaries. They advocated following a moderate course in part because they feared that Adams's brand of radicalism might bring about a restructuring of American society.[43]

The misguided effort to toss Adams out of the Massachusetts House in May 1772 helped subvert the political tranquility Tories prized. Hutchinson admitted that the attempt, which had little chance of success, "proved a disservice to government" because it "caused an alarm" among Whigs. In response, they labored mightily to reunite Hancock and Adams. It took the better part of a year to achieve that reconciliation. In the meantime, Hutchinson effectively removed what he labeled one of the Whig's "alleged grievances" by letting the General Court return to Boston. Hutchinson, who admitted his own questioning of the wording of a House pronouncement on the issue had produced "much uneasiness," claimed he acted "to prevent a dissatisfaction among the people of the province." It hardly seems mere coincidence, however, that the governor informed the legislators about the return on June 13, the day he finally admitted that the British were paying his salary.[44] The timing, it appears, was designed to dampen anger over the salary question. Hutchinson's ploy failed. The salary dispute gave Adams a powerful issue to improve.

Adams and his longtime ally Joseph Hawley, the two most zealous Whigs in the House, took the lead in producing a report and resolves that put Hutchinson on the wrong side of a fundamental constitutional issue. As Hutchinson noted, Adams and Hawley were "the principle persons" both when it came to framing the document and then "carrying it through the House." The report and accompanying resolves branded the paying of executive salaries "a dangerous Innovation" that violated the charter, the "most solemn Contract" that bound the British Crown and the people of Massachusetts. Indeed, "the Innovation is an important Change of the Constitution, and exposes the Province to a despotic Administration of Government." It was an action "in Derogation of the Constitution."

Hutchinson claimed that about a third of House voiced "great opposition . . . to the most material parts" of the report, but during the debates many Tory members "left the house and went home, despairing of success." That exodus might also have been related to the fact that the defenders of the colony's rights arranged for a roll-call vote, thus making each member's vote readily available for public scrutiny. The report and accompanying resolves passed eighty-five to nineteen on June 10, 1772.[45]

Although he wanted bolder resolves, Adams remarked that, "even as they now appear, I believe they chagrin him whom they call Governor." Samuel was right. Hutchinson conceded that the House's pronouncements might make people think their charter rights had been "invaded, and that the powers, which, in all free governments, ought to remain in the people, were, by act of the king, taken from them." On June 13, the House appointed a committee, which again included Adams and Hawley, to draft a petition and remonstrance to be sent to the king. It was to address the issue of the governor being supported "independent of the Grants and Acts of the General Assembly." The committee reported the next day. The House immediately approved having a copy sent to agent Benjamin Franklin, who was to present it to the king as soon as possible. That very afternoon, after telling the representatives that they had misinterpreted the Massachusetts Charter, Hutchinson adjourned the legislature.[46]

A mere adjournment of the House could not halt the growing controversy. It heated up considerably after the province learned in September that the British would also pay Massachusetts's superior court judges. Adams touched on this possibility in his 1764 instructions, openly broached this explosive issue again in the famous circular letter of 1768, and referred to it yet again in his subsequent propaganda blitzes. As Adams kept emphasizing, the question of the British compensating judges seemed especially troubling because of the nature of judicial appointments. The Crown appointed judges. In England judges received appointments for life during good behavior. In the colonies, however, the Crown could dismiss judges at any time for any reason. Making colonial judges financially dependent on the Crown thus raised the specter that they would do the monarch's bidding. The threat to judicial integrity touched a nerve with many people, not just committed Whigs. Of course, the Tory Peter Oliver, chief justice of the five-member superior court, viewed it differently. With some justification, he charged that the legislature used its power of the purse to undercut judicial independence. But most citizens, including those called Tory, did not see it that way. They considered the "innovation" of the British paying judges a threat to their liberties. The fact that the judges would be paid out of revenues derived from the tea duty made the problem even more nettle-some. Oliver, with his characteristic invective, underscored the importance of the issue when he asserted that the idea of the monarch controlling the salaries of superior court judges "mortified, chagrined, enraged & drove into right down Madness, *Adams* & all his Factious *Hydra*."[47]

Once the specifics of the new salary arrangements appeared in the press, Adams and other radicals leaped into action. In an October 5, 1772, news-paper diatribe Samuel pictured "the iron Hand of Tyranny" raised to "ravish our Laws and seize the Badge of Freedom." He pleaded, "Is it not High Time for the People of this Country explicitly to declare, whether they will be Freemen or Slaves?" Seeking to spark yet another flammable issue, Adams linked the defense of political liberty to the preservation of religion and the people's morals. As he called on "the *Body of the People*" to defend "their free Constitution," Adams declared that history was on America's side. Seldom, if ever, had even a small community of people "been kept long in Bondage, when they have unitedly and perseveringly resolv'd to be Free." To foster that necessary unity, Adams urged people to "converse together . . . and open our minds freely to each other" on the subject of the threat to American liberties. "Let it be the topic of conversation in every social Club. Let every Town assemble. Let Associations & Combinations be everywhere set up to consult and recover our just Rights."[48]

Adams's impassioned pleas were calculated to generate support for a powerful new Whig organizational tool. Whigs, as well as other groups, had long used correspondence committees, and Adams and other leading Whigs had routinely promoted the idea of establishing an intercolonial-correspondence system. While not abandoning the hope that an intercolo-nial network might one day be formed, Adams, Dr. Thomas Young, and possibly others in Massachusetts saw great potential in creating a town-based structure of committees of correspondence that would present a unified Massachusetts front against Britain's policies. Adams and his allies realized such a system could not be constructed until a sharp grievance presented itself. So they planned—Tories would say plotted—and waited for events that would let them implement their scheme. The volatile issue of who would compensate judges and Hutchinson's unwitting assistance afforded them the opportunity.[49]

In addition to composing newspaper items to lay the groundwork for a committee-of-correspondence system in Massachusetts, Adams helped circulate petitions that urged the selectmen to call a town meeting to deal with the issue of the salaries of superior-court judges. On October 27, the day before the meeting, Adams was already working to have other town meetings express their opposition to what he described as "the Incroach-ments of Tyranny, which now threatens its Completion." One of the peo-ple he contacted was Elbridge Gerry of Marblehead, who, upon entering the House in May, became an instant ally of Adams. Gerry agreed that the legislature, not the British, should pay judges. Samuel spelled out the plan. Boston Whigs would have the town meeting ask the governor to call the assembly into immediate session while also demanding that judges declare whether they would reject Britain's "odious" new remuneration system. Promising to keep Gerry informed, Adams revealed his true goal: "I wish we could arouse the continent."[50]

Boston Whigs did urge the town meeting to "expressly declare their natural & Charter Rights to their Representatives" and to press the gov-ernor to reconvene the legislature. When that moderate proposal did not garner support, the ardent Whigs apparently decided against broaching their more radical proposal of asking judges to declare themselves. The best the Whigs could get was the formation of a three-member committee, headed by Adams, charged with preparing an address to the governor to inquire if he had any knowledge about the Crown paying judges. Although Adams's committee denounced the idea of the British paying judges and reiterated the bedrock Whig argument that Parliament could not constitutionally tax the colonists, the address merely requested that the governor please inform the meeting if he had received information about the important issue of the British possibly paying judges. Given its deferential tone, it would have been hard to vote against the address. No one did.[51]

As promised, Adams immediately informed Gerry of the meeting's ac-tions. In doing so he entreated, "I wish your Town would think it proper to have a Meeting." Indeed, "Pray use your Influence with Salem & other Towns." Adams reasoned that, if the towns declared themselves, "our Enemies would not have it in their power to divide us." Expecting that Hutchinson would refuse to comment on the report about the judge's pay or would answer equivocally, Samuel sought Gerry's help. He urged Gerry to attend the meeting of the Superior Court in Salem and to ask the judges themselves whether the report of the British starting to pay their salaries was true. Adams clearly hoped to use the issue of judges' pay to foment resistance throughout Massachusetts. And he pushed for action outside the metropolis even before Boston's town meeting established the committee of correspondence that was the key to developing the new organizational system he and Young envisioned.[52]

As Adams anticipated, Hutchinson refused to confirm or deny the report that the British planned to pay judges. But, rather than equivocating as Adams thought he might, Hutchinson told the town meeting it should mind its own business, which he pointedly said did not include inquiring about imperial policies. Hutchinson, an experienced and often wily politician, should have realized his response would provoke the meeting. After considering the governor's comments, the meeting created a high-profile committee made up of Cushing, Adams, and Otis, who had at least temporarily regained his sanity. The meeting authorized the committee to draft a petition asking the governor to permit the General Court to meet, as scheduled, on December 2. Although Adams advocated even stronger action, the petition's moderation gave it broad appeal. After approving the petition unanimously, the meeting adjourned until November 2 to await Hutchinson's reply.[53]

Hutchinson played right into the great incendiary's hands. Although the town meeting had sent him deferential and moderate requests, Hutchinson again responded haughtily. Emphasizing that what he called the "Royal Charter" vested the power to call or dismiss the legislature in the governor, Hutchinson again lectured the meeting on its proper duties, which he stressed did not include meddling in the timing of legislative meetings. Adams had to smile with delight. Reiterating one of his cardinal political maxims, he informed Gerry that the meeting's requests of Hutchinson had been "so reasonable that in refusing to comply with them he must have put himself *in the wrong*, in the opinion of every honest & sensible man." As a consequence, "such measures as the people may determine upon to save themselves, if rational & manly, will be the more reconcileable even to cautious minds, & thus we may expect that Unanimity which we wish for." Adams was right. The town meeting responded to Hutchinson's blast by unanimously passing a resolution stating that the people had an absolute right to petition the king or his representatives for redress *and* to communicate their sentiments to other towns. At this point, Adams struck. He moved that Boston create a twenty-one-member committee of correspondence. It would issue a manifesto "to state the Rights of the Colonists and of this Province in particular, as Men, as Christians, and as Subjects" and also formulate a statement of grievances. This would be communicated to the province's towns and "to the World as the sense of this Town." The committee would ask every Massachusetts town to send "a free communication of their Sentiments on this Subject." Adams's wording ensured that the committee could function as a protest clearinghouse. The resolution spoke of the committee assessing infringements or violations of the colonists' rights as they "have been, or from time to time may be made." According to Rev. Samuel Cooper, "a Number of the most respectable Friends of Liberty in the Town," including every other Boston representative, opposed Adams's proposal. They said the other towns would not respond. After further discussion the more timid Whig leaders backed down, and Adams's proposal passed unanimously.[54]

Adams and Otis, now merely a shell of his former self, headed the committee. But prominent and wealthy moderates—including Hancock, Cushing, and William Phillips, who had replaced Otis in the House— declined to serve. For those who counseled accommodation, that was a mistake. As Richard D. Brown, the modern historian of the Boston committee, indicates, the committee was made up of staunch Whigs who recognized Adams as their leader. Indeed, eight of the twenty-one members reportedly belonged to the North End Caucus, one of the branches of the Boston Caucus. Adams and the other extreme Whigs had their instrument to rally and unify support for the Whig cause throughout Massachusetts.[55]

The Boston committee held its first meeting on November 3, 1772, and began the process Adams hoped would result in Massachusetts towns presenting a united front against Great Britain. As committee members drafted position statements, Adams kept sending personal letters to Whigs in other towns to promote the creation of similar committees and to get them to endorse the actions of the Boston Town Meeting. He believed that once the towns established correspondence committees and shared their thoughts, it would demonstrate that the people were "united in Sentiments." That would naturally produce "a Confidence in each other, & a plan of Opposition will be easily formed, & executed with Spirit." On November 14 Adams sounded even more like the great incendiary. Again calling on Gerry to increase support for a committee-of-correspondence movement, Adams expressed his desire to behold "the Love of Liberty & a Zeal to support it" enkindled in every Massachusetts town. Employing the same image, he later urged James Warren to spur Plymouth to action with the admonition that, "where there is a Spark of patriotick fire, *we* will enkindle it."[56]

On November 20 the Boston committee gave the town meeting its statement on the rights of the colonists, its list of grievances, and a copy of the letter to the other Massachusetts towns. Although drafted by subcommittees, each of the documents had been reviewed, revised as needed, and then approved by the whole committee. The section on rights, originally worked up primarily by Adams, essentially restated well-developed Whig arguments. Stressing and often quoting from Locke, Adams emphasized that the people had fundamental rights that could not be abridged. The statement gave extended and special attention to suggesting that

Americans' religious liberties might be as endangered as their political liberties. The manifesto was also notable for incorporating a claim Adams had been articulating more and more often: political officials were the "servants of the society." The lengthy list of grievances offered a dozen numbered sections each festooned with detailed evidence, some carefully drawn from other colonies. The covering letter asserted that Americans confronted "a constant, unremitted, uniform aim to enslave us." This official letter, unlike Adams's private correspondence, did not ask other towns to form correspondence committees, but it amounted to an invitation to do just that. It suggested that Boston's observations should "be laid before your Town, that the subject may be weighed as its importance requires, and the collected wisdom of the whole People, as far as possible, be obtained." The committee made it clear that Bostonians believed the people outside the metropolis would agree that the colonists' rights were in mortal danger and must be defended.[57]

After making a slight revision in the list of colonial grievances, the meeting unanimously approved the pronouncements and ordered them printed. The resulting pamphlet, which also contained messages exchanged between the town meeting and the governor, had a title that underscored the importance of lawful action: "*The Votes and Proceedings of the Freeholders and other Inhabitants of the Town of Boston, in Town Meeting assembled, According to Law.*" The committee members were authorized to send copies to the selectmen of every Massachusetts township and to whomever else they thought proper. It took ten days to get the pamphlets printed. Adams, always known for his industry, put enormous effort into creating a colony-wide communication system during this period. He kept up a steady correspondence with Whigs in several towns and pressed them to have their towns take immediate action. At the end of November Samuel informed Arthur Lee in England that, while the committee's pamphlets had not yet been sent into the interior, "other towns are in motion of their [own] accord." Adams could have added, but did not, that his letters urging action helped stimulate the movement.[58]

As he toiled to plant committees of correspondence throughout Massachusetts, Adams also found a way to champion his goal of forging an intercolonial network. In one of the few actions that marred the quiet period, Rhode Islanders had burned a British revenue ship, the *Gaspee*, in June 1772. Invoking a recently passed law that allowed colonists accused of such a crime to be tried in England, the British authorized a special commission to investigate the *Gaspee* incident. In late December, with the commission about to begin functioning in their province, Rhode Island officials asked

Adams for advice. Denouncing the commission's powers as a violation of the first principles of government, the British constitution, and Magna Carta, Adams counseled standing firm against the commission. Forcefully embracing the principle of unified colonial action, he suggested that Rhode Island's cause was the cause of all Americans; therefore, its assembly should send the other colonies a circular letter on this issue. This would "tend to the Advantage of the General Cause & R Island in particular." The Rhode Islanders, who consulted political leaders throughout the colonies, were thinking along similar lines. They sent out the type of circular letter Adams advocated.[59] It would take some time before the results of Rhode Island's circular letter could be known.

As 1772 ended, Adams kept up an extensive correspondence with people in England, in Massachusetts, and in other colonies. But above all he focused on getting the committee-of-correspondence system up and running. Observing that Samuel corresponded not merely with many in Massachusetts but with people in England and the other colonies, John Adams marveled, "his time is all employed in the public Service." The great incendiary and his colleagues on the Boston committee usually assembled once a week. They began by meeting from 5 p.m. to 7 p.m., and by early spring their gatherings extended to 9:30 or even later as the members, who jointly purchased and consumed Rhode Island beer, mixed committee work and conviviality. When responding to communications it received from the townships and districts of Massachusetts, the committee showed creativity by flattering the townships' wisdom and patriotism. To convey a sense of growing momentum, as additional townships contacted it, the committee heralded the growing number of responses. And as events worth "improving" occurred, the committee exploited them. Thus, when the news of the *Gaspee* investigation broke, committee members highlighted the new grievance in their missives.[60]

Leading Tories snickered when the Boston committee came into existence. At the same time Adams contemplated sparking "the Love of Liberty & a Zeal to support it" in every Massachusetts town, Hutchinson snidely observed that "to keep up a correspondence through the Province by Committees of the several Towns . . . is such a foolish scheme that they must necessarily make themselves ridiculous." By late November smirks turned into worried frowns. Finally realizing that the Boston committee was creating a powerful Whig organization throughout Massachusetts, Tories tried to sabotage it.[61]

Aaron Davis Jr. was, Adams believed, one of the would-be saboteurs. Four days after the town meeting approved the committee's statements on the colonists' rights as men, as Christians, and as subjects, Davis assaulted Dr. Young in print. Young, an important committee member who was a friend and close political ally of Adams, was known as an outspoken nonbeliever, an "infidel." Denouncing Young's irreligious moral chanter, Davis accused him of routinely cursing, swearing, and taking "God's name in vain." Linking Young's "Creed" to "the most thorough paced infidels, and violent oppressors of holy Religion," Davis argued that he personally "did not chuse to have any thing to do with measures, wherein I must fol-low the lead of such men as Dr. Young." By claiming that he supported the colonists' rights but only wanted to follow "men of probity, piety and real christianity," Davis seemed to invite the committee of correspondence to abandon Young.

Adams quickly rushed an extraordinarily vicious response into print. Writing as "Vindex," one of his well-known pen names, Samuel called Davis an "insect" who had produced a "stupid composition." Pointing out that Davis claimed he had long known about Young's irreligious character, he asked why Davis had waited to raise the issue. Samuel did more than imply that Davis had Tory leanings. It seemed odd that "*the cause of chris-tianity* abstracted from *political concerns* was not sufficient to awaken your resentment." In fact, "had not the *cause of liberty* found a busy *advocate* in the man you branded with *irreligion*, your abhorrence would probably never have found a tongue." Adams did not try to deny that Young was in fact irreligious. Instead, he snarled that the Whig's "thorough conviction of his political integrity" justified the doctor's leadership position. Thus, Young's religion is not what mattered. What mattered to Adams was that Young "has ever been an unwearied assertor of the rights of his countrymen: has taken the post of hazard, and acted vigorously in the cause of American freedom."[62]

The great incendiary's spirited embrace of Dr. Young illustrates a vital point: despite his deep personal commitment to an orthodox Puritan reli-gion, Adams's driving impulse was to protect the people's natural and con-stitutional rights, not promote his own religion. As John said of his cousin, "Mr. Adams lived and conversed freely with all sectarians, in philosophy and divinity. He never imposed his creed on any one, or endeavored to make proselytes to his religious opinions." Mercy Otis Warren, who knew Samuel well, offered a similar judgment. She remarked that he "was at the same time liberal in opinion, and uniformly devout; social with men of all denominations." John Adams and Mercy Otis Warren could have added that when it came to standing up for the defenders of American liberty or when it came to countering possible attempts to undermine the Boston

Committee of Correspondence Samuel had no problem defending an irreligious "infidel." And he also did not refrain from expressing his displeasure when Christian ministers failed to show what he considered the necessary vigor "in the cause of American freedom." For Samuel Adams, "political integrity" in the defense of the people's liberties trumped any concerns about an individual's religious views.[63]

Tory efforts to undermine Boston's committee of correspondence failed miserably. By early December Thomas Hutchinson was scolding himself for having believed that Boston's committee and its pamphlet would have "little or no effect." He concluded that, as a result of the committee's efforts, a "doctrine of Independence upon the Parliament" was "every day spreading and strengthening itself." Although Hutchinson probably overstated the case, the Boston committee's messages, especially on judges' pay, were clearly helping to rekindle Whig ardor as 1772 gave way to 1773. Indeed, although he never returned to the General Court, it was the question of who would pay judges that brought John Adams back into the political fray; the issue also influenced John Hancock's return to the political wars.[64]

By early January 1773 many Massachusetts communities had gone on record opposing British policy. The task was made easier because some Tories publicly conceded that it would endanger liberty to make judges depend on the Crown for their salaries. Hutchinson's anxiety about the impact of the expanding committee-of-correspondence system ballooned when he received reports that the radicals, having shown what could be done in Massachusetts, planned to have the Massachusetts House issue a circular letter aimed at creating an intercolonial correspondence system. That chilling thought goaded the governor into taking a major gamble.

For almost three years Hutchinson had endeavored to avoid giving Whig legislators issues they could exploit. He had been particularly careful about steering clear of the explosive question of what powers Parliament actually had over the colonies. But, frightened by the Boston committee's success and believing the radicals were plotting to establish an American committee of correspondence system, Hutchinson, as Adams described it, unexpectedly called the General Court back into session on January 6, 1773.[65] Supremely confident in his own intellectual prowess and unrivaled knowledge of Massachusetts history, the governor appeared in person and delivered an address, notable for his repeated use of "I," that centered on the question of the supremacy of Parliament.

Admitting that "the government is at present in a disturbed and disordered state," Hutchinson blamed the difficulties on the Whigs' failure to realize that "it is impossible the rights of English subjects should be the same, in every respect, in all parts of the dominions." History proved that, from the start, the colonies formed part of "the dominions of the Crown of England" and "were to remain subject to the supreme authority of Parliament." Therefore, the resolutions recently passed by various towns that "deny the supreme authority of Parliament . . . are repugnant to the principles of the [British] constitution." Pressing the legislators to admit the supremacy of Parliament, Hutchinson put the issue starkly: "I know of no line that can be drawn between the supreme authority of Parliament and the total independence of the colonies." Hutchinson expanded the argument by portraying what independence would bring. Shorn of British protection, the colonies would, he predicted, be gobbled up by a European power. Hutchinson openly challenged the General Court to prove him wrong. The governor's erudite address impressively marshaled the essential Tory arguments and voiced them in a calm manner. And his arguments were compelling—*if* one accepted the premise of Parliament's supremacy. Hutchinson certainly expected that, once they realized they were flirting with rebellion, the General Court and the people of Massachusetts would reject Whig ideas.[66] He miscalculated.

Samuel Adams was the chief author of the House's lengthy response approved on January 26, but it was a collective effort in which Joseph Hawley played a central role.[67] The House boldly maintained that, when created, the colonies were not annexed to the realm of England but were "at the absolute disposal of the Crown." Moreover, since the colonies were not annexed to the realm, "they are not a part of the kingdom and consequently not subject to the Legislative authority of the kingdom." The colonists could be subjected to Parliament's authority *only* if the Massachusetts Charter authorized that, and it did not. Since the charter did not establish Parliament's supremacy, Parliament could not assert it now. Nor could the British cite the fact that Parliament had recently taxed the colonists as a precedent because "whatever is originally in its nature wrong, can never be *sanctified*, or made right by *repetition* and use." This radical claim, a claim Hutchinson had warned that the legislature would adopt, amounted to a denial of Parliament's right to legislate for the colonies.

Hutchinson paid dearly for arguing that no line could be drawn between independence and accepting Parliament's supremacy. Following Adams's dictum of putting an opponent in the wrong, the House placed the onus on Hutchinson for anything the representatives might say on that score. "We cannot but express our concern," they intoned, "that your Excellency, by your speech, has reduced us to the unhappy alternative, either of appearing by our silence to acquiesce in your Excellency's sentiments, or of thus freely discussing this point." The representatives said that, if no line could be drawn, the colonists were either mere "vassals of Parliament" or "totally independent." Turning to history, the legislators maintained that the colonial delegates who negotiated the 1691 charter surely would not have reduced themselves to vassalage; therefore, they must have considered the colony independent.

After accusing Hutchinson of forcing the legislators to contemplate independence, Adams implied that the governor's address might necessitate calling an intercolonial gathering similar to the Stamp Act Congress. Indeed, drawing a line of distinction between the supreme authority of Parliament and the total independence of the colonies "would be an arduous undertaking, and of very great importance to all the other colonies." Accordingly, the legislators—even if they could discern a line of distinction—would not think of marking it out unless an intercolonial congress concurred in the analysis.[68] The great incendiary and his allies had once again found a way to point out the need for unified colonial action.

The governor counterattacked on February 16 by delivering a lengthy address laced with historical references buttressing his legal analysis. His scholarly effort merely caused the Council—which had also rejected the governor's analysis—and the House to draft additional pronouncements that restated, even more emphatically, the essence of their original responses. Hutchinson now realized he had initiated a controversy that, he lamented, "may be lengthened out to perpetuity." The governor also misjudged when he condescendingly told the members of the House that "nice Distinctions and legal Constitutions are far above the Reach of the Bulk of Mankind to comprehend." As the many responses sent to the Boston committee indicated, the province's citizens had a lucid conception of their fundamental rights. The problem for Hutchinson and the British was that the Massachusetts vision was not their vision. The overwhelming majority of Massachusetts citizens insisted that there were limits to Parliament's power, that Parliament had no right to tax underrepresented people such as themselves, and that the Crown should not pay colonial officials.[69]

Even as they engaged in a sophisticated constitutional debate with Hutchinson on parliamentary supremacy, Adams and his allies kept hammering on the easy-to-understand and sensitive issue of who would pay judges and the governor. Whigs recognized, as Adams put it, that the issue "was like Thunder in the ears of all but a detestable and detested few." In early February 1773 a House committee, with Adams as its driving force, called on the governor to say definitively whether the British were funding the judges' salaries. They justified this request with the accurate observation that the people were universally alarmed by reports that the Crown would control the salaries of the superior-court justices. Thus pressed, the governor, as indirectly and backhandedly as possible, finally admitted that the judge's salaries were now under the power of the monarch.

The House, with Adams as usual playing a central role, quickly accused the judges of wrongdoing if they accepted pay from the Crown. "No Judge who has a due Regard to Justice, or even his own Character," would let himself be placed under the "undue Bias" of depending on the Crown for his compensation. In the days that followed, the House pressed the judges to proclaim that they would accept their pay only from the House. Just before the legislative session ended, the House turned up the heat. It proclaimed that any judge who accepted a salary from other than the General Court had no real understanding of "the Importance of an Impartial Administration of Justice, that he is an enemy to the Constitution, and has it in his Heart to promote the Establishment of an arbitrary Government in the Province." Soon every one of the superior-court judges except Chief Justice Peter Oliver capitulated and agreed to the legislators' demands. The House also kept pressuring the governor to say he would only accept monetary support from the Massachusetts legislature. Following an established pattern, the House appointed a committee, naturally including Adams, to prepare a petition to be sent to the king "for the Redress of Grievances." The petition, which reiterated the House's constitutional claim that it alone should pay the salaries of the governor and superior-court judges, was approved unanimously on a symbolic day: March 5.[70]

The beleaguered Hutchinson had refrained from again commenting on parliamentary supremacy until March 6, 1773, the day he prorogued the legislature. That tactic hardly guaranteed the governor the last word, and it even played into Adams's hands. Believing the controversy supported their Whig positions, the representatives had already voted to have all the official pronouncements of both sides in the "Controversy" printed as a pamphlet. In a move that reflected the methods of the Boston committee, the clerk of every town and every district in Massachusetts as well as all members of the General Court were to receive a copy. The legislators did not fear having their debates with Hutchinson distributed throughout Massachusetts, and they were right. Hutchinson had committed a major tactical error. As Adams remarked to a fellow Whig, Hutchinson's defense of parliamentary supremacy "quickened a spirit of enquiry into the nature and end of government, and the connection of the colonies with Great Britain." When they learned what Hutchinson had done, British government officials winced. Hutchinson regretted having raised the issue in the first place, and that regret nagged him the rest of his life.[71]

With Adams serving as a vital member of each body and clearly functioning as the liaison between the two, the Massachusetts House of Representatives and Boston's correspondence committee increasingly worked in close harmony. Right after the legislature adjourned, the Boston Town Meeting responded to Hutchinson's suggestion that Boston had no right to concoct resolves on imperial policy or to urge other towns to adopt its views. The town meeting placed Adams at the head of a committee charged with preparing a report that would "vindicate" Boston against the governor's "gross misrepresentations and groundless charges." Adams drafted the lengthy report. Not surprisingly, it emphasized the crucial issue of judges' salaries and also put Hutchinson on the wrong side of another basic rights issue: the right of the people of Boston—or any Massachusetts community—to meet "together in a time of publick danger." Adams accused Hutchinson of attempting to keep the people "in ignorance of their danger, that they may be more easily and speedily inslaved." After unanimously approving the report, the meeting directed its correspondence committee to send copies to every town and district in the province.[72]

By early March 1773, Virginians had received copies of the Boston Town Meeting resolves on judges' pay, information on the establishment of Boston's committee of correspondence, and the pamphlet containing the addresses Hutchinson and the legislators had hurled at one another. Newspaper accounts about the *Gaspee* commission in Rhode Island had also reached Virginia. A member of Virginia's House of Burgesses indicated that the items sent from Massachusetts proved useful when the burgesses decided what must be done. They called for the development of intercolonial committees to gather and exchange information about Britain's flagrant attack on American liberties. The burgesses gave special attention to the threat of Americans possibly being transported to England for trial. As soon as it learned of the burgesses' actions, Boston's correspondence committee held a special meeting. On their own initiative, the committeemen decided that the letter containing the burgesses' resolves should be published as a circular letter and forwarded to every township and district in Massachusetts. Adams and the rest of the committee transformed the Virginians' actions into a ringing endorsement of Massachusetts's correspondence system. The Boston committee prefaced its April 9 circular with the flattering observation, "we congratulate you upon the Acquisition of such respectable Aid as the ancient and patriotic Province of *Virginia*." Reminding township officials of the value of correspondence committees, the circular contained the directive that it should immediately be given to the town's correspondence committee or, if none existed, to the selectmen so they could communicate it to the town.[73]

By the spring of 1773 Adams could honestly boast that Boston's correspondence committee had produced "Effects which are extremely mortifying to our petty Tyrants." As he later phrased it, the committee's efforts "had raised the Spirits of the People, drawn off their attention from *picking up pins,* and directed their Views to great objects." Fellow Whig Rev. Samuel Cooper observed that the Boston committee "had an Effect thro the whole Province beyond the most sanguine Expectations" of its friends. The great majority of Massachusetts towns had followed the committee's lead, said Rev. Cooper, and their actions proved that most people, not some small faction, believed "that their most essential Rights are violated." Adams observed that the towns and districts stressed "two capital Grievances": taxing the colonists without their consent and using that money to pay the governor and judges.[74]

The Rev. Cooper overestimated the groundswell of public action. By April 1773 slightly less than half the colony's townships and districts had responded to the Boston committee's missives. But momentum remained, and on April 12 Adams asserted that a great many Massachusetts towns, with more joining them every day, voiced full support for the positions taken by the Bostonians. In time, a majority of townships did react, but only 58 of the 260 townships and districts formed their own committees of correspondence. Although the committee network was never fully developed, the responses demonstrated that a clear majority of citizens opposed Britain's imperial policies. Equally important, the correspondence system provided a powerful organizational base when further action became necessary.[75]

In mid-April 1773, when he began exchanging letters with the noted Virginia Whig Richard Henry Lee, Adams was so exuberant about Massachusetts's committee-of-correspondence system that he wanted to clone it. Recounting its impressive achievements in Massachusetts, he recommended establishing a similar system in every colony. If that development occurred, it might well "promote that General Union, upon which the Security of the whole depends." Adams added that "I have often thought it a Misfortune, or rather a Fault in the Friends of American Independence and Freedom, their not taking Care to open every Channel of Communication." Reiterating a theme Whigs had often voiced and employing imagery he had publicly enunciated as far back as 1764, Samuel argued that, by creating an intercolonial-correspondence network, the united "Wisdom & Strength" of the whole continent could be "employed upon every proper Occasion." Three days later, writing to the committee in Duxbury, Massachusetts, Adams asserted that creating a two-tiered committee-of-correspondence system would "strike Terror into the hearts of those who would enslave us."[76]

What a difference a year made! In May 1772, deep into the quiet period, confident Tories tried to have Boston pitch Samuel Adams off its House delegation. Now in 1773, as the colony-wide election approached, Tories languished. At least in Massachusetts the quiet period was just a memory, and only a masochist would have challenged Adams's reelection. He garnered 413 of a possible 419 votes. When Thomas Cushing, the speaker of the House, could not serve as moderator, the town meeting elected Adams to that honorific post and, rather than refer to him as it normally did as "Mr. Samuel Adams," styled him "Mr. Samuel Adams, Esq."[77] The meeting also unanimously approved instructions produced by unflinching Whigs who heartily endorsed Virginia's plan of establishing intercolonial correspondence committees.[78] The next day Adams forwarded a copy of the proceedings to Arthur Lee with the comment that Boston's instructions served various good purposes, which included communicating Boston's "sentiments and spirit" to the other towns and beyond.[79]

As Tories feared, the annual election further weakened them. When the new General Court met in late May, Adams's days of struggling to improve on the flimsy issue of the General Court's meeting place had given way to controversies over judicial independence and the right to a jury of one's peers. Moreover, Virginia's call for creating intercolonial committees of correspondence was ready for action. And, if Governor Hutchinson proved foolish enough to renew the fight over parliamentary supremacy, that would supply yet more fuel to the growing resistance movement. Hutchinson understood the new realities. When he addressed the legislators on May 27, he uttered not a word about Parliament's powers.[80] It did not matter. The damage had already been done.

The new House took immediate action on Virginia's resolutions. On May 28, in what was probably a moment of extraordinary pleasure, and perhaps with a sense of accomplishment, Adams asked the House to approve resolves rooted in the fact that the representatives were "fully sensible of the Necessity and Importance of a Union of the several Colonies in America, at a Time when it clearly appears that the Rights and Liberties of all are systematically invaded; in Order that the joint Wisdom of the Whole may be employed in consulting their common Safety." Instead of the small correspondence committee the House normally appointed, the members now established a standing committee of fifteen that, as in the case of the earlier correspondence committees, included Samuel Adams. Adopting the language of Virginia's resolves, the Massachusetts House ordered its committee to obtain all possible information about the important issues separating Britain and the colonies and to share that information by maintaining correspondence "with our Sister Colonies." Again following Virginia's lead, the commission of inquiry in Rhode Island (the *Gaspee* commission) received special attention. The House directed that a circular letter containing its resolves be sent to every colonial assembly and that those assemblies be urged to join Massachusetts in supporting "the wise and salutary Resolves of the House of Burgesses in Virginia." Signaling the importance of their actions, the House approved its resolves with a roll call, thus making each member's position a matter of record. The members approved the resolves 119 to 4. As other colonies also followed Virginia's lead, one of the cherished goals of many Whigs, not just of Samuel Adams, was being accomplished. The development of intercolonial committees of correspondence provides a prime example of the way many colonists in many colonies worked together and shared ideas on the road to revolution.[81]

Massachusetts's committees of correspondence proved especially vital since Governor Hutchinson, like the governor of every royal colony, could simply refuse to call the legislature into session or could dismiss it at any time. The committee-of-correspondence system allowed Whigs to establish a form of shadow government that constituted a way station on the road to installing extralegal governments in Massachusetts. As Samuel later said in appraising the Massachusetts committee system for a leading Pennsylvania Whig, "by this Means we have been able to circulate the most early Intelligence of Importance to our Friends in the Country, & to establish an Union which is formidable to our Adversaries."[82] He hoped the other colonies would emulate Massachusetts.

In June of 1773, Samuel Adams orchestrated a political exposé that savaged Governor Hutchinson's political reputation beyond repair and helped fuel the American resistance movement. For months, Thomas Cushing, the speaker of the House, had possessed letters written in the late 1760s by Hutchinson, Andrew Oliver, and other friends of the British government. Cushing got the letters from Benjamin Franklin, the House's agent, on the condition that they neither be copied nor made public. Franklin claimed that he sent the letters to mollify Boston's anger at the British government and to give the British an opportunity to adjust its policies. If those were his motives, he badly misjudged what the great incendiary might do. Believing the letters would sink Hutchinson, Adams longed to expose them. He finally managed to publicize them by once again working closely with John Hancock. Samuel's ability to manufacture propaganda even won Hutchinson's grudging respect.[83]

Less than a week after the House supported Virginia's call for intercolonial committees of correspondence, Adams dramatically informed the representatives that he had matters of grave importance to communicate and requested that the gallery be cleared. Once that was done, Adams told the members he had obtained letters prejudicial to Massachusetts and had received permission to share them with the House provided the members stipulated the letters would not be copied or printed. The members agreed, and Adams read the letters. That afternoon the House turned itself into a committee of the whole and considered the correspondence. Hancock reported that the representatives had concluded the letters were designed "to overthrow the Constitution of this Government, and to introduce arbitrary Power into the Province." The House approved that statement by a vote of 101 to 5 and the next day appointed a nine-member committee, including Samuel Adams and other prominent Whigs, to further "consider" the letters. On June 9, as Hutchinson twisted slowly in the wind of circulating rumors, Hancock said he had acquired what apparently were copies of the infamous letters. The House initiated an elaborate process of authenticating the documents that, rather perversely, included inviting Hutchinson to become a part of the procedure. As Hutchinson justifiably complained, these maneuvers allowed Whigs to continue inflaming the public with vicious rumors about the still-unreleased contents of the letters. Those rumors made his actions seem "more and more criminal." Then, with the letters still unpublished, on June 16 the House passed resolves proclaiming that Governor Hutchinson and Andrew Oliver, the lieutenant governor, were unworthy of serving in those capacities. Therefore, the king should, the representatives urged, remove the two from office. Samuel Adams was, of course, placed on the committee charged with turning these resolutions into a petition to the king.[84]

Adams used the Massachusetts committee-of-correspondence system to promote intercolonial unity by spreading suspicion about the letters. On June 22 Boston's committee issued a broadside describing the uncovering of the letters as a very fortunate discovery that brought to light "the Plot" hatched "by our malicious and insidious Enemies." Calling up the image of providence aiding the original settlers of Massachusetts to escape tyranny, the committee claimed this discovery was yet another instance of "Providential Care." The resolves passed by the House in response to the letters supposedly showed the need for "the strictest Concurrence in Sentiment and Action of every individual of this Province, and we may add, of THIS CONTINENT." Clearly, said the committee, "the Good of the Whole should be the single Object of our Pursuit." By standing united, Americans "shall be able to defeat the Invaders and Violators of our Rights." The one violator named in the broadside was Governor Hutchinson. Massachusetts's religiosity and the traditional ideal of consensus were being blatantly exploited for Whig purposes. And, as Hutchinson groaned, all this happened without anyone directly quoting from any of the supposedly damning letters.[85]

Hutchinson was justified when he complained that his letters were being manipulated and that Adams engineered the manipulation. But the governor erred when he tried to dismiss his writings by saying they contained nothing more than what he had already said about Parliament's supremacy. When the letters finally became public later that year, Hutchinson could not escape the devastating repercussions of his claim that, for the colonists, "there must be an abridgement of what are called English liberties." That line alone was more than enough to convince many that Hutchinson cared little about American rights. He was vilified throughout Massachusetts, burned in effigy in Philadelphia and Princeton, and, as his modern biographer Bernard Bailyn discovered, "compared in verse to Catiline, Caligula, and Nero"—notorious political villains of ancient Rome.[86]

The assault on Governor Hutchinson, waged by all means fair and foul, culminated in the House approving a petition to the king by a vote of eighty to eleven on June 23. As drafted by Adams, the document assured the king that "Nothing but a Sense of the Duty we owe to our Sovereign, and the Obligation we are under to consult the Peace and Safety of the Province" could produce such a petition. Asserting that the House's goal was to restore harmony and goodwill between Great Britain and Massachusetts, Adams reprised themes he had often enunciated. He suggested that the difficulties between "both Countries" flowed from misinformation supplied over a long period of time by evil men in the province. These wicked individuals planned to annihilate America's liberties so they could gain wealth and political position. Governor Hutchinson and Lieutenant Governor Oliver were named as such miscreants and therefore should be replaced. Once again this was not mere propagandistic bombast. The letters Adams wrote to Arthur Lee in England must be viewed as statements penned with the knowledge that they might well be published. Still, writing to Lee, Samuel insisted that the notorious letters showed that "the plan for the ruin of American Liberty was laid by a few men born & educated amongst us, & govern[e]d by Avarice & a Lust of power."[87] Adams, like his major adversaries, honestly believed evil, self-interested men in Mas-

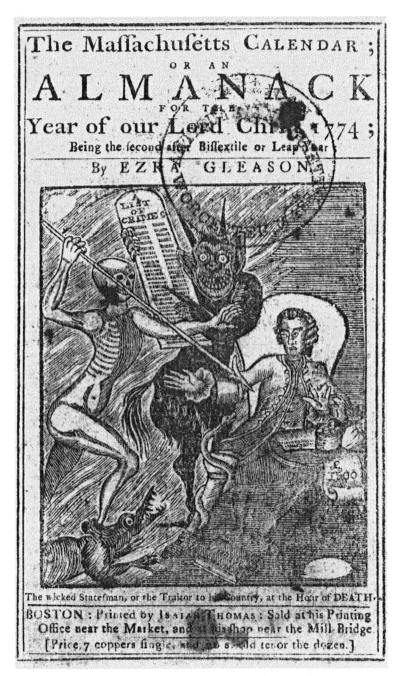

The wicked Statesman, or the Traitor to his Country, at the Hour of DEATH.

Paul Revere engraving of Thomas Hutchinson—"The wicked Statesman"—from the Massachusetts Calendar . . . 1774. Courtesy of the American Antiquarian Society.

sachusetts played a central role in fomenting conflict between the colonies and the mother country.

As he led the attack on Governor Hutchinson and his supporters, Samuel Adams continued, as the governor ruefully noted, to be innovative in "even small circumstances." According to Hutchinson, Adams had, over the course of four or five years, transformed the political language in Massachusetts. Under his direction the House of Representatives had come to refer to itself as "his majesty's commons"; the House debates were styled "parliamentary debates"; what had been known as "the province laws" were now heralded as "the laws of the land." In language, at least, Adams made it seem that Massachusetts had already achieved a significant degree of autonomy if not outright independence. His use of the phrase *both Countries* when referring to Great Britain and Massachusetts in the petition to the king conveyed the same message.[88]

By the time he prorogued the legislature in late June, Governor Hutchinson had been so beaten down by the unstinting attacks that he did not even mention the purloined letters, the question of judicial pay, or the petition asking for his removal.[89] The quiet period in Massachusetts had obviously ended. And by the early summer of 1773 Massachusetts had a powerful new Whig organization, the committee-of-correspondence network, ready to combat Britain's assaults on the people's liberties. The American colonists had not yet fully awakened from their political slumber, but vital issues such as the right to a fair trial, who would pay colonial officials, and the possible limits of Parliament's power simmered in the public consciousness. If the British miscalculated and renewed their assaults on American liberties, Samuel Adams could reasonably hope to garner many supporters to champion those liberties once he "improved" on British miscalculations.

6

BRITAIN MISCALCULATES AND THE GREAT INCENDIARY STRIKES

Even in the depths of the quiet period, Samuel Adams believed the British would, in time, provide him with opportunities to reignite the flame of liberty in America. The administration of Prime Minister Lord North did just that in 1773 and 1774. Lord North's bungling allowed Samuel and his political protégés to introduce additional innovative organizational methods. They shifted effective political power in Massachusetts into the hands of the people and, in the process, did rekindle resistance in America. In doing so, Adams came to emphasize that only the people themselves could save America's liberties. When the British subsequently responded to events in Massachusetts by lashing back in anger, Adams "improved" on events by using that response to help fuel the drive that finally produced an intercolonial congress that could lead a united colonial opposition to Britain's assaults on American rights.

The British stumbled into a confrontation with the colonists that finally shattered the quiet period when Lord North's administration devised a plan to rescue the British East India Company from bankruptcy. The company's economic woes arose in part because Americans often consumed smuggled tea. To deal with these interrelated problems, Parliament passed the Tea Act in May 1773. Under this law, the East India Company could consign its tea to a few colonial merchants, and the tea was subject only to the Townshend duty. In practice, that meant the East India Company could meet or even undercut the price of tea smuggled into America. From the British administration's perspective, the Tea Act seemed fair and brilliant. By disposing of tea that might otherwise rot in storage, the East India Company would be saved from bankruptcy while the Americans would drink inexpensive tea. And, by enticing the Americans into buying the company's duted tea, the colonists would be conceding that Parliament could tax them. The administration thus bet that the colonists, then as fond of tea as they later became of coffee, could not resist cheap tea. The politicians realized that their scheme might alienate colonial merchants squeezed out of the tea business. Still, the British government apparently believed that only tea smugglers, then headquartered in Philadelphia and New York City, might howl about the Tea Act.[1]

The North administration badly misjudged the situation. When news of the Tea Act reached America, opposition sprang up throughout the colonies, not just among smugglers. Philadelphia led the way. A massive town meeting of October 16 tore into the Tea Act in eight sharply worded resolutions that blended political principle with concerns about immediate economic interests. The meeting did not, of course, point out that the legislation threatened the livelihood of everyone from merchants to cartmen who smuggled tea. Rather, the meeting asserted that the Tea Act endangered all law-abiding classes and that low-cost tea would come at a horrific price. The reports of the meeting do not indicate whether any speakers raised the specter of the British monopolizing all manner of businesses from selling tea to manufacturing chinaware. But that example might well have come to mind. Philadelphians had already experienced how the British, and even more specifically the British East India Company, could use its economic power to threaten the city's economic well-being. In 1771, after Philadelphians started producing chinaware, the East India Company dropped its price on chinaware so low that only special appeals for support allowed the Philadelphia manufactory to survive. Thus ordinary citizens had reason to believe that the Tea Act might destroy their livelihoods just as it might ruin many honest merchants. And from the early 1770s on, Philadelphia's mechanics, those who manufactured for the local market, were well aware that boycotts could aid them materially. Philadelphia's mass meeting did explicitly assert that the Tea Act endangered America's liberties because it gave renewed vigor to the Townshend duty on tea. Adopting a tactic used against Stamp Act distributors, the Philadelphia meeting proclaimed that merchants who had signed on as consignees for East India Company tea must resign.[2]

Although opposition began in a tea-smuggling port, it spread throughout the colonies. The most dramatic and influential challenges occurred in Massachusetts as a result of innovative actions spearheaded by Samuel Adams. In a circular letter of October 21, prepared for the House's correspondence committee, Adams called the Tea Act a fresh grievance. This scheme, he warned, would destroy the colonial economy and also support Britain's claim that Parliament could bind the colonies in all cases whatsoever. Here and throughout the developing controversy Adams never lost sight of the goals of creating an intercolonial correspondence system and of achieving colonial unity. He asserted that, in the face of the new dangers, the colonies should be united in their sentiments. If any colony experienced an infringement of "the common Rights of all, that Colony should have the united Efforts of all for its Support." Thus he repeated his tireless refrain: all the colonies should establish committees of correspondence to achieve a unified defense of America's liberties.[3]

Because many Americans, not just radicals like Adams, believed the Tea Act threatened them, most Tories and royal officials in America tried to ignore the legislation. Thomas Hutchinson was not interested in doing that. Having had his credibility shredded by the publication of purloined letters, Governor Hutchinson was about to leave office and sail to England. Defending the Tea Act afforded him one last chance to defeat the radicals. And, if needed, the governor had military muscle handy: British troops were still garrisoned at Castle William; British warships dotted Boston's harbor. The governor also had an economic incentive to want the Tea Act implemented. A majority of the East India Company's Boston consignees were related to him by blood or marriage. The governor may not have been spoiling for a fight, but he hardly thirsted after compromise.[4]

Since Hutchinson had canceled its fall session, the General Court could not launch an assault on the Tea Act. So Adams and the Boston Caucus sprang into action. In late October the North End Caucus vowed to stop the sale of East India tea "with our lives and fortunes." On November 2 the members met at the Green Dragon Tavern. They vowed to ensure that no East India Company tea would be landed and established a committee to arrange for the public resignation of the tea consignees at the Liberty Tree at noon the next day. A handbill invited the freemen of Boston and adjacent towns to the proceedings. When the consignees indicated they would not come, the North End Caucus proclaimed itself "intolerably insulted." The members declared that, if the consignees failed to appear, they would be considered "enemies to their Country." On November 3 Boston's church bells started ringing at eleven o'clock, and the town crier called the people to the Liberty Tree. By noon, at least five hundred people—described by a proconsignee source as being mostly "people of the lowest class"—milled around the Liberty Tree, but the consignees refused to play their assigned part in the street drama.

About an hour later, a large crowd appeared before a warehouse where several consignees had gathered. William Molineux, a noted radical merchant who belonged both to the North End Caucus and the city's

committee of correspondence, walked at the head of the crowd. A delegation of nine, with Molineux as the spokesman, confronted the consignees.
Using words the North End Caucus had adopted the night before, Molineux said the people's heavy resentment would fall on the consignees if
they refused to resign. Shortly after the delegation left, some members of
the crowd rushed the warehouse; the merchants hurriedly barricaded themselves in a second-story room. Richard Clarke, a consignee who was there,
labeled this a "mob" action. Yet he also reported that no injuries occurred
and that, within thirty minutes of the altercation, the merchants walked out
of the warehouse, strolled up and down the street, and then went to their
homes—all "without any molestation, saving some insulting behavior from
a few dispicable persons."[5]

When the type of intimidation that had proved effective during the
Stamp Act crisis failed, the caucus turned to the town meeting. On November 5 it considered a petition that proclaimed the Tea Act a nefarious
plot aimed at destroying the colonial trade and exacting a tribute that would
crush the people's liberties. The petition's supporters cleverly asked if anyone wanted to defend the Tea Act. No one did. Pointedly embracing the
ideal of colonial unity, the meeting then unanimously adopted the "Judicious Resolves lately entered into by our worthy Brethren the Citizens of
Philadelphia." The meeting added additional resolves that admitted that
a few Boston merchants had violated the colonial agreement to boycott
all dutied tea. The meeting contended that unfortunate lapse encouraged
the British in their evil plan to use the Tea Act to subvert the colonies'
economy and liberties. Despite the claim that only a few merchants had
behaved so reprehensibly, the fact is the consumption of dutied tea had
soared in Boston during the so-called quiet period. Adams and others who
pushed for the meeting knew the boycott movement needed resuscitation.
Further emulating Philadelphia, the gathering then established committees
to inform the consignees that the town expected them to resign.[6] When
the consignees tried to evade the question by sending a message declaring
they lacked official knowledge of the East India Company's intentions,
the meeting unanimously branded the response "*Daringly Affrontive* to the
Town." The town's committee of correspondence was ordered to dispatch
reports of the meeting's actions to every town in the province.[7]

The town meeting assembled again on November 18 when the arrival
of East India Company tea seemed imminent. The meeting appointed a
new committee to demand the consignees' immediate resignation. When
the committee, which included Adams, visited the consignees, they promised to respond by three o'clock. They met the deadline but continued to

temporize. After unanimously voting the merchants' response unacceptable, the meeting immediately dissolved itself. Hutchinson said "this sudden dissolution struck more terror into the consignees than the most minatory resolves." "The inhabitants of Boston," the governor lamented, "were in possession of the powers of government."[8]

With Adams at its head as chairman, Boston's correspondence committee stretched its powers and assumed leadership of the anti–Tea Act efforts. Promoting the unity Adams considered essential, a subcommittee, on which he served, arranged to meet with the correspondence committees from four adjacent townships. At that November 22 conclave the five groups unanimously approved a circular letter drafted by a subcommittee on which Adams served. The letter described the Tea Act as having been devised for "the purpose of enslaving us." If allowed to stand, the Parliament's "avarice will never be satisfied until our own manufactures, and our own land . . . are taxed to support the extravagance and vices of wretches, whose vileness ought to banish them from the society of men." The act must, therefore, be resisted to save the colony's "happy constitution." Then, on its own, the Boston committee added a lengthy addendum designed to prove that the Tea Act would hurt all Americans economically.[9]

On November 28, as the Boston committee arranged for the printing and distribution of the joint call to action, the *Dartmouth* arrived in Boston harbor with a cargo that included East India Company tea. Although it was a Sunday, Adams convened the Boston committee in emergency session. The members pressured Francis Rotch, the owner of the *Dartmouth*, into withholding official notification of the ship's arrival until the last possible moment, November 30. That short delay allowed the committee time to arrange a gathering to prevent the tea from being landed. Adams quickly penned a circular letter asking the neighboring correspondence committees to ready their towns to help Boston save "this oppressed Country." The committees were invited to meet at Faneuil Hall on Monday at 9 a.m. and urged to bring supporters with them. Soon notices went up around town that cried out, "FRIENDS! BRETHREN! COUNTRYMEN! That worst of all plagues, the detestable tea . . . is now arrived in this harbour, the hour of destruction or manly opposition to the machinations of tyranny stares you in the face; every friend to his country, to himself, to posterity is now called upon to meet."[10]

An observer who attended this gathering later recalled that this mass meeting, which Adams was instrumental in organizing, and which with adjournments stretched over two days, styled itself "*the People.*" The meeting was, as Hutchinson observed, also called "the body." These designations echoed Adams's depiction of the masses as "the body of the people," the potent term rooted in the phraseology of John Locke. Governor Hutchinson admitted that several thousand people came together in an extraordinary meeting so large it had to move to the Old South Meeting House. This gathering of "*the People*" resembled a town meeting. But as an assembly of "*the People*" of greater Boston, it was not bound by the legal restraints imposed on town meetings.

Adams opened the proceedings by introducing a resolution demanding that the tea be returned to England in the same ship that brought it. When Rotch protested that he needed the governor's authorization to do that, Adams offered the *Dartmouth*'s owner some advice. After noting that cargoes and even vessels might be lost in storms, Samuel told Rotch he could argue he "was now compelled by a *Political* Storm to return the Tea." Indeed, he "might safely and honestly protest that he was compelled by a Mob of several Thousands to send the Tea back without the Duty's being paid and that it was necessary for the safety of his Person and Property so to do." Lest Rotch miss his less than subtle message, Samuel added that "the People" now had "the Power in their Hands" and would "carry their Resolutions into Execution at all Events." The meeting approved Adams's resolution, and Rotch promised to seek permission to reship the tea without any duty being paid. To ensure that the tea remained aboard the *Dartmouth*, "the body" created a twenty-five-member watch to guard the cargo. At this juncture, a spokesperson for the consignees announced that they had just received word from the East India Company and needed until the morning to respond. The body agreed to wait until the next day for their answer.[11]

When "*the People*" reconvened on November 30 the sheriff arrived with a proclamation from Governor Hutchinson ordering them to disperse. The governor subsequently reported that the meeting refused to let the sheriff read the announcement "until Mr. Adams signified his acquiescence." As the sheriff read, boos and hisses filled the air. Adams then denounced Hutchinson and his proclamation. Samuel argued that "a free and sensible People when they felt themselves injured would always and had a Right to meet together to consult for their own Safety." Moreover, the gathering was as orderly as the provincial assembly and even, as far as he could learn, of the House of Commons. After unanimously rejecting Hutchinson's demand, the body considered the consignees' letter. Pleading that they faced financial ruin if they returned the tea, the consignees volunteered to have it stored anywhere the people directed. Following motions by Adams, the meeting rejected the consignees' pleas and reaffirmed its demand that the tea be returned. Emphasizing that the tea must, in the meantime, remain under the people's control, Adams sounded a militant note. After remarking that he kept his gun in good working order and by his bedside "as every good Citizen ought," Adams raised the possibility that the meeting's guards might be assaulted. If that happened, he would "not hesitate," and he expected no other person would hesitate, to respond appropriately. The people, pledging to achieve their goals "at the Risque of their Lives and Fortunes," decreed that copies of the meeting's resolves should be sent to England and the seaports of Massachusetts.[12]

What Hutchinson described as these "bodies of the people collected together" frightened him. One saw in the November 30 meeting, he said, "a more determined spirit . . . than in any of the former assemblies of the people." Worse yet, everyone, including the lowest ranks of society, "had an equal voice." Orderly government had, the governor moaned, given way to a democracy of the people, an unsavory development that raised the threat of violent anarchy. Nevertheless, Hutchinson conceded that the mass meeting had been surprisingly orderly; "no eccentrick or irregular motions . . . were suffered to take place." He accounted for that by saying the undertakings "all seemed to have been the plan of a few, it may be, of a single person." Despite Hutchinson's implications, the man he called the greatest incendiary in the colonies did not manage everything by himself. A detailed account of these two later meetings provided by an eyewitness indicates that, while Adams was the most prolific speaker, several others joined him as "chief Speakers" at the mass meetings. Still, Hutchinson hit the mark when he underscored Adams's central role and proclaimed that "Adams never was in greater glory." Friend and foe alike understood that Samuel Adams was the leading figure in greater Boston's fight against the Tea Act.[13]

After the meeting of "*the People*" adjourned on November 29, Adams, speaking for the Boston correspondence committee, had ordered Rotch to have the *Dartmouth* moved to a town wharf. Rotch complied. Although Whigs controlled the tea ship, the custom officials could seize the cargo unless the Townshend duty was paid within twenty days. The grace period would expire at midnight on December 16. The antitea forces in New York and Philadelphia managed to avoid such problems because public pressure forced the consignees to resign and because government officials, wanting to avoid a confrontation, winked at the legal technicalities and allowed the tea to be returned to England without any duty being collected. But, given Governor Hutchinson's unflinching position, Boston's Whigs knew they must act decisively or the tea would be landed and the duty paid.

When two additional tea ships, the *Eleanor* and the *Beaver*, arrived, the local committees of correspondence, which had been holding daily joint meetings, ordered them tied up at Griffin's Wharf near the *Dartmouth*. As December 16, 1773—the day of decision—approached, Hutchinson believed "the town is as furious as in the time of the stamp act." The body of the people assembled again on December 14 and on December 16 to give the consignees and the owners of the tea vessels one last chance to return the tea without the Townshend duty being paid.[14]

The December 16 gathering truly was a meeting of "the body of the people" of greater Boston. Adams perhaps embellished somewhat when he asserted that "by common estimation" the total attending was at least seven thousand. Nevertheless, it is clear that about three thousand of the city's total population of approximately sixteen thousand joined the throng; another two thousand or so, some having traveled twenty miles to attend, came from areas outside Boston. Shortly before 6 p.m., with darkness falling, Francis Rotch reported that Governor Hutchinson would not let him reship the tea without paying the duty. Upon hearing that news, Adams declared that "he could think of nothing further to be done—that they had now done all that they could for the Salvation of their Country." Although it has often been claimed that these words gave the signal to destroy the tea, the evidence is inconclusive. Still, Adams's declaration prompted the shouts, "Boston harbor a tea-pot tonight!"; "Hurrah for Griffin's Wharf!"; "The Mohawks are come!" And right after Adams spoke, men disguised as Indians advanced on Griffin's Wharf. As they marched, Adams and the others who had been especially active in addressing the body remained very conspicuously behind in the Old South Meeting House. Adams even suggested that Dr. Young should present a speech, which he did for fifteen to twenty minutes. Only after the huge gathering of approximately five thousand had dwindled to one hundred or so did any of the leading Whigs stroll down to Griffin's Wharf. By then 90 to 130 men, who did their best to avoid damaging other property, were well into the task of breaking open 342 chests of East India Company tea and pitching it overboard. As a huge crowd watched, the "Mohawks" took about three hours to dump ninety thousand pounds of tea worth roughly £9,000 into the harbor. Adams, who was universally credited or blamed for leading the activities that produced this Boston Tea Party, proclaimed that it brought joy to all—"excepting the disappointed, disconcerted Hutchinson and his tools."[15]

The day after the Tea Party, Adams hastily prepared an account of the events. Paul Revere, who often served as an express rider in the Whig cause, rushed the message south to New York and Philadelphia. He com-

The Boston Tea Party as depicted in the frontispiece engraving of Francis S. Drake's Tea Leaves *(Boston: A. O. Crane, 1884).*

pleted the arduous round-trip by December 27. Samuel maintained that the news of the Boston Tea Party put starch into New York's antitea efforts. In late December, commenting on the fact that numerous areas of the colonies adamantly opposed implementation of the Tea Act, Adams happily asserted that the British government "could not have devised a more effectual Measure to unite the Colonies."[16]

Samuel Adams had ample reason to celebrate in late 1773. Throughout the quiet period, when so many other notable Whigs temporized, Adams had unrelentingly persevered in defending America's liberties and in trying to awaken his fellow Americans to the threats against their freedom. In the process, Adams took the leading role in forging a Massachusetts committee-of-correspondence network and in setting America on the road to developing a similar intercolonial system. He had played a crucial role in shattering the quiet period in Massachusetts and then in the other colonies. Now the rekindled flame of resistance and the growing unity among Americans might light the way to independence. Nevertheless, Adams understood that the British could douse the flames if they chose. As he and others in the colonies and Great Britain had repeatedly said, the change in British imperial policy in 1763 set the time of troubles in motion. If the British returned to the imperial system as it existed in 1763, the time of troubles would end no matter what the great incendiary did. Of course, to do that, the British would have to respond with moderation to the Boston Tea Party and would effectively have to back away from their claim that Parliament could bind the colonies in all cases whatsoever. Adams was sure the British would not do that. He believed they would continue to provide issues that, once "improved," might allow the newly established committee of correspondence networks to achieve the colonial unity he championed.[17]

Although Bostonians worried about how Britain would react to the Tea Party, that response would not be known for weeks or even months. In the meantime, fearing to do otherwise, Governor Hutchinson allowed the General Court to meet in late January. Adams quickly pushed the hot-button issue of judges' pay. By mid-February of 1774 the House had convinced every superior-court judge except Chief Justice Peter Oliver to agree that only the legislature could pay them. When Oliver refused to yield, the House impeached him as "an Enemy to the Constitution of this Province" and asked the governor in Council to remove him. Hutchinson naturally refused. As the governor recounted it, Adams devised a way around the problem. He visited the Council room as the head of a House committee; when officially informed that the governor was absent, Samuel maintained that he was presumed to be present. Adams's innovative argument served as the pretense for claiming that the House had impeached the chief justice in the presence of the governor and his Council.[18]

Adams soon engineered even more audacious assaults on established political practices. On March 7 the House adopted a resolve Adams drafted that claimed the governor and Council constituted a supreme court possessing the power to remove judges for crimes and misdemeanors. It went a giant step further by asserting that the powers of the Massachusetts governor and Council were so blended that the governor needed the Council's approval to negate laws. When this resolve was matched with Adams's assertion that the governor could be presumed to be in Council even when he was not, it meant that the governor's powers would effectively be transferred to the Council. These arguments continued Adams's extraordinary efforts to shift authority from royal officials to the people or to legal entities responsive to the people. His arguments were not merely radical, they were revolutionary and subversive.[19]

To fend off what he perceived as an Adams-led takeover of the government, Hutchinson, without warning, dispatched a message dissolving the legislature. Learning that the governor's directive was being read to the Council, the representatives employed a delaying tactic that proved useful more than once. After locking the door, they quickly endorsed several Whig measures. They declared that Hutchinson had opposed impeaching

Oliver because the governor was also in the monarch's pay. In addition, the representatives instructed their correspondence committee to send letters outlining the citizens' grievances to the other colonies and to the House's agent, Benjamin Franklin. Only then did the legislators open the door so the governor's message could be read.[20]

Before the winter legislative session was so abruptly terminated, Adams had once again found a way to turn an attack on the House's committee of correspondence to the Whigs' benefit. When the General Court reconvened in late January 1774 Hutchinson informed the legislators that the king disapproved of the House permitting a correspondence committee to function when the legislature was not in session. A House committee headed by Adams countered with a vigorous defense of the committee and the rights of all Americans. Adams, who authored the committee's response, pointedly declared that "the common Rights of the American Subjects" continued to face attack when colonial legislatures were not in session. Moreover, royal governors could call or dismiss legislatures whenever they desired; therefore, correspondence committees were necessary so the colonies could effectively unite to obtain redress of grievances. According to Adams, these committees helped achieve what he called the great end of government, which was "the Safety and Welfare of the People."[21]

Boston's committee of correspondence was already proving Adams's point by using the Tea Party as a reason for initiating regular exchanges with other New England colonies. This interchange of messages inspired William Goddard, who had printing interests in Philadelphia and Baltimore, to conspire with the Boston Committee of Correspondence, and especially with Samuel Adams, to create an American-run postal system. It would replace the tax-supported, and thus from the committee's view unconstitutional, royal mail system with a post office established, as Adams phrased it, "upon constitutional Principles." Ten days after Goddard arrived in Boston, the correspondence committee sent out a circular letter written by Adams. Speaking for the committee, he emphasized that Goddard's plan would do much more than counter an obnoxious, unconstitutional revenue act; the plan would help promote the necessary "Union of the Colonies" and also keep Whig communications safe from prying British eyes. Aided by this endorsement, Goddard quickly had the American postal system in operation from Baltimore northward. In the summer he extended it south of Baltimore. Anticipating these developments, Adams seemed justified in proclaiming in late March 1774 that "Colony communicates freely with Colony" and that colonial opposition to Britain's imperial policies had "become systematical." However, Samuel exaggerated when he added that the "whole continent is now become united in sentiment and opposition to tyranny."[22]

The creation of an intercontinental-correspondence network and the development of an American-run mail system were both part of a long-time effort by Adams and many other Whigs to develop a unified colonial response to the assault on American liberties. Believing America must also "cultivate and strengthen an Union" in the face of Britain's evil policies, Adams raised his voice in the growing chorus of advocates for holding an intercolonial congress. He had publicly espoused this idea for more than a year. John Hancock gave further support to the idea when he delivered the 1774 Boston Massacre oration, an oration Adams and others helped compose. In April, writing to Arthur Lee in London and probably expecting his comments would be shared, Samuel rhapsodized that "there is now a fairer prospect than ever of Union among the Colonies."[23]

Realizing the Tea Party might be viewed as criminal vandalism and thus undermine efforts to present a united colonial response to Britain's actions, Adams devoted considerable time to explaining and defending it. Using imagery he often employed, he candidly told James Warren that his goals were to "put our Enemies in the wrong" and "to be ready *for all Events*, that *we may make the best Improvement of them*." When writing for the Boston committee or crafting personal letters, Adams stressed that the Bostonians, aided by many from the countryside, "acted upon pure & upright Principle." The people did not want to destroy the tea, but the intransigence of the consignees, the customs officials, and especially of Thomas Hutchinson left them no choice. Moreover, since nothing but the tea had been destroyed, the Tea Party was not the work of a lawless multitude but "the people's rising in the necessary defence of their liberties."[24] While he did not specifically mention the Tea Party in a lengthy review of colonial grievances he sent to Benjamin Franklin, Adams reiterated the point that the colonists were merely responding to gross provocations. And once again he blamed the troubles on evil men in England and in the America. The colonists "wish for nothing more than permanent union with her [the Parent Country] upon the condition of equal liberty." That equal liberty involved protecting each colony's "Constitution," for the American people would never let the British "govern them arbitrarily, or without known and stipulated Rules." Despite the politically necessary claim of a desire to have permanent union with Great Britain, Adams embraced the idea of an autonomous America by boldly asserted that in America "Britain and the Colonies are considered as distinct Governments under the King." Actually, that view was not commonly held; it was a novel argument being advanced by only a very few radicals such as Samuel Adams and his cousin John.[25]

The Whig message that Great Britain was threatening America's liberty was spread by more than words. Paul Revere literally illustrated that, and Samuel Adams's ever-growing notoriety, when he engraved an image of Adams that appeared in the *Royal American Magazine* in April 1774. Despite its title, the *Royal American Magazine*, published in Boston, was a thoroughly Whig organ. Revere's engraving bristled with symbolism. The trumpeting angel represents fame; the smiling female figure of liberty with her liberty cap on a pole, stands on a thick volume of "Laws to Enslave

Paul Revere frontispiece engraving of "Mr. Samuel Adams" for the Royal American Magazine *of April 1774. Courtesy of the American Antiquarian Society.*

America"; a soldier of the Twenty-ninth Regiment, associated with the infamous Boston Massacre, lies on the ground clutching a serpent, while standing above him is a figure seemingly representative of Great Britain. Beneath the bust of Adams, one sees that he is both defending and relying on the great symbol of English liberty: the Magna Carta. Revere's thoroughly political depiction of Adams, like Samuel's own words, conveyed the message that Great Britain should stop assaulting American liberty.[26]

Adams believed that nothing would convince the British that they must abandon their theory of parliamentary supremacy if they wanted peace. He was sure they would not compromise. He even feared that the British might try to trick Americans by proposing that Parliament would exercise its full powers only in case of absolute necessity. And "to induce us to be thus submissive beyond the bounds of reason & Safety their Lordships will condescend to be familiar with us and treat us with Cakes & Sugar plumbs." That is why, as America awaited Britain's response to the Tea Party, Adams warned James Warren that the Whigs must be ready for anything.[27]

While he spoke of being prepared for any response, Adams assumed the British would react brutally to the Tea Party. At a time when destruction of private property could be a hanging offense, the Tea Party would surely outrage the British. Benjamin Franklin, the colony's agent, reflected the general view when he counseled the Bostonians to pay for the tea. Upon learning this, Adams reportedly remarked, "Franklin may be a good philosopher, but he is a bungling politician."[28]

British officials did turn livid when they learned about the Tea Party. Their outrage stemmed from more than the destruction of private property, horrendous as that was considered. The Tea Party proved all the more galling because it occurred in Boston, long considered the hotbed of sedition. Heartily supported by George III himself, Lord North's administration proclaimed Great Britain must take "effectual steps . . . to secure the Dependence of the Colonies on the Mother Country." Concluding that prior concessions had been a mistake, most British politicians accepted Prime Minister Lord North's argument that "we are now to establish our authority, or give it up entirely." The Earl of Dartmouth, who headed Britain's American Department, concurred. He concluded that, if the Americans refused to obey Parliament's laws, "they say in effect that they will no longer be a part of the British Empire." Even longtime defenders of the Americans, including Colonel Isaac Barré, agreed the Bostonians must be punished. The result was the Boston Port Act, the first of Britain's Coercive Acts. Except for allowing limited local shipping, it closed the port of Boston as of June 1, 1774. The port could not be reopened until several conditions were met. Boston must compensate the East India Company. In addition, the king had to determine that trade could be carried on safely and the customs officials could function without fearing for their lives. To tighten the screws of punishment, the Port Act also stipulated that Massachusetts's capital and the meeting place of the General Court would be shifted from Boston to Salem as of June 1. In addition, because Hutchinson had asked to be replaced, the British had another way to make Bostonians toe the line. George III appointed General Thomas Gage, commander of the British army in America, as the new royal governor.[29]

"The Bostonians in Distress" (London: Printed for R. Sayer and J. Bennett, November 19, 1774). Courtesy of the Library of Congress.

An English political cartoonist imaginatively illustrated how British officials anticipated the administration's firm response to the Tea Party would play out. The engraver's "The Bostonians in Distress" mocked the symbolism of the "Liberty Tree" as a rallying place for anti-British action by depicting Bostonians held captive in a cage dangling from the tree. Surrounded by British redcoats and cannon, the quarrelsome colonists were reduced to eating fish given to them by smiling, almost smirking, British jack tars. The desperately hungry Bostonians gobble down the fish and, seemingly in exchange, offer a bundle of "Promises"—one assumes promising better behavior. Aware of the Bostonians' reputation for being deeply religious, the cartoonist cited the section of Psalm 107 that concerns "Fools" who, "because of their transgression, and because of their iniquities, are afflicted." Expecting his readers to know the reference, the artist had one of the caged miscreants utter another part of the Psalm: "Then they cried unto the LORD in their trouble, *and* he saved them out of their distresses." Thus, in this cartoonist's mind, British might would force the foolish, immoral Bostonians to yield, and God intended them to yield.[30]

General Gage and the text of the Port Act arrived in early May, just after Boston's representatives to the House had been easily reelected. Flexing its now considerable political muscle and striving for a show of unity, Boston's correspondence committee quickly arranged for a May 12 joint meeting with the committees of eight neighboring towns. Just before that gathering opened, John Bowler, the speaker of the Rhode Island House of Representatives, informed the Bostonians that every colonial assembly except Nova Scotia's had indicated it would join in united action for "preserving the Liberties and promoting the Union of the American Colonies." This electrifying news heightened the possibility that the colonists might mount a truly unified effort to assist Boston and in the process forge a solid American resistance.[31]

The convention of towns chose Adams as chairman and approved sending all the colonies and America's port cities a circular letter he had written. The letter built on the premise that "Boston is now Suffering the stroke of Vengeance in the Common cause of America." If Boston failed to resist, every American colony would find its freedom endangered. Indeed, the Port Act was "Intended to intimidate and subdue the Spirits of all America." But "the joint efforts of all" could frustrate this cruel act. The greater Boston committee also endorsed a circular letter that would be forwarded to all Massachusetts towns. Although it did not specifically call for an economic boycott, the letter suggested as much by contending that, if America stopped trading with Great Britain, "the British manufacturer must *emigrate* or *starve*."[32]

The Boston Town Meeting convened in special session the next day and endorsed the proposals advanced by the greater Boston committee. With Adams serving as moderator, the meeting also voted to send a circular letter not just to Massachusetts towns but to all the colonies as well. The town meeting agreed unanimously to exhort all the colonies to "come into a joint Resolution." The colonists should agree that until Parliament repealed the Boston Port Act they would neither import anything from Great Britain nor export anything to Great Britain or the West Indies. Doing this would "prove the Salvation of North America & her Liberties." On the other hand, if the colonies carried on trade as usual, "the most Odious Oppression" would likely crush "Justice, Social Happiness & Freedom" in America. The Bostonians thus asked other colonists voluntarily to suffer Boston's fate because doing so would defend all the colonies. The meeting instructed Adams to have the news of its actions carried to the seaports and other American colonies. Paul Revere rushed south with the call for waging economic warfare.[33]

In letters to Whig colleagues in various colonies Adams spelled out the logic behind the movement for commercial warfare. Americans should take the offensive by making Britain "share in the miseries which she has unrighteously brought upon us." America should adopt a nonimportation and nonconsumption program so British manufacturers as well as British merchants would suffer. Adams believed a trade suspension "should be pushd as far as it will go & as speedily as possible." And the colonists could not delay launching their economic reprisals until an intercolonial congress met. His theme became "A Congress is of absolute Necessity," but "the present Emergency" required the immediate adoption of economic warfare.

Adams emphasized that America's merchants could not be entrusted with carrying out the suspension of trade. Because their immediate self-interests were at stake, some merchants would hold back; others would actively oppose the endeavor. As a result, Adams increasingly counted on the "yeomanry"—as evidenced in the meetings of "the body of the people"—to make nonimportation and nonexportation work. He told Charles Thompson, a leading Philadelphia radical, that only the yeomanry's virtue could "finally save this Country." He voiced the same thoughts to Silas Deane, a Connecticut Whig. The fact was, he maintained, a suspension of trade could achieve great success only if America's yeomanry enforced it. And if the plan was to have any chance of success, the colonies must aid Boston quickly lest "Misery and Want" cause the people "to yield to Tyranny."[34]

In late May of 1774, with Adams in the moderator's chair, Boston's town meeting began waging economic warfare on the mother country. The meeting placed Adams at the head of a committee to prepare a "Non-Consumption agreement" and then furnish every Boston family with a copy. The agreement should call on Bostonians to abstain from buying any British-manufactured goods that could be obtained from local producers. Reflecting Adams's belief that the yeomanry must spearhead the economic resistance, each family should "totally desert those who shall Counter-work the Salutary Measures of the Town." The town's correspondence committee was to inform the rest of Massachusetts of these actions so the nonconsumption movement could spread throughout the province.[35]

By the time Boston produced its nonconsumption agreement, talk of holding an all-colonial congress percolated throughout the colonies. Adams planned to get the newly convened General Court, which opened on May 25, to endorse and arrange for the congress. But Governor Gage suddenly adjourned the legislature on May 28 and told it to reconvene in Salem on June 7. This unexpected development prevented Adams from raising the issue. During the brief recess, however, Samuel unlimbered his pen and touted the idea that a congress must be held. He even asked Silas Deane if Connecticut's assembly could postpone its adjournment so the two colonies might act in concert in promoting a congress.[36]

When he wrote to William Checkley, a friend and relative of his first wife, to congratulate him on the birth of a daughter, Adams waxed eloquent on the possibilities of a united American resistance. Confronted with "the Malice of Tyranny," he found it "a consolatory thought, that an Empire is rising in America." He hinted at his own hankering after independence when he added that Britain "by her multiplied oppressions is now accelerating that Independenency of the Colonies which she so much dreads, and which in the process of time must take place."

Dwelling on the influence of the birth of a child, Samuel speculated that the new father had added cause to participate "in the Struggles of your Country, as you hope your Infant will outlive you, and share in the Event." "We live in an important Period, & have a post to maintain, to desert which would be an unpardonable Crime, and would entail upon us the Curses of posterity." The allusion to posterity, so common in Adams's writings, is telling. It suggests that, while Adams did not yearn for material prosperity, he did want the approbation of posterity. And he believed, as he had said before, that "the Man who nobly vindicates the Rights of his

Country & Mankind shall stand foremost in the List of fame." By pressing for immediate economic reprisals against Great Britain and by championing a colonial congress to unify America's resistance, Adams believed he was fulfilling his duty to posterity and helping to ensure his historical immortality.[37]

The situation changed dramatically before the General Court could reconvene in Salem. On June 1, which ironically was the day Thomas Hutchinson sailed for England, never to return, the Boston Port Act took effect. When the town's clocks struck high noon, the port was officially closed. To mark the sorrowful day, Bostonians walked the streets in mourning attire and the city's church bells tolled. As Adams hoped they would, many Americans expressed solidarity with Boston. Christopher Gadsden, Adams's longtime South Carolina correspondent, wrote on behalf of the Charleston committee of correspondence. Saying we "most sincerely feel for and sympathize" with you in Boston, the committee members stressed they were "thoroughly sensible that you are suffering for your activity and Spirit in the Common Cause" of all Americans. The Charlestonians pledged to send aid equivalent to one thousand barrels of rice.

In Virginia the House of Burgesses proclaimed that to defend American rights the people should express support for "the City of *Boston*, in our Sister Colony of *Massachusetts*." To do that, the Burgesses passed a resolution consciously modeled on Puritan forms. It decreed that Virginians should "set apart" June 1 "as a Day of Fasting, Humiliation, and Prayer." The Burgesses turned those words into symbolic action. They gathered together at ten o'clock on the morning of June 1 and, led by their speaker and the Mace, marched solemnly to the Williamsburg church where they heard a prayer and sermon "suitable to the Occasion." The people of Norfolk sent encouraging words. "Our hearts are warmed with affection for you"; the Bostonians could "be assured we consider you as suffering in the common cause, and look upon ourselves as bound by the most sacred ties to support you."

Colonists elsewhere expressed similar sentiments. Annapolis and Queen's County in Maryland each issued lengthy statements saying the Bostonians were suffering to defend the rights of all Americans. Christopher Marshall, an ardent Philadelphia Whig who was soon working with Samuel Adams, described how his city responded on what he called "the day when the cruel act for blocking up the harbor of Boston took effect." Many Philadelphians expressed their support for the Bostonians by shutting their shops and staying close to home. The bells of Christ Church were muffled "and rung a solemn peal at intervals, from morning till night." Ships' flags flew at half-mast. The city's various houses of worship were crowded, and people listened to divine services and discourses appropriate to the occasion. Repeating almost verbatim what the *Pennsylvania Packet* reported, Marshall remarked that "sorrow, mixed with indignation, seemed pictured in the countenance of the inhabitants and indeed the whole city wore the aspect of deep distress." Despite such verbal support and pledges of aid, June 1, 1774, was a bad day for Boston. June 2 was worse.[38]

On June 2 Bostonians learned that Parliament had passed two additional Coercive Acts. The editors of the *Boston Gazette* published the texts four days later. The Massachusetts Government Act, flagrantly overriding Massachusetts's 1691 charter, decreed that the provincial Council would now be appointed, not elected. And while the charter accorded the councilors a significant role in selecting and dismissing provincial officials, the new act made the royal governor solely responsible for appointing and dismissing all judges, sheriffs, and other magistrates, including justices of the peace. In addition juries could now be selected by the appointed sheriffs rather than, as they had been, elected. The law was also designed to emasculate the Massachusetts town meeting as a forum for protesting British policies. As of August 1, 1774, except for the annual meeting to elect local officials, no town meeting could occur unless the governor preapproved the agenda. The second piece of legislation, an act "for the impartial Administration of Justice," struck most colonists as anything but impartial. Under this law, if the governor so directed, the trial of anyone charged with committing a crime—including murder—while suppressing a riot in Massachusetts could be shifted to another colony or even to Great Britain.[39]

Writing to Richard Henry Lee, an infuriated Samuel Adams labeled the Massachusetts Government Act an unabashed attempt "to destroy our free Constitution" and replace it with "an absolute Government." Knowing the Virginian would share his letter, Adams ruminated about the frightening possibility of the British using the act "as a model of Government" for "the whole Continent." As for the so-called Administration of Justice Act, it was merely a way of "screening from Punishment any Soldier who shall Murder an American for asserting his Right[s]." Adams exclaimed that the Bostonians were not "in the least Degree intimidated." And they were buoyed by the fact that each day brought new evidence that all the colonies considered them as suffering in the common cause. Yet again promoting the ideal of the colonies acting as one, he asserted that Lord North had not counted on "the Effects of an Union." Samuel expressed the hope that a general congress would be held and that "America" would "agree in one general Bill of Rights."[40]

Confronted with the shocking new assaults on colonial rights, Boston's correspondence committee, acting on its own authority, fashioned what it called a Solemn League and Covenant. That name alluded to an alliance formed against King Charles I during the English Civil War. The plan, apparently authored principally by Dr. Joseph Warren, Adams's closest friend and political ally, was sent off to all Massachusetts towns on June 8. The Solemn League and Covenant laid out a strident program of economic warfare. The people should come together and solemnly pledge to stop all commerce with Great Britain. No one should buy any British imports that arrived in America after August 31. To promote colonial manufacturing, as of October 1 no one should even use anything manufactured in Britain. The names of persons who refused to sign this or a similar pledge should be published so the patriots could boycott and ostracize them—*forever.* This agreement would remain in force until Parliament rescinded the Port Act and restored Massachusetts's charter rights.

The Solemn League and Covenant translated Adams's pronouncements about the yeomanry saving America into an action program. The people, not the merchants, would wield the effective power in an economic war to safeguard American rights. Significantly, Adams and the other committee members tried to make it appear that their plan originated in the countryside. Tories and merchants, who generally denounced the plan, saw through that sham. On June 17 the town meeting endorsed the committee's actions and directed the committee to write to all the other colonies to inform them of Boston's spirited resistance through the nonconsumption agreement. The communication should also emphasize that Boston was "waiting with anxious Expectations for the Result of a Continental Congress; whose Meeting we impatiently desire, . . . & in whose Determinations we shall chearfully acquiesce." Moderates tried to counterattack ten days later by asking the town meeting to censure and disband its correspondence committee. Adams left his post as moderator long enough to defend the committee. The debate stretched on so long that the meeting adjourned until the next day when the anticommittee resolution lost "by a great Majority." The town meeting then considered a statement thanking the committee for its "upright Intentions" and "honest Zeal." The official records of the meeting graphically highlighted that the statement praising the committee passed "by a *Vast Majority*."[41]

As Adams helped formulate the Solemn League, he wondered whether Americans would see the Massachusetts Government Act and the Administration of Justice Act as attacks on one colony or "as part of a plan to reduce them all to Slavery." Given Adams's theory that a political leader could not arouse the people unless they believed their rights were endangered, that was a crucial question. Since Adams and other radicals already believed a conspiracy was afoot to trample America's liberties, the question became, What would America's political moderates, including those with Tory leanings, think of the two new acts? The response of John Rowe was typical and revealing. Although a Whig, Rowe was also a political trimmer and wealthy Boston merchant who had socialized amiably with Governor Hutchinson. Rowe's diary consists mainly of social chitchat. When commenting on political issues, he rarely wrote more than a brief line or two offering little or no analysis. His June 1 entry on the Boston Port Act taking effect fits that description. But when he learned about the Massachusetts Government Act a day later, Rowe confided to his diary that the "Act strikes the very Charter Granted to this Province by King William & Queen Mary." He predicted that the act would produce "many Evils" in Massachusetts "& sour the minds of most of the Inhabitants thereof. I am afraid of the Consequences that this Act will Produce. I wish for Harmony & Peace between Great Britain Our Mother Country & the Colonies— but the Time is far off. The People have done amiss & no sober man can vindicate their Conduct [in the Tea Party affair] but the Revenge of the [British] Ministry is too severe."[42]

When a man like John Rowe agreed with Samuel Adams that the British had mounted an unreasonable assault on basic rights, it suggested the great mass of colonists likely believed Great Britain was threatening American liberties. And these new Coercive Acts *did* threaten American liberty. The Administration of Justice Act swept aside the ideal of trials by local juries, a principle that stretched back to the Magna Carta of 1215. The Massachusetts Government Act was more frightening. If Parliament could unilaterally alter the Massachusetts Charter, it could, as Adams argued, do the same with any colonial charter. Even Edward Shippen, a moderate Pennsylvania Tory, graphically warned that the acts aimed at Massachusetts also contained the names of the other colonies "written with lime juice & only want the heat of fire to make them legible." If that happened, the colonial charters, which most Americans considered their constitutions, could offer no real protection against tyrannical actions. Because these latest in what came to be called the Intolerable Acts were perceived as genuine threats to all the colonies, the warnings Adams had long been enunciating resonated throughout the colonies.[43]

The two new Intolerable Acts heightened support for holding an intercolonial congress. Adams's political adroitness in helping ensure that the congress took place provides a case study of how he carried the workings

of the Boston Caucus into legislative endeavors. On June 9, having protested against being forced to assemble in Salem, the Massachusetts House
placed Adams at the head of a nine-member Committee on the State of the
Province and charged it to give special consideration to the Port Act. Every
committee member except Daniel Leonard, who had increasingly come
under the sway of the pro-British court party, was a committed Whig.
Fearing Leonard would divulge their radical plans so Governor Gage could
quickly dissolve the legislature, Adams and the rest of the members hid their
intentions. Robert Treat Paine, a committee member, who recounted the
events decades later, explained how it was done. When the committee held
its regular meetings, the members focused on how to respond to the Port
Bill, which demanded that Boston pay for the tea destroyed during the Tea
Party. To throw Leonard off guard, the other committee members "talkd
very favorably of paying for the tea" because the cost of doing so would
be small when measured against the "Sufferings" the Port Bill inflicted on
Boston. Paine marveled that "it would be hard to describe the Smooth &
placid Observations by Mr. S. Adams, Saying it was an irritating affair,
& must be handled Cautiously; that the people must have time to think &
form their minds, & that hurrying the matter would certainly create such
an Opposition [to paying for the tea] as would defeat the matter; & many
Observations of this kind." The other Whigs on the committee took the
same line, and soon Leonard, "the Oblique member of that Committee,"
came to think the members would recommend "obedience to the *Port
Bill*." This charade unfolded in three afternoon meetings that extended into
the early evenings.

While Leonard was thus being beguiled, what Paine called "Another
Committee of vastly more importance" began operating in secret. Paine
indicated that only those House members who had clearly proven "their
opposition to the British Aggressions of Tyrannick Govt." were allowed to
attend. As soon as the meetings of the Committee on the State of the Province adjourned for the evening, all of its members, except Leonard, rushed
to the room where a "Self Created Committee" met. Once Adams and the
others arrived, the doors were closed and "all the Subjects of Grievances"
"freely & fully" debated. After several evenings of this, the self-created
committee spelled out a detailed plan of action. The Massachusetts House
should arrange for holding a "General Congress of all the Colonies to meet
on the Subject of their Grievances." Following Adams's usual practice, a
set of resolves to achieve this objective were crafted for presentation to the
House. The secret committee then selected the five members it wanted
Massachusetts to send to the general congress: James Bowdoin, Samuel

Adams, Thomas Cushing, John Adams, and Robert Treat Paine. The committee also agreed that the cost of sending these delegates should be covered by an assessment levied on a number of towns. The final order of business concerned how this plan, which Paine emphasized "was as yet a profound secret," could be implemented. Since the proposals needed to be submitted to the House, Leonard would have to be gotten out of the way lest he tell the governor who could then derail the Whig's carefully formulated scheme. Paine, who like Leonard practiced law in Bristol County, undertook the task. He convinced Leonard that they should ride to Taunton to help with cases at what was a very busy time for the Bristol Court of Sessions. Paine assured Leonard they could do this and return to the General Court before any important business came up for action. Leonard agreed, and the two rode out of Boston on Saturday, June 11, to spend the next week in Taunton.[44]

With Leonard safely away, and after getting the gallery cleared and the House door shut and locked, Adams addressed the House on June 17. Ostensibly speaking for the Committee on the State of the Province, Adams proposed that all colonies send delegates to a congress that would convene in Philadelphia on September 1, 1774. The congressmen would deliberate and recommend measures "for the Recovery and Establishment of their just Rights and Liberties civil and religious, and the Restoration of Union and Harmony between Great-Britain and the Colonies." Having agreed that a circular letter containing this resolution would be forwarded to every colony, the House chose five men to represent Massachusetts at the congress: Thomas Cushing, Samuel Adams, John Adams, Robert Treat Paine, and James Bowdoin, who declined the appointment due to ill health. Knowing Governor Gage would not authorize spending £500 to pay the delegates' expenses, the House took the extraordinary step devised by the secret Whig committee. The representatives recommended that Massachusetts's towns use their regular tax base to determine their share of the £500 and then forward that sum to Cushing in Boston. Doing that removed the governor from the taxing process and denied him his charter-given veto power. Thus, the House took the actions scripted by the Adams-led self-created committee that had itself emulated the Boston Caucus.

Sometime during these June 17 deliberations a House member feigned illness, was allowed to leave, and rushed to alert Gage to what was happening. The governor hastily scrawled an order dissolving the General Court and sent his secretary, Thomas Flucker, to read it to the House. But with Adams in possession of the key, Gage's secretary could do nothing more than read the governor's directive before the locked chamber door. As

Flucker rambled on in vain, the representatives, having completed arrangements for a congress, passed a resolution supporting economic warfare. The House urged the people to stop consuming British goods "until the publick Grievances of America shall be radically and totally redressed." Only then was the door unlocked and opened so Flucker could again read Gage's order dissolving the legislature. Leonard learned of these dramatic developments as he was riding back to Boston.[45]

Shortly after he dismissed the legislature, Governor Gage reportedly tried doing what Thomas Hutchinson had declared impossible—bribing Samuel Adams into forsaking his principles. In June 1774 Gage had two reasons to hope Adams might be bought off. As part of an ongoing military buildup, army units arrived in midmonth and bivouacked on Boston Common. That deployment helped fuel a growing speculation that Adams, and others too, would be seized and whisked to England for trial and punishment. Indeed, Samuel's political ally John Hawley of Northhampton was soon saying that Samuel should be warned that "our top Tories here give out most confidently, that he will certainly be taken up before the Congress." The possibility of being hauled away to an uncertain fate blended with a second consideration: the Adams family's shaky economic position. Since Adams was relatively poor for a person of his public stature, the loss of his salary as clerk of the House left questions about how the Adams family would subsist. That was the situation in late June when, according to Hannah Adams, Gage sent a Colonel Fenton to visit her father. Fenton verbally presented Gage's confidential offer. If Adams stopped opposing Britain's policies, he would receive "great personal advantages" and "make his peace with the King." As Hannah recounted it years later, having heard this proposal, her father responded, "Sir, I trust I have long since made my peace with the King of kings. No personal consideration shall induce me to abandon the righteous cause of my country. Tell Governor Gage it is the advice of Samuel Adams to him no longer to insult the feelings of an exasperated people." While it is not clear if it happened during this exchange, there is credible evidence that at some point the British offered Adams the princely sum of at least £1,000 a year during his lifetime and possibly for that of his son too. As his rebuke of Gage's emissary reveals, Samuel treated such offers with contempt.[46]

Given the political tradition of preferment, the conditions in late June 1774, and his lack of knowledge about Adams, it made sense for Gage to tender Adams an offer. Thomas Hutchinson had known better. Neither threats nor inducements would dissuade Adams. They would not work for the same reason Samuel Adams could not, in the quiet period, emulate John

Adams and John Hancock and eschew politics to pursue personal economic gain. Samuel meant what he repeatedly said in public and private: he believed he had a duty to defend the people's constitution and liberties. The British assault on the Massachusetts Charter, a constitution that protected the people's rights, represented for Adams both an immediate political horror and the culmination of a conspiracy to destroy colonial liberty. Because many colonists were coming to share Adams's views, colony after colony agreed to attend the congress Massachusetts said should meet in Philadelphia on September 1. Thus, as the summer unfolded, Adams had reason to believe, as he said in mid-July, that the colonies would create "one firm Band of Opposition to the oppressive Measures of the British Administration." When he wrote that in a letter to a Georgia Whig, Samuel signed it as "Your Friend and Fellow Countryman." And he used the same nationalistic close when writing to Whigs in Pennsylvania, Virginia, and South Carolina.[47]

During that summer of 1774 Adams also diligently labored to make it possible for Bostonians to hold out against Britain's attempt to force them into submission through misery and want. He actively sought charitable donations from throughout the colonies and helped distribute the contributions in greater Boston. Fearing a lack of jobs might spark counterproductive violence, he also helped increase employment opportunities, especially for the poor. To do that, the Boston Town Meeting launched several public-works projects.[48]

In August, as he prepared to attend the intercolonial congress, Adams himself became the beneficiary of an anonymous gift, a complete gentleman's wardrobe. John Andrews, a Boston merchant who described the arrival of the clothes and accessories, noted that Adams also received a gift of money. In addition, individuals replaced the family's dilapidated barn and repaired the Adams home. Writing to a friend, Andrews said he mentioned the examples of generosity bestowed on Adams "to show you how much he is esteemed here. They value him for his *good* sense, *great* abilities, *amazing* fortitude, *noble* resolution, and *undaunted* courage."[49]

While others worried about his appearance and his family's comfort, Adams thought about keeping an organized resistance going in Massachusetts. He helped arrange a convention of towns like the one he had promoted in 1768 to oppose the arrival of British troops. To circumvent the prohibition against unapproved town meetings, Adams and Dr. Warren devised a plan for holding county meetings. By the end of August, with Dr. Warren being the driving force, delegates from four counties had produced an outline for a provincial congress that would effectively become the extralegal government of the colony. Significantly, the delegates suggested that the provincial congress should urge the people to sharpen their military training and preparedness.[50] As he prepared to travel to Philadelphia to attend the intercolonial congress, Adams knew he could count on Dr. Warren and other ardent Whigs to keep the Massachusetts flame of resistance alight.

7

THE HELMSMAN OF
AMERICAN INDEPENDENCE

When Samuel Adams and the other Massachusetts delegates climbed aboard a coach on August 10, 1774, for the journey to Philadelphia to attend the Continental Congress, he was leaving Massachusetts for the first time in his life. He hoped the congress would fashion a unified and vigorous resistance that would lead to independence. But, contemplating what awaited him in Philadelphia, Samuel knew that two decidedly different groups had promoted the congress. Radical Whigs wanted the congress to pursue the kind of vigorous resistance embodied in the Solemn League and Covenant. On the other hand, moderates, including most merchants in the major cities, did not want to suffer severe business losses or flirt with rebellion. In fact, some moderates, especially those in New York, had pushed for a congress to undermine the radicals' demands for initiating economic conflict with the British. As the Massachusetts delegates traveled south and conversed with other colonial leaders during their nineteen-day trip and then mingled with other delegates once they arrived in Philadelphia on August 29, it became clear that ardent Whigs and moderates had different agendas. The congress would surely turn into a crucial test of strength between the groups.

The situation proved all the more nettlesome because Samuel Adams and his fellow Massachusetts delegates had to walk a political tightrope that figuratively stretched from backcountry Massachusetts to Philadelphia. The delegates wanted their province to resist the British actively, and they wanted the congress to adopt vigorous countermeasures against Britain. At the same time, the Massachusetts contingent believed that attaining colonial unity, especially among the congressional delegates, was essential to the American cause; therefore, to keep timid Whigs and Tories from undermining unity, the people of Massachusetts must show prudence and forbearance.

But Massachusetts's landholders were threatening to cast prudence and forbearance aside. Adams had long maintained that Britain's claims of parliamentary supremacy could endanger the colonists' landholdings. He raised that specter in his precocious 1764 instructions, and during the quiet period he had chided landholders for being "too unconcern'd Spectators" in the fight against the British policies that threatened all colonial property, including land. In the fall of 1774, however, the message of lands being endangered resonated rather too well and threatened to produce extreme actions that might scare moderate delegates and thus undermine unity at the intercolonial congress.[1]

On September 12 Dr. Joseph Warren wrote to inform the Massachusetts delegates that the people, especially farmers, feared "molestation" of their lands. The fear was so strong that many in Massachusetts, and almost everyone in the western counties, wanted to overthrow the established government and return to the first Massachusetts charter. Under the 1629 charter the people elected the governor. Warren stressed that many people believed that, even if the 1691 charter were fully restored, "the possession of their lands may be rendered precarious by any alterations in the charter which parliament shall think to make." He pleaded, "I beg you would give me immediate advice." Adams had to consider that question within the framework of fostering a strong resistance effort in Massachusetts without having that resistance alienate congressional moderates. Upon reflection, Adams suggested that Warren strive to unite the people behind creating a government based as much as possible on the current Massachusetts Charter. Reminding Warren that "there is a charm in the word 'constitutional,'" Adams counseled prudence and moderation so the British, not the colonists, would appear the aggressors. He wanted to put the onus on the British because, as he often reiterated, "it is a good Maxim in Politicks as well as War to put & keep the Enemy in the wrong."[2]

A paucity of sources makes it difficult to fathom the inner workings of the First Continental Congress. The delegates adopted a solemn pledge of secrecy, and their official published journals contain only a bare-bones record of actions taken. Although the sources are frustratingly scanty, the congress that met from September 5 through October 26, 1774, clearly split into two factions—the moderates and the determined Whigs. Moderates dominated the important New York and Pennsylvania delegations; Joseph Galloway of Pennsylvania emerged as a chief spokesman of that faction. Although the moderates believed America had grievances against the British, they were committed to maintaining union with Britain. Thus they supported petitioning for redress but, as Galloway put it, strove "to avoid every measure which tended to sedition, or acts of violent opposition." Moderates disliked economic warfare, especially since, in their view, it would be, as Galloway stressed, implemented "by illegal conventions, committees, town meetings, and their subservient mobs, which would soon put an end to all order, and destroy the authority of Government."[3]

Despite Galloway's assertions, firm Whigs were hardly anarchists, even if some, including Samuel Adams, would have happily shifted political power downward. The more radical Whigs, who dominated the Massachusetts and Virginia delegations, were themselves not in total agreement. In 1774, according to the Rev. William Gordon, few colonists shared Samuel's conviction that America must become independent. And while most colonists, the Massachusetts delegation among them, disliked the Quebec Act of June 1774 and lumped it with the Intolerable Acts, the Virginians hated it with a special passion because the law effectively stifled the plans of innumerable land speculators. Many Virginians were, therefore, determined to emasculate the law. Indeed, considering all of Britain's actions well into 1774, Richard Henry Lee of Virginia proclaimed the Quebec Act "the worst grievance." Even allowing for differences, ardent Whigs agreed on two crucial general points. They believed, as Whigs had argued since the time of troubles began in the mid-1760s, that Parliament could neither tax the colonists nor bind them in all cases whatsoever. They also maintained that the colonists must do more than petition for redress; they must use economic and other forms of coercion to force the British into acknowledging the Americans' fundamental rights.[4]

Even before the congress officially convened on September 5, Galloway caught a glimpse of what he was up against. He was the speaker of the Pennsylvania Assembly and, in that capacity, offered the delegates the use of the Assembly Room of the colony's State House. The city of Philadelphia, or the carpenters who owned the building, offered Carpenters' Hall, a private, not public, structure. Having asserted that the Assembly Room was "a much more proper Place," Galloway was bothered when the delegates rejected his offer to meet on what would have been his home turf. Writing at the time all this was transpiring, Connecticut delegate Silas Deane claimed that Galloway "insists" on the congress meeting in the State House's Assembly Room. "But as he offers, the other party oppose," Deane added. His use of the term *party* illustrates that different groups of delegates knew they had antagonistic agendas.[5]

Galloway got an even nastier jolt when the congress began official deliberations on September 5. The delegates selected Charles Thompson, one of Adams's correspondents, as their secretary. The moderate Galloway, who called Thompson's election a surprise, had maneuvered to keep him off the Pennsylvania delegation. Galloway did that because he considered Thompson "one of the most violent Sons of Liberty (so called) in America." John Adams endorsed that view when, having met him, he recounted that "this Charles Thompson is the Sam. Adams of Phyladelphia—the Life of the Cause of Liberty, they say." Galloway was dismayed both by the selection of Carpenters' Hall and the election of Thompson, who received a unanimous vote. Galloway explained to a fellow moderate that this unanimity came about because "the New Yorkers and myself and a few others, finding a great Majority [for Thompson], did not think it prudent to oppose it." He then added that "both of these Measures, it seems, were privately settled by an Interest made out of Doors" and were advocated by "the Bostonians." Galloway was already starting to learn that he was dealing with men, especially Samuel Adams, who had a flair for political intrigue.[6]

While they were pleased with the way the congress commenced, the Massachusetts delegates realized that they themselves posed a danger to the congressional unity they longed to achieve. Samuel later observed that some congressmen considered Massachusetts "intemperate and rash" and its delegates too domineering. His political acumen helped blunt such negative views. As the delegates began their second day of deliberations, Thomas Cushing recommended opening the following session with a prayer. Several speakers said the delegates' differing religious persuasions made any joint worship impossible. At that point, Samuel rose and remarked that "he was no Bigot, and could hear a Prayer from a Gentleman of Piety and Virtue, who was at the same Time a Friend to his Country." Adding that he had heard that the Reverend Duché, an Episcopalian, was such a man, Adams moved that he be invited to speak. The motion carried, and Adams's ecumenical attitude softened the hostility some delegates had toward Massachusetts.

Speaking in private, George Read, a delegate from Delaware, called Adams's motion a "Masterly Stroke of Policy." That stroke was enhanced by the fact that on the evening before Duché spoke, news—incorrect, as it turned out—reached Philadelphia that British warships had bombarded Boston. In that charged atmosphere, Duché offered a rousing patriotic prayer. The psalm of the day (Psalm 35) made his presentation especially inspiring. Psalm 35, as Duché would have read it, implores the Lord to "fight thou against them that fight against me" and defiantly beseeches, "Let them be as dust before the wind, and the angel of the Lord scattering them."[7]

A delighted Samuel Adams wrote to Dr. Warren and praised Duché's performance as demonstrating the clergyman was "a warm Advocate for the religious and civil rights of America." Once again underscoring that support of American rights mattered more to him than religious affiliation, Samuel used the example of Duché to stress that "many of our *warmest Friends* are *Members of the Church of England.*" As perhaps he anticipated, Dr. Warren saw to it that Samuel's comments appeared in the *Boston Gazette.*[8]

The masterful stroke of having Duché give the opening prayer set the tone for the congress, but Adams improved on events by employing what Galloway called "continual expresses" between Philadelphia and Boston. Before the congress's committees and subcommittees had even submitted reports, Paul Revere arrived in Philadelphia on September 16 with the results of the Suffolk County convention. The convention had sent a letter to General Gage that alleged Bostonians were being subjected to military oppression. More important, the convention had approved a lengthy list of grievances. These Suffolk Resolves depicted the Coercive Acts "as the attempts of a wicked administration to enslave America" and boldly asserted that the citizens need not obey unjust laws. The resolves, which advocated nonimportation and nonconsumption, called for holding a provincial congress in Massachusetts and outlined ways for governing that ignored the Coercive Acts. Pointing out that the people of Massachusetts had not engaged in riots or tumults, the resolves emphasized that "we are determined to act merely upon the defensive, so long as such conduct may be vindicated by reason and the principles of self-preservation, but no longer."

The Suffolk Resolves jolted moderates. In Galloway's mind, the claim that Parliament's laws could simply be ignored constituted "a complete declaration of war against Great-Britain." He was horrified when on September 18 Congress approved a general endorsement of the Suffolk Resolves. And, following the pattern Adams had established during his clerkship of the Massachusetts House, Congress directed that its endorsement and the Suffolk Resolves be printed in newspapers. Over the next ten days Congress called on Americans to cancel orders for merchandise and to begin nonimportation of goods from Britain on December 1.[9]

In desperation, moderates proposed a Plan of Union drafted by Galloway. It envisioned the formation of an American legislature that would have to vote its approval before acts of Parliament could take effect in America. Galloway presented this plan on September 28, and it generated two days of heated debate. As Adams saw it, the Plan of Union, like calls for petitioning rather than waging vigorous economic warfare, amounted to a delaying tactic that could lead to the loss of American liberties. Radicals effectively quashed Galloway's plan by tabling it and went so far as to delete any trace of the plan and the discussion of it from their official records. Congress then expanded the program of economic warfare by decreeing that, if America's grievances had not been redressed by then, Americans would stop exporting goods to Great Britain beginning in September 1775.[10]

Radical Whigs dealt moderates another sharp blow when Congress issued its Declaration of Rights on October 14. Although much of the declaration reiterated established Whig arguments, it broke new ground by explicitly denying that Parliament had *any* right to legislate for the colonies. Delegates like Galloway considered that yet another treasonous action. The congress softened its radical pronouncement by saying the colonists would cheerfully allow Parliament to regulate the empire's trade—so long as no taxes were involved. Even as modified by this concession, the congress's renunciation of Parliament's power marked a major advance along the road toward casting off British control.[11]

Less than a week later, the congress formulated an "Association" to enforce its program of economic warfare. The congress stressed that each step in the plan—nonimportation, nonconsumption, and then nonexportation—would be implemented unless Britain abandoned the "ruinous system of colonial administration, adopted by the British ministry about the year 1763, evidently calculated for inslaving these Colonies, and with them, the British empire." Taking the Massachusetts committee-of-correspondence model in hand, the congress declared that citizen committees should be chosen in every town, city, and county in America and charged with ferreting out anyone who violated the agreement. The names of such "enemies of American liberty" would be published so the people could "break off all dealings with" them. The endorsement of extralegal entities went even further. The congress recommended that the enforcement committees, as well as provincial conventions, "establish such farther regulations as they may think proper" to achieve the aims of the association.

The Association devastated moderates. The only consolation they achieved, and it was a minor one, came from the stipulation that Association committees should be elected by those eligible to vote for members of the colonial assembly. Since every colony had a property requirement to vote, the congress's directive, if followed, would stop poor people from determining who served on those committees. Although the Association constituted a disaster for them, many moderates believed they had to accept it. As Galloway later explained to Parliament, he signed the Association agreement to prevent "the violent part of Congress" from adopting even more "violent measures."[12]

The First Continental Congress took some actions that could be described as aiming at reconciliation. The delegates, accepting a proposal advanced by moderates, petitioned the king for redress of grievances. In addition, the congress presented addresses to the English and the American people. These pronouncements spoke of wanting reconciliation. But given the congress's frontal assault on Britain's economic interests and the way the Association promoted extralegal entities, no one could deny that the ardent Whigs had carried the day. As Governor Gage informed his superiors in November, the congress's proceedings "astonish and terrify" the king's supporters, and yet they appeared to lack the fortitude necessary to counter them publically. To ensure that the resistance program did not wither, the delegates authorized holding another congress if the British rejected this congress's positions. If needed, that second Continental Congress would convene in Philadelphia on May 10, 1775.[13]

Many delegates contributed to the triumph of the zealous Whigs in the Continental Congress of 1774. Acting on instructions Adams would have been proud to have authored, the Virginia delegation played a central role. Its instructions praised the noble Bostonians for defending American rights and denounced Gage's implementation of the Massachusetts Government Act as "the most alarming Process that ever appeared in a British Government."[14] Even within the Massachusetts delegation, Samuel shared the limelight with his cousin John. Nevertheless, the reaction of moderates in the congress illustrates why Samuel Adams came to be seen as the person who steered America toward independence. When Joseph Galloway assessed what had happened in that congress of 1774, he traced the achievements of what he called the "violent party" to one person—Samuel Adams. Galloway saw Adams as "a man, who though by no means remarkable for brilliant abilities, yet is equal to most men in popular intrigue, and the management of a faction." In short, Samuel Adams had the skills of a master politician. In addition, Galloway joined many others who expressed amazement at Samuel's energy and dedication. Galloway observed that Adams "eats little, drinks little, sleeps little, thinks much, and is most decisive and indefatigable in the pursuit of his objects." Having lost more than one tussle with Adams, Galloway came away almost transfixed by what he considered Adams's evil political genius. "It was this man," Galloway opined, "who by his superior application managed at once the faction in Congress at Philadelphia, and the factions in New England."[15]

Galloway, like Hutchinson and others before him, erred in attributing major Whig triumphs solely to Samuel Adams. Adams did not, could not, direct the politics of Massachusetts and the congress all by himself. But Galloway's reference to the management of factions accurately reflects the fact that in the congress Samuel effectively employed the political skills he had sharpened in the Boston Caucus, the Boston Town Meeting, and the Massachusetts House. Above all, Samuel pursued his political goals with an unflinching single-mindedness that impressed his allies and exasperated his foes. Adams carefully planned ahead, as when he and Dr. Warren devised plans for holding provincial conventions. And, always seeking to improve on events, a process that included putting his enemy in the wrong, Adams helped arrange the express communications between Massachusetts and Philadelphia that allowed Whigs to build on the Suffolk Resolves and the reportedly outrageous actions of Governor Gage's soldiers.

In the congress of 1774, as in Massachusetts, Samuel achieved fame not only for his extraordinary energy and remarkable clarity of vision, but also for what Galloway later called "Adams's art." Contemporaries agreed that Adams exhibited an amazing, perhaps unparalleled, ability to lobby other delegates and make arrangements for pursuing joint objectives. Given the praise—and hatred—American politicians lavished on Adams's political prowess, it is hardly surprising that many British politicians shared Galloway's assessment of Samuel's extraordinary political skills. Josiah Quincy, one of the ardent young patriots Adams mentored, learned about Adams's exalted reputation in person. In December 1774, writing from London and having met with a wide array of leading British politicians, Quincy told his wife that the estimation of Samuel Adams "runs very high here. I find many who consider him the first politician in the world."[16]

Throughout his arduous labors in the 1774 congress, Samuel Adams had a special source of strength—his wife. We can only catch glimpses of the relationship between Samuel and "Betsy," as he called Elizabeth. A letter she sent Samuel in September, written in a clear, forceful style, provides some of those glimpses. Even given the stilted language of the day, the love and warmth the two shared is evident. Saying she had written three letters and impatiently awaited news from him, Elizabeth observed, "indeed (my dear) I am never more happy than when I am Reading your letters or scribbling to you my self." Calling herself "your affectionate Wife," Elizabeth let Samuel know that "I long for the happy day when you will return . . . [although] I know it will be to a new Scene of Cares." Her reference to the struggles that lay ahead underscores another vital aspect of Samuel and Elizabeth's relationship: both were fervent, articulate Whigs. She denigrated the lying, "the infamous," Thomas Hutchinson. Ruminating about Tories who had flocked to Boston, Elizabeth informed Samuel that "the once happy Boston is now become a den of thieves, a Cage of Every unclean Bird—[tea] consignees, Commissioners, and tools of every denomination have made this town their ark of safety."[17]

By the time Samuel returned to Elizabeth on November 9, 1774, the government of Massachusetts had been transformed—but not in the way Parliament envisioned when it passed the Massachusetts Government Act. Governor Gage had dissolved the General Court even before it could meet. The representatives, joined by others selected at town meetings, had countered by forming a provincial congress that usurped the province's taxing power and set Massachusetts on a war footing. Under Dr. Warren's energetic leadership, the Provincial Congress's Committee of Safety continued military preparedness after the extralegal gathering adjourned in late October. One goal espoused by the Provincial Congress was to have at least a fourth of their men ready to march "at the shortest notice." Soon the Provincial Congress started calling them "the minute men," citizen soldiers who would literally stand ready to fight at a moment's notice.[18] Having long trumpeted the need for military preparedness, Adams applauded these efforts. Corresponding with Dr. Thomas Young in mid-October, Samuel remarked that "I have written to some of our Friends to provide themselves without Delay with Arms and Ammunition, to get well instructed in the military Art, embody themselves & prepare a complete Set of Rules that they may be ready in Case they are called to defend themselves against the violent Attacks of Despotism."[19]

When it reconvened on November 23, the Provincial Congress added Adams and the province's other Continental Congress delegates to its Committee on the State of the Province, which formulated recommendations for the rest of the members to consider. Three days later Adams was placed on a committee to devise how to keep up a correspondence with Montreal and Quebec as a way of acquiring intelligence. Drawing on what was by then a well-established technique, the committee recommended, and the Provincial Congress agreed, to establish a committee of correspondence to communicate with Canadian inhabitants. The goal was to gain timely intelligence about developments in that area. Samuel, who was already known for his strong interest in Canada, was placed on that committee. The Provincial Congress also reelected the four men who had represented Massachusetts at the First Confederation Congress to attend the Second Continental Congress and added John Hancock to the delegation. Before dissolving their gathering on December 10, the delegates endorsed the Continental Association, stressed the importance of dramatically expanding a wide range of American manufacturing, and exhorted the militia to become skilled soldiers. To keep their powerful extralegal form of government functioning, the delegates authorized the citizens to elect a second Provincial Congress and scheduled it to meet on February 1, 1775.[20]

Despite the limitations the Massachusetts Government Act imposed, the Boston Town Meeting, with Samuel Adams serving as moderator, devised a way to continue operating. Using the ruse that its meetings were merely adjournments of a meeting held before the new regulations took effect, the town meeting functioned into 1775 without submitting its agenda for the governor's approval. In early December 1774, Boston's citizens appointed Adams and the city's other noted Whigs to a sixty-two-member Committee of Inspection to enforce the Association and the Continental Congress's other directives. The committee was also directed to respond to a letter produced by Governor Gage that, according to the town meeting, was riddled with gross errors that unfairly maligned Boston. And, at the end of the month, the Boston Town Meeting officially elected Samuel Adams to be one of its delegates to the Second Provincial Congress scheduled to convene in February. As he assumed yet more duties in the Whig cause, Adams remained active on Boston's Donations Committee. Here, as always, he sought to improve on events and promote intercolonial unity. When he sent letters of thanks to those who had contributed to the relief of Bostonians, Adams routinely emphasized that, sustained by the noble assistance of "sister Colonies," the people of Massachusetts would persevere in their defense of the rights of all Americans.[21]

To heighten patriotic ardor, Adams and his fellow Whigs continued the tradition of having an oration delivered on the anniversary of the Boston Massacre. In 1775 that seemed a dangerous undertaking. Rumors circulated that Boston's leading Whigs might be arrested, and people knew Governor Gage had more than twenty-two hundred redcoats available for the undertaking. Indeed, as Adams phrased it just before the oration was to occur, "Every Art has been practicd to intimidate our leading Men on the popular side." So it took courage for Dr. Warren to deliver the speech and for Adams to preside at the ceremony since he thought "we may possibly be attackd in our Trenches."[22]

The events of the March 5, 1775, oration illustrate more than courage. They show how Adams could, as he so often did, turn a difficult situation to the Whigs' advantage. As the people gathered at the Old South Church, Adams anticipated trouble. It came in the form of a large number of British officers. As Samuel remembered, "I took Care to have them treated with Civility, inviting them into convenient Seats &c that they might have no pretence to behave ill, for it is a good Maxim in Politicks as well as War to put & keep the Enemy in the wrong." Adams's report, confirmed by other accounts, had the officers behaving "tollerably well" until Dr. Warren finished and the usual motion was offered to arrange for the next anniversary commemoration. That motion prompted hissing from the officers. Adams believed this was done to provoke an incident and thus break up the meeting. Despite some exchanges of unpleasantries, Adams recounted that "order was soon restored & we proceeded regularly & finished."[23]

When Dr. Thomas Bolton soon thereafter published a mocking parody of the Boston Massacre oration tradition, he gave a sense of just how frighteningly important Samuel Adams was in the view of contemporary supporters of the king. Depicting the leaders of "the Sons of Liberty of this degenerate age" as "sachem, or Indian chiefs," Bolton, himself a Bostonian, took special aim at Adams as "the first of these chiefs." The Tory doctor mockingly described Samuel as "a *sachem* of vast elocution" who "retails out syllables, sentences, and eulogiums, &c. to draw in the multitude." For Bolton and his friends, the problem was that "it can be attested that what proceeds from the mouth of A—ms is sufficient to fill the mouths of millions in America." Turning hopeful, Bolton added, "but it is prophesied that the time is near at hand, when the *frothy food* will fail them."[24]

During the winter and spring of 1775 Samuel labored hard to crush such Tory hopes by devoting his energies principally to the Second Provincial Congress and to preparing for war. Again working closely with Dr. Warren, he gave special attention to Canada. In mid-February, probably at Adams's urging, the Provincial Congress authorized Boston's correspondence committee to solicit the support of influential men in Montreal and Quebec. Warning them that their rights were also endangered, Adams urged Canadians to send delegates to the Second Continental Congress scheduled to convene in May. John Brown, a recent Yale graduate then living in western Massachusetts, carried these letters. He went north on February 21 with the committee exhorting, "We hope you will make utmost Dispatch to Canada, as much depends upon it." Adams and Dr. Warren counted on Brown being more than a mailman; they instructed him to assess the military situation. Brown did so in late March and advised that Fort Ticonderoga in New York must be captured as soon as hostilities began. Fortunately, said Brown, New Hampshire men stood ready to undertake the task. Capturing Fort Ticonderoga would serve the patriots in two vital ways. The fort occupied a strategic location on the route between Canada and the American colonies, and it had many cannons, a vital weapon in short supply among the colonists.[25] Adams concurred with Brown's analysis and promoted an attack on Fort Ticonderoga when the appropriate time came.

Adams also prepared for the seemingly inevitable hostilities by seeking alliances with Native Americans. In early April he chaired a Provincial

Congress committee charged with establishing favorable relations with the Indians of the Six Nations. The committee wrote to the Reverend Samuel Kirkland, a noted missionary who worked with the Mohawks, urging him to convince the Mohawks, and through them the rest of the Six Nations, to join the colonists. If that proved impossible, he should attempt to keep the Indians neutral. Adams drafted a lengthy letter for Rev. Kirkland to give the Mohawks. Adams tried, as he did in his letters to Canadians, to convince the Native Americans that "you as well as we, are in danger." Warning that the British wanted the colonists' and the Indians' lands, Adams urged the Mohawks "to whet your hatchet, and be prepared with us to defend our liberties and lives." Given the American colonists' dismal record of breaking promises made to Native Americans and the colonists' virtually unrelenting efforts to take over the Indian's lands, Adams's pronouncements had a hollow ring.[26]

As a member of the powerful Committee on the State of the Province, Adams's efforts to form alliances extended to the New England colonies. On April 8 the committee urged the Provincial Congress to send delegates to Connecticut, Rhode Island, and New Hampshire with a proposal that they join Massachusetts in creating a New England army. The Provincial Congress overwhelmingly assented and began the process of forming this consolidated force before adjourning on April 15, 1775.[27]

After the Provincial Congress adjourned, Adams and John Hancock, the new member of the province's congressional delegation, traveled to Lexington to spend a few days with the Reverend Jonas Clark. According to reports, British troops wanted to arrest Adams and Hancock. Despite such speculation, Adams believed that if troops marched it would be to capture military stores, not individuals. As the two men rested in Lexington, it was not yet clear how the British intended to respond to the colonists' demands. They soon learned.

The actions of the First Continental Congress convinced the British that only brute force would bring the Americans, and more particularly the people of Massachusetts, to their senses. In November 1774, responding to the Suffolk Resolves and the Continental Congress's support for these radical pronouncements, Lord Dartmouth, conversing with Thomas Hutchinson, proclaimed that Massachusetts was "plainly in a state of revolt or rebellion." King George III agreed. "Blows," he said, must decide whether the colonists would "be subject to this country or independent." By mid-February 1775 the king had officially declared Massachusetts in a state of rebellion, and measures expanding Britain's army and navy had been approved. In fact, the fatal step occurred even earlier. Lord Dartmouth hoped that a vigorous use of force would stop what was "an actual and open Rebellion" in Massachusetts and keep it from spreading to the rest of New England. So on January 27 he had issued orders for General Gage to arrest the principal leaders of Massachusetts's Provincial Congress. He also advised Gage to capture military supplies colonists had taken from British depots. Although he left the implementation of these directives to Gage, Lord Dartmouth made it clear that Gage would face severe censure if he failed to act decisively. Dartmouth's letter reached Gage on April 16, 1775; he took immediate action. Gage ordered about seven hundred troops to move, as secretly as possible, to Concord, where colonists had stashed military stores. Despite Dartmouth's instructions and recent reports about possible arrests that swirled around the colony and caused many leading Whigs to flee Boston, Gage's plan did not include having soldiers capture Samuel Adams or any other Whig leaders.

The British operation began on the evening of April 18. Adams and Hancock received word of the British troop movement about midnight. When the soldiers appeared in the vicinity early on the morning of April 19, Adams and Hancock were prevailed upon to move to the nearby village of Woburn to avoid capture. It is not clear whether the two men heard the exchange of gunfire between the redcoats and the Lexington minutemen that turned protest into war. But, according to the historian Rev. William Gordon, who talked with him later in 1775, as Adams and Hancock moved through the fields Samuel proclaimed, "*O! what a glorious morning is this!*"[28]

Adams naturally put the British in the wrong when he penned comments on "that memorable Battle" of April 19. "I rejoyce," he professed about a month later, "that my Countrymen had adhered punctually to the Direction of the General Congress, and were at length driven to Resistance through Necessity. I think they may now justly claim the Support of the confederated Colonies." Adams displayed his imaginative use of language and his sense of America as a country by referring to the British troops as "the Rebel Army" and the Americans who sided with the British as "the Rebels." The Americans were fighting "the mercenary Soldiers of a Tyrant." And, as Adams often reminded those to whom he wrote, the tyrant George III and his ministers had "resolvd to persevere in their Attempts to enslave us."[29]

After hostilities commenced, Adams made a revealing thematic change in his writing. During the political sniping that preceded the war Adams had rarely invoked religious imagery. Once war erupted and throughout the war years, though, he routinely employed religious allusions. He was also much more inclined to see, and seek, God's intervention in America's affairs. In May 1775, praising Massachusetts for observing a day of fasting and humiliation, he proclaimed that "it is upon the Blessing of God *alone* that we must depend for the happy Issue to our virtuous Struggle." In November he proclaimed that "Righteous Heaven will surely smile on a Cause so righteous as ours is, and our Country, if it does its Duty will see an End to its Oppressions." Samuel even expressed the belief that "Divine Vengeance" would come crashing down on the tyrannical George III because "all-gracious Heaven cannot be an indifferent Spectator of the virtuous Struggles of this people."[30]

Samuel wrote about "Divine Vengeance" while attending the Second Continental Congress. Except for a five-week recess the congress took to avoid the August heat, Samuel toiled in the congress from the spring of 1775 through the formal declaration of independence and beyond. The 1775 recess, which allowed him to make a quick trip home, provides an example of his famous physical stamina. Believing it would benefit Samuel's health, cousin John urged Samuel to join him in returning to Philadelphia by horseback. Although he had rarely been on a horse, Samuel agreed. He completed the three-hundred-mile journey with relative ease. In fact, by the end of the trip Samuel was, according to servants who traveled with him and John, the better horseman of the two.[31]

As Samuel labored in Philadelphia, his family was much on his mind, and his concern naturally increased because the war was being fought in Massachusetts. Samuel's apprehension intensified after June 12, 1775, when Governor Gage offered a pardon to the American rebels who laid down their arms. Samuel Adams and John Hancock were the only rebels explicitly excluded from the offer; their offenses were deemed so villainous that they must be punished. Samuel shrugged that off when writing to "My dearest Betsy" by quipping that "Gage has made me respectable by naming me first amongst those who are to receive no favor from him." He could not, however, simply dismiss the fact that his family was in the battle zone for, as he conceded to Betsy, "my great Concern is for your health and Safety." Samuel's anxiety probably intensified when he learned that his closest friend and political soul mate, Dr. Joseph Warren, had been killed on June 17 at the battle of Bunker Hill. Writing to Elizabeth, Samuel said he found solace in remembering that Dr. Warren "fell in the glorious Struggle for the publick Liberty." Samuel tried to ensure his family members' safety by having the Adams family move to Dedham, some twenty miles outside of Boston. The younger Samuel Adams, however, had remained in Boston after completing his medical training, and he could not now get out. Samuel pleaded with Elizabeth for any news of his son and expressed elation when he learned in late June "that my dear Son has at length escapd from the Prison of Boston."

Samuel's concern for his only son, a son "for whom my Anxiety is great," led him to ask James Warren to assist young Samuel in securing an army post if he did not yet have one. Samuel tempered his request by saying Warren should help young Dr. Adams only "as far as he shall appear to have merit." When Samuel received reports about his son behaving well on the battlefield, he wrote to Elizabeth, "Nothing gives me greater Satisfaction than to hear that he supports a good Reputation."[32] Samuel's insistence that his son earn a position on merit as well as his emphasis on the importance of deservedly acquiring a good reputation reflected his own deep concern with being worthy of the public trust and doing one's patriotic duty.

Throughout the weary months in Philadelphia, Samuel inquired about everyone in the family household. He asked to be remembered not only to his family and friends but also to Surry, the family servant, and to Job, an apprentice boy. On occasion, Samuel exchanged letters with his son and with his daughter, Hannah. And, as in the days of the Congress of 1774, he drew strength from the support of his wife. Although many of the couple's letters have not survived, they wrote regularly. Each pleaded for more letters, and each waited, as Samuel put it, "impatiently" for the other's letters to arrive. The simple truth was, said Samuel, "it is painful to me to be absent from you" and the arrival of "your Letters would in some Measure afford me Reliefe." One feels the warmth of their affection in a letter that also conveys a sense of the long hours he spent at his desk after the congress adjourned for the day. Samuel closed a letter of June 28, 1775, saying, "Pray my dear let me have your Letters more frequently—by every opportunity. The Clock is now striking twelve. I therefore wish you a good Night."

Elizabeth was far more than an affectionate wife to Samuel. In an age when few marriages reflected anything approaching equality, Samuel and Elizabeth's union was built on a great measure of equality. Samuel praised Elizabeth's "Prudence" and counted on her "usual Discretion" in difficult times. Elizabeth also had a real hand in managing the family's finances. Samuel wrote from Philadelphia that "when I am in Want of Money I will write to you." And while most men—and women—stressed that women should not be involved in politics, Samuel and Elizabeth shared a passion for it. When Samuel wrote to his dearest Betsy saying "We must be content to suffer the Loss of all things in this Life, rather than tamely surrender the publick Liberty," he was writing to another staunch Whig. Elizabeth commented on the politics of the day when she wrote to Samuel. And he responded to a letter from Elizabeth—unfortunately one of the many that have not survived—with the comment, "I am much pleasd my dear with the Good Sense and public Spirit you discoverd in your Answer to Maj^r Kains Message." Far from wanting Elizabeth to eschew politics, he lamented the congress's secrecy rule and told her, "I wish I could consistently inform you what is doing here." Samuel did send Elizabeth accounts of the latest intelligence from England as well as clippings on politics from the Philadelphia press. And when Thomas Paine's polemical *Common Sense* appeared, he promptly sent Elizabeth a copy and even urged James Warren to ask to borrow her copy.

Pride as well as love glistened when Samuel recounted to Elizabeth how a Roxbury man "wrote me that he had often met with you and was surprised at your Steadiness & Calmness under Tryal." Samuel was not surprised. As he said, "I am always pleasd to hear you well spoken of, because I know it is doing you Justice." Elizabeth's strength and political drive, as well as her love, helped sustain and nourish Samuel, for theirs was a symbiotic relationship and both labored to defend American liberties.[33]

Samuel's efforts to further the American cause in the Second Continental Congress during the crucial period from the outbreak of war through the formal declaration of independence cannot be recounted with anything approaching precision. The Second Continental Congress continued both the secrecy rule and the policy of providing minimal reports about deliberations. Because of his understandable concern about keeping sensitive political information from falling into an opponent's hands, Adams revealed little in his letters. Moreover, he often did not keep copies of his own correspondence. And John Adams recounted how his cousin, when they were about to leave the congress in the summer, would get out his scissors and "cut up . . . whole bundles of letters almost into atoms and throw them out the window, to be scattered by the winds." In the winter "he threw whole handfuls into the fire." "Whatever becomes of me," Samuel explained, "my friends shall never suffer by my negligence."[34]

Despite the paucity of sources, it is clear that Samuel Adams remained a dominant, and perhaps the dominant, figure in the congress. Although he never carried a gun or commanded troops, he played a significant role in military efforts, especially in the first two years of the war. Adams revealed his keen concern about military matters even before he began serving in the Second Continental Congress. As he traveled to Philadelphia in late April 1775, he and John Hancock stopped in Hartford. They met secretly with the Connecticut governor and Council to help arrange an attack on Fort

Ticonderoga. The attack resulted in the capture of that strategic location and its invaluable cannon in early May.[35]

As a congressman Adams devoured military intelligence and devoted himself to strategic planning. He quickly came to the conclusion that New York and Canada were vital and that the British planned to cut the colonies in half by driving through New York. Reflecting Adams's concern about the province, the congress placed him on a committee to determine what military measures should be taken in New York. Having already implored Canadians to join their southern neighbors, Adams was a natural to work on the committee drafting an appeal to the Canadian people. Adams also took a special interest in naval power. He served on the committee delegated to consider the possibility of developing an American navy, and he lobbied for creating such a force. When the congress approved building thirteen warships in December 1775, Adams said, "I wishd for double or treble the Number." He did not push for a bolder shipbuilding program out of fear that doing so might produce divisive acrimony in the congress.

When he considered it necessary in the opening phase of the war, Adams did press his fellow congressmen for decisive action. He did that when supporting a motion put forward by his correspondent and political ally Richard Henry Lee of Virginia. In October 1775 Lee recommended that the congress stop the British mail service in America. Adams supported Lee's proposal by bluntly proclaiming, "I am for stopping the correspondence of our enemies." The congress refused to take that step in the fall of 1775, but Adams's stance offered yet another example of his desire to challenge British authority and to prosecute the war vigorously.

Adams's deep interest in military matters was reflected in the many important assignments the congress gave him as the war progressed. He served on a committee charged with obtaining military stores, especially ammunition. Samuel took this task seriously and even forwarded designs for a powder mill to Massachusetts. He was quite active on committees that assessed the defensive needs of various colonies and on the powerful committee, created in December 1775, that evaluated the applications of all who sought to become officers in the Continental Army. His fellow congressmen could expect Adams to approach that task with a willingness to obtain military talent from any quarter. Months earlier he had helped secure the appointment of British-born Charles Lee as a general. Making that appointment might, Adams believed, induce English officers to volunteer "in the Cause of Liberty in America." Adams's contributions to military success did not go unnoticed. Thomas Jefferson, who served with Adams on important military committees, proclaimed that Adams "had, I think, a greater share than any other member in advising and directing our measures in the Northern war."[36]

As he labored to make the American war machine run smoothly, Adams also struggled to convince everyone he dealt with that the hope of reconciliation with Great Britain "is the Rock which endangers the Shipwreck of America." Samuel hammered on the theme that the British remained determined "to establish arbitrary Government in the Colonies by Acts of Parliament and to enforce those Acts by the Sword." Chastising so-called moderates for exacerbating America's problems, he argued that any British talk of possible reconciliation on reasonable terms was a ploy. It was designed to divide Americans and give the British a better chance of enslaving America. If Americans acted on the belief that Britain wanted reasonable reconciliation, "it would be a Delusion leading directly to Destruction."[37]

For Adams, independence offered the only alternative to political slavery. He also claimed that America actually became independent on April 19, 1775. Indeed, "the Moment we determin'd to defend ourselves by Arms against the most injurious Violence of Britain we declar'd for Independence." Given his views, Samuel lamented that the congress did not issue a formal declaration of independence as soon as hostilities broke out, and its continued reluctance to do so nettled him. He did not press more aggressively for a declaration for the same reason that he kept counseling Massachusetts residents to be prudent and remained silent when the congress authorized fewer warships than he would have liked. Samuel was well aware that it would take time "to convince the doubting and inspire the timid" members of the congress. As he said in one of his favorite aphorisms, one must "let the fruit hang till it is ripe."[38]

Although he had long emphasized that a politician could not control events, Adams developed and pursued a vision of how Americans should defend their liberties and ultimately achieve independence. The first step involved organizing new governments in each of the colonies. Adams advocated creating new governments because he believed doing so would have a domino effect leading to the establishment of an American confederation, the second vital step in his plan. He theorized that once the people of a colony installed their own government, "the Colonies will feel their Independence." When that occurred, "the Way will be prepared for A Confederation, and one Government may be formed with the Consent of the whole." America would thus become "a distinct State composd of all the Colonies with a common Legislature for great & General Purposes." Creating a confederation government was, for Adams, linked to obtaining the foreign assistance Americans needed to fight the world's greatest military power. As soon as hostilities commenced, Americans sought, and received, some military supplies from abroad. But Adams judged, and rightly so, that to win independence, Americans must secure full alliances with foreign powers. Such alliances would, he reasoned, naturally follow once Americans established a true continental government. These developments—creating new provincial governments, forming a continental government, and forging alliances with other nations—would culminate in, and be crowned by, a formal declaration of American independence.[39]

From Adams's perspective, the congress began moving toward his ultimate goal of independence on June 9, 1775, when it responded to a letter from the Massachusetts Provincial Congress. Proclaiming that Britain was waging war against the "peaceful and loyal subjects" of Massachusetts, the congress authorized the people of Massachusetts to disobey any act of Parliament that altered the colony's charter. The people did not owe any allegiance to officials, such as the appointed governor and lieutenant governor, who were endeavoring to subvert the charter. Given these points, the congress, in language that reflected Adams's stated position, instructed the people of Massachusetts to form a government that conformed as nearly as possible to the spirit and substance of the colony's charter. Accordingly, the Provincial Congress should call on the townships to elect representatives who would then elect a council. The council would exercise the governor's powers until the king appointed an executive who would govern according to the charter.[40]

Since George III had no intention of replacing Governor Gage, the congress's recommendations smacked of independence. Still, in June 1775 Massachusetts was a war zone, so what happened there did not necessarily establish a precedent for other colonies. That is why Adams rejoiced when the movement for creating new governments spread. In mid-October New Hampshire citizens asked the congress what should be done about their nonfunctioning government. The congress responded on November 3 by authorizing the colony's Provincial Congress to "call a full and free representation of the people." If those representatives deemed it necessary, they should establish a government designed to produce happiness while securing peace and good order in the province. The new government would function during the present "dispute" with Great Britain. The same day the congress took that action it appointed a committee to assess the situation in South Carolina. Since Adams served on that committee, it is hardly surprising that it reported back the very next day and, using language of the just-adopted resolution concerning New Hampshire, recommended that South Carolina be authorized to form a new government. The congress agreed.[41]

The events of November 4 made Samuel wildly optimistic. That evening he wrote to James Warren and reported, "I believe the Time is near when the most timid will see the absolute Necessity of every one of the Colonies setting up a Government within itself." Almost giddy with delight, Adams prophesied that George III and the British administration "will necessarily produce the grandest Revolutions the World has ever yet seen. The Wheels of Providence seem to be in their swiftest Motion. Events succeed each other so rapidly that the most industrious and able Politicians can scarcely improve them to the full purposes for which they seem to be designd." Samuel even proclaimed he should be replaced since "Men of moderate Abilities, especially when weakened by Age are not fit to be employed in founding Empires." Adams's continuing handiwork in helping to establish new colonial governments belied his self-deprecating comments. Responding to the royal governor's declaration of martial law in Virginia, in early December the Committee on Virginia, which Adams chaired, recommended that the congress invite Virginians to form their own government. Reflecting the approach Samuel had used in the Massachusetts House, the Adams committee framed its proposal in the same language the congress employed when it invited New Hampshire and South Carolina to establish new governments. The congress adopted the committee's recommendation.[42]

Although new provincial governments were being authorized, Adams soon admitted he had been too optimistic when he proclaimed that "the Wheels of Providence seem to be in their swiftest Motion." As 1775 drew to a close, the congress had not yet moved toward creating a confederation government, much less toward declaring independence. Samuel complained to James Warren, "We go on here by Degrees, though not with the Dispatch I could wish." However, events in the new year quickly dispelled Samuel's gloom. On New Year's Day 1776 a British fleet bombarded Norfolk, Virginia. When the news reached Philadelphia on January 7, Americans expressed outrage. Believing that "Mankind are governed more by their feelings than by reason" and that events often exerted a controlling influence on politics, Adams suggested that the cannonading of Norfolk would do far more than reasoning could to bring about a confederation.[43]

Americans became even angrier when they learned of George III's response to the congress's pleas for redress of grievances. A copy of the king's pronouncements appeared in the Pennsylvania *Evening Post* of January 9. The king, doing what Adams said he would, insisted that the Americans must accept Britain's authority. The colonists had to realize, the king stressed, that only "submission" and "allegiance" would end hostilities.

Believing many deluded Americans wanted independence, George III announced that the British military presence in America would be increased so it could force the colonists to yield. Proclaiming that the king's speech proved that George III had "a wicket Heart," Adams asked, "What have we to expect from Britain, but Chains & Slavery?" For Samuel the answer was obvious. Americans should "act the part which the great Law of Nature points out" and declare independence. By chance, the *Evening Post* carried the king's speech on the same day Thomas Paine's stunning pamphlet *Common Sense* appeared. In powerful yet simple language ordinary people could understand, Paine savaged monarchy in general and George III in particular. And, much to Adams's delight, Paine constructed powerful arguments for America's declaring its independence.[44]

The events of early January scared congressional moderates and spurred them to action. Led by James Wilson of Pennsylvania, the moderates called for the congress to disavow any thoughts of American independence. Adams of course opposed that proposal. Wilson's initiative fueled Adams's anger at the failure to create a confederation government. By mid-January he even raised the possibility of forming a continental government made up just of the colonies "inclined to it." He indicated that he had informed Benjamin Franklin that "I would endeavor to unite the New England Colonies in confederating, if *none* of the rest would joyn in it." Samuel claimed that Franklin approved of this plan and said "he would cast in his Lot among us" if Adams could get a New England confederation formed. Such extreme measures proved unnecessary. Wilson's effort to put the congress on record as opposing independence soon vanished under a wave of indifference.[45]

To fuel the growing sentiment for independence among ordinary Americans, Adams once again utilized the press. Writing for a Philadelphia paper in mid-February under his well-known "Candidus" signature, Adams built a case for independence. He began by praising Paine's pamphlet and then mounted a frontal attack on the assertion that the colonists might yet reach a peaceful reconciliation with Britain. Although it was still the congress's official position, Adams brutalized the idea that the empire might find peace if Britain returned to the pre-1763 imperial system. In the first place, said Adams, Britain would not consider returning to the old ways. And, even if the British did agree, America's constitutional status would still be too vague, too precarious. That was especially true because, according to Adams, George III wanted to establish an absolute tyranny over *all* the people of the British Empire, not just over Americans. Turning to those who warned that Americans faced a protracted, bloody war if they declared

independence, Adams boldly asserted that "the puling, pusillanimous cow-
ards" had it backwards! Declaring independence, he reasoned, constituted
"the only step that can bring the contest to a speedy and a happy issue."
Why? First, once they declared independence Americans would be on an
equal footing when negotiating with Great Britain. Second, the nations of
Europe, especially the maritime nations, "will find it in their interest (which
always secures the question of inclination) to protect a people who can be
so advantageous to them." Cleverly posing the question in a way that put
his opponents in the wrong, Adams challenged the proponents "of returning to a state of dependence on Great Britain" to argue their case openly.
To counter such efforts even before they might appear Adams again put
his opponents in the wrong by calling up, as he so often did, one's duty
to posterity. "Shame on the man who can court exemption from present
trouble and expense at the price of their own posterity's liberty!"[46]

By mid-April 1776 Samuel openly spoke of linking the creation of a
solid confederation to declaring independence and forming alliances with
powerful nations. It was, he argued, time to embrace independence "and
under God trust our Cause to our Swords." In late April, after reviewing
the situation in each colony, he informed Rev. Cooper that "the Ideas of
Independence spread far and wide among the Colonies." Given that many
American communities were, in fact, issuing their own calls for independence, Samuel's claim was not mere propagandistic hyperbole. But the
congress had to be convinced to declare independence, and events seemed
to be working toward that end. Adams informed Cooper the British were
expected to attack in the South. Samuel anticipated that prospect with pleasure because the South was well prepared to defend itself and because he
believed such an attack would hasten independence. "One Battle would,"
he asserted, "do more toward a Declaration of Independence than a long
chain of conclusive Arguments in a provincial Convention or the Continental Congress."[47]

As a formal declaration of independence seemed within reach, Adams
found it horrifying that enlistments were flagging in New England. On
May 12 he pleaded with James Warren to spur recruiting. As he discussed
what might be done to achieve that goal, Adams's missive provided a summary of methods he employed to convince the people that their rights were
in danger and, consequently, to move Massachusetts and America toward
his cherished goal of independence. He asked, "Do our [Massachusetts]
Countrymen want Animation at a Time when [all] is at Stake! Your Presses
have too long been silent. What are your Committees of Correspondence
about? I hear Nothing of *Circular Letters—of joynt Committees*, etc., etc."

"Such Methods," Adams reminded his fellow Whig, "have in times passed raised the Spirits of the People, drawn off their Attention from *picking up pins*, and directed their Views to great objects."

The "great object" Adams strained toward so passionately seemed tantalizingly close in early June. By the 6th of that month Adams knew his close political ally Richard Henry Lee would introduce a resolution calling on the congress to declare the colonies independent. Since he desperately wanted that resolution adopted unanimously, Adams did not want events in Massachusetts spooking timid congressmen. The night before Lee's resolution of independence was presented Adams wrote to James Warren and implored him "to exert your Influence to prevent unnecessary Questions in the [Massachusetts] Assembly which may cause Contention. Now if ever Union is necessary—Innovations may well enough be put off, till publick Safety is secured."[48]

On June 7 Lee offered the resolution that embodied the goals Samuel Adams had been advocating. The resolution declared the colonies free and independent, stipulated that foreign alliances should be formed expeditiously, and directed that a plan of confederation be produced. Although it postponed the vote on Lee's proposal until July so delegates might obtain instructions on independence, the congress appointed a committee to draft a declaration of independence. Less than a week later, the congress established a committee, made up of a congressman from each colony, to formulate a plan for a confederation government. Samuel Adams represented Massachusetts. The congress then created yet another committee and instructed it to prepare treaties that could be proposed to foreign powers. Then on July 2 the congress proclaimed that "these United Colonies are, and of right, ought to be, Free and Independent States." Two days later the delegates approved the language of the Declaration of Independence. At least on paper, Adams's dream of American independence had been achieved.[49]

A deflated and defeated Joseph Galloway, who had resigned from the congress in May 1775 and who ultimately cast his lot with the king, thought he knew who above all should be blamed. Galloway maintained that some members of the congress constituted a "faction" that "ever had independence in their view" and Samuel Adams was "the great director of their councils, and the most cautious, artful and reserved man among them." But, said Galloway, as soon as America's independence was declared Adams openly boasted that "he had laboured upwards of twenty years to accomplish" it. William Allen, a Philadelphia loyalist, offered the same analysis when, in January 1777, he claimed that Adams "has often publically boasted in Philadelphia of late, that for 20 Years he has been inculcating his republican Opinions among the young Gentlemen in & about Boston, and that he now saw the happy Fruit of it." Sounding like Peter Oliver, Allen went on to observe that, "of all the men he ever knew, this Adams is the most capable of leading or inflaming a Mob. He has vast Insinuation, & infinite Art, by wch he has been able to impose on most Men."[50]

While opponents such as Thomas Hutchinson, Peter Oliver, and Joseph Galloway overstated his control, there is no question that Samuel Adams played a prodigious role in the movement that led to declaring independence. From 1764 on, his single-minded determination to defend the constitutions that protected the people's liberties and his consummate political skills set him apart from other American Whigs. Writing in April 1774, and not for public consumption, John Adams called his cousin Samuel perhaps "the most elegant writer, the most sagacious politician, & celebrated patriot" of anyone who had figured in the struggle for American liberties in the ten years since the time of troubles began.[51] John was marveling at the political skills Samuel had employed and sharpened in the Boston Caucus, the Boston Town Meeting, the Massachusetts legislature, various extralegal committees, and as political author. Mercy Otis Warren, the sister of James Otis and the wife of James Warren, in an 1805 history of the American Revolution pictured Samuel as "indefatigable; calm in seasons of difficulty, tranquil and unruffled in the vortex of political altercation; too firm to be intimidated, . . . his mind was replete with resources that dissipated fear, and extricated in the greatest emergencies." Adams had, she noted, "stood forth early, and continued firm, through the great struggle, and may justly claim a large share of honor, due to that spirit of energy which opposed the measures of [the British] administration, and produced the independence of America."[52]

Whigs who served with Samuel Adams in the congress during 1775 and 1776 offered similar and even stronger assessments.[53] Speaking in 1780 of having worked in the congress with him since 1774, Richard Henry Lee said of Samuel, "I have found him uniformly firm, sensible, and attached to the cause of America upon the best principles." Decades later Dr. Benjamin Rush of Pennsylvania, who joined the congress in July of 1776 and left it in late February 1777, offered a general assessment of Congressman Adams. Voicing generally agreed-upon themes, Dr. Rush proclaimed that the then near fifty-five-year-old Samuel "possessed all the vigor of mind of a young man of five and twenty" and that "both friends and enemies agreed in viewing him as one of the most active instruments of the American Revolution." Samuel "seldom spoke in Congress, but was active in preparing and doing business out of doors." Elbridge Gerry also attested to Samuel's ability to be influential with fellow delegates when conversing outside as well as in the congress.

One gets a sense of Samuel in action "out of doors" from a report of how he spent the evening of Sunday September 25, 1775, when a few congressional delegates and friends spent the night socializing. Samuel fell into what his cousin called a lengthy "Disputation" with John Houstoun, a newly arrived Georgia delegate. The issue was how quickly and thoroughly America's military forces should take the offensive in the manner of "an open War." John Adams, who discussed the events of the evening in his diary, found it natural that Houstoun would enter into disputation since he was a lawyer. Perhaps forgetting that Samuel had spent time preparing to enter the law and had for decades devoted himself to reading political theory and history, John added that his cousin "is not a Whit less detected to it [disputation] than the Lawyers." The important point is that Houstoun and Samuel "disputed the whole Time in good Humour." Clearly Samuel enjoyed the give and take of political debate and could do it in a manner not likely to antagonize a potential ally.[54] That is one reason Samuel won fame for his ability to forge alliances.

Speaking decades later of his cousin's work in the congresses, John Adams also emphasized how Samuel worked behind the scenes to achieve his goals. Sounding like Joseph Galloway, John depicted Samuel as a less than brilliant man who was, nevertheless, a brilliant politician. According to John, his cousin "had the art of commanding the learning, the oratory, the talents" of the best among his colleagues. Moreover, Samuel practiced his art "without anybody's knowing or suspecting he had it, but himself and a very few friends."[55] Reflecting on the Second Continental Congress, which he joined in June 1775, Thomas Jefferson offered a strikingly similar assessment of Samuel's methods. Jefferson's description also reveals that Samuel used tactics he had honed in the Boston Caucus and the secret committee of the Massachusetts House Whigs in 1775. Jefferson observed that Samuel "was constantly holding caucuses of distinguished men . . . *at which the generality of the measures pursued were previously determined on—and at which the parts were assigned to the different actors, who afterwards appeared in them.*" And while John Adams was a "*Colossus*" in debate, he had "very little part" in Samuel's caucuses.

Addressing the issue of Adams the speaker, Jefferson, who stressed that Samuel was "immovable in his purposes," agreed with the general view that he "was not of fluent elocution." Yet he "commanded the most profound attention" when he rose to speak because he was "so rigorously logical, so clear in his views, abundant in good sense, and always master of his subject." Offering a general summary of Samuel Adams the congressman, Jefferson maintained that, "for depth of purpose, zeal, and sagacity, no man in Congress exceeded, if any equalled Sam. Adams; and none did more than he to originate and sustain revolutionary measures in Congress." In fact, said Jefferson, "I always considered him as more than any other member the fountain of our important measures." Intriguingly, Jefferson offered his most-telling assessment of Adams in conversations that focused on Richard Henry Lee. Since Adams was not the subject of the discussion, there was no reason for Jefferson to give undue emphasis to his importance. Nevertheless, Jefferson emphatically attested that, if there was any helmsman of the American Revolution, "Samuel Adams was the man."[56]

8

"ZEALOUS IN THE GREAT CAUSE": WINNING INDEPENDENCE

Declaring independence was, Samuel Adams emphasized, not the same as securing it. From the day Congress proclaimed independence until Britain officially recognized America as an independent nation, Samuel Adams followed the advice he gave all Americans. He was, as he urged others to be, "Zealous in the great Cause." As he continued to help fashion a military capable of winning independence on the battlefield and the seas, Adams also industriously strove to create a continental government and gain the foreign assistance he considered essential to winning the War for American Independence. For Congressman Adams the great cause involved more than winning independence. The great cause also involved establishing that independence on a firm geographical foundation that would allow the Americans' posterity to flourish. As he put it when writing to James Warren, "we shall never be on a solid Footing Till G[reat] B[ritain] cedes to us what Nature designs we sh[ould] have or we wrest it from her."[1]

As a member of Congress, Adams continued to play a key leadership role in the military conduct of the war once independence had been declared. He served on many important committees, including the Marine Committee, and the Board of War and Ordnance, the major committee on army affairs. Samuel worked so exhaustively creating an effective military and developing viable strategies that some analysts in Britain linked him to the most infamous military opponent of England's monarchy. One commentator called Adams "the would-be *Cromwell* of *America*"; another dubbed him "the Cromwell of New England." In America, Thomas Jefferson, thinking back on the work of Congress, expanded on his assertion that no member matched Samuel Adams "in advising and directing our measures, in the Northern war" by adding, "Indeed, in the Eastern States, for a year or two after it began, he was truly the *Man of the Revolution*."[2]

Knowing that winning independence required an adequate military, Adams worked diligently to provide the tools of victory in what he routinely called "the great" or "the glorious" cause. He pushed for keeping army enlistments up and for meeting the supply needs of the armed forces, including the small navy. The difficulties of maintaining an effective army in the field forced Adams to advocate measures that bumped against his fear of military power. Believing the military cast of mind endangered liberty, he had long advocated using militias, citizen soldiers who served for limited periods under their state's control. While he still championed the militia, Adams understood, as he later phrased it, that the vicissitudes of war presented the revolutionaries with "a Choice of Difficulties." His own eyes quickly convinced him that America needed professional soldiers. He reached that conclusion in August 1776 after visiting the troops in New York and speaking with George Washington, the commander in chief of the Continental army. Writing to a fellow congressman, Samuel proclaimed "it would be a pity" to lose experienced troops. He recommended offering a more generous bounty—$20 and a hundred acres of land—provided a soldier enlisted for at least three years. On September 16, with Samuel back in Philadelphia, Congress authorized a $20 bounty for noncommissioned officers and soldiers willing to serve during the present war. A sliding scale of land grants offered ordinary soldiers the hundred acres of land Adams had recommended.[3]

Making long-term enlistments more attractive did not help the immediate situation, and it soon turned grim. As the leaves changed color and fell in 1776, British forces, including Hessian mercenaries, smashed through sections of New Jersey and Pennsylvania, raping and pillaging as they went. By early December Adams spoke of the British tyrant "summoning the powers of earth and hell to subjugate America." Soon thereafter most congressmen fled Philadelphia as a British force drew near. Adams and three colleagues who had not yet left the city learned the enemy had just put ten thousand men into Rhode Island. Calling it their "Duty," they informed General Washington about the incursion and, observing that the area lacked a commanding general, recommended he appoint either General Horatio Gates or General Nathaniel Greene. The congressmen pointed out that each man was well known in the region and that might make recruiting easier. America's military prospects seemed so bleak even the indomitable Washington lamented on December 18 that "I think the game is pretty near up."[4]

By the time Congress reassembled in Baltimore shortly before Christmas, the military situation seemed almost hopeless. As Thomas Paine said in

"The Crisis," "These are the times that try men's souls." A desperate Congress ordered Adams and two other members to propose appropriate action. They recommended—and on December 27, 1776, Congress agreed—that Washington be accorded extraordinary powers to make the army function. Those emergency powers, which would expire in six months, allowed Washington to make every effort, including giving bounties, to spur enlistments and secure supplies for the army. The congressmen explained that they took this drastic step because they had confidence in Washington and because of the abysmal military situation.[5]

Victories at Trenton and Princeton, together with the fortuitous British decision to shut down the campaign for the winter, eased the immediate danger. And the near disasters of 1776 caused the American commander in chief to reassess his approach to the war. By the spring of 1777 Washington was following what Adams and others labeled "the Fabian Method" because it emulated the great Roman general's military strategy. As Adams reported, Washington now attacked only when his army had the advantage. In the meantime, smaller units harassed and diminished the British forces by continual skirmishes. In a May 12 commentary on the strategy Samuel turned historian and compared Fabius's situation when battling Hannibal with the situation in America. In doing so Adams built the case for taking more aggressive action during the skirmishing around Brunswick, New Jersey. In a July 15 comment on the events in New Jersey Adams returned to the same theme. Observing that the Americans had mustered a considerable and confident force, Samuel, without naming him, implicitly criticized Washington for not adopting "more of an enterprizing Spirit." Claiming rather disingenuously that "I possess not the least Degree of Knowledge in military Matters, & therefore hazzard no opinion," Samuel proceeded to hazard an opinion. Saying he wanted "our Country" to "speedily enjoy the Fruits of the present conflict—an established Independence and Peace," he declared, as he often did during the war, that God helps those who help themselves. In offering this analysis, Adams admitted that "my Temper is rather sanguine" and, therefore, "I am apt to be displeasd when I think our Progress in War and Politics is Slow."[6]

Despite his grousing about the New Jersey campaign, Adams understood the value of the Fabian strategy. In mid-June 1777 he commented on speculation that the British planned to attack what was in effect the American capital. Assessing the possible British capture of Philadelphia, Adams asked, "what will it avail them unless they beat our Army?" And he defiantly added, "this I am fully perswaded they will not do." As he openly embraced this central tenet of the Fabian strategy, Adams added, "I confess that I have always been so very wrong headed as not to be over well pleasd with what is called the Fabian War in America." He now predicted that America's warriors faced "a long and moderate War."[7]

His increasing acceptance of Washington's Fabian strategy is important for understanding Adams's possible involvement in what came to be called the Conway Cabal—a conspiracy supposedly launched in the winter of 1777–1778 to dump Washington as commander in chief. The reputed plan was to replace him with someone like General Gates, the celebrated leader of the crucial victory at Saratoga in October 1777.

The story of the so-called Conway Cabal as it relates to Adams necessarily begins with his response to General Philip Schuyler's misadventures as the commander of the Northern Department in the spring and summer of 1777. The Northern Department centered on the American-Canadian frontier in New York and included the vital Fort Ticonderoga. Adams, among others, believed that Schuyler, a New Yorker based in Albany, would have made a good quartermaster or commissary but that he was ill suited to command fighting forces. One problem stemmed from Schuyler's haughty, aristocratic style; it irked many and helped foment discontent among his officers and troops, especially the New England militias. That made it difficult for him to recruit troops and to get them to reenlist. Worse yet, based on his performance in the 1776 campaign Schuyler had acquired a well-deserved reputation for hunkering down in Albany, his home and headquarters, rather than personally venturing into the field. General Schuyler's flaws were exacerbated because both troops and matériel were in short supply in the spring of 1777.[8]

In July, when British forces under the command of General John Burgoyne advanced on Fort Ticonderoga, the American commander, General Arthur St. Clair, faced two equally devastating choices. As he said, "if I evacuate the place, my character will be ruined; if I remain here, the army will be lost." To save his small army, St. Clair abandoned Fort Ticonderoga on July 6, 1777. As the commander of the Northern Department, General Schuyler bore the ultimate responsibility for the debacle in New York. The Continental Congress moved quickly to replace Schuyler, and Adams openly acknowledged that he took an active part in the effort. On July 29 Congress ordered that an inquiry be conducted into the recent reverses in the Northern Department. Then, on August 1 Congress relieved Schuyler of command in the Northern Department and directed Washington to select a replacement. Attempts to defend Schuyler failed above all else because, as Adams put it in a scathing denunciation penned even before the full scope of the disaster was known, "*he was not present with his Army.*" As

Schuyler's fellow New Yorker George Clinton later observed, Schuyler's "cursed attachment to the comforts of Albany and doing the fighting business by proxy for two campaigns, has destroyed him."[9]

The day after Schuyler was dismissed-Adams joined congressmen from Massachusetts, New Hampshire, Rhode Island, and Connecticut in writing to Washington and urging him to give the Northern Department command to General Gates. They reasoned that "no Man will be more likely to restore Harmony, order & Discipline, & retrieve our affairs in that Quarter." Indeed, "he has on Experience acquired the Confidence, & stands high in the Esteem of the eastern States & Troops." When Washington, who disliked being involved in such appointments, asked the Congress to excuse him from making the choice, the members took matters into their own hands. On August 4, by a vote of eleven states, Congress selected Gates to command the Northern Department. If Adams voiced arguments he had made two weeks earlier in a letter to Richard Henry Lee, he would have urged his fellow congressmen to appoint Gates because "he is *honest* and *true*, & has the Art of *gaining the Love of his Soldiers* principally because he is *always present* with them in *Fatigue & Danger*." For Adams, the contrast with General Schuyler could hardly have been sharper.[10]

After Gates took charge, reports from the Northern Department soon brightened. And when the Americans, with militiamen playing a crucial role, achieved the stunning and momentous victory over General John Burgoyne's army at Saratoga in mid-October, Gates suddenly became America's hero. His achievements in battle seemed to contrast favorably with the recent setbacks Washington had experienced at the battles of Brandywine in September and Germantown in early October 1777. Given these developments it is hardly surprising that some revolutionaries grumbled about Washington's recent reverses and that speculation arose that some might want the commander in chief replaced.

Washington and his immediate staff become convinced that Gates or General Thomas Millfin, or both, aided in some way by General Thomas Conway, plotted to replace the commander in chief. As December gave way to January 1778, Washington brilliantly used an unflattering letter from Conway to shift the focus away from his own seeming lack of success. And the commander in chief soon received assurances that, despite fears to the contrary, there was no plot afoot in Congress to replace him. On January 15 Henry Laurens, the president of Congress, said that congressional criticism of Washington amounted to "little more than tittle tattle" and most certainly did not include a movement to oust him. Reviewing what had transpired in the supposed cabal to replace him, Washington himself remarked in May 1778 that he was "well informed that no whisper of that kind was ever heard in Congress." And the evidence of any concerted effort to remove Washington as commander in chief is so thin that the modern-day historian John Ferling, who has written extensively both on Washington and the war, rightly speaks of "the nonexistent Conway Cabal."[11]

While it did not stop political opponents from trying to smear him with what he later denounced as "the fabricated Charge" that he was anti-Washington, there is no evidence that Samuel Adams wanted a new commander in chief. He was not even in Congress from mid-November 1777 through mid-May 1778 when the so-called Conway Cabal plot was supposedly in progress. Adams stated his position in a January 1, 1778, letter to Richard Henry Lee that assessed what had happened in the Middle Department under Washington's command in 1777. Observing that the army had not experienced any "shameful Defeats," Samuel nevertheless lamented that "a promising Campaign has . . . ended ingloriously." Carefully noting there were some exceptions, Adams placed the blame on "a miserable Set of General Officers." Calling for the dismissal of unnamed "cowardly or drunken officers," he asked, "Is there not Reason to fear that our own Commander in Chief may one day suffer in his own Character by Means of those worthless Creatures?" In Adams's judgment, that was no small concern. Asserting that the reputation of the American commander in chief "is of the greatest Importance to our Armies," he urged, "let us promote this Winter a strict Scrutiny into the Causes of this unfortunate Campaign." Here, to help support the great cause, Adams's concern was for protecting Washington's reputation, not trying to replace him. Samuel continued to hope, as he put it in the spring 1778, that "an early Stroke" would inflict "a mortal Wound" on the British. But he understood the military realities, and that meant supporting the commander in chief and accepting the Fabian strategy. Indeed, in September of 1778 Adams went so far as to praise the American generals who "are wisely following the unpopular Steps of Fabius or Count Daun." The reference to Count Daun was especially significant. He was an Austrian general who, although criticized for being overly cautious during the Seven Years' War that ended in 1763, had won praise for thwarting the military goals of his enemies and thus helping preserve his nation.[12]

No matter what strategy they followed, the revolutionaries needed to field an experienced army, and Adams continued, as he had in 1776, to pursue that goal vigorously. As early as April 1777 he decried the "mortifying" problems caused by one-year enlistments and spoke of the need to form "a permanent Army for the future." In 1779 he supported the Massachusetts program of offering a $300 bounty to men who reenlisted for the duration of the war. When he happily reported to John Adams in early 1780 that many soldiers had rejoined, Samuel sounded positively militaristic. Maintaining that a soldier's "Courage" in combat often sprang from military discipline, Adams exclaimed that Washington would soon have the best American army ever, because the longer soldiers served, the more disciplined they became. By the end of 1780 Samuel asserted that Americans had no choice but to support Congress's plan of forming a permanent army to win the war. More than four years of fighting had convinced him that no person "in his Senses who wishes the War may be carried on with Vigor" would prefer temporary drafts of militia "to a permanent and well appointed Army!"[13] Adams thus demonstrated that, despite his distrust of the military, he could be flexible if the cause of independence required it.

When personally confronted with the need to make a command decision, Adams showed his willingness to carry on the war aggressively. In June 1780 Adams and Elbridge Gerry, another Massachusetts delegate, met by chance in Hartford and learned that a large British force was threatening the strategic fortifications at West Point. The two congressmen ordered General John Fellows, commander of Massachusetts's Berkshire County militia, to secure provisions, get wagons wherever he could, and quickly march his forces to relieve West Point. While admitting they acted "*without Authority*," Adams and Gerry assumed that the state's legislators would, given "the very critical Situation of the Army," approve of their conduct. They were right.[14]

The zealousness Adams brought to the great cause impressed the Marquis de Chastellux, a French major general serving in America. Recounting a lengthy conversation they had in December 1780, Chastellux remarked that "I experienced in his company the satisfaction one rarely has in society, or even the theater, of finding the person of the actor corresponding to the role he plays." Echoing views held by both Whigs and Tories, Chastellux described Adams as "a man wrapped up in his object, who never spoke but to give me a good opinion of his cause and a high idea of his country. His simple and frugal exterior seemed intended as a contrast to the energy and scope of his thoughts, which were wholly focused upon the republic, and lost nothing of their warmth by being expressed with method and precision, just as an army, marching towards the enemy, appears no less daring for observing the laws of tactics."[15]

Wanting all Americans to be as wholly focused as he was, throughout the war years Adams used his considerable skills as political polemicist—as propagandist—to foster zealousness in the great cause.[16] He wrote "private" letters for others to use in support of positions he advocated, just as he similarly used letters sent to him. Adams occasionally read letters he received to government bodies, or he inserted appropriate extracts in the press. The optimistic military forecasts he routinely put in his private correspondence formed part of his propaganda efforts. Thus, more than once in 1777 he suggested that one major American victory might well "put a glorious End to the present Campaign & very probably the War." In early 1778 he wrote of longing for America's forces to begin the military campaign "very early the next Spring." In mid-1780 one of his propagandistic newspaper essays used eye-catching type to proclaim that, if amply supported, America's soldiers had a "GOLDEN OPPORTUNITY" to make the current campaign "DECISIVE and GLORIOUS." Adams constantly exhorted the people of Massachusetts, of New England, of America to be "Zealous in the great Cause," and he lavished praise on them for pouring labor and money into the war.[17]

When he wielded his pen to bolster the war effort, Adams highlighted two core arguments: America was defending her liberties against a barbarous enemy, and more than American liberty was at stake. He made the link emphatically at the end of 1776 when America's military situation seemed almost hopeless. Adams boldly asserted that the tyrant George III wanted to subjugate America because "the lamp of liberty" burned there and nowhere else. By the summer of 1777, adapting the phraseology of Thomas Paine's *Common Sense*, Adams was proclaiming that America's great cause was "the Cause of Mankind." Indeed, liberty was under assault around the globe, so the friends of liberty looked to America as an asylum. America was thus on a dual mission for freedom: "We are contending for the Rights of our Country and Mankind."[18]

Strident propaganda efforts seemed necessary because less than a majority of Americans actively supported the war. To his dismay, thousands attempted to maintain what Adams called "a dastardly and criminal Neutrality." And a significant minority of Americans, at least one in five and possibly as many as one in three, yearned to remain in the British Empire and worked to make that happen. The British thought these loyalists, those Americans the revolutionaries maligned as Tories, could prove decisive. Adams shared the British view. His fears centered on Tories who might surreptitiously undermine the war effort. He soon came to believe they were more dangerous than loyalists who took up arms. By early 1777, and then throughout the rest of the war, Adams carried the argument further. "The secret Machinations" of Tories, he asserted, posed a greater threat to the glorious cause than the British military did. All manner of Tories must, he insisted, be squelched.[19]

Adams began translating his strident anti-Tory views into congressional action even before independence was declared. In December 1775 he took full advantage of being appointed to chair a small congressional committee on how to overcome the problem of soldiers being jailed for minor debts. Based on the Congress's statement that such actions might have occurred either by "inattention to the public good" or "with a design to retard the recruiting service," his committee decided to formulate general policies for dealing with Tories. Congress approved the report in early January 1776. It called on citizens to educate any well-meaning but uninformed Americans who were being deceived by Britain's supporters. For their part, the local governmental units, including conventions and committees, should speedily adopt measures "to frustrate" the "mischievous machinations" of those working against America. All Tories should be disarmed; "the more dangerous" should be locked up or forced to post bonds for their good behavior. Since Adams's hatred of Tories never subsided, it is no surprise that he was one of the initial appointments to a committee of five created in October 1776 to prepare a plan "for suppressing the internal enemies of America, and preventing a communication of intelligence to our other enemies." This group evolved into the congressional "committee for suppressing toryism."[20]

The major antiloyalist efforts occurred at the state and local levels. So, even while he attended Congress, Adams kept pressing for vigorous action back home. Massachusetts did quickly pass a test act that incorporated the Adams committee recommendations. All free adult males were required to take an oath of allegiance to the Revolution. Those who refused would be disarmed; moreover, they could neither hold public office nor posts as teachers or ministers. The extralegal committees and local magistrates would enforce these regulations. Adams soon called for sterner measures. Writing home in early 1777, and often thereafter, he insisted that measures, "and the most vigorous ones," must be taken quickly "to root out these pernicious Weeds." If the Tory weeds were not ripped out, America's struggle would be in vain. When these hints failed to produce results, Adams escalated his rhetoric. In June he proclaimed that Tories should be cast out of society. Although it took longer than he wanted, a September 1778 Massachusetts law banished upward of three hundred Tories by name and threatened them with death if they returned. In April 1779 the Massachusetts legislature authorized the confiscation of Tory property.[21]

While he considered patriotic fervor and the suppression of internal enemies essential to winning independence, Adams believed that forming a confederation government was also a prerequisite to securing true independence. He was therefore gratified when Congress finally appointed a committee in early June 1776 to produce a frame of government for the confederation. He was, no doubt, happier yet when Congress placed him on it. The committee did not keep a record of its deliberations, so Adams's contributions are not known. However, it is clear the members clashed sharply over many provisions. The committee issued its recommendations a month later. The title of the proposal, "*Articles of confederation and perpetual union*," highlighted the fact that "The United States of America" was a "Confederacy." To protect their liberties and promote "their mutual and general Welfare," the states were creating "a firm League of Friendship," not a unified national government. The states that formed this perpetual union would retain "sole and exclusive" control of their internal affairs, provided their actions did not conflict with the Articles. The voting system and the rules for amending the Articles underscored that the government was a confederation: no matter what its size or wealth, each state would have a single vote in Congress and, once the Articles were adopted, *every* state must give its approval before the Articles could be altered.

The proposed frame of government obviously reflected America's colonial experience. As members of the British Empire, the colonists expected a central government to control foreign policy and mutual defense. The committee charged with crafting America's constitution was, however, understandably determined to deny the central government the kinds of coercive powers that had produced the time of troubles and then revolution. Accordingly, the confederation government could station troops in forts, but it could not maintain standing armies. Except for financing a postal system, Congress could "never impose or levy any Taxes or Duties." The state legislatures would meet the confederation's financial needs by supplying funds based on a formula linked to a state's population. The confederation government was not, however, given any power to force states to comply with its requests for money.[22]

Adams hoped Congress would "speedily digest" the confederation proposal. Yet, despite his repeated efforts to stop congressional dallying, it took more than a year just to revise the plan before sending it out for adoption. As Samuel indicated, two major questions delayed the approval of "a Matter of very great Importance." Congressmen from populous and wealthy states typically argued that voting power should reflect a state's population or wealth. Representatives from smaller states defended the established one state, one vote system. The other problem flowed from a simple statement in the Articles that gave Congress power to settle land disputes between the states. Some colonial charters contained wording that allowed states to claim lands as far west as the Union could expand. States with such charters, especially Virginia, did not want Congress deciding land matters.

While the Articles of Confederation that Congress sent to the states in November 1777 retained the essential features of the original plan Adams helped draft, some significant modifications had been made. The taxing formula was changed so assessments would be based on the value of each state's lands and improvements to the land rather than its population. In addition, Congress's revisions clarified two important points. Congress would still have authority to settle land disputes arising from colonial charters or colonial land grants; however, the brief statement in the original plan had given way to a complicated system for adjudicating land disputes. In addition, a revised Article 2 spelled out unequivocally the principle of state's rights: "Each State retains its sovereignty, freedom and independence, and every power, jurisdiction, and right, which is not by this confederation expressly delegated to the United States, in Congress assembled."

Adams proclaimed himself reasonably satisfied with the revised Articles of Confederation. With its careful limitation of the central government's power the Articles seemed well suited to ensuring that the government could not endanger the people's liberties. The Articles' emphasis on state sovereignty—an emphasis Adams approved—reflected the fact that the revolutionaries had dual loyalties. Although they thought of themselves as Americans, at least to the extent of supporting the Union, many gave a preference to their state. This penchant could be seen in the sharp debates in Congress about how land claims would be settled. It could be seen in the fact that many Americans, including Adams, kept referring to their state as their "country."[23]

Because Massachusetts had enlarged the size of its congressional delegation and developed a rotation system so members could take breaks from their duties, Adams was able to return to Boston in late November 1777 and remain there until early May 1778. The Boston Town Meeting put him to work almost instantly. On December 7 he was appointed to draft a petition to the General Court to allow the town to appoint more tax assessors. He quickly did so. Once at home, though, Adams devoted most of his attention to promoting the adoption of the proposed confederation government. He resorted to his established lobbying techniques to achieve this goal. Samuel wrote letters to his correspondents that emphasized the importance of approving the Articles. Putting a positive spin on

the question while reflecting his own belief that compromise was necessary when forming governments, he said he expected the General Court
would approve the plan, "even those parts which it may be wishd had been
different." This would be done "for the Sake of that Union which is so
necessary for the Support of the great Cause." He also drafted a resolution,
which the Boston Town Meeting unanimously approved in late January,
that proclaimed the Articles "well adapted to Cement the Union of the . . .
States." The town meeting translated those words into action by instructing
its representatives to vote for the Articles.[24]

Samuel Adams rejoined Congress in time to sign the Articles of Confederation. The importance Adams attached to the event shines in a letter
he penned to Elizabeth on July 9, 1778. "I now write at the Table in Congress, having just put my Hand to the Confederation with my [Massachu-
setts] Colleagues & the Delegates of seven other States." He indicated that
two more states had also agreed to sign. Owing in large measure to concerns about western land claims, however, the Articles were not officially
implemented until March 1781, when Maryland became the thirteenth
state to approve them.[25]

The formal establishment of the confederation government could not
obscure the fact that the revolutionaries were awash in economic difficulties. Despite foreign aid and loans, the revolutionaries had to issue paper
money. Soaring inflation, especially in 1778 and 1779, created economic
havoc, and numerous attempts to regulate prices failed. To remedy the
problems on a long-term basis, Adams advocated levying high taxes and
reducing the amount of money in circulation. At the same time he insisted
that the people should be sensitive to the needs of the poor. But Americans generally opposed high taxes. Given what was at stake in "the great
Cause," Adams found it irksome that people were unwilling to sacrifice for
the public good and for the good of posterity.

As the war dragged on, Adams grew increasingly convinced that
some revolutionaries were selfishly pursuing their own economic interests.
When circumstances reduced the supply of food, greedy people drove up
the prices by withholding goods from the market. Public anger soon boiled
over, and at least three dozen food riots erupted by the end of 1779. More
than 40 percent of these riots took place in Massachusetts, and half of those
happened in Boston. Samuel Adams was not involved in these disturbances;
indeed, he was not even in Boston when food riots occurred there. Once
again the evidence demonstrates that people did not need the influence of
someone like Adams to form crowds to deal with crucial problems that

touched their vital interests and that seemed to require their immediate action.[26]

While Adams reviled the monopolizers, he was no enemy of free enterprise. As he and others had repeatedly pointed out over the decades, his beloved Boston was a commercial town. Adams also acknowledged that conducting trade in wartime conditions was both risky and expensive. Therefore it was, he remarked, only "natural" that businesspeople would want a substantial profit. Nevertheless, all people had a duty to protect liberty, and, when liberty was in mortal danger, the people should not let "private Interest" compete with the larger interest "of the great Community." Writing in early 1778 from Boston, he lamented that "the Spirit of Avarice . . . prevails too much in this Town." Still, he exonerated the ordinary people—the yeomanry—by proclaiming that the evil "rages only among the few, because perhaps, the few only are concernd at present in trade." It was merchants, the same kind of people who had so often undermined colonial-era efforts to protect liberty, who too often shirked their duty as citizens.

Although Adams did not initiate the food riots in Massachusetts, he seemed to endorse them. In January 1778 he said he considered the suppression of monopolizers nearly as crucial as supplying the American army. Discussing how that might be done, Adams observed that price-control legislation seemed ineffective. He then suggested that if "the Popular Indignation" could be raised "to a suitable Pitch," the price gouging would stop. He proclaimed himself ready to join in any measure that would achieve that goal. Adams did not have to direct crowd actions to use the threat of them as a club against monopolizers.[27]

Believing that "A Citizen owes everything to the Commonwealth," Adams naturally detested businesspeople and politicians who tried to enrich themselves through monopolies. Their behavior was the exact opposite of what he considered appropriate. A public figure should be guided by "the pure Motive of serving his Country" and "promoting the public welfare," not by "private or Selfish Considerations." Those who truly loved their country would, he maintained, willingly make any sacrifice necessary to protect it. He put the idea succinctly when he declared that "My first Concern is for the Honor & Safety of my Country." In 1778 Adams had summed up his ideals of public service, ideals he believed he measured up to, when he exclaimed, "It would be the Glory of this Age, to find Men having no ruling Passion but the Love of their Country, and ready to render her the most arduous and important Services with the Hope for no other Reward in this Life than the Esteem of their virtuous Fellow Citizens." And in late 1780, as he contemplated retiring from Congress, Samuel wrote to his dear Betsy, "you are Witness that I have not raisd a Fortune in the Service of my Country. I glory in being what the world calls, a poor Man."[28]

Even as he vigorously strove to help create the confederation government and thwart those who sought to enrich themselves at the expense of their endangered country, Adams expended tremendous energy in the effort to acquire the foreign assistance he considered vital to winning independence. Since it had long contended with Britain for dominance in Europe and North America, Adams believed that "France is the natural ally of the United States." At first France willingly aided the revolutionaries, but not openly and only on a limited basis lest she be drawn into war with Britain. Still, the arms and powder France supplied in the early phases of the war proved crucial to the American forces.[29]

Once independence was declared, his fellow congressmen, recognizing Adams's ardor on the issue, placed him on the committee charged with obtaining foreign aid. Adams crafted many letters intended for French eyes or ears. He pointed out numerous reasons why France's "true Interest" dictated helping America instantly and to the utmost. Still, according to Adams, military success, not words, finally swayed the French. He believed the astounding American victory at Saratoga in October 1777, where a British army of more than five thousand surrendered, finally convinced the French to enter an alliance with America. France did that, Adams reasoned, lest the British make "Overtures" that would lead the Americans to compromise with Britain. When news of the French treaty of alliance reached America in the spring of 1778, Adams was ecstatic. Congress acknowledged his diligence in pursuit of a French alliance by putting him on the three-member committee that arranged the formal welcome for Conrad Alexandre Gérard, France's first ambassador to the new nation. Samuel wrote to James Warren about the irony of someone like himself, who was "so little of the Man of the World," being placed on a committee "to settle Ceremonials." Nevertheless, Adams gladly accepted the assignment. He believed that, because the ceremony might set precedent, it was of some importance to agree on "forms that are adapted to the true *republican* Principles." After Adams and Richard Henry Lee personally escorted Gérard into the Congress's chamber in the Pennsylvania State House, the ceremonial acceptance of his credentials as the first ambassador ever appointed to the new United States of America took place on August 6, 1778.[30]

As a realist Adams understood that America required the aid of France. So, as he later told his cousin John, Samuel consciously employed his pen to blunt negative comments that could weaken the newly formed alliance and thereby give aid and comfort to the British. Although he had in the past occasionally employed anti-Catholic rhetoric himself, once the alliance was completed Samuel decried those who expressed anti-Catholic sentiments. Writing to James Warren, he asserted that it was the king's partisans who were most prone to shout about "the Danger of Popery." So, as Adams presented it, those who voiced religious "prejudice" against "our new Connection" to France aided the Tories or were Tories. Samuel was especially sensitive to the vital assistance the French navy could provide. When hurricane winds and inferior numbers caused the French admiral Compte d'Estaing to withdraw his fleet from a planned attack against the British in Rhode Island in the fall of 1778 and consequently endangered American ground forces, Adams did his best to quell the anti-French grousing of many New Englanders. He defended d'Estaing's withdrawal as militarily reasonable, and he also bluntly called it "impolitick in the Extreme" to traduce the French admiral. Adams's efforts on behalf of first acquiring French aid and then avoiding rifts in the alliance were amply rewarded in the battle of Yorktown in October 1781. French assistance, in the form of a naval fleet as well as ground troops, proved essential in achieving the decisive victory that, when he heard the news, caused the British prime minister, Lord North, to moan repeatedly, "Oh God, it is all over!" It took almost another two years to achieve the final peace, but Lord North was right.[31]

Although he courted French aid, labored to make the alliance function smoothly, and at the end of the war heaped praise on France as the "faithful Ally" whose assistance made achieving independence possible, Adams had no illusions about the Catholic monarchy. He knew the French had not assisted the revolutionaries for altruistic reasons. Nations, he insisted, pursued foreign policies "consistent with their Ideas of their own Interest." Adams certainly believed America should follow that dictum. In April 1783 he articulated his own sense of what America's long-term foreign policy should be. Contemplating what the American people should do in a peacetime world, Adams said, "I hope we shall never intermeddle with the Quarrels of other Nations." An independent America should, he believed, pursue a course of judicious international neutrality.[32]

Given his own realpolitik, Adams acted on the belief that American foreign policy should be based on America's interests, which, in Adams's mind, often neatly coincided with the interests of New England and especially of Massachusetts. The revolutionaries, he insisted, could accept peace only on terms that "shall be honorable & safe to our Country." Independence was a "mere Charm" unless America secured "those Advantages" necessary to maintain that independence. Because he considered having access to the fishing waters off Newfoundland one of those advantages, he relentlessly strove to obtain it. From the opening of hostilities he cast covetous eyes northward. He advocated annexing Canada. Looking south, he also mentioned acquiring Florida. His suggestions about gobbling up land and his occasional declarations about America as an "empire" seem to stamp him as a keen expansionist. Yet Samuel explicitly denied that America fought for empire. In his case, that was true. He did not advocate acquiring Canada so America could create an empire. He wanted the territories as bargaining chips America could "exchange" to secure its vital interests. In August 1780, when the war was going poorly in the South, Samuel suggested to the French ambassador what might be done if the British held Georgia or South Carolina when peace negotiations occurred. Adams suggested that, if the Americans controlled Nova Scotia, it could be traded to the British to ensure that Georgia and South Carolina were returned. Despite these diplomatic musings, Samuel coveted Canada, or at least Nova Scotia, to ensure that Americans, especially New Englanders, could continue to fish Canadian waters. As he indicated, the possession of Canadian territories would be "a great & permanent Protection to the Fishery." Adams's concern about the fisheries glistened in the congressional committee report on getting foreign assistance he helped draft in late 1776. The report stipulated that, if they wrested Newfoundland, Cape Breton, and Nova Scotia from Britain, the French and Americans would share the fishery equally while excluding all others.[33]

Throughout the war years Adams thought of acquiring lands to protect the invaluable fisheries. Congress gave him an excellent opportunity to translate his desires into policy when it placed him on the committee charged with formulating America's war goals. The committee report of February 1779 listed several points as "absolutely necessary for the safety and independence of the United States." The right to fish in Newfoundland waters and to cure fish on the shore must, the report indicated, "be reserved, acknowledged, and ratified to the subjects of the United States." And while the committee recommended acquiring Nova Scotia and Florida, its report also suggested those lands were expendable. If Britain ceded Florida, Congress could sell it to Spain. Any claims to Nova Scotia should be sacrificed if doing so gave America an equal share in the fisheries. Nova Scotia was valuable as a bargaining chip, not for itself. Congress debated the recommendations until August 1779 and then, at a time when Adams was in Boston on leave, issued instructions that waffled on the question of the fisheries.[34]

French officials were determined to counter Adams's unrelenting efforts to ensure that any peace treaty guarantee American rights to the fisheries. They did that because they coveted the fisheries for France and because they did not want the American desire to secure them to prolong the war. As Congress was trying to hammer out its position on the issue, the French turned to the Reverend Samuel Cooper, the well-known Boston Whig and Adams's frequent correspondent. Cooper needed no urging to champion the alliance with France both orally and in publications. He, like Samuel, had long emphasized that the revolutionaries needed French assistance to win independence. But Cooper, as his French handler John de Valnais put it, had a "penchant for gold," and that penchant made him willing to do much more than merely promote French-American cooperation. When de Valnais approached him in January 1779 with the suggestion that the French government would give him a yearly stipend for promoting French interests, the reverend asked for the huge sum of £200 a year in specie. De Valnais recommend acquiescing to Cooper's extraordinary demand because "such an eminent man deserved to be bought, even at this price." It quickly became obvious that the French hired Cooper in large measure, as de Valnais put it, "to destroy the influence of Mr. S. Adams in this state." Given Adams's standing in Massachusetts, Cooper had to proceed surreptitiously. Still, by June of 1779 de Valnais reported good success in "ruining him [Samuel Adams] in the opinion of several important men who are even his best friends and sole supporters." Despite this and continuing reports of the reverend's supposed success, events proved it was not so easy to sabotage either Adams or his position on the fisheries. Nevertheless, because Cooper remained on the French payroll until his death in late December 1783, he continued to do the bidding of the French government by trying to undermine Adams in the eyes of his fellow citizens even after Samuel left Congress.[35]

The so-called Deane-Lee controversy of the late 1770s demonstrates the complex interrelationship between acquiring French aid, protecting the fledgling nation's vital geographical interests, and Samuel Adams's unflinching concern for putting country above personal gain. Silas Deane, whose avarice was at the core of the controversy, represented Connecticut in Congress from 1774 into January 1776. While in Congress Deane served on the Secret Committee for purchasing war materials. As a member of that committee he developed close personal and economic ties with men like

Robert Morris and other leading merchants from the mid-Atlantic region who believed they had every right to mix government and personal affairs to enrich themselves. In March of 1776 the Secret Committee sent Deane to France to establish himself as a merchant and acquire trade goods suitable for Indians; he was to get a 5 percent commission on the transactions he arranged. At the same time, although he did not understand French, the Congress' Committee of Secret Correspondence authorized Deane "to transact such business commercial & political" as the committee entrusted to him. Deane, who craved wealth and lived as lavishly as possible, soon unscrupulously blended his business affairs with those of the government. He also continued his speculation in American land. By July 1777 there were rumblings about recalling him. Declaring that Deane had no authority to enter into such accords, on September 8 Congress repudiated agreements he had made with foreigners seeking to join the American army. Then on November 21, 1777, Congress recalled Deane.

In August 1778, fueled by complaints lodged by Arthur Lee, another diplomat serving the nation in Europe, a suspicious Congress finally began interviewing Deane about his business activities. As the process unfolded over the months, bitter accusations roiled Congress. When Deane published a letter in December 1778, the issue turned into a vitriolic battle of accusations hurled about in newspapers and pamphlets. Deane tried to defend himself in part by attacking Arthur Lee and, as far as an outraged president of Congress Henry Laurens was concerned, the "dignity of Congress." Laurens told his fellow congressmen that Deane's letter contained material "highly derogatory to the honor and interests of these United States." Despite all the heat it generated, the controversy subsided with a whimper in August 1779 when the Congress effectively ended its investigation of Deane's tangled expense accounts by merely resolving that Deane "be discharged from any further attendance on Congress."[36]

Samuel Adams took no part in the print warfare and had been away from Congress for almost two months when it finally discharged Deane. However, because the controversy became linked to the issue of the fisheries and also what boundaries the new nation would have, Samuel did become deeply involved in aspects of the fray. In part to try to extricate himself from the charges leveled against him, Deane did his best to ingratiate himself to Gérard, the French ambassador. Gérard had no special interest in defending Deane, but he was determined, as evidenced by the hiring of Rev. Cooper, to stop Samuel Adams and his supporters from making America's right to use the fisheries a precondition for ending the war. So Deane's attack on Arthur Lee and his relatives, close allies of Adams, served Gérard's purposes.

A newspaper essayist who ventured into print in late June 1779 provides a sense of the congressional infighting involved in the Deane-Lee fracas and how Adams continued to use his well-honed organizational methods. The author of the essay was probably former Congressman Edward Langworthy of Georgia, who served in Congress for most of the period from November 1777 through mid-April 1779. James Lovell, a Massachusetts congressman who worked closely with Adams and the Lee family during the Deane-Lee controversy, made sure that Samuel, who had recently returned to Boston, received a copy of the essay. Intriguingly, Lovell told Adams the piece offered "a history of you & your Clubs."

Writing under the signature "O Tempora! O, Mores!," Langworthy bemoaned the workings of what he called a congressional "club" that functioned as "a junto." Claiming that "the foundation of this junto was laid during the sitting of the first congress," Langworthy noted that he did not plan to present a "history of this junto." Rather, he wanted to warn the American people that for over a year this "club," despite being a minority in the Congress, had been able to "retard, delay, and even obstruct every [congressional] proceeding." Accordingly to Langworthy, the members of the club "meet regularly, debate upon, and adjust the manner of their proceedings; and congress, at all times, being a fluctuating and changing body, these men, acting in concert, are able to keep back or obstruct any measure whatever, until, by absence of some members, and the division of others, they can, with a small majority, carry the vote as they please."

Langworthy, though, overstated the power of what Lovell referred to as Samuel's congressional "Clubs." His diatribe did not give enough weight to the fact that there were fundamental, and in some cases irreconcilable, differences among congressmen. State concerns, regional concerns, differing worldviews, and even individual aspersions all played their part. The lengthy struggle to get the Articles of Confederation adopted, the difficulty in agreeing on what the United Sates would demand in a peace treaty, and the Deane-Lee controversy itself illustrate the clash of interests and perceptions that often made congressional politics of the day so acrimonious. Nevertheless, Langworthy accurately described methods Adams had skillfully used over the decades to achieve his political goals.[37]

As he surveyed the unfolding controversy in January of 1779, Samuel was not surprised by Deane's duplicity. Thinking back on when he served with him in Congress, Samuel maintained that, if Deane had any political principles, "I could never learn them." Adams then added a comment that could hardly have been more damning, coming, as it did, from one who had asserted that a public official should, after careful self-scrutiny, honestly be able to say that "he has had in his View no private or selfish

Considerations, but has ever been [guided] by the pure Motive of serving his Country." Samuel sneered that Deane's "Views always appeared to me commercial & interested." Sadly, Deane was merely one of many such covetous men. Adams feared that what he called a combination of political and commercial men were "aiming to get the Trade, the Wealth, the Power and the Government of America into their own Hands." Two weeks later he voiced his suspicions more emphatically: "I am sorry to be obligd to think, that a Monopoly of Trade, and not the Liberty of their Country, is the sole object of some Mens Views. This is the Cake which they hope shortly to slice and share among themselves." By late February he was even more apprehensive. He warned that men were plotting to grab America's best land as well as monopolize its commerce. They must be resisted, just as the fisheries must be protected, or else independence, once achieved, would be a sham.[38]

Although the final military victory had not yet been achieved and the fisheries had not yet been secured, by 1781 Adams believed the time had finally come to retire from Congress. Adams felt justified in leaving Congress in part because by March 1781, when he formally asked to be replaced, the great cause was doing very well at the continental level. All the original states had—finally—approved the Articles of Confederation. Spain and Holland had become belligerents in the war against Britain, thus brightening the long-term military situation. The optimism that Samuel Adams voiced in that decisive year of 1781 was shared by many who supported the Revolution. Indeed, even before the decisive victory at Yorktown in October, Americans were offered a depiction of "America Triumphant and Britannia in Distress" that celebrated the free American nation Samuel Adams was helping to bring into existence. The explanation that accompanied "America Triumphant" gloried in "America sitting on that quarter of the globe with the Flag of the United States displayed over her head; holding in one hand the Olive branch, inviting the ships of all nations to partake of her commerce; and in the other hand supporting the Cap of Liberty." And while "Fame [was] proclaiming the joyful news to all the world," poor, defeated Britannia, "attended with an evil genius," was "weeping at the loss of the trade of America." The idea that Europe's trade would stream into America was underscored by images of French, Spanish, Dutch and other ships crowding an American harbor.[39]

The portrayal of "America Triumphant and Britannia in Distress" matched well with arguments Samuel, and others, had advanced during the movement toward independence. It was trade, he had argued as early as 1764, that made the colonies valuable to Great Britain; therefore, En-

"America Triumphant and Britannia in Distress" (Boston, 1782). Courtesy of the Library of Congress.

gland would, if she persisted in trying to tax the unrepresented colonists, soon find her strength and glory being eclipsed. Still, even allowing for the fact that "America Triumphant and Britannia in Distress" was a complex depiction, if he saw it Samuel might have noticed there was no mention of the fisheries he considered so vital not merely to New England but to American interests. As he prepared to leave Congress, Samuel certainly was well aware that the fisheries still needed protecting. But he knew, and as France's diplomats ruefully discovered, he could direct that effort from Boston. In addition, as he had repeatedly asserted and honestly believed, Massachusetts had many men, such as James Lovell, who could perform admirably in Congress.

The Samuel Adams who spoke longingly of rejoining his family and tasting "the Sweets of Retirement" found the thought of permanently returning home attractive for many reasons. He was approaching his sixtieth birthday and had taken to referring to old age creeping up on him. Those

Facsimiles of Samuel Adams signatures over time reproduced from William V. Wells's Life and Public Services of Samuel Adams (1865).

who knew him said he possessed a strong constitution but hard work was taking its toll. As he aged, the Adams family malady, likely palsy, grew progressively worse. The involuntary movements of his hand and head increased; his speech became more halting. Writing letters was an essential part of his political work, and by late 1780 he complained that his shaking hand was unfit to guide a pen. Specimens of his writing show he was right. Samuel had also recently experienced major bouts of ill health, as had Elizabeth a year before.[40]

After he retired from Congress in the spring of 1781, Samuel no longer needed to exchange letters with his beloved Betsy, the woman he told his daughter Hannah was "a rich Blessing" to them both. In one sense that is unfortunate. What can be discerned about Samuel and Elizabeth's evolving relationship comes primarily from their correspondence. The letters they exchanged from 1776 through mid-1781, like their earlier letters, reveal a loving relationship. As before, each pleaded with the other to write more often, and Samuel once remarked that he would not consider it a burden if he received six of her letters at once. And when Elizabeth had sufficiently recovered from an illness so she herself could write, Samuel said getting her letter was "like cool Water to a thirsty Soul." Samuel expressed concern about the family members' safety and comfort as they moved about to avoid the British. Each of them routinely inquired about the other's health, and Samuel gently chided Elizabeth because one of her letters did not "expressly" tell him she was well. He insisted she must always do that. Yet Samuel withheld medical news he knew would worry her. Even as he scolded Elizabeth for not reassuring him about her health, he altered his letter by expunging a statement that Philadelphia "has for some time past been a complete Hospital, and many are still sick."[41]

The relationship between Samuel and Elizabeth, as well as his general view of the place women should have in society, became clearer in these years. Although he did not indicate that he was giving his personal view of a woman's proper role, Samuel once noted that society dictated that women should occupy a subordinate position. In November 1778, having given Thomas Wells permission to marry "the dear Girl whom I pride myself in calling my Daughter," Samuel wrote to Thomas with advice about marriage. "The Marriage State," he observed, "was designd to complete the Sum of human Happiness in this Life." Maintaining that it required "Judgment on both Sides" to discern the proper conduct toward each other, Samuel remarked that, "though it is acknowledgd, that the Superiority is & ought to be in the Man, yet as the Management of a Family in many Instances necessarily devolves on the Woman, it is difficult always to determine the Line between the Authority of the one & the Subordination of the other." His own suggestion was "not to govern too much." He seemingly endorsed a sense of equality by adding that, "when the married Couple strictly observe the great Rules of Honor & Justice towards each other, Differences, if any happen, between them, must proceed from small & trifling Circumstances."[42]

On two occasions, though, Adams embraced traditional stereotypes about women. Knowing Congress had fled Philadelphia in December 1776 to avoid the onrushing British, Elizabeth wrote Samuel that she "was greatly alarmd" to hear about the British occupation. That prompted Samuel to observe, "I have long known you to be possessd of much Fortitude of Mind. But you are a Woman, and one must expect you will now and then discover [the] Timidity so natural to your Sex." And in a letter of August 1777 Samuel ended a discussion on military matters with the comment, "But I forget that I am writing [to] a female upon the Subject of War."[43]

Despite his occasional articulation of contemporary and stereotypical views about women, Samuel increasingly relied on Elizabeth's active participation in political matters. Their letters demonstrate the gradual but steady change. Writing in late 1776 Samuel mentioned that "it has not been usual for me to write to you of War or Politicks." He revealed, though, that Elizabeth wanted to discuss such issues by adding, "but I know how deeply you have always interrested yourself in the Welfare of our Country and I am disposd to gratify your Curiosity." In early 1777 he paid her the compliment of saying he would willingly have his letter intercepted and passed into the hands of General Howe so "that from the Quotations I have made from yours he might see the unconquerable Spirit of a Boston Female." By February 1777 Samuel was leaving his expense vouchers under Elizabeth's control. In March he suggested he might be trying her patience with long letters about politics, but he wrote them nonetheless. It was in the late summer of 1777 that he mentioned not writing about military affairs to a woman. Intriguingly, he was well into that discussion of military matters before figuratively catching himself writing to a woman about military topics. And he seemed to dismiss his own stereotypical observation by immediately interjecting the comment that "I know your whole Soul is engagd in the great Cause." As 1778 progressed, Samuel no longer mentioned any possible lack of interest on Elizabeth's part because she was a woman, and he filled his letters to her with commentary on the war and the political scene.[44]

Samuel drafted Elizabeth into active service by the end of 1778. Deep into a lengthy letter on public matters, he indicated that he had read and then sent James Warren a recent publication concerning the political struggle raging between Silas Deane and Arthur Lee. He requested, "I wish you would invite him to a Dish of Tea, and desire him to let you see it [the publication] and my Letter which inclosd it." For her part, "You may read this Letter to him and other Confidential Friends, but dont let it go out of your own Hands." The general societal view still held that women should not even think about politics, much less participate in them. Thus Samuel's request that Elizabeth engage in political discussions is telling. His request was, in fact, remarkable because he spoke of "other Confidential Friends" without naming them. Samuel trusted Elizabeth to know who should or should not be allowed to peruse his letters. In March 1779 he sent her a letter containing extracts from one written by Arthur Lee. Samuel reiterated his faith in Elizabeth's political judgment by telling her that she could show Lee's comments "to such of my Confidential Friends as you think proper." What makes that letter even more illuminating is the fact that it came in response to one from Elizabeth in which she urged Samuel to resign his post as Massachusetts secretary of state. He responded not with anger but with the comment that her "Wish" that he resign "perfectly coincides with my own Inclination."[45]

Elizabeth's active participation in Samuel's political world reached a pinnacle in 1781 shortly before he retired from Congress. Ironically, it involved the Rev. Samuel Cooper, who Samuel did not know was pocketing French gold in return for slandering him. In a letter covering various political matters, Samuel told Elizabeth that his old friend had stopped writing although Samuel had requested specific information. Having expressed the hope that Cooper did not find the correspondence troublesome, Samuel sounded a hostile note. He observed that, as Elizabeth knew, he was inclined to retaliate when someone chose to stop writing. He then added that when he thought an old friend had done wrong, "I let none know it, but him & you." Samuel told Elizabeth she could let Cooper, but no one else, read the letter. So Samuel shared his thoughts with Elizabeth on a special basis, and he left it up to her to decide whether she wanted to initiate contact with her husband's offending friend. She did and with good success. Surely in part to cover his anti-Adams efforts, Cooper resumed writing to Samuel and praised Elizabeth for how she communicated the original letter to him. "I am glad she did it in a Manner so acceptable," Samuel noted. "Indeed," he added, "I never found Reason to doubt her Discretion." By the time Samuel left Congress to return home to Boston, he was rejoining a spouse who had become an active partner in his political endeavors.[46]

Samuel, who last participated in congressional activities on April 25, 1781, probably left Philadelphia later that month. He did so even before his replacement delegate arrived on June 12. There was a special reason for Samuel to rush home. On Friday, June 1, his daughter, Hannah, and Thomas Wells, the younger brother of Samuel's dearest Betsy, officially announced their intention to marry.[47]

The Samuel Adams who rejoined Elizabeth in the spring of 1781 was serious about retiring from Congress. In 1782, when once again appointed to the post, he recounted his lengthy congressional service and asked to be excused, which he was. And once having quit Congress and again taken up residence in Boston, Adams never again ventured out of Massachusetts. However, even as he contemplated leaving Congress, Adams did not contemplate retiring from politics. He merely planned to confine himself to what he called a more limited sphere. So he accepted election to the Massachusetts House on May 16 and was soon elevated to the presidency of the Senate, but he declined a position on the Governor's Council.[48] Even as he moved into this more limited sphere, Samuel had no intention of abandoning his efforts to achieve victory in the great cause and to rest independence on a secure foundation. He most certainly made sure Congress did not forget about the fisheries.

Once he returned home, Samuel bombarded American leaders with letters on the fisheries issue. He insisted that New England's and America's vital interests required that access to the fisheries *must* be guaranteed in any peace treaty. In August and September 1781 he spelled out his logic in letters to Thomas McKean, then the president of Congress. Samuel pointedly reminded McKean, who represented Delaware but had extensive ties to Philadelphia, that the fishing banks were at least as important as the South's tobacco and rice or the great wheat fields of Pennsylvania. Adams stressed that all Americans benefited from the fisheries. Since an independent America would have an extensive shipping trade, it followed that the nation would need a strong navy to protect that trade. A navy required seamen. That is where the fisheries came in because, as Britain could attest, "*the Fishery* is a grand Nursery of Seamen." Indeed, where would America find "a Nursery for Seamen but in the Fishery?" Adams was not inventing arguments to suit an immediate political goal. He had long been an acknowledged advocate of the American navy and even served a period as chairman of the congressional naval board. And, given America's history, no knowledgeable person, least of all a sophisticated mid-Atlantic lawyer such as McKean, could deny that America expected to carry on an extensive shipping trade. It seemed logical, as events eventually proved, to emphasize that America would need a navy to protect its interests. To increase the political pressure, in late 1781 Adams chaired a Boston Town Meeting that enunciated the same profisheries points in a circular letter that called on New England's towns to spread the word.[49]

Exasperated French diplomats testified to Adams's effectiveness and to the fact that he did not have to be in Congress to wield considerable influence in that body. In early 1782 the Chevalier de la Luzerne, the second French ambassador to the United States, complained that Adams "has employed all the influence he can bring to bear on the other [congressional] delegations to induce them to support the claims of Massachusetts." Reflecting the commonly held European view of Adams's role in fomenting the revolution, the ambassador added that "Mr. Samuel Adams, who at the beginning of this revolution directed in an astonishing manner the movements of the people by forming them into Committees," was doing it again. He was adapting the same machinery to the fisheries issue, and, unfortunately, it was working. New Englanders, having been riled up, had held many meetings. According to Luzerne, several reasonable and moderate congressmen had informed him that they knew the New Englanders "and the difficulty of stopping them once they were in motion."[50]

François Barbé de Marbois, the secretary of France's legation, offered a similar analysis in March 1782. Adams was "making every effort" and pouring "his constant labors" into ensuring that any peace treaty protected New England's use of the fisheries. If thwarted, Adams would then employ "all his resources, all his intrigues," advocating the conquest of Canada and Nova Scotia so he could secure the same result. Sounding rather like Adams's prewar opponents, the secretary argued that Adams "takes pleasure in troubles and difficulties" and "glories in forming a party of opposition." Yet, even as he denounced Adams as a supposedly incorrigible rebel, Marbois admitted that Adams could not have selected a better issue to sow the seeds of violent opposition in New England. Marbois, like Luzerne, realized that New Englanders generally, not just Samuel Adams, considered the fisheries essential. Thus, although the French, like the British before them, wanted to blame the undesirable uproar on Adams's evil manipulations, they had to admit that, while he orchestrated the political fight, it was successful because the people believed their personal interests were at stake. Indeed, said Marbois, Adams "has excited the imagination of the inhabitants of Massachusetts to an extraordinary point. The Almanacs, the Gazettes expound the importance of the fisheries." The campaign Adams spearheaded aimed to pressure the French into defending America's fishery rights whether they wanted to or not. In the end, the French did not have to take a resolute stand because America's peace-treaty negotiators got the British to stipulate that an independent America would have "Liberty" to use the fisheries.[51]

Great Britain agreed to a preliminary peace treaty on November 30, 1782, and formally acknowledged America's sovereignty and independence in the Treaty of Paris signed on September 3, 1783. This was the day the American revolutionary had anticipated longingly when, writing to Elizabeth in 1777, he spoke of "the happy Day when Tyranny [shall] be subdued and the Liberty of Our Country shall be settled upon a permanent Foundation." Once he knew independence was at hand, Samuel expressed his sense of accomplishment by saying, as well he might, "We have done our Duty. Future Generations can never curse the present for carelessly surrendering their Rights."

When he spoke of doing one's duty, Samuel Adams was talking about more than finally achieving American independence and gaining what he called the gifts of nature necessary to sustain that independence. As early as December 1775 Adams stressed that independence would be worth little if his country of Massachusetts did not create a government and a society that would protect the people's liberties. So, even as he worked at the continental level in the great cause, Samuel simultaneously worked to promote virtue in Massachusetts and to create a new state constitution that would, by protecting the people's rights, be worthy of being jealously defended.[52]

9

"THE PRINCIPLES OF LIBERTY":
THE MASSACHUSETTS SCENE

Even before independence had been declared, Samuel Adams reached the conclusion that Massachusetts must create a new frame of government. Reflecting his core political values, he called for "the Establishment of a Government upon the Principles of Liberty, and sufficiently guarding it from future Infringements of a Tyrant." The reference to the future underscored one of Adams's abiding goals: working for posterity, for the "millions yet unborn." As he pondered how to formulate a government that would protect liberty, Adams reached the conclusion that Massachusetts's society, as well as its government, needed to be transformed. He came to stress that the Massachusetts revolutionaries had a duty to foster "Virtue" because virtue was "the Soul of a republican Government." So, even as he labored in Congress and worked to establish a new government for his "Country" of Massachusetts, Adams spent considerable time contemplating how "the Virtue of my Countrymen may be secured for Ages yet to Come" and trying to turn his contemplations into reality.[1]

As Massachusetts was the first colony to reshape its government under congressional authorization, Adams considered its performance crucial. The people of Massachusetts had more than an opportunity to establish good government; they had an awesome responsibility to all Americans to do so. As a consequence of Congress's directive, from the summer of 1775 into the early winter of 1776 Adams spent considerable time ruminating about the nature of government and then endeavoring to translate his thoughts into action. "I have," he admitted, "a strong desire that our Colony should excell in Wisdom and Virtue." In the heady days of late 1775 Samuel dared hope that Massachusetts's legislators might emulate the Senate of Areopagus in ancient Athens. Its actions were so "eminently upright" that foreign governments asked it to mediate disputes.[2] Events soon tempered Adams's optimism. Rather than emulating the superlative Athenian senate, the Massachusetts House and Council bickered over control of the militia. Each body seemed more concerned about grasping power than promoting the public good. Only the forceful intervention of Samuel and his cousin John, who both wrote home and stressed that Congress would not become embroiled in the dispute, kept the unseemly quarrel from reaching Congress. The fall elections of 1775 also proved disappointing. Elbridge Gerry reported that some voters made their choices based on a candidate's wealth. Samuel, who considered the right to vote a sacred trust, found that mortifying. "Giving such a preference to riches is," he lamented, "both dishonourable and dangerous to a government."[3]

The views Adams articulated in the fall and early winter of 1775 and 1776 were not idle philosophical musings. As Samuel told James Warren, "we live in a most important Age, which demands that every Moment should be improvd to some serious Purpose."[4] Adams crafted his letters, especially those to Warren and Gerry, so his friends could use them to persuade Massachusetts's inhabitants and legislators to support the ardent Whig positions Adams, Warren, and Gerry advocated. All of Samuel's observations reflected his belief that the Massachusetts government must rest on the consent of the governed and must protect the people's liberties. He also continued to reiterate that the people themselves must be constantly vigilant so they could thwart unworthy or, worse yet, tyrannical politicians who might subvert liberty.[5] Adams highlighted a number of specific issues as he contemplated how government and society might be constructed.

He dwelled on the military. While admitting that government might occasionally have to rely on seasoned military men, he still insisted that "a standing Army, however necessary it may be at some times, is always dangerous to the Liberties of the People." There were ways, he maintained, to check the inherent danger the military posed. The legislature must control the military, and that requirement held true for the American army. Adams stressed that the militia must remain a vital part of the military because the militia constituted the "natural Strength" of a free country. He reasoned that, since they were "free Citizens," militiamen would not trample their own rights but would, instead, steadfastly defend them from outside attackers. Maintaining state militias and keeping them under the control of the individual states would, Adams stressed, help safeguard the people from the military power.[6]

As he pondered how to deal with potential evils, more than the military bothered Adams. The process of government itself contained inherent dangers. Reiterating a commonplace view, Adams intoned that "all Men are fond of Power." Indeed, the love of power did not evaporate merely because men entered legally constituted legislatures. Even legislators, he warned, often coveted more power than the public wanted them to possess. Fortunately, Massachusetts had, he noted, found ways to bridle the corrosive lust for power. Each branch of the legislature could thwart the excesses of the other. The legislators were, in turn, kept in check through annual elections. Adams considered annual elections a special bulwark for protecting liberty because the legislative power "frequently reverts into the hands of the People from whom it is derivd." Provided the voters scrutinized the nominees and those who held public office, yearly elections made public officials truly accountable. For Adams, theory and history demonstrated that Massachusetts must have a republican government that incorporated appropriate checks and balances. At the same time, this government must rest on the consent of the governed and also give the people control over their elected political servants. In defending the principle of power flowing from the people, Adams lamented that he found some men *"every where"* who were "afraid of a free Government, lest it should be perverted, and made Use of as a Cloke for Licentiousness." Putting such men on the wrong side of the issue, Adams eviscerated their logic by observing that "the fear of the Peoples abusing their Liberty is made an Argument against their having the Enjoyment of it."[7]

Adams gave special attention to plural officeholding, a vexing problem in colonial Massachusetts illustrated most egregiously by Thomas Hutchinson serving in all three branches of the government at the same time. While conceding that an attack on plural officeholding would cause inconveniences, Adams urged both Gerry and Warren to at least ensure that no one could hold political posts "incompatible with each other." He was particularly adamant about ensuring that no official could exercise both legislative and judicial powers. The evil of plural officeholding must, Adams insisted, be confronted, and "it is my opinion that the remedy ought to be deep and thorough."[8]

No matter what issue he assessed, when thinking about the nature of government in late 1775 and early 1776 Adams eventually linked the topic to the question of moral character. His intense focus on character was probably influenced by his heartfelt responses to the dramatically different actions of two talented young men he had befriended and promoted as defenders of America. In mid-October Adams had to face the shocking news that Dr. Benjamin Church had sold out to the British. That disheartening revelation and the contrast it presented to Dr. Joseph Warren's patriotic death at Bunker Hill accentuated the importance of the question of character. As he discussed what should be done in Massachusetts, Adams repeatedly stressed one point above all: "virtue is the surest means of securing the public liberty." "Virtue" is not self-defining. In addition, Adams often spoke of the virtues necessary to preserve liberty. Still, he defined "private" virtue as "the Feeling of moral Obligations" in one's "private Connections." When referring to what he labeled political virtues, Adams specifically mentioned fidelity to one's country and opposition to bribery, luxury, and extravagance. Writing later and more generally of republican virtues that elected officials ideally should possess, he mentioned piety, justice, moderation, temperance, simplicity, industry, and frugality.[9]

Samuel, who maintained that one's actions in private life typically paralleled what one did in public life, used the sad case of Dr. Church to illustrate the tie between personal and public virtue. Church's infidelity to his wife had been "notorious" before the betrayal of his country was discovered. For Adams, the lesson was clear: those who were upright in their personal lives were not likely to be unfaithful to their country. He carried that idea further by repeatedly asserting that the disposition and manners of a people—their virtue or lack of it—determined whether they were fit for freedom or for slavery. In fact, he maintained that no country could long retain its freedom unless "Virtue" was "supremely honord." He later provided a strong illustration of the importance he placed on virtue when he remarked to Elizabeth that "My Children cannot imagine how much Comfort I have in believing they are virtuous." Massachusetts *must* find ways to promote virtue.[10] Adams suggested looking to the past.

In the fall of 1775, in letters to James Warren, Adams spoke of "the golden opportunity of restoring the ancient purity of principles and manners in our country" and emphasized education as the key to securing good government. Invoking Massachusetts's noble ancestors, Samuel claimed the founders of the colony had laid an excellent foundation for defending liberty by quickly establishing an extensive public-education system. Given the importance he assigned to education, Adams was horrified to learn that some Massachusetts towns had closed their local schools, reportedly because of the high cost of the war. In lines obviously intended for many eyes, Samuel urged society's leaders to impress upon the people the necessity of continuing to support an education system "well calculated to diffuse among the Individuals of the Community the Principles of Morality, so essentially necessary to the Preservation of publick Liberty." Adams sought to clinch the argument, and give the supporters of public education valuable ammunition, by proclaiming that "no People will tamely surrender their Liberties, nor can any be easily subdued, when Knowledge is diffusd and

Virtue is preservd. On the Contrary, when People are universally ignorant, and debauchd in their Manners, they will sink under their own Weight without the Aid of foreign Invaders."[11]

Adams even incorporated the idea of education for good government into his January 1776 proposal that Boston help overcome America's lack of trained military officers by establishing a military academy. The young men who displayed military potential should, Adams emphasized, learn more than the art of war. They should be "taught the Principles of a free Government, and deeply impressd with a Sense of the indispensible Obligation which every member is under to the whole Society." Thus, as Adams envisioned it, the academy would inculcate republican ideals as well military knowledge. Although he raised the possibility more than once, Boston did not establish a military school.[12]

Adams considered religion essential for developing people's morals. Yet in 1775 and 1776, when he focused on formulating governments, he only occasionally linked religion to his quest for attaining a virtuous society. In fact, he did not specifically join the two until the spring of 1776 when he wrote to John Scollay, a longtime selectman of Boston. After expressing joy about the British finally quitting Boston, Adams reprised his theme of the previous fall by speaking of "the happy opportunity of reestablishing ancient Principles and Purity of Manners." He maintained that one of Britain's goals had been to destroy the people's "Sense of true Religion & Virtue" so the British could more easily enslave Boston. Stressing that God rewarded—or punished—communities according to their general character, he argued that "the publick Liberty will not long survive the total Extinction of Morals." Without specifying exactly what the officeholders ought to do, Adams reminded Scollay that Boston's morals depended on the selectmen's vigilance.[13]

Adams was a religious man, an old-fashioned Puritan in the eyes of many, who believed in family readings from the Bible. He told his future son-in-law that "Religion in a Family is at once its brightest Ornament & its best Security." And Samuel was famous for always attending Sunday church services. Indeed, when the Continental Congress, then meeting in York, Pennsylvania, did not hold a religious service in its chapel, he regularly attended services at the German church even though he did not understand German. Like most other Americans, Adams considered public support for religion appropriate, and in late 1776 he commented to Elizabeth that "I wish we were a more religious People." Although he believed in public support for religion, Samuel Adams considered religion primarily a personal and family matter.

During the war, Adams often did mention God's intervening hand. When Elizabeth saw God's hand in the transforming victory at Saratoga, Samuel agreed and also observed that "Religion has been & I hope will continue to be the ornament of N. England." But, while he spoke during the war years of God's intervention, he rarely used such imagery before the fighting commenced. This suggests that he deemed religious appeals especially appropriate, and potentially powerful, during wartime. And, for all his emphasis on providential intervention, Adams also repeatedly asserted that God helped those who helped themselves.[14]

In assessing Adams's motivation, many authors have highlighted the fact that Adams spoke of Boston becoming "the *Christian* Sparta." It is unwise, however, to place great emphasis on this single reference. Too often that comment has been forced to bear an interpretive weight it cannot sustain. The phrase appears *only once* in all of Adams's published writings; moreover, Samuel did not call for creating the Christian Sparta. Rather, he used the term in a December 1780 letter in which he complained bitterly about Bostonians, including "Men of Religion," living a life marked by extravagant entertainments complete with "Superfluity of Dress & Ornamentation." Adams's reference to Boston's possible religious transformation was, thus, meant to reprove the Boston of late 1780. After recounting many examples of Boston's vices, Adams lamented, "But I fear I shall say too much. I love the People of Boston. I once thought that City would be the *Christian* Sparta. But Alas! Will men never be free! They will be free no longer than while they remain virtuous. [The political philosopher Algernon] Sidney tells us, there are times when People are not worth saving. I pray God, this may never be truly said of my beloved Town."[15]

Since he normally tried to influence people by holding up the image of a nobler standard, Adams's reference to "the *Christian* Sparta" may have been no more than a effort to reform his beloved, but far-too-unvirtuous, Boston. The evidence shows that, when he spoke of promoting religious ideals, he had in mind the maxim of doing unto others as you would have them do unto you, not of championing a specific faith. John Adams was right when, as already noted, he later stressed that Samuel "lived and conversed freely with all sectarians" and "never imposed his creed on any one, or endeavored to make proselytes to his religious opinions." The evidence shows that, despite his own personal religiosity, when it came to government developing a virtuous citizenry, Adams looked to the schoolhouse every bit as much as he looked to any church.[16]

The observations Adams advanced in the fall and early winter of 1775 and 1776 constituted a primer on forming a republican government and cultivating the virtues he believed a republican society needed to survive. He did not alter his basic views as the war progressed and as Massachusetts continued to have difficulty creating a new frame of government. But his thoughts were naturally colored by the process of seeking independence, by seeing it declared, and by the travails of war. Some of his concerns, especially about the issue of character, intensified in the lengthy period it took for Massachusetts to implement a new constitution—a process that stretched into 1780.

When Adams contemplated the sundry problems involved in shaping Massachusetts's government and society, he shuddered at the example being set by John Hancock. As his contemporaries and historians agree, Hancock cared little for political idealism. He craved the sunshine of public adulation. He sought popularity, which gave him a sense of self-worth. Politically, Hancock was a moderate Whig, but he resembled a well-oiled weather vane. He easily shifted positions according to the prevailing winds of public opinion. If he could not feel how those winds blew, he wavered and avoided taking a firm position.

Hancock demonstrated his character and values by how he responded to being president of Congress, a largely ceremonial post. He reveled in the visibility and status that accompanied the presidency, and he exploited the office for his own purposes. Upon leaving Congress in the summer of 1778, Hancock insisted on delivering a valedictory address that would, seemingly, require a flattering response from Congress. And, despite manpower problems, Hancock pressed General Washington to provide a military detachment to escort his carriage to Boston. Samuel Adams was appalled. He and his cousin John had sponsored the fabulously wealthy Hancock for the office of president to counter Tory claims about Whigs being a pack of poverty-stricken rabble-rousers. Now Hancock was acting like a pompous aristocrat, not a virtuous republican. Moreover, he had already disappointed Samuel by not actively championing independence and by opposing the effort to form an alliance with France. The political friendship between the two, which had been cooling, turned frigid.

Hancock received his military escort and arrived in Boston looking like a very important personage indeed. Once at home, he staged a gala reception and continued a lavish lifestyle. No doubt to his chagrin, it took time for the statement of gratitude he expected from Congress to arrive. It was delayed because of opposition led by Samuel Adams. He observed that two others had served as president and neither had made a parting speech or received the thanks of Congress. Congress did eventually vote Hancock a statement of thanks, but only by a six-to-four margin. Even more insulting, under Adams's leadership Massachusetts voted *against* issuing the pronouncement. As Robert Finkelstein, a biographer of Hancock, indicated, "this galling insult was not forgotten."[17]

Over the next few months Adams received numerous reports detailing Hancock's aristocratic lifestyle, his hubris, and his quest for popularity. Samuel was able to confirm the reports in person because he was in Boston during the early months of 1778. For Adams, the evidence screamed that Hancock was undermining republican virtues. Moreover, Adams believed that Hancock, who knew it was not true, spread the ludicrous rumor that Samuel was involved in a conspiracy against George Washington. So it is not surprising that, when asked about Hancock having returned to Congress on June 19 but then permanently leaving it less than three weeks later, Samuel offered a less than full-throated defense of his colleague. Remarking that the actions of "a great Man" were often subjected to misleading interpretations when they might be easily explained, Samuel merely quoted Hancock as saying he quit Congress because of "His own Want of Health & the dangerous Illness of his Lady." And Samuel added that he hoped the newspapers erred in reporting that Hancock had made his grand entrance into Boston on a Sunday. It was obvious whom Samuel had in mind when he soon thereafter denounced Whigs who exhibited "an insatiable Desire . . . to establish a Popularity in order to obtain the Splendor or Emoluments of Places, or that vanity of vanities the Breath of Applause."[18]

In a September 1778 letter Samuel Savage, who wanted to reconcile Adams and Hancock, commented on Boston having "become a new City" owing to its "exceeding Gayety of Appearance." That report made Adams livid. He responded by warning that luxury and extravagance would destroy the virtues necessary to preserve the people's liberty and happiness. He was not subtle about blaming the lamentable developments on Hancock. Adams pointed to John Hancock's staging an extravagant, and perhaps illegal, entertainment at the close of the review of the Boston militia. Samuel rhetorically wondered when they might "again see that Sobriety of Manners, that Temperance, Frugality, Fortitude and other manly Virtues" that had once been "the Glory and Strength of my much lov'd native Town." A month later Adams rebuffed another of Savage's calls for a reconciliation by again carping about Hancock's lavish gatherings. Ostentatious entertainments were, Samuel groused, incompatible with the present serious times, especially since many of the state's citizens could barely subsist. In Adams's mind Hancock grossly compounded the evil by inviting Tories to his galas and thus blurring the lines between Whigs and Tories. Adams soon depicted John Hancock as the second coming of Thomas Hutchinson.[19]

Adams believed Hancock's vain pursuit of popularity helped unleash a torrent of vices more likely than the British to destroy liberty. It was time, said Adams, for those who wanted to transmit the blessings of liberty to their posterity to unite in support of public virtue. In pursuit of that goal, Adams again employed his pen in a lobbying effort to generate support for education. Elaborating on arguments he had advanced in 1775, Samuel expressed sorrow that some Massachusetts communities reportedly found maintaining schools too costly. Appealing to pride, Adams said he wished anyone who questioned the necessity of maintaining the education system could hear the comments of sensible and public-minded Southerners. They showered compliments on Massachusetts for having always provided instruction for the young. In fact, Virginians had become so convinced of the importance of education that they reportedly planned to establish a public-education system. These wise Southerners understood that "if Virtue & Knowledge are diffusd among the People, they will never be enslavd. This will be their great Security. Virtue & Knowledge will forever be an even Balance for Powers & Riches."[20]

While Adams glorified virtue and education, Hancock looked for ways to become governor of Massachusetts. He began forging a powerful coalition that included archconservatives Adams detested. Hancock did not want Adams's virulent anti-Toryism cutting into his potential power base. Hancock's blurring of the lines between Whig and Tory, a development that made Adams seethe, paid dividends in the May 1778 elections. Adams's close friend and staunch political ally, James Warren, had been speaker of the House of Representatives; but, with Tories voting in Plymouth for the first time in seven years, Warren could not even win reelection to the House. Hancock's political strategy aimed to reduce the political influence of any prominent leaders who might oppose him. Part of the plan entailed circulating the negative reports about Adams supposedly wanting Washington replaced as commander in chief. Samuel argued that the man who "fabricated the Charge did not believe it himself" and that, while he helped spread the ludicrous rumor, Hancock knew it was not true. When his dearest Betsy mentioned political slanders being hurled at her beloved husband, Samuel comforted her by claiming that every honest and sensible man who knew him would attest to his having acted with honorable consistency. Moreover, "the Censure of Fools or Knaves is Applause."[21]

Despite his defiance, Samuel realized that returning to Massachusetts for a while would give him a chance to wash off the political mud that had been pitched at him. But it was not personal concerns that convinced him in mid-1779 that he should go home for an extended time. Adams believed the interests of Massachusetts, and of America, required him to journey to Boston. He feared that Massachusetts's zealous efforts in the great cause could be jeopardized by the state's continuing inability to form a new constitution, an inability that threatened to plunge the state into chaos. Dissidents in the western counties of Berkshire and Hampshire had shut down courts in 1775, ostensibly because the state's government had not been established by the people and thus did not rest on the consent of the governed. In September 1776 the legislators recommended having the next General Court produce a constitution, and nearly 75 percent of the townships that responded agreed. Some townships, however, maintained that the state's constitution must be drafted by a separate convention elected solely for that purpose. While the legislators rejected this plea, they did stipulate that the proposed constitution would be presented to the towns for their approval. Thus, although not created by a separate convention, the constitution would reflect the bedrock republican ideal of government resting on the consent of the governed. The General Court produced a constitution in 1778, but the overwhelming majority of voters (9,972 of 12,055) and townships (147 of 178) rejected it, above all because it lacked a bill of rights. Facing further threats of violence from the western sections of the state, the General Court admitted defeat in February 1779 by asking whether the people wanted a separate constitutional convention. The answer was already apparent. Although he did not say it openly, it seems likely that Adams contemplated helping Massachusetts achieve the new constitution he believed the state had to have for its own good, for the good of the Union, and for the great cause.[22]

Adams left for Boston on June 15, 1779, the day the General Court officially authorized the voters to select delegates for a constitutional convention that would commence on September 1. Boston sent a dozen delegates to the convention, and Samuel was the top vote getter of the group. He played a vital role in creating the Massachusetts Constitution. He served on the convention's thirty-member committee charged with formulating a constitution. The Committee of Thirty turned the job of producing a first draft over to a subcommittee made up of Samuel Adams, John Adams, and James Bowdoin. Unfortunately, this committee did not keep a record of its deliberations. In fact, the three men did not even preserve a copy of what they produced. The closest available approximation of the subcommittee's document is the draft constitution the Committee of Thirty forwarded after making revisions.[23]

John Adams asserted, and most analysts have accepted his claim, that he was the "principal Engineer" of the constitution. That may be true, but it would be absurd to think Samuel Adams and James Bowdoin had no significant input. In addition, both the Committee of Thirty and the full convention made modifications, some of them significant. Also, John Adams implied that the subcommittee did not draft what, with major revisions, became the controversial Article 3 of the Declaration of Rights, which dealt with religion. And, in part because John Adams left for Europe in early November, the task of getting the convention to approve the proposed constitution fell primarily to Samuel. Even more important, the document presented to the Committee of Thirty was undeniably the work of many minds, not just the three-member drafting committee. Before any drafting began, the convention delegates emphatically articulated three basic points: the state's constitution must include a declaration of rights, the government must be "a free Republic," and, "it is the Essence of a free Republic, that the people be governed by fixed Laws of their own Making." In addition, the Massachusetts Constitution obviously drew on earlier documents and political systems. Its Declaration of Rights incorporated ideas and even specific language from Virginia's influential 1776 Declaration of Rights. The proposed structure of government owed a good deal both to the 1691 charter and the constitution Massachusetts's voters rejected in 1778.[24]

Despite the paucity of evidence, three salient points are indisputable. First, Samuel Adams believed constitutionmaking required compromise. As emphasized in "An Address of the Convention . . . to their Constituents," which he coauthored, "we may not expect to agree on a perfect System of Government," and therefore one's special interests should give way "to essential Principles, and Considerations of general Utility." Second, he approved of the constitution's main features.[25] Third, the constitution contained specific, innovative features that reflected Samuel's concerns about protecting the people's liberties by looking to the past and by promoting virtue, especially through education.

The 1780 Massachusetts Constitution was thoroughly Whig, thoroughly republican, in its statement of ideals. The document's language proclaimed it "a social compact" voluntarily entered into by the people to provide them "with the power of enjoying, in safety and tranquillity, their natural rights and the blessings of life." If the government failed to protect those rights, "the people have a right to alter the government, and to take measures necessary for their safety, prosperity, and happiness." The Declaration of Rights stretched to thirty detailed articles. It included the cardinal theoretical statements that all power resides originally in the people and that every member of society had a right "to be protected . . . in the enjoyment of his life, liberty and property, according to standing laws."[26]

Although John Adams wanted the governor to have an absolute veto, the most notable features of the constitution Massachusetts adopted in 1780 were its separation of powers and its well-developed system of checks and balances. As Samuel, but not John, desperately wanted, elections would occur annually. Voting was restricted to free males aged twenty-one and older who were worth £60 or who owned land, a freehold, yielding at least £3 a year. These requirements actually raised the property requirements above what they had been in colonial days. The two-branch legislature was again called the General Court. Representatives had to own a £100 freehold or be worth at least £200; senators had to possess a freehold worth at least £300 or be worth £600. To reflect the ideal of equality, the size of a township's House delegation was based on population. The Senate was limited to forty seats distributed with some attention given to the size of a county's population. The House and Senate had to concur before a bill went to the governor, who was assisted by an advisory Council selected primarily from among the ranks of the Senate. The Committee of Thirty version gave the governor an absolute veto, a provision John Adams adamantly championed. However, as finally approved, the governor's veto could be overridden by a two-thirds vote of the General Court. Judges, who were appointed by the governor with the advice and consent of the Council, were guaranteed reasonable salaries and would hold their posts during good behavior.[27]

Parts of the constitution are especially relevant for understanding Samuel Adams's views on the role of virtue and religion in protecting the people's liberties. The draft constitution, which required that the governor be a Christian, stipulated that the people had a "duty" to worship "the SUPREME BEING." Moreover, the constitution justified public support for religion by proclaiming that "Good morals" were "necessary to the preservation of civil society." Those sections of the proposed constitution were easily accepted by the delegates. That was not the case with the Committee of Thirty's version of Article 3 of the Declaration of the Rights of the Inhabitants. The committee's Article 3 stipulated that the legislature could authorize using tax moneys to support public worship and could enjoin all citizens to attend religious services, "provided there be any such teacher [i.e., minister] on whose ministry they can conscientiously and conveniently attend." That limitation on public support for religion added weight to the constitution's strong statement on freedom of conscience written into Article 2. It stipulated that anyone who did not "disturb the public peace, or obstruct others in their religious worship" would themselves not be "hurt, molested, or restrained" from worshiping "GOD" according "to the dictates of his own conscience."

While it retained that Article 2 statement on freedom of conscience, the full convention found parts of the Committee of Thirty's Article 3 unacceptable. The existing laws made the Congregational Church the established state religion in fact if not in name, and the majority of delegates insisted on keeping it that way. After lengthy and contentious debates, the convention revised the mechanics of public support for religion. As finally approved, Article 3 effectively kept the Congregational Church as the state church and also restricted public support of religion to Protestant ministers. As those who pushed for greater religious freedom emphasized then and later, the revisions to Article 3 seemed to limit, and contradict, the statement on freedom of conscience. It only guaranteed that peaceful and law-abiding Christians "shall be equally under the protection of the law."

The evidence indicates that Adams would have preferred the original Article 3, which, if enacted, would have moved Massachusetts further along the road toward religious toleration. Certainly his earlier strident defense of the zealous, but irreligious, patriot Dr. Thomas Young suggests Samuel would have preferred the original Committee of Thirty wording on religious issues. And his fall 1778 denunciation of a Christian who would "destroy the peace of others . . . because they differ from him in Matters of mere opinion" matches well with John Adams's insistence that Samuel did not try to impose his religious views on others. However, to get the proposed constitution through the convention Samuel accommodated the majority position and also put the best possible spin on the outcome. The convention's address he coauthored downplayed the acrimony the lengthy debates about Article 3 generated by maintaining that the delegates had achieved "much more Unanimity than usually takes place in disquisitions of this Nature." That statement, while perhaps literally true, effectively distorted the record, but Samuel Adams was making history, not writing it.[28]

The constitution's noncontroversial pronouncements on education and the encouragement of literature are particularly important for delineating Samuel Adams's thoughts on how the government should promote virtue. These sections contained ideas and language he had often employed when promoting education and accentuating the essential role virtue played in a free society. The constitution lauded Massachusetts's sagacious ancestors for supporting a general education system. The constitution proclaimed that "Wisdom, and knowledge, as well as virtue, diffused generally among the body of the people" were "necessary for the preservation of their rights and liberties." In provisions that also reflected Samuel's emphasis on providing education for the many, not just the few, the constitution declared that legislators and magistrates must forever cherish and support the public schools, the town grammar schools, and Harvard College. The government was also to encourage private organizations that promoted "agriculture, arts, sciences, commerce, trades, manufactures and a natural history of the country." More revealing when it comes to virtues Adams and others wanted to champion was the pronouncement that the state's public officials must seek "to countenance and inculcate the principles of humanity and general benevolence, public and private charity, industry and frugality, honesty and punctuality in their dealings, sincerity, good humor, and all social affections, and generous sentiments among the people."[29]

The Massachusetts Constitution of 1780, which was formally adopted in June and took effect in October, did not create a "democratic" government, nor did it truly protect religious freedom. It was, however, thoroughly republican. It was built on the ideal that government must rest on the consent of the governed. It did embrace the principle that the people must be governed by "fixed Laws of their own Making." As Samuel often stressed, annual elections gave the voters a ready check on their elected officials. In addition, when compared to the 1691 charter the constitution provided a government with better checks and balances. The new government would have what Samuel considered the necessary energy without being likely to endanger the people's liberties. From his perspective, the constitution seemed well worth defending because it was founded on what he called "sober Republican Principles."[30]

A discussion Samuel had in December 1780 with the Marquis de Chastellux, the French major general who was so impressed with Adams when they first met earlier that month, helps elucidate Adams's view of the constitution and politics in general. The lengthy conversation was, the Frenchman indicated, interrupted only by a glass of Madeira, a dish of tea, and the arrival of another lodger. Chastellux opened the discussion by expressing "anxiety" about the new American state constitutions, especially the Massachusetts document. Confusing Pennsylvania with the Bay State and not realizing that the Massachusetts constitution actually toughened the property requirements to vote, Chastellux said he considered it dangerous to let virtually every male taxpayer vote for legislators. It might do for now "because every citizen is about equally well-off, or can become so in a short time." But time would produce greater economic inequality and endemic political problems because those with property would have "the real force." The state would then face "the two equally dangerous extremes of aristocracy and anarchy." Chastellux suggested it would have been wiser to allocate power based on ownership of property.[31]

Adams, of course, readily agreed that one should consider future generations, not just the present moment. Yet, while admitting it was not perfect, he heartily defended the new constitution. He began by recounting how it was created through a wonderful process that included a specially elected convention, analysis by the voters, and then the return of the document to the delegates for final revisions. "If two-thirds of the voters approved it, it was to have the force of law, and be regarded as the work of the people themselves." It would, in sum, be a republican constitution built on the consent of the governed. Samuel added that, of the twenty-two thousand votes cast in the state, far more than two-thirds favored the new constitution. He proudly asserted that the last time a constitution came into being in such a legal manner occurred in the days of Lycurgus—nine centuries before the birth of Christ! Adams's glorification of the process and document are open to challenge. Some sections of the constitution may not have gotten the required two-thirds approval. In counting votes, the delegates may have used creative accounting. Adams was, nevertheless, right to stress the significance of how Massachusetts formulated its constitution. The eminent constitutional historian Andrew C. McLaughlin maintained that "the fully developed convention" process first used in Massachusetts constituted "the greatest institution of government which America has produced." It "answered in itself," said McLaughlin, "the problem of how men could make government of their own free will."[32]

Responding to Chastellux's anxiety about the distribution of political power, Adams explained the logic of the system. Voicing what for him was at the heart of the dispute with Great Britain, Adams argued that "a state is never free except when each citizen is bound by no law whatever that he has not approved of, either directly, or through his representatives." Accordingly, "every citizen must . . . have a part in elections." Although Adams claimed the suffrage requirements would not bar any citizen from voting, some citizens, which at the time meant free adult males, could not meet the property requirement. Adams, therefore, still accepted the established view that voters should have a material stake in society. In short, they should own property. The commonplace nature of that requirement is demonstrated by the fact that, when they created new constitutions in this era, none of the American states extended the vote to all adult freemen. Pennsylvania and North Carolina came the closest to eliminating the property requirement. At a time when taxes were levied on property, not income, these two states let free adult male taxpayers vote.

Having maintained that all citizens would have a voice in the laws that governed them, Adams focused on who could represent the people. He stressed that the House of Representatives constituted "the people themselves represented by their delegates." Therefore, the property requirements for serving in the House should not be, and in Massachusetts were not, set too high. According to Adams, "thus far the government is purely democratic." But the democratic power, like all power, must be checked. And the members of the House were especially prone to letting their "passions and whims" influence them. The Senate and the governor, advised by his Council, provided the necessary "moderating power." Here, explained Adams, is where the holders of property had a balancing power. Senators could reject a House bill, and it required "considerable property" to serve as a senator. Moreover the governor could veto a bill, although the legislature could, after "fresh examination," override the veto by a two-thirds vote. Adams maintained that this process provided the balance necessary to produce sound legislation without destroying "the authority of the people."[33]

Chastellux marveled at how Adams's pronouncements contradicted his popular image. Adams had often been "reproached with consulting his library rather than present circumstances, and of always proceeding by way of the Greeks and Romans in order to reach the Whigs and Tories." However, said Chastellux, Adams's studies of the ancients did not keep him from being pragmatic or from paying close attention to present circumstances. The French general also commented on what he considered this revolutionary's amazing transformation. Adams had supposedly moved from being "the most extravagant partisan of democracy" to being a person who accentuated the importance of a mixed government.[34] Chastellux was right to maintain that Adams often planned for the future by looking to the past, that he was sensitive to present circumstances, and that he could be flexible and pragmatic. But the Frenchman missed important subtleties, and he was wrong about Adams having undergone a political metamorphosis.

Samuel Adams had "democratic" tendencies. They were reflected in his glorification of the people's role in creating the Massachusetts Constitution, in his strident insistence that the people had a right to elect public servants who were duty bound to work for the public good, and in his emphasis on the importance of annual elections. His defense of what he called the "simple Democracies" of New England's towns reflected his democratic proclivities. But if one defines democracy as all adult citizens having equal voting rights and an equal right to run for office, Adams was no democrat. He never argued that propertyless people should have the vote. He even tempered the "democratic" notion of majority rule. While he emphasized that the majority must govern, he never argued that the majority was always right. If the majority or their representatives acted on what he called "their first emotions," they might well take inappropriate action or produce poor legislation. The unreasonable will of the majority must be checked just as the potential tyrant must be checked. His praise for the careful checks and balances of the Massachusetts Constitution reflected his publicly expressed belief that "a Power without *any* Restraint is Tyranny" and that liberty could be assailed by the many as well as the few.[35]

In July 1780 Samuel said the "great Business" of ratifying Massachusetts's new frame of government "was carried through with much good Humour among the People, and even in Berkshire," which had been a disruptive force since 1775. As the months went by, Samuel continued to report that the new constitution met with general approval. Still, he saw the adoption of a constitution as merely a first step toward creating the virtuous society he considered essential to preserving liberty. Because he believed history proved that legislators and magistrates "have always had a mighty Influence on the People," he placed great importance on the upcoming special elections scheduled for September. Adams believed the election of the first governor would be extraordinarily significant because he "may probably have it in his Power to do more good or more Hurt than any of his successors."[36]

Shifting political coalitions, rather than well-organized political parties, waged electoral battles in the Massachusetts of the 1780s. In 1780 announcements in the press made it clear that John Hancock and James Bowdoin were the principal candidates for the governor's post. Before returning to Congress, Adams voiced his anti-Hancock views to anyone who asked. When he learned that Hancock had won the election easily, Adams was distressed; nevertheless, he put the best face on the result. If Hancock was "a wise & virtuous" governor, Adams would salute him and happily see him reelected. And if Hancock proved a poor choice, the people would see their error and avoid making the same mistake again.[37]

Knowing John Hancock as he did, the reports Adams received about Hancock's behavior when he was inaugurated and how he acted in the weeks that followed quickly confirmed what Samuel had expected would happen. Deeply worried that Governor Hancock's extravagant lifestyle might undermine republican virtue, Adams began working immediately to secure his defeat in the first regular election under the new state constitution, which was scheduled for April 1781. Adams filled his letters with derisive commentary that could be used against Hancock when he ran for reelection. They bristled with allusions to Hancock acting like a monarch. Clearly trashing Hancock, Adams fretted that the people might select politicians who liked "Levity," "Foppery," "Vanity & the Folly of Parade." He considered "Pomp & Show" tools of aristocracies and monarchies. Adams knew the kind of men he wanted to hold public office. Massachusetts would be set on a solid footing and flourish provided the elected officials were "Men of Wisdom & Knowledge, of Moderation & Temperance, of Patience Fortitude & Perseverance, of Sobriety & true Republican Simplicity of Manners, of Zeal, for the Honor of the Supreme Being & Welfare of the Common Wealth."[38] In Samuel's eyes, Hancock did not come close to meeting these exalted standards.

The special elections that launched the new Massachusetts government also disconcerted Adams for very personal reasons. Samuel adhered to the standard view that people should not put themselves forward as candidates for political posts. He prided himself on never asking for votes and on doing his duty without considering whether he might benefit materially. He also denounced plural office-holding as a pernicious practice that must be curbed. Despite these views, in addition to his elected posts, since 1775 Adams had served as secretary of state of Massachusetts, an appointive post that made him responsible for producing state documents. And he retained the position even though spending most of his time in Congress meant he had to employ a deputy to perform the secretary's duties in Massachusetts. Given how extensive plural office-holding was during the war, Adams sinned much less in that way than most leading Massachusetts Whigs. It is also true, using a standard Adams applied, that the post of secretary did not necessarily conflict with Adams's other duties. These points do not, however, alter the fact that when it came to *his* plural office-holding Adams had been ignoring his own argument about cutting deep and eliminating the evil.[39]

When the post of secretary of state became an elective position in 1780, Adams's political friends assumed the voters would keep him in the office. However, John Avery, the man who had actually done most of the secretary's work, won the September election. For the first time in years, Adams was not elected to any Massachusetts political office. The only post he now held was that of congressman. Adams's friends rightly blamed Hancock for conspiring against him, and Samuel himself was clearly knocked off stride by the public's seeming lack of faith in him. Although he spoke of "that Retirement from publick Cares, which my Country seems to point out for me," he quickly regained his balance. Samuel said he regarded Avery highly and would hold no grudge against him, and he meant it. More important, Adams analyzed his own political loss in a way that revealed his keen grasp of human nature. When James Warren informed Adams that "the Tongue of Malice" had been employed against him, Samuel figuratively turned the other cheek. The slanderous comments would, he said, merely make him all the more careful to avoid doing anything that could justly be criticized. Revealing judicious insight, he added, "We are apt to be partial in our own Judgment of our selves. Our Friends are either blind to our Faults or not faithful enough to tell us of them."[40] Adams's understanding of human nature helps explain his extraordinary ability to work with others to devise political agreements.

His loss in the secretary of state election also caused Adams to reflect on how a politician should view public service. Responding to Elizabeth's anger over the slights he had received, Samuel maintained that in a free republic the people possessed the absolute right of voting for any candidate they pleased. No person should expect a government post merely because he had held office before. What a public servant had was a duty to do everything possible to promote "the Cause of Liberty & Virtue." If the people wanted to replace him, the public servant should accept that decision and gracefully retire to private life. This American revolutionary believed he had adhered to those standards. A year before, thinking of his fellow citizens of Boston and of Massachusetts, Samuel had asserted that "in their Service, I began my political Race. I have ever kept their Interest in View."[41]

Samuel Adams was anxious to leave Congress in 1781 and return home in part because he thought that Boston and Massachusetts required his presence to help fight the growing level of vice he believed Hancock did so much to foster. Adams put the issue bluntly when writing to James Warren. Observing that "Power is intoxicating" and implying that the new governor was already tipsy, Samuel stated that "our Country will stand in Need of its experienced Patriots to prevent its Ruin." Having spent months firing off letters that suggested Hancock's high-flying lifestyle eroded republican virtue, Adams took a more direct approach: he once again resorted to a weapon he had often used in the run-up to independence. Samuel turned to the press. Before leaving Philadelphia, Samuel drafted two essays for the *Boston Gazette*. The first of the commentaries, each styled "Extract of a Letter from the Southward," appeared in print on April 2, 1781—election day in Massachusetts.[42]

The election-day letter, clearly part of Adams's continuing efforts to promote and protect a government based on "the Principles of Liberty," constituted a primer on voting and good citizenship in "free Republics." Adams's analysis highlighted a concern many Americans shared: the fear that political factions and political parties would form and consequently destroy good government. Adams offered the readers advice on how to ensure that Massachusetts would never "sink into the Violence and Rage" that came with political parties. The responsibility rested with the citizens, who when voting exercised "one of the most solemn Trusts in human Society." The voters must be devoted to the constitution, not to individuals. For the benefit of the republic, the voters, and their posterity, Adams hoped that "the great Business of Elections will never be left by the Many, to be done by the Few." Accentuating the ideal of virtuous republicanism, he spoke of embracing "that Simplicity which is the Ornament and Strength of a free Republick." Making a thinly veiled reference to Hancock, he wrote that political servants who still reveled in monarchical pomp or who thirsted after "Adulation" were unworthy candidates for public office. Adams drove that point hard by celebrating the fact that annual elections let people correct their "Mistakes."[43]

If Adams thought his first letter would affect the elections, he misjudged badly. Hancock and his candidate for lieutenant governor, Thomas Cushing, romped to victory in all parts of the commonwealth. Hancock got every vote cast in Boston; Cushing garnered over 96 percent of Boston's votes. Adams could not have been shocked by Hancock's victory, only its magnitude. Samuel knew that the ideal of achieving consensus still exerted real influence in Massachusetts. He was also well aware of Massachusetts's tradition of reelecting public officials. So, realistically, Adams could not have expected the voters to reject Hancock. Still, given his views on promoting republican virtue, Adams had to try to influence the 1781 election.[44]

The second essay Adams forwarded to the *Boston Gazette* demonstrated his understanding of political reality, which indicated that Hancock would win. The letter was written before the election but not published until after the results became known. Adams added to his primer on voting by saying he trusted that each voter had expressed his honest views rather than having "prostituted" his vote to please a friend or a patron. Adams devoted most of his energy to trumpeting his often-stated ideal that the people's vigilance could check evil officeholders. Citizens must, he said, monitor their public servants by inquiring "freely, but decently," into their conduct. Adams offered a detailed example from Swedish history to illustrate that even good men might abuse their power if they were not watched carefully. He literally highlighted his basic thought: "*There is no restraint [on politicians] like the pervading eye of the virtuous citizens.*"[45]

Adams planned to follow his own advice about keeping careful watch on public servants, especially Governor Hancock. Samuel also intended to reform a Boston that James and Mercy Otis Warren, Elbridge Gerry, and the Reverend Samuel Cooper had long been describing as being awash in gaiety. They reported that the Bostonians, especially the wealthy and even ministers, were, alas, eagerly adopting the gaudy social trappings of monarchy. Because he believed Massachusetts's liberty was not yet set on a firm foundation and was in grave danger from the likes of Hancock, Samuel Adams's political race had not yet run its course by the time he retired from Congress and returned to Boston. Indeed, upon his return to Massachusetts in 1781 he was elected to the state Senate and served in it, most of the time as its president, until he become lieutenant governor in 1789.[46]

When Samuel arrived back in Boston in the spring of 1781, his own eyes convinced him that simple republican virtue was not a hallmark of his beloved native city. Assembly balls and other fashionable amusements, extravagant displays of wealth, and even gambling enjoyed widespread popularity. Although he sought to quell the growing profligacy, he did not share the enthusiasm some displayed for using proscriptive legislation to promote piety. Instead, he continued to emphasize the importance of fostering virtue by providing a public education to all children. In December 1781 the Boston Town Meeting appointed him chairman of a committee charged with assessing the city's public school system. Five days later he remarked that one of the committee's interests was "the better Education of female Children." Samuel was apparently speaking only for his committee; the town meeting had not mentioned educating females. The town meeting put an additional member on the Adams committee in March 1782 and sharpened its charge by asking the group to determine whether some new arrangement would improve the public-school system.[47]

Two years elapsed before the Adams committee presented its analysis to the town meeting. When it finally appeared, Adams's imprint was obvious in both the report's arguments and its language. It opened by applauding the wisdom of the people's venerable ancestors for constructing an extensive education system that ranged from simple writing schools to Harvard College. Turning the colonial founders into education democrats, the committee report proclaimed that "Our free Schools seem to have been intended for the Benefit of the Poor and the Rich." Indeed, the founders supposedly wanted to place all children on an equal footing by giving them the same educational opportunities. The report emphasized that these original goals, which benefited the whole community, should still guide Boston's actions.

The Adams committee attributed its slowness in presenting a plan to the difficulty of determining how many children attended Boston's schools and, accordingly, recommended conducting a school census. The town meeting approved. The committee also maintained that truancy was a problem and that some of the absent children injured their minds and virtue by gambling. The town meeting accepted the committee's proposal that it deal with these problems by carefully investigating the moral character of anyone seeking to open a private school. The committee's investigation also found that some public-school teachers shortened the instructional hours so they could earn extra income tutoring. The committee said the practice of shortening instructional hours should be halted but balanced that by declaring that Boston must pay its teachers a living wage. Again the town meeting concurred.

The Adams committee report of April 1784 addressed two potentially divisive topics: providing education for the poor and for females. The committee recommended that, pending the completion of the school census, the Overseers of the Poor assist the poor so that even the most destitute child could attend school. This program would have applied to all children, including females. Aware that controversy swirled around the idea of offering females a general education, the Adams committee approached the issue gingerly. It merely said the question of educating females "required particular Consideration." The members trod no further than suggesting that females would become more useful members of society if they received schooling. The town meeting sidestepped these controversial proposals by deferring them for possible future action. In the next few months of 1784 the meeting increased teachers' salaries and also agreed to establish a new school in the city's southern section. Thus, although the Adams committee successfully pushed some education reforms, it had not realized the goal of ensuring that all the city's children could receive instruction in the public schools.[48]

It would obviously take time for the limited, but important, educational reforms to produce significant changes in the nature of Boston's society. And from Adams's perspective, that society was continuing its slide into antirepublican habits. Although plays had been outlawed in Massachusetts and Boston long before the American Revolution and remained illegal into the 1790s, some people sponsored theatrical performances, a form of amusement Samuel believed undermined republican virtues. That was but one of the problems. Writing to his cousin in the summer of 1785, Samuel informed John that he would be surprised if he could behold the fancy carriages, ostentatious furniture, and fantastic extravagance that abounded in Boston and the rest of the Commonwealth. Samuel complained that "the Pride & Vanity of Dress" infected all classes and thus blurred the distinction between the poor and the rich. These regrettable facts convinced Samuel that many people were imitating the English by indulging "in every idle Amusement & expensive Foppery" that might ruin a young country.

Despite his laments, Samuel thought the prospect for reforming society was improving. John Hancock had decided to retire, at least temporarily, from the governorship and left office in 1785. James Bowdoin, the man Samuel supported in the first governor's race, defeated Hancock's handpicked replacement, Thomas Cushing. Governor Bowdoin earned Adams's praise by quickly issuing "A Proclamation, for the Encouragement of Piety, Virtue, Education and Manners, and for the Suppression of Vice." Admitting he had long wished to see Hancock leave the governor's chair, Adams allowed himself to hope that, with a new chief magistrate and others setting better examples, the people of Massachusetts "may *perhaps* restore our Virtue."[49]

Samuel Adams nurtured that restoration of virtue above all by continuing to dwell on the importance of providing every child with a public education. It took another four years, but in 1789 Adams and his allies achieved dramatic support for, and transformations in, the education systems first of Massachusetts and then of Boston. In June the General Court passed one of the most influential education acts in American history. Sections of the act read like a compilation of arguments Adams had been trumpeting for years. All who instructed youths were to emphasize "the principles of piety, justice, and a sacred regard to truth, love of their country, humanity and universal benevolence, sobriety, industry and frugality, charity, moderation and temperance, and those other virtues which are the ornament of human society, and the basis upon which the republican Constitution is structured." The students needed to learn that such virtues tended "to preserve and perfect a republican Constitution and to secure the blessings of liberty, as well as to promote future happiness." And students must also be made to understand that the vices that undermined such virtues had a marked tendency "to produce slavery and ruin." Reestablishing the kind of colonial education system Adams so praised, the legislature decreed that all towns with at least fifty families must maintain a town school; larger communities must also support grammar schools. As in Boston, government officials were to ensure that only persons of good moral character became teachers.[50]

The 1789 act did not address the question of educating females, but in the fall of that year Boston's town meeting finally faced the issue. Spurred by a petition calling for reform that would include educating both sexes, the meeting appointed a Committee of Twelve, one from each ward, to report on the petition. When Bostonians held high executive state posts, they were not expected to serve on town-meeting committees. Samuel, who by then was the state's lieutenant governor, did the unexpected. Reflecting his long-standing commitment to expanding educational opportunities in Boston, "His Honor Sam¹. Adams, Esq." represented the city's Ninth Ward.

The Committee of Twelve recommended creating an elected school committee that would run an education system open to girls as well as boys. Three Reading Schools would teach reading and the proper use of English; three Writing Schools would offer the instruction in writing and arithmetic usually taught in the town schools. These schools, open to all children ages seven through fourteen, would be located to serve the northern, central, and southern sections of Boston. Another school would prepare students for university studies. Stressing that these innovations would require little increased spending, the committee boldly asserted that the great and obvious advantages that children in general, and females in particular, would derive from the plan "would abundantly compensate & Justify a far greater expence." Despite its plea for educating both sexes, the committee did not advocate full equality. Boys would attend school all year round; girls would only receive instruction for six months each year. And the report's language suggested that the college preparatory school would be open only to males.

In October 1789 the town meeting approved the committee's plan and authorized developing Boston's "new System of Education." Despite offering females less than equal educational opportunities, after a lengthy effort in which Adams figured prominently Boston had taken the greatest strides yet made in a major American city toward providing free public education for both sexes. Few contemporary American leaders supported creating a public-education system; far fewer advocated providing a general education to girls as well as boys. Samuel's strong efforts on behalf of educating all children illustrated his firm commitment to his often-stated belief that education was crucial to perpetuating a republican government. Upon reflection, it is hardly surprising that he championed education for females. He had always prized and lauded the influence his elder sister, Mary, had on him. Even more important, from the 1760s on, at a time when many New England adult women were not literate, Samuel knew the joys of a wife who could read and write. Moreover, he had come to rely on Elizabeth as a partner in political endeavors as well as in those things normally considered within the sphere of women.[51]

At the same time Adams and his allies began achieving educational reform in the mid-1780s, Samuel had to lead the effort to squash attempts to alter—to destroy—Boston's own constitution. For more than a century Boston had been governed by town meetings, a system that gave the citizens a direct vote in determining how their city functioned and allowed for meetings to occur as often as seemed necessary. But as proponents of incorporation had maintained for decades, the town meeting, which functioned through elected committees, could often be less than efficient. In the spring of 1784 several leading citizens decided the inefficiency must stop. They submitted a petition to have Boston incorporated and run by a mayor and council system. This request came at a time when many urban elites in America touted the glories of incorporating cities. But those who championed the people's right to participate actively in governance typically considered incorporation schemes aristocratic power grabs. Adams, truly a man of the town meeting, believed that Boston's government gave the people the power to preserve their liberties. Refusing to let Boston's republican constitution be ripped apart in the name of efficiency, Adams led the city's anti-incorporation forces. He did it not merely to defend his beloved native town but also to safeguard town-meeting government throughout New England. As he stated when writing to a citizen of Connecticut, Samuel believed that the people could not be enslaved or even significantly injured so long as they retained and made "good Use" of "those simple Democracies in all our Towns that are the Basis of our State Constitutions."[52]

No one could rival Samuel Adams's knowledge of how to make good use of a town meeting's democratic features. The proincorporation forces came into the May 11, 1784, meeting expecting they could convince the people to approve their plan to ask the General Court to incorporate Boston. Under the proposed incorporation plan, town meetings would occur only three times a year and the city would be governed by a mayor, twelve aldermen, and twenty-four common councilmen. All of these officials would be elected annually. The spokesman for the incorporation forces, Joseph Barrel, claimed this system would eliminate several "grievances" caused by the present "town constitution." It would also benefit everyone by putting an end to the "multiplicity" of town meetings that gobbled up the people's time. Having listened to the arguments for incorporation, Adams, the only anti-incorporation speaker cited in the newspaper account of the meeting, laid out the case against demolishing Boston's constitution. Claiming that Boston's constitution had served the people well for more than a century, Adams argued it was not necessary to destroy the town's system of government to deal with any grievances the city faced. Samuel warned that the plan being proposed "carried with it the appearance, and might in its consequences be instrumental to the introduction of aristocracy." Citing what had happened to republics in Rome and Greece, Adams asserted that "a love of novelty, and a desire for change had been," in other nations, "an avenue through which aristocracy has entered." Maintaining that some Americans hankered after aristocracy, Samuel proclaimed himself "too great a friend to democracy" to ever want to see that oppressive form of government introduced into America. Having put his opponents on the wrong side of a basic-rights issue, Adams asserted that "all the advantages that could possibly accrue to the town from its being incorporated, would be derived from a proper display of the powers of the present system."

While the backers of the incorporation plan pressed for an immediate vote, the best they could get was the appointment of a committee to consider their petition and, if necessary, report a plan for a different form of government. Adams was listed first and Barrel second on the roster of the committee's thirteen members. Brushing aside Adams's objections, this high-powered committee soon formulated two incorporation plans. They were presented to the June 4 town meeting. This apparent incorporation victory melted away after what a newspaper report described as a lengthy discussion rather than a debate. Instead of voting on the incorporation proposals, the meeting authorized the publication and distribution of the proposed plans to *every* household in the city. That eight-page pamphlet was to, and did, urge all the inhabitants to attend a June 17 town meeting that would take action on the proposals.

The newspaper account of what happened at the crucial and well-attended meeting lends credence to a later claim that a coalition had been formed days before to defeat any incorporation scheme. When Barrel began speaking on June 17, he was quickly challenged for allegedly having cast aspersions on the actions and integrity of the town's selectmen. Barrel denied that accusation and started to review the supposed economic woes of the town, but he was "obliged to desist by reason of the continual callings for '*the question*'"—which would force a vote. Several people tried to steer the discussion back to the merits of the incorporation plans, "but their arguments were drowned in the incessant shouts and demands for '*the Question*.'" As chants of "*No corporation*," "*No Mayor and Aldermen*," "*No Innovations*," reportedly echoed throughout the structure, "many gentlemen of character left the Hall." Soon thereafter the moderator gained enough control to ask for a show of hands, and the incorporation motion was defeated. The brief official minutes of the June 17 Boston Town Meeting include almost none of these details. They merely indicate that, after "some warm altercations," the idea of asking to have the city incorporated failed "by a great Majority." A motion was then made to dissolve the meeting immediately; although "contested," it carried.[53]

In August of 1784 the town meeting took action that seemed in accord with Adams's assertion that whatever might ail the governance of the city could be corrected under its present constitution. The August 17 meeting appointed a committee to consider whether the city's bylaws needed revising and, if so, to recommend action. That committee did not undertake a thorough revision of the bylaws but in October was authorized to ask the General Court for enlarged powers in formulating bylaws. As the weeks passed and nothing significant happened, the proincorporation forces tried a backdoor approach. On December 13 the *Independent Ledger*, which was openly proincorporation, carried the comments of a "Well-Wisher." The essayist maintained that, since the town had not asked to be incorporated, and since many problems still existed, the town meeting should elect a selectman from each ward. These twelve men should be paid to meet every week and be given more power so they could address the many troubles the city faced. Five days later, another writer built upon Well-Wisher's comments to argue that real efforts must be made to enforce existing laws *or* the town's system of governance should be entirely changed. He buttressed this argument with the claims that the city was being overrun with free Negroes who needed to be supervised. He insisted that, if such supervision did not occur, the free Negroes would likely fill up the almshouse and thus drive up the cost of poor relief. Underscoring the commonly held perception that Samuel Adams was leading the anti-incorporation forces, this essayist adopted the pen name "NOT ADAMS."[54]

As the months passed, these and other proincorporation efforts did not spur significant changes in either the city's bylaws or its constitution. In September 1785, more than a year after it had been formed, the committee charged with considering the possible revision of Boston's bylaws was once more pressed to report on its progress. Rather than supporting this request, the town meeting short-circuited it. Offering the intriguing claim that the six-member committee was too large and its members too busy to complete their work in any reasonable time, the town meeting abolished the committee. The meeting then appointed yet another committee. Its mandate was to revise the city's bylaws, make any modifications it considered necessary, and report back to the town meeting as soon as possible. Since the new five-member committee was chaired by Samuel Adams, the proincorporation forces were hardly likely to applaud these actions.[55]

Obviously believing, and correctly so, that they were being outmaneuvered and could not count on the Adams committee to do what they wanted, the proincorporation forces decided to start over. They circulated a petition calling for a town meeting to consider "That it may *once more* be made a Question, Whether this Town shall be Incorporated with City privileges?" The official notification for the meeting declared that a large number of inhabitants had signed that petition, and a newspaper account indicated that more than a hundred people had signed.[56] When the October 26, 1785, meeting opened, Samuel Adams was unanimously chosen as moderator. Once the petition had been read, he quickly used his position as moderator to put his opponents on the defensive. The *Massachusetts Centinel* reported that "on the Hon. Moderator's calling for its *fathers* to inform the town what the object of their *wishes* really were, no one appeared." A period of silence reportedly soon gave way to "the buz of—What is to be done." After an effort to dismiss the petition failed, the meeting agreed to appoint a committee to take the petition into consideration, to develop a plan for the future government of Boston, and to lay it before the town meeting. The nine-member committee, which included known proponents and opponents of incorporation, was once again headed by Samuel Adams.

Less than three weeks later the new Adams committee reported that it had met repeatedly but could not agree on a plan. The proincorporation forces countered by calling for the creation of yet another committee. It would consider possible defects in the town's constitution and how to remedy them *other than by incorporation*. That wording implied that only incorporation could correct major defects in how Boston was governed. The advocates of incorporation got their committee. Unfortunately for them, Samuel Adams was yet again elected to chair the committee, which reported back on November 30. It indicated that, after holding three meetings and having fully considered the matter, it could not find any defects in Boston's constitution. The town meeting voted its approval and politely, but firmly, told the incorporation petitioners to withdraw their request.

The separate bylaws committee, which Adams chaired, soon undercut one of the central arguments for destroying Boston's constitution. The committee did produce a thorough revision and expansion of the city's bylaws, which the town meeting started considering on December 6, 1785. As he repeatedly indicated, Adams was not against improving the governance of his beloved native town, but he was determined to thwart those who wanted to destroy the Boston Town Meeting's simple democracy. And thwart them he did. Although the incorporation forces did not give up, they were long frustrated; Boston was not finally incorporated as a city until 1822.[57]

As his efforts in helping to create the Massachusetts constitution and in defending Boston's constitution demonstrated, Samuel Adams could be flexible. But he never wavered from his commitment to crafting or maintaining republican constitutions that protected the people's liberties. And, holding firm to his view that a free republic like Massachusetts needed a virtuous citizenry to survive, he called for promoting virtue, especially through education. In doing so, he did more than celebrate the importance of expanding educational opportunities for all children. He played a central role in achieving significant educational advancements both in Boston and the commonwealth. In all these ways this American revolutionary labored, as he put it, "to secure the blessings of equal liberty to the present and future generations." But Samuel Adams did not, could not, limit himself merely to being concerned about the local world. In part because events in Massachusetts became embroiled in continental politics, because of his fame as an American revolutionary, and because of his commitment to the Union, Adams was inexorably drawn into contentious debates about how the nation itself would be governed.[58]

10

"AN IDOLATER OF
REPUBLICANISM" AND THE
NATION'S CONSTITUTION

As his ongoing defense of the fisheries illustrated, Samuel Adams remained active in continental affairs even after he left the Congress.
His concern for promoting virtue and protecting republican constitutions
naturally drew him into continental politics in the 1780s. He simply could
not avoid getting caught up in the increasingly acrimonious disputes about
reforming or even abolishing the Union's Articles of Confederation. In
dealing with such issues, Adams continued to be guided by his belief that
the people deserved a constitution that defended their rights and that, once
having such a constitution, they must guard it resolutely. As a perceptive
and noted foreign visitor declared upon meeting him in 1788, "if ever a
man was sincerely an idolater of republicanism, it is Samuel Adams."[1]

His fear that the return of loyalists who had abandoned America during
the Revolution would threaten republicanism certainly caused Adams to
look beyond his state. In 1783, as he contemplated the possible remigration
of loyalists, Adams adhered to the strident positions enunciated by Whigs
during the 1760s and early 1770s. Time and again, Bostonians had said
that those who undermined the cause should be ostracized *forever*. Adams's
actions proved that, for him, the prewar diatribes were not mere propagandistic bombast. Adams considered the refugees anti-American, antirepublican, and politically dangerous. He prophesied that, if allowed to return,
Tory refugees would join forces with evil politicians and undermine the
Union's republican governments. Moreover, if the loyalist wretches came
back, "Mutual Hatred and Revenge" would produce "perpetual Quarrels
between them & the people & perhaps frequent Bloodshed." Some of these
vile but cunning refugees might gradually regain public standing and form
factions in support of a foreign nation. In November 1783, believing that
such factions might already be endangering America, Adams wrote to his

diplomat cousin John, who was still in Europe. Samuel argued that every effort must be taken to counter the Tories' "evil Effects." Because he both hated Tories and considered them dangerous, Adams expressed pleasure when he learned that the peace treaty his cousin John had helped negotiate could be interpreted as giving individual states the right to bar loyalists from returning. Samuel worked to make that a reality in his home state. As the head of a committee appointed at the end of the war to craft instructions for the city's representatives, he persuaded Boston to endorse strong anti-Tory positions. The town meeting proclaimed that, whether they fought for the king or merely sought the shelter of his forces, Tories were "Conspirators against the Rights and Liberties of America and of Mankind." The "Traitors" who had fled America should never be taken back.[2]

Hostile British actions reinforced Samuel's already adamant stance on the loyalists. By late 1784 it had become obvious that Britain was flagrantly violating the peace treaty by keeping troops in frontier posts on American territory. Samuel maintained that Britain even seemed ready to threaten the Union's eastern territory and might attempt to stop Americans from using the fishery. It appeared to him that, when Great Britain signed the Treaty of Paris ending the war, "she seems to have meant Nothing more than a Truce." Given that, surely Tory refugees should be barred from returning to America. Britain's belligerent actions helped perpetuate the anti-British sentiment that had permeated wartime America and made it easier to beat back attempts to ease harsh antiloyalist laws.[3]

The actions of American military men helped fuel Adams's concern about loyalist refugees joining antirepublican political factions. In May 1783 officers of the Continental Army formed a "Society of Friends" and named it for Lucius Quinctius Cincinnatus, the famous Roman general who, after leading the armies to victory, refused any special honors and returned to his life as a farmer. While any Continental Army or French officer could join the Society of the Cincinnati, militia officers were not automatically entitled to membership. The society could, whenever it chose, bestow honorary membership on individuals. As an initiation fee, members had to contribute a month's pay to the society's coffers. The local branches could, if they wished, levy additional financial tithings.

Adams and others who denounced the society maintained that it debauched the ideal of Cincinnatus. The group adopted regalia that included a gold eagle medal and a wide blue ribbon so its members could, as the founders phrased it, "be known and distinguished." The society embraced hereditary primogeniture by letting a member's eldest son join. Worse yet, the constitution of the Cincinnati, as most called the group, suggested it would become politically active. The society's mix of aristocracy and militarism terrified Adams and others, including Thomas Jefferson, John Adams, Elbridge Gerry, and James Warren. Supplying his cousin John with ammunition, Samuel depicted the district and state conventions of the Cincinnati as trying to usurp the powers of the state legislatures, the Congress, and other government officials. Samuel warned that, "being an Order of *Military* Men," the Cincinnati might soon try to enforce their resolutions and in the process possibly destroy America's free governments.

As a determined republican who believed one must ardently defend established constitutions that guarded the people's freedom, Samuel Adams became an anti-Cincinnati activist. He was instrumental in convincing the Massachusetts legislature to denounce the Cincinnati as an aristocratic threat to republicanism. To spread the message, in April 1784 he dispatched letters to Elbridge Gerry, an equally firm opponent of the Cincinnati, who was serving in Congress. Samuel ominously warned that the formation of the Cincinnati constituted "as rapid a Stride towards an hereditary Military Nobility as ever was made in so short a Time." Since it would be politically unwise to disparage the officers as nothing more than power-hungry aristocrats, Adams claimed he was sure that few, if any, of the Cincinnati's founders had evil intentions. The real danger would come from the officers' progeny. They might want to transform the pageantry of nobility into the real thing. For individuals who might dismiss these arguments, Adams conjured up a frightening scenario. By letting foreigners into their ranks, the Cincinnati increased the danger that "a foreign Influence might prevail in America."

Since the revered George Washington endorsed the Cincinnati, and since Adams respected and trusted Washington, he carefully noted that Washington must not think the Cincinnati posed a danger to liberty. Washington justified Samuel's trust. When the anti-Cincinnati firestorm erupted, Washington responded by quickly recommending several changes in the society's constitution. The hereditary features should be eliminated; anything that had a political tendency should be expunged; provisions should guarantee that the group's money could not be used for political purposes. In May 1784 the first general meeting of the Cincinnati endorsed Washington's recommendations.[4]

Although anti-Cincinnati sentiment quickly subsided, Adams and many others were not reassured. Writing to Gerry in 1785, Samuel evoked an image he had used in the 1760s against the British. He declared that the changes approved at the 1784 general meeting made the Cincinnati *more* dangerous because the society "is the same serpent still, but it hides its sting." Moreover, the state Cincinnati organizations rejected the alterations Washington recommended and that the first general meeting had approved. So, despite Washington's efforts, the Cincinnati retained its dangerous militaristic and aristocratic features and, in Adams's view, stood ready to unleash its power to influence and possibly control America's legislatures. Adams and Gerry kept trying to convince Congress that it must go on record as opposing the Cincinnati. Congress did not act, and in time the Cincinnati proved that the extreme fears raised by its foes were wrong. Nevertheless, in the early 1780s fervent republicans could not foresee that the Society of the Cincinnati would evolve into a benign organization. So, given his cardinal rule that one must watchfully defend the people's rights and the people's republican constitutions, Adams's anti-Cincinnati campaign made sense.[5]

Although decidedly unhappy about Congress's failure to oppose the Cincinnati, Adams consistently advocated the necessity of backing the confederation government. His support for the central government stemmed from the fact that it was a confederation of sovereign states. Like many other Americans, Adams, who considered himself a citizen of both the United States and Massachusetts, had a well-developed sense of dual citizenship. Thus, while he constantly referred to Massachusetts as his country, he could also tell a South Carolinian that "We are Citizens of the United States & our Interest is *one*." Given this view, he regularly expressed concern for upholding "the honour of congress" because Congress "is and must be the cement of the union of the states."[6]

Adams's support for the confederation government was especially evident in the positions he took on the volatile issue of giving America's military officers pensions. While he was still a congressman, Congress debated the question at length before finally, in October 1780, offering half pay for life to officers who would serve for the duration of the war. This was done to keep experienced officers in the field. Although he zealously supported most proposals that bolstered the revolutionaries' military power, Adams, whose fear of a military establishment was legendary, balked at what he considered a dangerous bow to the military. He voted against the half-pay-for-life proposal, but he was in the minority.[7]

Once the war was safely won, strong sentiment welled up for reneging on the proffered officers' pensions. The anger festered even after March 1783 when the Congress "commuted" the lifetime pensions to full pay for five years. In July the Massachusetts General Court expressed its displeasure in a letter to Congress, and the state's delegates struggled for months to find a way to reverse the earlier decision. In September, as public protests over commutation flared, especially in Connecticut, Adams responded to a question from a Connecticut "Gentleman" about where he personally stood on the matter. If, as seems likely, the questioner anticipated receiving an anti-Congress blast, he misjudged. Although Adams had opposed the pensions in 1780, he now backed Congress unflinchingly. Knowing his comments might be used in the commutation fight, Samuel offered reasons for supporting Congress's actions. He intimated that five-year pensions were preferable to lifetime pensions in part because they were less likely to perpetuate militaristic attitudes. Also, on the basis of the claim that officers supposedly missed economic opportunities open to fellow citizens at home, the pensions seemed just and reasonable. In addition, commutation would probably be cost-effective when measured against the original promise of half pay for life. For Adams, such considerations mattered less than the principle of defending Congress when it exercised legitimate constitutional powers. Congress had been created, he pointed out, so the joint wisdom of the states could protect "our just Rights & Liberties." When an army became necessary because Britain waged war against those rights, Congress had the constitutional responsibility and undoubted right to decide how to support the army, and a congressional majority voted for the pensions. The Congress did that because granting pensions seemed absolutely necessary to the war effort. The states, therefore, must support Congress's actions even if some people considered the actions inappropriate. Adams added the forceful reminder that "an *honest* Man" would understand that "States as well as individual Persons are equally bound to fulfill their engagements."[8]

While he consistently advocated the importance of backing Congress, Adams's responses to possibly altering how Congress functioned sprang from a basic principle. He measured every major suggestion by this question: will it possibly undermine liberty? If his answer was yes, he opposed it. Thus, early in the war, he had voted to create boards of war, ordnance, navy, and finance that would be run by skilled persons who were not members of Congress. He did so because he believed the change would improve efficiency without endangering liberty. However, in 1781 he voted against a congressional plan that effectively shifted major responsibilities from congressional committees to executive departments headed by a powerful superintendent. He was particularly leery of creating a superintendent of finance and pleaded with his fellow congressmen to oppose the idea. He feared a superintendent of finance might gain a "highly dangerous" and "undue influence" both in Congress and in state legislatures. Alluding to the extraordinary power the British finance minister wielded, Adams predicted that even an angel-like financier might become so influential he could control Congress. One proponent of the new system countered by saying that "the breath of congress could annihilate the financier." Adams shot back, "the time might come, and if they were not careful it certainly would, when even congress would not dare to blow that breath." To protect the people's liberty, he preferred keeping the clumsy and often inefficient committee system rather than risk having power consolidated in one person's hands. A majority of Adams's fellow congressmen disagreed. They voted the executive system into existence.[9]

Whenever the question of revising the Articles surfaced, Adams tempered his desire to ensure that the continental government could function effectively with an abiding concern about not undermining liberty. By the time he left Congress in mid-1781, it was already painfully evident that Congress could not rely on the states for the funds necessary to run the Union's government. Adams found that disconcerting in part because he considered it sound policy for governments to discharge their debts "with all possible Speed" so future generations would not be encumbered. Accordingly, Adams supported the 1781 and 1783 proposals to give Congress a measure of financial security by letting it levy impost duties. Indeed, although justifiably famous for being politically upright, Adams was accused of underhanded shenanigans in support of the 1783 proposal. In a letter Gerry sent to a Massachusetts legislative committee Adams chaired, Massachusetts's congressmen proposed that the state refuse to approve the impost unless Congress adopted several positions favorable to the state. In effect, the delegates recommended blackmailing Congress. An Adams committee member pocketed the unsavory letter, and Massachusetts approved the impost proposal in October 1783.

Soon thereafter politicos charged that Adams and the other two members of the committee purposefully suppressed the letter. The legislature launched an investigation, and Adams apologized profusely. He maintained that the crush of his work as Senate president, his ill health, and the fact that Congressman Stephen Higginson had already briefed the General Court on the delegates' ideas explained his failure to ensure that the legislators received the letter. Adams escaped censure; the committeeman who pocketed the letter did not. Adams told Gerry that "mere forgetfulness" caused the problem and that the complaints against him sprang from political animus. Samuel predicted that the "Clamour" would evaporate as soon as the next election was over. Gerry accepted his friend's explanation. Adams was, in fact, seriously ill when the incident occurred in September 1783, and, as he prophesied, it did him no lasting harm. Nevertheless, when all allowances have been made, the fact remains: his action, which did support the effort to increase Congress's powers, was negligent and possibly devious.[10]

Although they garnered strong support, the 1781 and 1783 impost proposals both foundered because a single state could scuttle the amendment process. So Congress remained financially impotent. It also could not effectively regulate the Union's commerce. Once peace returned, Americans fell into old habits and resumed trading with Britain. As Adams lamented, the British consequently refused to negotiate a commercial treaty because they already had the benefit of America's trade without making concessions. In part to give Congress leverage against the British, many Americans advocated granting Congress the kind of commercial power Britain once exercised. Formal proposals on the matter surfaced beginning in 1783. Adams supported granting Congress commercial powers. In the fall of 1785, he reminded Gerry that, when Massachusetts and New Hampshire tried to use navigation acts to force nations to enter commercial treaties with the United States, neighboring states had not taken similar action. That left the two activist states "suffering by their own honest exertions for the general interest." Thus Congress's inability to regulate commerce had exacerbated economic woes in Massachusetts. It seemed obvious that Congress should have "sufficient Power to regulate the Trade of the States with foreigners."

Some Americans insisted that the confederation should not be granted additional powers. Others thought that only a vigorous consolidated national government could meet America's needs. Adams belonged to neither camp. He was willing, even anxious, to give the confederation government the power necessary to function. But he also assessed each recommended change by asking himself if it might undermine what he called the Articles' objective of promoting "Liberty." Thus, in September 1785, when he called for giving Congress commercial powers, he held that Congress could be granted "properly *guarded*" powers "without endangering the Principles of the Confederation." However, he balked at the idea of undertaking a full revision of the Articles. Adams feared such a revision might transform the central government into a dangerous monolith. In one of the numerous political letters he sent for Gerry's use in 1785, Adams argued that a general revision of the Articles seemed not only unnecessary but dangerous. Samuel warned that the confederation's commitment to liberty could be lost in at least two possible ways. If the people were not watchful and attentive, a few scheming men might grasp the government; or a revised frame of government might be couched in "such ambiguous Terms" that it could be interpreted in ways that would harm or even destroy liberty.[11]

Adams's desire to modify rather than totally revise the Articles ran into problems that touched him personally as he strove to preserve Massachusetts's constitutional government. The problems were rooted in economic difficulties. Although the war thoroughly disrupted the Massachusetts economy, people, particularly farmers, derived some economic benefit from the presence of American and French forces. Then, as the fighting shifted to the South in 1780, the military market shrank dramatically. The economic dislocations touched all Massachusetts inhabitants, but western farmers, many living on the economic margin, felt especially squeezed by the loss of markets. The General Court appeared to exacerbate the economic woes. Starting in 1779 and continuing into 1780, the legislature levied heavy taxes to meet financial obligations to its own citizens and to Congress. Although the policy of heavy taxation pinched the people, Adams considered the pinch necessary. The revolutionary generation must not shirk its duty; it must not burden posterity with a massive debt.

People, particularly in the westernmost counties, did more than grumble. Facing hard times and in many cases imminent bankruptcy, citizens flooded the General Court with petitions in the early 1780s. They pressed for tax relief and insisted that the supply of money be increased. In 1781 and into 1782 extralegal conventions met to demand action. By the spring of 1782 crowd actions disrupted some government functions in western Massachusetts. In April a crowd shut down courts in Hampshire County. One of the leaders, Samuel Ely, reportedly urged the people on with the cry, "Come on my brave boys, we will go to the wood pile and get clubs enough, and knock their gray wigs off, and send them out of the world in an instant." Some people defended the judges, and bloodshed was prevented. The efforts to capture and punish Ely, however, raised the possibility that violence might bubble up again.

The General Court responded with a hard fist encased in a soft glove. In midsummer 1782 the legislators suspended habeas corpus for six months but also declared that, for one year, certain goods—including livestock, grain, and marketable lumber—would be legal tender. In addition, the General Court dispatched three legislators, headed by Senate president Samuel Adams, to hear the westerners' complaints. During July and August of 1782 the legislature's committee attended town meetings and then met with a special convention of towns. Westerners aired their grievances and called for redress. But the convention also thanked the General Court for listening and, more important, called on everyone to support constitutional government. Given this development, the legislature applauded the Adams committee and enacted a general pardon that excluded only Ely. Major uprisings were averted, but sporadic crowd action continued to flare, and ad hoc conventions began springing up in the eastern as well as the western sections of the state. The gatherings did more than criticize the Massachusetts government. They often opposed giving Congress the right to levy an impost, and many harsh words were uttered about the impropriety of Congress granting pensions to military officers.[12]

Although Adams believed the people's grievances should be considered, his response to the ongoing challenges to constitutional government was predictable. While he still proclaimed that citizen watchfulness was a political virtue and one of the greatest securities of liberty, he also observed that some men, under the guise of being watchful patriots, were assaulting everything the governments did and using conventions to stir up "Discord & Animosity." Adams, who feared anarchy as well as tyranny, stressed that, while citizen watchfulness was vital, it was equally true that "there is Decency & Respect due to Constitutional Authority." Adams also pointed out that, while methods being used in the 1780s were methods he had employed in the 1760s, there was a fundamental difference. In the 1760s the people used county conventions and popular committees to defend the right of being governed only by laws their own representatives produced. Now the people had a constitution that guaranteed their legislators and other public officials would be annually selected in free elections; therefore, county conventions and popular committees challenged, rather than defended, constitutional rights.[13]

By 1785, in part due to an improving economic situation, the danger posed by firebrands such as Samuel Ely and by ad hoc bodies appeared to have subsided. The quiet was misleading, though, especially in western Massachusetts, where large numbers of people still labored under a heavy burden of debt. In 1786, when the General Court refused to issue paper money and also enacted a hefty tax hike, calls for holding conventions to produce reforms morphed into open rebellion. The rebels, who had their greatest strength in the two westernmost counties of Berkshire and Hampshire, organized themselves into military units led by veterans of the war. One of the principal rebel commanders was Daniel Shays, a former Continental Army captain, and the uprising became known as Shays's Rebellion. The first spasm of violence occurred in late August when armed men shut down the courts in Northampton in Hampshire County; crowds soon disrupted courts in several other counties. Adams and the Boston Town Meeting tried to halt the disturbances. In early September, with Adams serving as moderator, the meeting appointed a committee, headed by him, to address the governor. The committee recommended that, in addition to communicating directly with the governor, a circular letter should be sent to the state's townships. The town meeting agreed. The lengthy letter, apparently drafted principally by James Sullivan, was designed to convince the dissidents that they should renounce violence and support constitutional government. Echoing Adams's sentiments, the circular letter stressed that any real grievances could be—and to protect the rights of posterity must be—redressed by using the established constitutional process.[14]

Two days after the town meeting approved these pronouncements Governor Bowdoin, having consulted his Council, directed the General Court to meet in a special session starting on September 27. He asked the legislators to find ways to stop the courts from being subjected to the kind of crowd actions that had already produced "many tumults and disorders." The General Court, which included Senator Adams, responded with a series of laws that allowed those who had disrupted the courts to be pardoned on a promise of good behavior. But the laws also gave the government strong powers to deal with any future disruptions. In addition, the legislature took actions that offered at least temporary relief from the pressure of paying taxes in specie and from draconian debt collection. Finally, before adjourning in November, the legislature issued a lengthy report that reviewed the economic situation and sought to justify government expenditures. And, in words Adams would applaud, the General Court reminded the people that "in a republican government the major part must govern: if the minor part governs, it becomes an aristocracy: if everyone opposes at his pleasure, it is no government, it is anarchy and confusion."[15]

Words and legislative modifications proved ineffective. The uprising spread. In January 1787 about fifteen hundred rebels commanded by Shays threatened to capture the federal arsenal at Springfield. They might have succeeded had not Massachusetts fielded an army of more than four thousand that stopped them, but only after an exchange of fire left the blood of two dozen rebel farmers soaking into the snow. Four were killed, at least twenty wounded. Organized resistance sputtered on into February, and fear of a renewal of violence lingered well into the summer.[16] For Samuel Adams, Shays's Rebellion constituted perhaps the ultimate horror: the people waging war against a constitution that protected their liberties and provided them with effective legal means to redress grievances. Once the rebellion was crushed, most politicians, sensing that the public wanted mercy, endorsed clemency for the rebels. Adams refused to pander to the popular mood. He reportedly said the ringleaders should be hung because, "in monarchies, the crime of treason and rebellion may admit of being pardoned or lightly punished; but the man who dares to rebel against the laws of a republic ought to suffer death."[17] In fact, while some death sentences were handed down and some men actually marched to the gallows before being reprieved, none of the insurgents was executed for his role in the insurgency.[18]

Shays's Rebellion figured prominently in the eventual destruction of the Articles of Confederation and the subsequent creation of a truly national government. Americans who wanted to revamp the Union's government skillfully exploited the fear that accompanied Shays's Rebellion. Exaggerated reports of rebellion brewing throughout New England helped convince George Washington, the most admired and trusted man in the Union, to attend the convention Congress authorized to recommend changes in the Articles. The convention that met in Philadelphia from May into September 1787 disregarded its instructions and drafted a totally new constitution. Congress, which by then rarely had enough members to function, followed the convention's recommendation and called on the states to have elected ratification conventions vote on the proposed Constitution. The people of Massachusetts, like those throughout the Union, disagreed sharply over the merits of the new governmental framework. In fact, opinion in the Union divided about equally on the question of adopting it. In Massachusetts, a state that the pro-Constitution forces knew they had to carry, a majority of the citizens favored rejecting the convention's document.[19]

Believing Adams would oppose the new Constitution, its staunch Massachusetts supporters contemplated trying to block his election to the state's ratifying convention. They abandoned the idea in part, as Christopher Gore noted, because "those who are in favor of the constitution feard the consequences of opposing S.A.'s election." They reasoned, Gore noted, that if Adams were not a delegate, he might openly attack the Constitution and also surreptitiously influence groups of delegates. If he attended, his arguments could be countered more easily; moreover, as Gore admitted, Adams could not be defeated at the polls. Boston's caucuses had, supposedly for the first time, been totally united on a ticket that included Adams and several others Gore considered to be less than committed supporters of the proposed Constitution. As concerns about Adams's possible opposition mounted, pro-Constitution forces plotted to neutralize him. In January 1788, just before the ratifying convention opened, almost four hundred Boston artisans and tradesmen met and proclaimed that no delegate should even think about trying to amend, much less oppose, the new Constitution. That message was, supporters of the proposed Constitution emphasized, designed above all to try to influence one man: Samuel Adams.[20]

Adams *did* dislike the proposed Constitution. He expressed his general views in a letter to his old political ally Richard Henry Lee in early December 1787. "I confess, as I enter the Building I stumble at the Threshold. I meet with a National Government, instead of a Federal Union of Sovereign States." Adams was right. The framers of the Constitution had replaced a federal constitution with one that, while retaining some federal features, created a national government. However, in a brilliant propaganda maneuver that still controls how the terms are used, the nationalists appropriated the popular term *Federalist* for themselves while tarring anyone who raised questions about the new Constitution with the derisive and misleading label *Anti-Federalist*.

Adams used basic Anti-Federalist arguments against the Constitution. After suggesting that America was too vast and the interests of its people too diverse to be governed effectively by a single national legislature, Adams played the aristocracy card. Maintaining that "the Seeds of Aristocracy" lay "like a Canker Worm . . . at the Root of free Governments," he asserted that those seeds began germinating even before the War for Independence ended. The clear implication was that the new Constitution sprang from an ongoing aristocratic plot to subvert free republican governments. Having attempted to place the so-called Federalists on the wrong side of basic rights issues, Adams pitched the idea of amending rather than annihilating the Articles. He did that by elaborating on the central points he had made in September 1785 when arguing against a general revision of the Articles. Adams maintained that, with adjustments, the Articles, which protected America's liberty, could serve the people well. Going to the extreme of adopting a new frame of government was, he argued, unnecessary and dangerous.[21]

Despite his strictures against the proposed Constitution, Adams knew the confederation government was woefully underpowered. In addition, he could not deny that the process being used to replace the Articles was the same republican process he glorified when it was used to create the Massachusetts constitution. He therefore could not simply reject the new Constitution. In early January 1788 Adams intimated to Christopher Gore that he planned to attend the ratifying convention with an open mind. In fact, Gore noted that Adams said a government could be formed from the proposed Constitution—*but only if the document were amended*. Gore, an intense Federalist who was convinced Adams would vote against the proposed Constitution, dismissed Adams's comments. He should not have. Adams considered moderation a republican virtue and had acted with restraint when he helped create the Massachusetts constitution. He had also urged the people to exercise moderation when considering the proposed state constitution. Indeed, whenever he approached the question of forming a government, Adams had always shown a willingness to compromise where it could be done without endangering liberty. Moreover, he always stressed the impossibility of achieving either perfection or everything one desired in a government. Had Gore not been so closed-minded himself he would have realized that Adams would likely be open-minded and judicious at the ratifying convention.

Gore's own recent experience with Samuel should have given credence to Samuel's comment about a willingness to be open-minded. Christopher's father, John Gore, a painter and color merchant, had left his family behind and fled Boston with the British forces in March 1776. He returned in 1785 and in June 1787 petitioned the legislature asking to be naturalized; that request, supported by patriotic notables including James Bowdoin, was granted, and, as a consequence, John once more became an American citizen. Despite his detestation of loyalists, Samuel did not oppose John Gore's request. He took that position because Gore's two sons had supported the Revolution and the wife and daughters John had abandoned. Samuel later told Christopher that, because of his pure regard for him, he was always willing to allow John Gore to return. Had Christopher considered Samuel's reasonableness in the case of his loyalist father, he could have offered a better forecast of how Samuel would behave at the ratifying convention.[22]

For most of the convention, which opened on January 9, 1788, Adams stayed out of the debates and functioned, as he put it, more as "an auditor, than an objector." Nathaniel Gorham, a committed Federalist delegate to the ratifying convention, appeared to acknowledge that fact on January 20. He seems to have placed Adams on a list of delegates who "appear to be determined to hear all that can be said on the subject—& then vote as they think right." Another ardent Federalist, Henry Knox of New York, used almost identical language when he said that Adams was on that list of thoughtful swing voters.[23] Adams's actions at the convention support that judgment and his own claim about being an auditor, not an objector. When he did participate in the convention's activities, Samuel evenhandedly followed precedents established during the process of drafting and adopting the Massachusetts constitution. He successfully urged the delegates to invite Elbridge Gerry, a member of the Philadelphia convention, to answer delegates' questions about how the Constitution came into being. Federalists interpreted that as a hostile act because Gerry had refused to sign the Constitution and then publicly explained why. In urging that Gerry attend, Adams was, in fact, following precedent. When the Boston Town

Meeting discussed the proposed Massachusetts constitution in 1780, it had asked constitutional convention delegates to attend so they could answer the citizens' queries.[24]

While passionate Federalists disliked his support for bringing Gerry into the ratifying convention, fervent Anti-Federalists disliked Adams's response to one of their tactics. When they began deliberations, the delegates agreed to discuss the proposed Constitution paragraph by paragraph. However, as the convention progressed, leading Anti-Federalists tried to change the rules. Realizing they had the votes to defeat the Constitution and not wanting to risk slippage in their ranks, they moved to stop debating each paragraph. Adams opposed the motion, and it lost. His action not only supported the idea of fair play but also adhered to the town-meeting precedent of examining vital documents such as a proposed constitution paragraph by paragraph before voting on it.[25]

On two additional occasions when he spoke, Adams displayed an evenhandedness that again favored the Federalists. When a pro-Constitution speaker commented on the *"anarchy"* of Shays's Rebellion, an opponent attempted to silence him by claiming that the discussion was not germane. Adams was among those who disagreed, and the pro-Constitution speaker was allowed to continue. Similarly, Anti-Federalists tried to exploit the fact that the Constitution stipulated that the slave trade could be outlawed by Congress, but only after a twenty-year interval. They chastised the framers of the Constitution for not banning the slave trade immediately. Adams was one of the delegates who, because the framers had set a specific date for potentially voting the slave trade out of existence, "rejoiced that a door was now to be opened for the annihilation of this odious, abhorrent practice in a certain time."[26]

As the convention progressed, Adams thus demonstrated a judicious, fair-minded, and pragmatic approach. The problem for devout Federalists and Anti-Federalists was that neither camp wanted to compromise. Each side desperately wanted to win because each thought that the ultimate fate of the Constitution depended on what happened in Massachusetts. Federalists were especially averse to admitting that the Constitution might contain any fundamental defects lest that admission open the door for holding a second constitutional convention. Some Anti-Federalists throughout the Union were calling for that second gathering as a means of killing the proposed new government.[27]

Believing they must carry Massachusetts, Federalists swallowed hard and compromised. They struck a deal with the very popular John Hancock. He had been elected president of the convention but had not attended, supposedly because his gouty condition forced him to stay in bed. As cynics noted, by not attending the convention, Hancock avoided having to take a position. According to the steadfast Federalist Rufus King, the pro-Constitution forces trolled for Hancock's support in part by dangling the possibility that he might become the first president of the new United States government. After all, if the Anti-Federalist-leaning Virginia did not ratify, George Washington would be ineligible. Hancock bit, and the Federalists reeled him on board. Federalists considered Adams's support imperative, and they did convince him to back the compromise arrangements. But, intriguingly, King did not mention any offers being made to catch him. Adams apparently joined in the arrangement on the basis of the merits of the case. Under the compromise, Federalists pledged to exert their influence to have a group of amendments added to the Constitution. In exchange for that pledge, Hancock and Adams would advocate outright, rather than conditional, ratification. Federalists hoped that, with "the weight" of both Hancock and Adams, they could secure ratification.[28]

Hancock left his sickbed and attended the convention for the first time on January 30, 1788. The next day he dramatically recommended approving the Constitution, but with the understanding that amendments would be added once the new government began functioning. Hancock offered nine amendments. By prearrangement, Adams moved that Hancock's proposals be adopted. Adams focused on the first proposed amendment, which said that "it be explicitly declared, that all powers not expressly delegated to Congress, are reserved to the several States." This was, for Adams, the crucial amendment. It would, as much as possible, ensure that the new Constitution would meet the standard he had enunciated in 1785. The Union's frame of government should not be couched in ambiguous language that might be construed in ways that would threaten liberty.

Knowing many Anti-Federalists faulted the proposed Constitution for its failure to include a bill of rights, Adams proclaimed that Hancock's first amendment "appears to my mind to be a summary of a bill of rights." He forcefully reminded the delegates that the amendment matched well with the crucial §2 of the Articles of Confederation and would be used to stop the federal government from creating laws "beyond the power granted by the proposed Constitution." In endorsing the compromise, Adams also observed that, when considering great and controversial issues of government, a person had to show respect for differing views. One had to weigh all the facts and be guided by mature judgment. He added that if Massachusetts ratified the Constitution with the understanding that amendments would be added, other states would probably follow suit. Thus, the country could reap the immediate benefit of a more vigorous central government while also anticipating that the Constitution would be altered to alleviate the concerns of those who, like himself, had serious reservations about it.[29]

Days later, just before the ratification vote, Adams tried to protect basic liberties even more explicitly. He moved that the proposed amendment limiting the national government to the powers "expressly" delegated to it be expanded by adding, "And that the said Constitution be never construed to authorize Congress to infringe the just liberty of the press, or the rights of conscience; or to prevent the people of the United States who are peaceable citizens, from keeping their own arms; or to raise standing armies, unless when necessary for the defence of the United States, or of some one or more of them; or to prevent the people from petitioning in a peaceable and orderly manner, the federal legislature, for redress of grievances; or to subject the people to unreasonable searches & seizures of their persons, papers, or possessions." This lengthy addition, which amounted to a bill of rights, reflected Adams's concern that a good constitution must protect the people's liberties. This proposal, though, reportedly caused real consternation, so Samuel withdrew it lest it scuttle the compromise he supported. When another delegate put his proposal forward again, Adams had to vote against it to protect the compromise agreement.[30]

Even with the backing of Hancock and Adams, the pro-Constitution forces feared they might not win. Their anxiety was justified; the final vote proved agonizingly close. With both Hancock and Adams voting to ratify, Massachusetts approved the Constitution 187 to 168. As the leading Federalist delegates conceded, they probably would have failed had they not obtained the support of the two famous patriots. Although the vote was tight, once the votes were in, a number of Anti-Federalist delegates declared that, since the majority had approved it, they would now support the adoption of the Constitution.

Adams swung over to the proratification group for several intertwining reasons. He always believed that government must have the power needed to perform its constitutional duties. And no one could deny that the piecemeal efforts to revise the Articles had repeatedly failed—and would probably continue to fail. Even more important, Adams firmly believed that the people had the inherent right to alter or abolish a constitution. Moreover, although the framers undeniably violated Congress's instructions, the Constitution would be subjected to a thoroughly republican ratifying process. So, if ratified, the new frame of government would rest on the consent of the governed. But what mattered most to Adams was the fact that Massachusetts Federalists had agreed to help add amendments

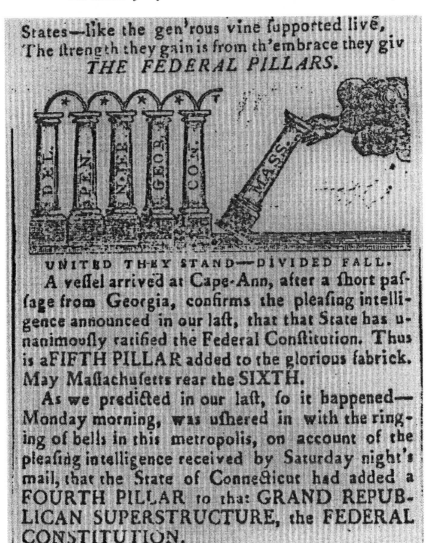

States—like the gen'rous vine fupported live,
The ftrength they gain is from th'embrace they giv

THE FEDERAL PILLARS.

UNITED THEY STAND—DIVIDED FALL.

A veffel arrived at Cape-Ann, after a fhort paffage from Georgia, confirms the pleafing intelligence announced in our laft, that that State has unanimoufly ratified the Federal Conftitution. Thus is a FIFTH PILLAR added to the glorious fabrick. May Maffachufetts rear the SIXTH.

As we predicted in our laft, fo it happened—Monday morning, was uffered in with the ringing of bells in this metropolis, on account of the pleafing intelligence received by Saturday night's mail, that the State of Connecticut had added a FOURTH PILLAR to that GRAND REPUBLICAN SUPERSTRUCTURE, the FEDERAL CONSTITUTION.

"The Federal Pillars" from the Massachusetts Centinel *(January 16, 1788).*

that would, he hoped, wring the ambiguity out of the Constitution. And since he believed, correctly as it turned out, that other states would follow Massachusetts's lead, Adams had good reason to think the new Constitution would be amended to protect the people's liberties.[31]

As he helped move Massachusetts toward approving a constitution that transformed the nature of America's central government, Adams's own life was, unfortunately, also being transformed. On January 17, just over a week after the ratifying convention began deliberations, his son died at the age of thirty-seven. The younger Samuel's health had declined while he was serving in the war, and he returned home to live in semiretirement. Given his reference to parents hoping their children would outlive them, and given his emphasis on fashioning a society and government for the benefit of one's posterity, the loss of his only son devastated Samuel. Some attributed Adams's general silence at the convention to the trauma of his son's death. That probably was not the case, but as of January 1788 Adams's own posterity consisted of his daughter, Hannah, and her children. The death of Samuel Jr., ironically, provided Samuel and Elizabeth with the greatest financial security they had known in their married life. He willed securities to his father that were worth approximately $12,500, a huge sum for that day.[32]

At the same time he lost his only son, Samuel was reestablishing a political partnership with John Hancock. Adams's antagonism toward Hancock had been softening, perhaps because Hancock did not exert the determining influence on society Adams thought the first governor of Massachusetts might. By the time the new Constitution was proposed in 1787, Samuel and John had reconciled socially. Their political reconciliation stemmed from their similar views on the new Constitution. Elbridge Gerry expressed the crucial point when he remarked that, "with all his foibles," Hancock was "yet attached to the whig cause." Samuel agreed, and soon he and Hancock were once again functioning as a political team.

Jacques Pierre Brissot de Warville, a French traveler who visited Boston in July 1788, documented the rapprochement. He observed that Adams "is the best supporter of the party of Governor Hancock." While the Frenchman did not attempt to explain why the two men had formed a close alliance, he offered hints. Although Hancock craved popularity, he still possessed the "spirit of patriotism" he had displayed at the start of the Revolution. Brissot de Warville, who like Chastellux before him found Adams remarkable, also ventured a comment on what motivated Adams, this "idolater of republicanism." Brissot de Warville marveled that he had never met any man who so exemplified the characteristics of his stated political persuasion. Adams "has the excess of republican virtues, untainted probity, simplicity, modesty, and, above all, firmness; he will have no capitulation with abuses; he fears as much the despotism of virtue and talents, as the despotism of vice."[33]

Brissot de Warville was right to hearken back to the patriotism of the struggle against Britain. From Adams's perspective, something of a similar struggle went on from the ratification of the new Constitution through the rest of his active political career. Adams had wrestled with the British serpent because he believed it threatened to kill America's liberties. Adams reunited with Hancock because both men, whatever else motivated them, feared the new national government might emulate the British government and attack basic rights. Together they would make Federalists live up to their promises to defang the Constitution by attaching language that would limit the potentially sweeping powers of the national government.

Adams's concerns about the Constitution forced him to reconsider his retirement from national office. Samuel, who believed that people should neither solicit nor campaign for a political office, let his name be put forward as a candidate for the United States House of Representatives. In the special December 18, 1788, election for what was dubbed the Suffolk District, Adams was opposed by Fisher Ames, a bright, articulate, but very young lawyer who lived in Dedham. Adams's supporters, confident of victory, stressed that "this venerable patriot," "this consistent republican," was an able and experienced politician. He would give Massachusetts real weight in the new Congress while protecting the people's economic interests and liberties. The young Ames, it was argued, might have potential but could not measure up to the great Samuel Adams. Adams was depicted as a friend of the poor, and *"if he has a prejudice in his politicks, it leans to the rights and privileges of the common people."* According to their public endorsement, more than a hundred tradesmen and mechanics met in a caucus and pledged to support Adams. "An Elector" attempted to offer a general summary when he said "let us unite in the choice of Mr. ADAMS, whose *venerable name* will give importance to the country; whose *exertions* will add energy to government, and whose *prudence* will guarantee the rights & liberties not only of his constituents, but of the people of the whole confederation." Given the charge that Adams was not steadfastly behind the new Constitution, the use of the term *confederation* seemed to suggest that some Adams voters were, in fact, less than enthusiastic supporters of the new national government. A few pro-Adams scribes took the low road by saying that "every old Tory" and the haughty aristocrats, supposedly often one in the same, opposed their candidate.[34]

Fisher Ames's proponents, while typically conceding that Adams played a noble and courageous role in winning independence, time and again charged that Adams's support for the new central government was suspect. "Constitutionalist" did that skillfully by dutifully praising Adams "for his firmness and intrepidity, in the hour of danger" and for undeniably being "a distinguished patriot of 75." But Constitutionalist emphasized that in December 1788, the issue that mattered was where Adams stood on "the New

Constitution." This commentator asserted that Adams's "advocates" could not give a satisfactory answer to the essential question, "is he *now* a firm, dedicated Federalist?"—which in 1788 meant an enthusiastic supporter of the new national government. On a related theme, some pro-Ames authors actually had the audacity to float the suggestion that Adams did not know much about trade and commerce, topics of vital importance to commercial centers such as Boston. Special appeals were made to convince tradesmen and mechanics, groups traditionally seen as Adams supporters, that this time they should abandon him for their own economic good. Confronting the issue of Ames's youth, some who recommended him emphasized that their brilliant candidate was no younger than Adams when he first served in the legislature. The day before the election, "Mentor" tried to turn the tables on the age issue by proclaiming that age had "impaired" Adams's judgment. Another Ames supporter employed dirty tricks. On the very day of the election, "Marcus" rushed into print the scurrilous claim that Adams "has written several letters to the southward, for no other purpose, than to vilify the character of the great and immortal WASHINGTON, and thereby hinder his election as our Chief and Father."[35]

The election results proved shocking. Ames did more than win; he beat Adams 445 to 439 in Boston.[36] In the immediate postelection days, Adams backers offered a range of excuses. It was claimed that some of Adams's friends thought he would not accept the post if elected; some of his friends supposedly did not vote for him because they wanted to keep his talents employed in Boston; the voter turnout was so disgracefully low in Boston that "thy neighbours will consider thee as verging to the low scale of an insignificant Fishing Town." "Bostoniensis," who said he had just recently returned to Boston after years abroad, howled at length about the voters' ingratitude and poor judgment in spurning the "*American* Cato." He lashed out at Ames as an inexperienced unknown who "*was Son to the Almanack-maker.*" Cleverly adopting Adams's signature, "Candidus" offered a skillfully measured pro-Ames response to that ill-tempered diatribe. He praised Adams's "honour" and "candour" even as he offered a lengthy, vigorous defense of Ames and his impressive abilities.

Adams could not stand idly by as supporters spewed venomous insults merely because he had lost a fair election. In a statement that appeared the same day Candidus's essay was published, Samuel made sure the people understood his concern for fair play in republican elections. Adams denounced Bostoniensis's aspersions by having the editors of the *Massachusetts Centinel*, the newspaper most associated with opposing him, inset the following announcement: "We are authorized to say that Mr. S. ADAMS, alluding to a late paper, wishes never again to see his own merit, if he is thought to have any, held up to the prejudice of any virtuous man. If A.B. has merit, why the inquiry, what his father was? especially if he also bore the character of an honest man."[37]

While Ames's election might at first glance seem baffling, the results made sense. Bostonians, like the people in America's other major cities, overwhelmingly supported the Constitution. Urbanites of all classes wanted a powerful central government that could further their economic interests. Since Adams seemed more concerned about shackling the power of the new government than exploiting it, Ames's views on the Constitution more closely matched those of his new constituents. Indeed, given how strongly most American urbanites backed the new Constitution and the leaders who had championed its adoption, Adams actually did rather well in Boston.[38] Also, the low turnout—caused in part by miserable snowy weather and also possibly by overconfidence among Adams's backers—probably made a real difference. Less than nine hundred Bostonians cast ballots in the December 18 special election. The spring elections of 1788 had brought out about 1,500 Boston voters. And just five months after the special election, more than 1,800 people voted in Boston. In that hotly contested election, Hancock and Adams ran as a team for governor and lieutenant governor, and each amassed more than 1,200 votes, a two-to-one victory margin in Boston. Adams took office as lieutenant governor in May 1789 and was annually reelected for the next four years. Perhaps in part as a consequence of that, Harvard awarded him an honorary LLD in 1792.[39]

Even though he lost the special election for the United States House of Representatives, Adams continued to pursue a twofold objective in national politics. He wanted to make the United States Constitution a document worth defending because it protected the people's rights. For Adams that required amending it, ideally by limiting the national government to the powers expressly delegated to it. At the same time, he believed in the rule of law. He had, after all, voted to ratify the Constitution. So Adams's dual goal included protecting the Constitution even as he sought to modify it.

In 1789, as Congress considered possible amendments, Adams employed the well-established tactic of using private letters to achieve political ends. He wrote to Richard Henry Lee and Elbridge Gerry, who were both serving in the United States Congress, and laid out the case for supporting alterations. Knowing some Federalists used the argument that the Constitution might be cluttered up with multitudes of special-interest amendments, Adams stressed that no amendments should be added to suit "partial or local considerations." What he sought, Adams indicated, were amendments that applied to every American. He stressed that, as much as possible, state sovereignty must be retained because it was the safeguard of the citizens' private and personal rights. He called, above all, for eliminating the "ambiguous Expressions" in the Constitution that might, in time, be used to subvert liberty. As he did at the Massachusetts ratifying convention, Samuel underscored the importance of the word *expressly*. Having spoken of Massachusetts as a sovereign and independent state, he added a pointed clarification. "I say *sovereign & independent*, because I think the State retains all the Rights of Sovereignty which it has not expressly parted with to the Congress of the United States—a federal Power instituted *solely* for the Support of the federal Union."[40]

The campaign to amend the Constitution ultimately produced the Bill of Rights, which was added to the Constitution in December 1791. Adams could have gloated, and his political supporters certainly did, that the lengthy amendment he proposed at the Massachusetts ratifying convention contained most of the guarantees found in the Bill of Rights. However, for Adams the crucial Tenth Amendment was defective. Rather than limiting the central government to those powers *expressly* delegated to it, the amendment merely said that the powers not delegated to the national government were reserved to the states or the people. The failure to include that one word—*expressly*—created the constitutional ambiguity Adams loathed and the opportunity to enlarge national powers he feared. To get it ratified leading Federalists, including Alexander Hamilton, claimed the Constitution created "a limited" government with circumscribed powers. However, by 1791, with Hamilton leading the way, nationalists changed their minds and conveniently determined that the Constitution contained implied powers. George Washington accepted that interpretation.[41]

As the battle over implied powers unfolded, Samuel Adams seemingly confronted a dilemma about accepting or attacking the Constitution that fervent nationalists were twisting into a document more to their liking. He had, however, voted for the Constitution, and it had been approved by the people's representatives in ratifying conventions. In addition, as promised by its Massachusetts proponents, the document had been amended to include a Bill of Rights. Adams considered the amendments deficient, but they had been added. Given the fact that the Constitution rested on the consent of the governed, given his firm commitment to the rule of law when the people possessed a constitution that gave them the means to redress perceived grievances, Adams actually did not face a dilemma. He would support the Union's new government while continuing to keep careful watch lest it turn into a liberty-destroying serpent.

11

"THE CONSISTENT REPUBLICAN" IN THE TURBULENT 1790s

Once the Bill of Rights was added, no sane politician would dare suggest the Constitution should be overthrown. And, despite the protestations of some political opponents, Samuel Adams did not want to destroy the Constitution he voted to accept and that had been sanctioned by the vote of the people. Still, the question of adding yet more amendments remained very much alive when Adams became acting governor of Massachusetts in October 1793 and then won election in his own right. Indeed, as chief executive of Massachusetts Adams was as determined to keep careful watch lest the Union's new constitution be turned into a liberty-destroying serpent, as he was determined to support that constitution. And as governor of Massachusetts he continued to champion ideas of government and ways of life he believed would promote liberty and equality and benefit posterity. He remained, as admirers often remarked, the "Consistent Republican."[1]

Samuel Adams's political importance changed dramatically when Governor John Hancock died in office on October 8, 1793. Lieutenant Governor Adams was suddenly thrust into the position of acting governor at the very time inflammatory political issues roiled the new nation. By the time he took over the governorship, differences over national economic policy and how to interpret the powers of the central government had given rise to two emerging political parties. The Federalists championed economic policies that aided commercial forces and those who already had economic power. They were the political thinkers most likely to find implied powers in the Constitution and to favor transferring as much political control as possible to the central government. Federalists also typically believed the nation benefited from close ties with Britain. Their opponents came to be called Republicans. They advocated economic policies that benefited average people. Republicans opposed the possible consolidation of power at the national level; they did not want the aristocratic few to control the nation. Republicans maintained that it was not only wrong but inherently dangerous to assert that the Constitution had implied powers. In Massachusetts, members of the party called themselves "Republican Federalists" or simply "Republican" and emphasized that they espoused "the cause of Democratic Republicanism." Once he assumed the governorship, Samuel Adams was seen as the state's leading Republican and as such functioned as a lightning rod for local Federalist party anger.[2]

When he became the acting governor of Massachusetts in early October 1793, Adams inherited a thorny situation linked to issues of special interest to him. The first issue involved the extent to which the states retained sovereignty under the new Constitution. The second pertained to loyalists and whether they could regain property confiscated during the War for Independence. The troubles began when Alexander Chisholm, a resident of South Carolina, sued the state of Georgia in the United States Supreme Court. Chisholm aimed to gain control of property Georgia had confiscated from a loyalist. Asserting that the Supreme Court did not have jurisdiction over the sovereign state of Georgia, its government refused the Supreme Court's summons to a trial. In February 1793 the court rejected that argument in its *Chisholm v. Georgia* decision, which held that the United States Constitution did allow a citizen of one state to sue the government of another in a federal court.

Massachusetts was dragged into the fray when William Vassall, a noted and wealthy loyalist banished under the state's antiloyalist law of 1779, emulated Chisholm. Vassall sued the state of Massachusetts in federal court; he wanted his confiscated property returned. It was the assault on state sovereignty that a dangerously ill John Hancock alluded to when he wrote to "My Friend" Samuel Adams on August 31, 1793. Saying "I am alarmed," Hancock proclaimed that "it is full time for serious considerations and resolute exertions" to challenge those "attempting to establish a system foreign to your ideas & mine." Using language he knew Samuel would applaud, Hancock heralded his own determination by pledging, "I feel for my Country & will not give up the liberties of the people to the last drop of my blood." Samuel responded by saying that Hancock's letter "cheer'd the Spirit and caused the blood to thrill thr'o the veins of an Old Man."

Governor Hancock, warmly supported by Adams, did take a resolute stand on the issue of state sovereignty. He called the General Court into special session on September 18, 1793. Informing the legislators of the suit against the state, Governor Hancock said he had refused, and would refuse, to appear in any court until the issue of jurisdiction was settled. While Hancock avoided offering the legislators his opinion on the issue of jurisdiction, he clearly invited them to support his position and to assert state sovereignty on the question. The legislators responded by instantly voting their approval of Hancock's refusal to appear in court to answer Vassall's suit. Then on September 27 they directed Massachusetts's United States senators and representatives to push for an amendment to the Constitution that would "remove any clause or article of the said Constitution which can be construed to imply or justify a decision that a State is compelled to answer any suit by an individual or individuals in any Court of the United States." The General Court asked the governor to communicate with the executives of the other states so they could pass the Massachusetts resolutions on to their legislators for possible action.

Because Hancock died less than two weeks later on October 8 without having taken further action, it fell to Adams to craft a circular letter to accompany the General Court's resolutions. He did so as expeditiously as possible. On October 9, 1793, Adams sent his circular letter, along with copies of Hancock's speech and the proceedings of the General Court, to the other states. Samuel held that "the claim of a Judiciary's authority over a State possessed of *sovereignty*" was too important to be accepted "without the most serious deliberation." He praised the General Court for having "treated the subject with an attention commensurate to the importance of the power demanded." Reiterating the legislators' words, Adams declared that the judicial power being demanded was unnecessary and "dangerous to the peace, safety and independence of the several States." Indeed, it was "repugnant to the first principles of a federal government." Sensitive as he was to precedent, Adams added his own endorsement of the General Court's actions by saying that "the support of the federal government is an object of high importance in the mind of every true friend of the Union; but it is easily discerned, that the power claimed, if once established, will extirpate the federal principle, and procure a consolidation of all the governments." Lest there be any question where he stood, Adams noted that, while it was his duty to forward the General Court's resolves, he was doing so "with great chearfulness, because my opinion fully accords with the determination of the Legislature who requested it." He urged the executives of the other states and their legislatures to join Massachusetts in working for a constitutional amendment that would forever negate the Supreme Court's *Chisholm* decision.

The position staked out by Massachusetts and Adams was both bipartisan and popular. Many Federalists in other states as well as in Massachusetts thought the Supreme Court had gone too far in its *Chisholm* decision. As a result, Congress acted quickly; on March 4, 1794, it recommended that the Constitution be amended. As Massachusetts requested, the proposed amendment declared that "The Judicial power of the United States shall not be construed to extend to any suit in law or equity, commercial or prosecuted against one of the United States by Citizens of another State, or by Citizens or Subjects of any Foreign State." The amendment proved so popular that ten states ratified it by the end of 1794, and by February 1795 the necessary three-fourths of the states had approved it. But the amendment was not officially certified as part of the Constitution until 1798. When it was certified, the Supreme Court decreed that the Eleventh Amendment applied to past as well as future cases.[3]

Even as the Eleventh Amendment was wending its way toward being added to the Constitution, Samuel Adams was increasingly drawn into the political wrangles spawned by the French Revolution. Americans of all political persuasions celebrated when the French Revolution began in 1789 and especially when the French National Assembly issued the famous Declaration of the Rights of Man and Citizen in August. The extension of religious liberty to French Protestants in late 1789 and then the stripping away of the Catholic Church's privileged position in 1790 were popular measures, especially among New Englanders. Most Americans expressed pleasure when the French king, Louis XVI, was made a constitutional monarch and France became the Republic of France in September 1791. Well into the fall of 1792 even the *Columbian Centinel*, the Boston voice of the emerging Federalist party, carried items that praised the French Revolution. The wide-ranging support for the French Revolution and the Republic of France was evident in the numerous celebrations held throughout the nation. In Boston, Lieutenant Governor Adams figured prominently in such fests. The most famous public celebration of the French Revolution held in Boston occurred on January 24, 1793, when, amid other festivities, Adams presided over a gala banquet in Faneuil Hall.[4]

The close-to-universal support for the French Revolution crumbled when Americans learned that the revolutionaries had executed Louis XVI in January 1793 and then declared war on Great Britain, Holland, and Spain in February. Reflecting their pro-British predilections, Federalists denounced the French revolutionaries' actions. Republicans continued to voice support for the sister republic. And, starting in the spring of 1793, so-called Democratic Republican societies, dedicated to backing the French

Revolution and prompting the ideals espoused in the 1789 Declaration of the Rights of Man and Citizen, began springing up in America. The largest and most influential, the Democratic Society of Pennsylvania, was formed in the spring of 1793; its Boston counterpart, the Massachusetts Constitutional Society, began functioning in late 1793 and issued a constitution and declaration of purpose on January 13, 1794. These societies modeled themselves on the famous and increasingly radical Jacobin clubs of revolutionary France. Federalist disdain for the French Revolution and those they considered its American champions deepened almost immeasurablty once word arrived that, starting in mid-1793 and continuing into the summer of 1794, radical French revolutionaries oversaw the execution of thousands deemed to be enemies of the state. Since Jacobins were seen as the instigators of this terror, the term *Jacobin* took on an ominous meaning. For Federalists, *Jacobin* became an all-purpose scare term depicting horrible and often deadly radicalism.[5]

When France went to war with Great Britain, Holland, and Spain in February of 1793, the French government thought it would benefit if the United States were technically neutral in the conflict. France therefore did not try to invoke the 1778 treaty of alliance between the two countries and thus bring the United States into the war as a belligerent. And the Washington administration, given America's vital interests, was determined to stay out of the European conflict. So President Washington issued a declaration of United States neutrality on April 22, 1793. While Americans typically favored neutrality, members of the nation's emerging political parties had decidedly different views of what was best for America now that Europe was aflame.

The volatility of the political and diplomatic situation intensified when a new French ambassador, Edmond C. Genêt, reached America in April 1793. Soon, in accord with French plans, but in defiance of America's official neutrality, Genêt had surrogates in several states outfit privateers to prey on enemy shipping. In Boston the French vice-consul, Antoine C. Duplaine, got the privateer *Roland* into service by late July. The diplomatic squabbles that emerged out of this flaunting of American neutrality unleashed a torrent of newspaper missives as Federalists strove to denounce Genêt and the French Revolution. For their part, most Republicans tried to distance themselves from Genêt while still defending the French Revolution. Understandably outraged by the French diplomats' actions, Washington and his cabinet agreed in early August of 1793 that Genêt had to be recalled. Then, in October, the president revoked Duplaine's diplomatic privileges for gross violations of American neutrality. His transgressions included allowing a federal marshal to be detained on board a French man-of-war in Boston harbor and having French military personnel take control of a prize ship that was in the process of being reclaimed through a legal proceeding. On December 5 President Washington told Congress about the dismissals of the French diplomats. In addition, he informed the legislators about British actions that also flaunted American neutrality.[6]

Since he did not became acting governor of Massachusetts until early October 1793, Adams avoided direct public involvement in the increasingly acrimonious relations with the French diplomats. Federalists, especially rabid ones, nevertheless believed Adams was a dangerous American Jacobin. Christopher Gore, who was determined to arrest French diplomats for violating American neutrality, believed that Governor Hancock was willing to support him in that effort. Gore claimed that he had learned that Lieutenant Governor Adams "was bitterly oppose'd to my interfering" and that Adams had convinced Hancock to do nothing to assist Gore. Leading Massachusetts Federalists, who were determined to thwart him, accepted such flimsy allegations as proof that Adams was indeed a pro-France Jacobin.[7]

Once he became acting governor, Adams was very quickly drawn into the political and diplomatic morass. Thomas Dannery, who replaced Duplaine as French vice-consul in Boston, appealed to Adams for assistance in November 1793. Citing the French-American treaty and a consular convention, Dannery asked the acting governor to use his "coercive" power to assist him in keeping a French privateer, the *Marseilaise*, from sailing out of Boston harbor. When Adams failed to respond positively, the vice-consul renewed his request. Adams replied on November 27, 1793. Using the style of address French Revolutionaries preferred, Adams directed the letter to "Citizen Dannery" and opened by saying, "it gives me greet pleasure that we can communicate with each other, and though differing in our sentiments, can yet retain that mutual Friendship, and our attachments to the interest of both Republics." Then softness gave way to legalistic hardball. "Whatever I do as commander in chief of this Commonwealth," Adams said, "I am to justify myself by the Treaty, or conventions, and I do not find any facts alleged, or evidence offered in your application on which I can be authorized to act coercively." He muted that rejection by inviting the vice-consul to point out to him if something in the Treaty had "escaped my attention." That invitation was, however, coupled with a demand that Dannery supply specific facts and demonstrate how the treaty or conventions applied to them. One did not have to be a skilled diplomat to understand that Adams would continue to politely, but firmly, decline to assist Dannery.[8]

The members of the general public, whatever their political leanings, were not privy to the exchange between Adams and vice-consul Dannery. Thus people could not use Adams's response to gauge how his support for the French Revolution might influence his actions as acting governor. But everyone who was interested could reasonably anticipate that Adams would discuss the French Revolution and its consequences when he presented his first formal address as acting governor to the General Court that convened on January 17, 1794. Adams offered the legislators an extended commentary on his own political philosophy as well as on the workings of America's republican governments. In doing so, he did, in his own time, speak directly to aspects of the French Revolution.

Adams opened his speech by expressing sorrow over the death of Governor Hancock and by observing that his fellow citizens had often given "strong testimonials of their approbation of his important services." Obviously reflecting on Hancock's recent support for state sovereignty rather than his less laudable behavior in the early 1780s, Adams remarked that the people "may certainly profit by the recollection of his virtuous and patriotic example." Then, exclaiming that he would look to God for "wisdom," Adams pledged to the legislators that "The [Massachusetts] Constitution must be my rule, and the true interest of my Constituents, whose Agent I am, my invariable object."

Having made that promise, Adams launched into an analysis of recent political history. He started by noting that, before independence was achieved, the people of the Commonwealth "possessed the entire sovereignty within and over their own territories." That changed when the various states formed "a Federal Constitution" that, Adams stressed, left "all powers not vested in Congress . . . in the respective States to be exercised according to their separate Constitutions." Painfully aware that the Tenth Amendment was, from his perspective, defective because it did not include the essential word *expressly*, Adams proclaimed that unremitting caution should be used to ensure that neither the federal government nor the state governments encroached on the other's constitutional rights. And Adams seemed to suggest the new Constitution was still a work in progress by asserting that "Honest men will not feel themselves disgusted, when mistakes are pointed out to them with decency, candor and friendship, nor will they, when convinced of truth, think their own dignity degraded by correcting their own errors." Given that he had recently added his own enthusiastic endorsement of the General Court's call for what became the Eleventh Amendment, Adams's listeners could hardly have disagreed even if they did not share his view of just how narrowly proscribed the powers of the central government should be.

Turning to the Massachusetts constitution, Adams began by stressing that it emphasized the ideals of liberty and equality. He proved that by quoting extensively from the first article in the constitution's Declaration of Rights, which proclaimed that "all men are born free and equal, and have certain natural, essential and unalienable rights." That quotation allowed Adams, as he had done so often over the decades, to trumpet the Lockean concept of government being a compact formed by the mutual consent of people seeking to protect their natural rights. Adams maintained that the Massachusetts constitution coincided well with the goal of protecting rights because it declared that "Government is instituted for the common good; not for the profit, honor or private interest of any one man, family, or class of men." And, of course, all inhabitants of the state who met the qualifications established in the constitution had the right to vote or be elected to public office.

At this point, Adams advanced a bold argument that linked fundamental political principles directly to America's republican governments. He did more than quote an ideal of the Declaration of Independence, which he rendered as "all men are created equal, and are endowed by their Creator with certain unalienable rights." He asserted that, since the Declaration of Independence had been ratified by all the states, "the doctrine of Liberty and Equality is an article in the political creed of the United States."

Adams followed that stunning formulation with what proved to be a segue into comment on the French Revolution. Adams began obliquely by praising the United States Constitution's prohibition on granting titles of nobility. He applauded that provision because such titles, if allowed, might in time introduce "the absurd and unnatural claims of heredity and exclusive rights." Making that point allowed him to move smoothly to the observation that "the Republic of *France* have also adopted the same principle, and laid it as the foundation of their Constitution." Alluding to the French having endured abuse from their king and nobility, Adams saluted the French people for having now "placed every man upon the footing of equal rights." And, surely anticipating that his listeners knew he was quoting the French Declaration of Rights of 1789 so admired by Americans, Samuel added that "'All men are born free, and equal in rights,' if I mistake not, is their language." Since that wording was strikingly similar to the Massachusetts Declaration of Rights that he had recently cited, unless they wanted to open themselves to the charge of being monarchists who advocated aristocratic government, it would have been hard for even the most rabid Federalist to publically denounce Adams's embracing of these ideals of the French Revolution. That was doubly true because, immediately after quoting the Declaration of Rights, Adams suggested that, however different the French and United States constitutions might be, both "agree altogether in the most essential principles upon which legitimate governments are founded." Making it logically impossible to tar him with the deadly internal violence gripping France, Adams then added, "I have said essential principles, because I conceive that without Liberty and Equality there cannot exit that tranquility of mind, which results from the assurance of every citizen, that his own personal safety and rights are secure."

While many Federalists, at least among themselves, continued to wail about Adams's supposed Jacobin radicalism, his skillfully modulated references to the French Revolution seemed positively tepid when compared to how the General Court responded to his speech. Agreeing with Adams's comments on the essential principle of all men being born free and equal, the legislators sprinted past acting governor Adams in praising the unfolding French Revolution. "Nor can we refrain," they gushed, "from expressing our affections for that nation who assisted us in time of our adversity, and with whom we are in alliance; and our sincere wishes that they may succeed in the defence of their country, and in the establishment of peace and good Government, founded on the principles of Liberty, and the Rights of Man." Based on his address and the General Court's response, by Federalist standards acting governor Adams was a temperate, moderate supporter of the noblest ideals of French republicanism and the Massachusetts legislators were a bunch of dangerous Jacobins.[9]

No matter how judiciously moderate Adams sounded or acted, committed Federalists did not trust him. They waited for him to reveal his true Jacobite self. Adams did venture into the political thicket of the French Revolution on February 19, when he issued the traditional spring proclamation for "a day of Public Fasting, Humiliation and Prayer." Declaring that the holding of such a day was "highly becoming all people, especially those who profess the Christian religion," Samuel called upon the people of Massachusetts to suspend all unnecessary labor and recreation on April 17. Adams specifically beseeched God to help the people experience a good harvest as well as other benefits and "to continue and confirm our civil and religious liberties." He expressed the hope that the federal government and all of the state governments would "under their respective Constitutions . . . be led to such decisions as will establish the liberty, peace, safety, and honor of our country." Adams evinced his deep religiosity be closing with "and above all, to cause the Religion of Jesus Christ, in its true spirit, to spread far and wide, till the whole earth shall be filled with His glory."

Adams directly addressed the French Revolution in his appeals. He beseeched the Lord "to inspire our friends and allies, the Republic of France, with a spirit of wisdom and true religion, that relying on the strength of His Almightily Arm, they may still go on prosperously till their arduous conflict for a government of their own, founded on the just and equal rights of man, shall be firmly crowned with success." Ardent members of the emerging Republican Party might have found that a rather lukewarm defense of the French Revolution, but for most Federalists it was too warm.[10]

Given the upcoming election for governor scheduled for Monday, April 7, Samuel Adams's January address and his February proclamation took on special importance. Politicos, both Federalists and Republicans, considered that election extraordinarily important. Massachusetts had a tradition of reelecting a governor so long as he was willing to serve; therefore, whoever became governor in 1794 might well hold the office for a lengthy period. The 1794 elections, like those before them, followed a well-established, if rather bewildering, etiquette. Candidates did not declare their interest in running for office. Rather, "friends" of the potential candidate supplied newspapers with the name of a person they wanted elected to a specific office. Indeed, while the fringe candidates in what one writer accurately styled "the Electionary Ball" of 1794 were soon effectively eliminated, eight men were nominated for governor and eight for lieutenant governor. Those put forward as candidates were not expected to campaign or even to confirm that they would serve if elected. As one political commentator put it, candidates would be "too modest" to announce that they would serve if elected. So, odd as it now seems, the voters sometimes could not be sure their preferred candidate would serve if he won. That is why supporters who put a name forward might add a comment such as "there is no doubt" the nominee would accept the post.[11]

As Federalists contemplated the 1794 contest for governor, they faced a daunting problem. Because Adams was the sitting lieutenant governor and everyone agreed he was a true hero of the American Revolution, it seemed likely that the state's voters would have a natural tendency to vote for him to become governor. The Federalists' pick for the office, William Cushing, understood this when he remarked in late February 1794 that there were "many weighty reasons" that made him reluctant to undertake the "arduous task" of being a candidate for governor. "There is," he observed, "our good Lieut. Governor, who stands in the direct line of promotion, and who has waded through a sea of political troubles and grown old in labors for the good of his country. Why not he!"[12] Given this situation, Massachusetts Federalists, led by the influential Boston contingent, devised a novel strategy to deny Adams the governor's chair. They pledged to vote for him to continue as lieutenant governor. This proposal, first floated in the principal Federalist organ the *Columbian Centinel* on March 8, was reiterated throughout the election season and even more just before the polling took place. As they reported it, more than five hundred Federalists met at Faneuil Hall on the afternoon of March 28 and voted unanimously to support Adams for lieutenant governor and William Cushing for governor. That meeting created a committee of twenty to prepare and distribute ballots for these men as well as those nominated for the Massachusetts senate.[13]

Federalists surely realized that their plan of neutralizing Adams by getting him reelected as lieutenant governor was a long shot. So they offered a range of reasons, including his advanced age, why Adams should not be governor. But the Federalist's central theme rested on the assertion that Adams and his Republican supporters were too friendly toward the French Revolution and likely to embrace the radicalism of the Jacobins. When a meeting of the state's Federalists advanced William Cushing's name as a suitable person for governor, the endorsement was signed "Union" and proclaimed that "the people of this Commonwealth cannot wish to elect as their Governor, the leader of any party. The exigencies of the times demand a man, whose qualities are calculated to unite all parties." That was a clear swipe at Adams who was seen as the leader of the Massachusetts Republicans. Although they did not list the offices Cushing had held, which included having been chief justice of Massachusetts, the Federalists lauded Cushing's experience as a judge. Obviously trying to appeal to those who were angered by Adams's harsh attitude toward Shays's rebels, the endorsement statement praised Cushing's "humane conduct during the late insurrection." While this opening salvo for Cushing did not attempt to tie Adams to French extremism, the editor of the *Centinel* printed the endorsement right above "Song, Sung at the Jacobin Club." Other efforts to draw comparisons between Cushing's opponents and radical Jacobins soon followed. Clearly alluding to the Massachusetts Constitutional Society, "Trimsharp" remarked that Cushing's "excellent character" would not recommend him to "certain men of a certain *Club*" who wanted a governor who would "*bend*" to their "schemes."[14]

Men who supported Adams played into the hands of those seeking to link him to the excesses of the French Revolution. On March 19 the *Centinel* carried an announcement issued by a number of leading Republicans who planned to hold a civil festival in honor of recent French military victories. The group noted it had obtained the selectmen's approval and had asked Acting Governor Adams to attend and to arrange for a military parade as part of the celebration. The very next day a writer in the *American Apollo* argued that it would be wrong for the commonwealth's chief magistrate to order such a military display. Doing so, he warned, could be "construed as disapproving the neutrality of the American States, in the present controversy of the European nations" declared by President Washington. Realizing they had unwittingly opened Adams to a potentially damaging charge, the planners of the celebration beat a hasty retreat. Less than a week later the pubic learned that the proposal for the celebration had been suspended.[15]

The major efforts to smear Adams, especially for supposedly being too friendly with French and pro-France radicals, occurred shortly before the balloting took place. On March 25 a *Salem Gazette* writer savaged Adams as "the Chief of the Jacobin Club" that supposedly "thunder out destruction to every thing federal and rational." On April 2 "Querist," having argued that Adams was too old and having reminded voters that he had often quarreled with Hancock, unleashed a barrage of allegations. Above all, he attacked Adams for supposedly working hand in glove with what Querist called the Constitutional Club. Querist even claimed that Adams had backed Genêt against President Washington. "An Independent Republican," whose piece appeared in the same issue of the *Centinel*, tried to document that pernicious accusation. He offered an extract of an Adams letter of October 22, 1793, that praised Genêt's "warm affection towards our country, as well as your own." An Independent Republican emphasized that the letter had been written "more than two months after the President had demanded the recall of Genet." The next day, the *Independent Chronicle*, the major Republican paper, carried a sharp rejoinder. The writer labored mightily to explain the letter away. He stressed that, if it was genuine, the letter had been written before there was any public declaration of Genêt's recall. Thus, when he wrote it, Adams's letter was nothing more than "a letter of *common civility*." Doing his best to counter any further use of this or similar correspondence, the author closed by arguing that the distortion of such an innocent letter at election time demonstrated the deep hatred some men harbored toward Adams.[16]

In the last issue of the *Centinel* to appear before the election, "Querist" again claimed that Adams was favorably inclined to Genêt, who by that time most Americans loathed. And "Civis" charged that Adams's "friends" had failed to answer any of the questions, especially the alleged support for

Genêt, that had been raised about Adams. "I therefore ask," Civis intoned, "whether any man in his sober senses can vote for Mr. A for Governor." This writer then patronizingly added that one hoped Adams would be retained as lieutenant governor because he would have few duties and yet receive a good salary. Thus "the remainder of Mr. A's life may be made serene and happy." Civis held that Adam's "friends ought not to expect more for him." Maintaining that he honored Adams's "early and patriotic exertions in the cause of our country," Civis added "but there is a duty which we owe ourselves." Reemphasizing his basic point, he claimed that "there are so *many* concurring circumstances which render Mr. A. a very improper person for Governor, that I am sure the good sense of the people will be against electing him."[17]

While they piled argument upon argument to convince voters that Samuel Adams should not be governor, the Federalists employed surprisingly little ink building up their own candidate's credentials. At first glance, that seems odd. William Cushing came from a venerable political family; he had served as the chief justice of the state's supreme court. Even more impressive, he was, in 1794, an associate justice of the United States Supreme Court. There was, however, good reason for Federalists to keep their praise for Judge Cushing as general as possible and to downplay his being on the Supreme Court. As Republicans reminded the voters over and over again, as a member of the Supreme Court Cushing voted with the majority in the *Chisholm v. Georgia* case; he had agreed that an individual could sue the state. The shorthand terms for this were "Suability of the States" or just "State Suability." Less than a week after Federalists first publically recommended Cushing for governor the *Chronicle* carried a blistering attack on his role in the *Chisholm* decision. "Consistency" alluded to and cleverly expanded the Federalists' claim that the voters would reject Adams because he was "the *leader of a party* in favor of Republicanism." He opined that "I will venture to conjecture that they will never give their suffrages in favor of the *leader of a party*, who have pledge themselves to overthrow the Sovereignty of the State Governments." Following the established pattern of trying to deploy particularly damaging evidence late in the election season, the recurring assault on Cushing's support for "Suability of the States" reached a crescendo on March 31 when the *Chronicle* carried an extract of the judge's opinion in the *Chisholm* case. Referring to the impact of the court's ruling, Justice Cushing had remarked that "'it may be insisted, that this will reduce States to mere corporations, and take away all sovereignty. As to corporations, all States whatever are corporations or bodies politic. The only question is—What are their powers.'"

Cushing's supporters desperately tried to defuse what they perhaps belatedly realized was a potentially explosive situation. By late March, referring to the fact that the proposed Eleventh Amendment had just been sent to the states, Federalist writers argued that the issue of state suability had become moot because Congress had decisively taken action to reverse the *Chisholm* decision. Even that limp defense—which had to concede that the *Chisholm* decision was almost universally detested—lacked punch. The Cushing forces also had to endure attacks based on the fact that the voters were scheduled to decide whether to alter the state constitution in 1795. Republican penmen gleefully raised the specter of a Governor Cushing clashing with the General Court and pushing ideas that would undermine the state sovereignty that many Americans, not just Republicans, prized. As Adams might have phrased it, Republican political writers had managed, with Cushing's help, to plant him firmly on the wrong side of a basic-rights issue.[18]

While the Republicans' main thrusts against Cushing focused on his position on state sovereignty, pro-Adams commentators also suggested that Cushing might not accept the governorship if elected. Naturally, pro-Cushing forces countered that Judge Cushing would, of course, accept the post of governor if elected. On April 5, just as the voting was about to occur, a *Centinel* essayist revealed the Federalists' sense of frustration over the issue. "An Elector" denounced unnamed *Chronicle* "scribblers" who supposedly kept complaining Cushing had never confirmed that he would serve. An Elector then asked whether it had even been ascertained that Adams would take the position. Having added that one could not expect either candidate to make a public declaration, he, predictably, assured his readers that "there is not the smallest doubt" that Cushing "would obey the call of his fellow citizens" if elected.[19]

While Federalist politicos tried to link Adams to the worst horrors of the French Revolution, Republican writers routinely claimed that many of Cushing's supporters were not only selfish but also dangerously subservient to Britain. That line of argument had a good chance of resonating because British assaults on American shipping were, even the *Centinel* reported, so numerous that "the papers from every quarter are filled with accounts of the depredations on the commerce of the United States by the British." Hyping both anti-British sentiment and Adams's unquestioned glorious role in the movement to independence, the editors of the *Chronicle* reminded their readers of the horror of the Boston Massacre. Another writer worked the same theme by offering an anecdote of Adams's memorable confrontation with Governor Hutchinson and Colonel

Dalrymple in the immediate aftermath of the massacre. Yet another, "An Elector," proclaimed that "old and young Tories" opposed Adams. One supporter validated his endorsement of Adams as "this Best of Men and of Patriots" by signing himself "An Independent Farmer, and one of the Minute Men of '75."[20]

Republican authors also strove to turn the issue of Adams's age to their advantage. In the first week of electioneering "A Voter" raised the usual arguments about Adams's magnificent role in achieving independence and his unflinching commitment to "republicanism and the rights of man." Since "he never forsook us," the people should back him "while he has ability to execute the office of chief magistrate." To prove that Adams did indeed still have all the strength and ability needed to be governor, A Voter reviewed the work of the most recent General Court. One could, he maintained, see Adams's strength of mind by considering the speech he gave at the opening of the legislative session. As this writer reported it, Adams delivered that speech entirely from memory without once looking at his prepared text. Moreover, in what was a busy legislative session, the acting governor performed his duties with dispatch. Three weeks later another pro-Adams writer, having proclaimed that "the only objection of any weight against Mr. Adams is his age," also recounted how Adams had performed during the latest session of the General Court. Commenting that the first signs of age-related mental failure appear in the memory, the author quickly absolved Adams of any diminution on that score. While he did not claim quite as much for Adams's memory as A Voter had, this writer asserted that Adams delivered his "lengthy and truly patriotic address entirely from memory, not having occasion to recur to his manuscript scarcely in one paragraph." This proved that Adams did not have "the least traces of old age" and that he still exhibited prodigious "intellectual power." Like A Voter, this author stressed that Adams's work with the legislature was done quickly and well. That good and expeditious work included returning a lengthy bill to the General Court accompanied by Adams's objections. And what happened? Both branches of the legislature unanimously agreed to his amendments.[21]

Reports published in the pro-Cushing *Centinel* just two days before the election rhapsodized about its candidate's alleged momentum. A Hingham author asserted that more than 90 percent of that town's voters would support Cushing for governor and Adams for lieutenant governor. The *Centinel* editor, Benjamin Russell, told readers that "we are assured, by a gentlemen of respectability, who left the county of *Worcester* on Thursday last, that the citizens in favor of Mr. Cushing, as Governour, increase in numbers daily. They say he is the real man of the people." For their part, when they printed their election-day issue, the editors of the *Chronicle* openly urged Massachusetts voters to "show both your Patriotism and Gratitude" by casting a ballot for Adams for governor.[22]

In a letter written on April 7 a Boston "Gentleman" recapped the election and described that day's voting at Faneuil Hall. He reported that both the friends of Adams and of Cushing "appeared very sanguine in their success which consequently excited the exertions of both parties." The friends of each candidate "confronted those of the other, and toe to toe, they each of them delivered their several tickets." Espousing his own Republican position and support for Adams, the gentleman lamented the fact that in the run-up to election day "every exertion was made against this patriot" and "no means was left untried to prejudice the citizens against him." The writer assured his friend that when the balloting took place, not a single Tory voted for Adams while "the true, genuine Old Whigs of '75 felt animated with the warm glow of affection for the old patriot." The Boston gentleman certainly had reason to say, as he did, that it would now be more difficult to assert that Boston was always hostile to Republicans. In Boston Adams outpaced Cushing 1,400 to 894, and he carried the state 14,465 to 7,159.[23]

Having been elected in his own right, Adams once again elucidated his philosophical principles when he addressed the new General Court on May 31, 1794. Singing the praises of annual free elections, through which the citizens expressed their own sovereignty, he gushed that in taking part in "that great transaction" the voters "must surely have felt their own dignity." Painfully aware of the growing political rancor evident in the recent election, Adams appealed to a sense of moderation and commitment to the rule of law. Using arguments he had long advanced, he offered the soothing comment that, whatever a voter's sentiments might have been about the candidates, "each elector having given his suffrage according to the dictates of his own conscience must enjoy the consoling reflection of having honestly done his duty."

Knowing that President Washington's December address to Congress had decried British assaults on American neutrality and that British depredations had increased in the intervening months, Adams swiped at the nation from whom Americans had won their own independence just over a decade before. In the process, he offered a more thoroughgoing endorsement of the French Revolution. Calling the European conflict "a war of Kings and Nobles against the equal Rights of Man," Adams pointedly stressed that Great Britain was fighting on the side of monarchists who hated the very idea of people forming their own republican governments. And, while the United States had followed a policy of strict neutrality, Britain had unleashed her naval forces to commit "depredations on our lawful and unprotected commerce." Adams reported that the situation was so bad that the Federal Government, while still hoping for peace, was making the necessary preparations to wage war against Britain. He opined that, if war were to come, the strength of the Union would be able "to reduce an unreasonable enemy to terms of Justice." Adams then turned to what he considered the Union's goals for peacetime. Summarizing his core political and social ideals succinctly, Adams declared that those goals were "to secure the blessings of equal liberty to the present and future generations."[24]

Given how Britain was assaulting the rights of America and its shipping as it warred with France, Adams gave an accurate image of Britain. The United States was in fact dangerously close to going to war with Great Britain in the spring of 1794. Nevertheless, for pro-British Federalists, Governor Adams's words branded him as a dangerous opponent of the national government. But his actions said otherwise. In that spring of 1794 the Washington administration provided Governor Adams with a copy of an act of Congress that called for building fortifications in Boston harbor. Having forwarded the law to the General Court, Adams addressed the issue on June 4. He told the legislators that the ancient fort on Castle Island was well located but, by Massachusetts law, had been used as a prison since 1785. So he could not, even if he wanted to do so, transfer control of the fort to the United States. Governor Adams offered a plan that would support the principle of state sovereignty while also complying with the federal law. He urged the legislators to transfer the convicts from Castle Island and fund the repair of the now-dilapidated fort. This course of action would meet defensive needs while keeping the fort, as it had been, under the control of Massachusetts. Doing that, he suggested, would serve "the interest of the Commonwealth, in particular, and the United States in general."[25]

Governor Adams dealt those who considered him an enemy of the national government yet another blow in early November 1794. He did that, perhaps with an inner smile, by complying with another request from the central government. In an October 10 letter, Secretary of State Edmund Randolph had asked Governor Adams to take measures to ensure that the seventeenth article of the Treaty of Amity and Commerce with France be strictly enforced. That article stipulated that, except in the case of unexpected life-threatening emergencies, French vessels captured in wartime could not be brought into an American port. Observing that he was acting "in compliance with the request of the Government of the United States,"

Adams directed all Massachusetts officials diligently to enforce the treaty article. Invoking "the faith of Nations, and the solemnity of National Treaties," the governor said "I have reason to expect that the good people of the Commonwealth will cheerfully afford their aid in support of the Laws of the land."[26]

Passionate Massachusetts Federalists, seemingly stymied by the fact that Governor Adams was complying with the national government's requests and firmly embracing the necessity of supporting the rule of law, struggled to find a way to attack the man they considered the leader of the state's Republicans. The Reverend David Osgood, who has accurately been described as being "preeminently a political preacher," thought he saw an opening when Governor Adams, following tradition, called for an autumn fast day in 1794. In October Adams issued a proclamation declaring November 20 a day of public thanksgiving for "rendering to the Father of all Mercies the just tribute of Gratitude and Praise" for "his manifold Mercies." Adams specifically asked the people to thank God because Massachusetts had escaped dangerous illnesses that afflicted other parts of the nation, had enjoying a good harvest, and because "our Fishery" had prospered. God should also be thanked because "He hath continued to us the inestimable blessing of his Gospel, and our Religious, as well as Civil Rights and Liberties." When he took his parishioners through Adams's proclamation point by point, Osgood agreed with Adams's observations. But Osgood then said he was struck by the fact that Adams's proclamation did not even mention the federal government. He used that as a pretext for suggesting that Adams shared the sentiments of the Democratic Republican societies that, according to Osgood, wanted to destroy the nation's government.[27]

The Reverend Osgood's message, which was aimed more at Democratic Republican societies in general than at Governor Adams, resonated in Federalist circles. But, given Adams's clear, unequivocal response to what was called the Whiskey Rebellion, it would have been hard, logically impossible, to sell the idea that he wanted to destroy the central government. Indeed, Adams's public response to the rebellion demonstrated his unflinching commitment to defending republican constitutions. The Whiskey Rebellion occurred in the summer of 1794 when western Pennsylvanians, angered by what they justifiably considered an outrageously unfair national excise tax, terrorized tax collectors, stopped mail deliveries, and disrupted court proceedings. Leaders of the emerging Federalist Party shouted that the anarchy in Pennsylvania must be stopped. President Washington understandably concurred and in August decreed that a force of 12,900 be dispatched to crush the uprising. By the time the huge army arrived, the rebellion had evaporated. These developments gave those who opposed the expansion of national powers an opportunity to castigate the national government and the Federalist Party. Thomas Jefferson, the acknowledged head of the Republican Party, sarcastically dismissed the Whiskey Rebellion with the airy observation that "an insurrection was announced, and proclaimed and armed against, but could never be found."

Although he was a supporter of Jefferson and was considered the leader of the Massachusetts Republicans, Adams responded differently. In the official address he delivered to the General Court in January 1795 Governor Adams voiced the same ideals he had articulated when confronting Shays's Rebellion. He observed that the whiskey "insurrection" against the excise tax challenged "an act of the Federal Government." That was unacceptable because, however much people might detest specific legislation, it "is constitutionally an act of the people, and our Constitutions provide a safe and easy method to redress any real grievances." Adams elaborated by forcefully stating what, for him, was the fundamental principle of democratic republicanism: "No people can be more free [than] under a Constitution established by their own voluntary compact, and exercised by men appointed by their own frequent suffrages." Given that, Adams bluntly asked, "what excuse then can there be for forcible opposition to the laws?" If real grievances existed, the people's freely elected representatives would find "a constitutional remedy." These pronouncements made it clear why Governor Adams praised the vigorous actions President Washington took to quash the insurrection and why Adams also asserted that those measures were "supported by the virtue of citizens of every description."[28]

While Federalists hoped that Osgood's political sermon would hurt Republican legislative candidates in 1795 elections, they accepted that fact that it would be futile to try to unseat Governor Adams or his lieutenant governor, Moses Gill. The *Centinel*, which had bristled with assaults on Adams in 1794, was devoid of such material in the spring of 1795. Even more revealing, readers of the *Centinel* did not encounter a campaign for any Federalist gubernatorial candidate. On April 3 "A Friend to the Two Patriots" said that those who had opposed Adams and Gill in 1794 had let it be known that they would make no effort to unseat either man. Taking no chances, A Friend urged supporters of the two "patriots" to be diligent and to vote. That plea hardly seemed necessary given the Federalist non-campaign for governor; every indicator pointed toward Adams winning reelection handily. He did. In the April 1795 election Bostonians cast 2,043 votes for governor. Samuel Adams got 2,008 of them; the next closest vote getter received 10.[29]

H. B. Hall engraving after John Johnston's 1795 painting of Governor Samuel Adams. Courtesy of the Frick Art Reference Library.

As he tended to do, the newly reelected governor used his next address to the General Court to ask the legislators and the people of Massachusetts to reflect on the nature of republican government and on the rights and duties it entailed. Reiterating what was for him a core belief, Adams stressed that "the sovereignty of a nation, always of right, resides in the body of the People." The legislators, together with the magistrates who carried laws into effect, were merely the people's "public agents." They had a duty to cooperate for the benefit of their constituents. Massachusetts officials should therefore focus on "the great objects of securing the equal rights of the citizens, and rendering those constitutions which they have voluntarily established, respectable and efficacious." Such reflections were especially appropriate because, as he reminded the legislators, the citizens of the Commonwealth had recently had to grapple with the question of possibly revising the state constitution. Expressing some of his often-voiced themes, Adams remarked that "the conduct of the citizens on this occasion, has given full proof, that an enlightened, free and virtuous people, can as a body, be the keepers of their own Liberties, and the guardians of their own rights." Having called for a "due observance of the Laws . . . constitutionally made" by either the Massachusetts or the Federal government, Adams closed with a statement that in many ways summed up his core ideals. "Let us," he urged, "transmit our Liberties, our Equal Rights, our Laws and our free Republican Constitutions . . . to those who are coming upon the stage of action, and hope in God, that they will be handed down, in purity and energy, to the latest posterity."[30]

Adams's commitment to supporting an established republican constitution amendable by the people caused him, over time, to embrace the United States Constitution more warmly. An acknowledged master politician, Adams had always been sensitive to the tone as well as the precise meaning of words. In the early 1790s he was fastidious about describing the central government as the "Federal Government." Doing so underscored his commitment to preserving the ideal of state sovereignty as much as possible. But in his fall 1795 thanksgiving proclamation Governor Adams asked the people to thank God "that he hath in his Good Providence united the several States under a National Compact formed by themselves, whereby they may defend themselves against external Enemies, and maintain Peace and Harmony with each other."[31]

By the time he addressed the General Court in January 1796, Adams lavished real praise on the national constitution. He observed that the people had voluntarily formed both the United States and Massachusetts Constitutions. And these constitutions were, he stressed, founded upon the same principles, including "the great fundamental political truth that all power is derived from the people." Later that same year, again speaking to the legislators, Adams referred to the United States Constitution's preamble goal of establishing a more perfect Union and invoked what for him was a sacred concern, the duty to posterity. He asserted that the American people had a responsibility to preserve the Union "and transmit it unbroken to posterity." He clasped the Constitution even more firmly by declaring it was in the people's "lasting interest" as well as "their public safety and welfare" to preserve the more perfect Union. That fall in the traditional thanksgiving proclamation Adams again celebrated the fact that both the state and national constitutions possessed the vital ingredients of democratic republicanism. Both constitutions were "formed by ourselves, and administered by Men of our own *free Election*."[32]

Adams's increasing admiration of the United States Constitution did not mean he had reconciled himself to an all-powerful central government. For Governor Adams the idea of adding liberty-preserving amendments, like the Eleventh Amendment, remained very much alive. So, even as he embraced the United States Constitution more firmly, Adams invited the people to consider altering it. In the 1796 address in which he lauded the national constitution he also opined that America's revolutionary governments must be considered "*experiments*" and "wisdom" dictated that the people should often think about "first principles." If the citizens discovered their rights were being undermined by either the state or the national constitution, the people should alter the offending document. Looking again to the needs of posterity, he prophetically warned that if either the federal or state governments "infringed" on the other's "Constitutional rights" for any period of time, America might eventually experience "such convulsions as may shake the political ground upon which we now happily stand." This American revolutionary never lost his zeal for trying to ensure that the national constitution would function to secure the blessings of equal liberty to the present and future generations, not become a potential liberty-killing serpent.[33]

Although he continued to raise the possibility of amending the national constitution, Adams did not think the Massachusetts Constitution, which kept earning not only his but general approbation, was in any way materially defective. As a state executive Adams focused on what he considered crucial issues for promoting liberty and equality and securing them for posterity. He demonstrated his concern about protecting basic rights—and his ability to acknowledge personal error—by how he dealt with the question of selecting replacement presidential electors. In November 1796 the General Court passed a resolution allowing the state's presidential electors to replace any of their number who might die or resign. Adams signed the resolution the day he received it but soon reconsidered. As best he could, he erased his name from the resolution. The next day he explained his actions. Saying he had approved the resolution prematurely, he maintained that permitting electors to fill vacancies in their own ranks "appears to be dangerous to the Liberties of the People, and ought not to form a precedent in a free government." He urged the legislators to find a way to deal with the problem that was more consistent with the spirit of Massachusetts's republican government. On the following day, Adams returned to the issue by emphasizing that he sought to avoid establishing a dangerous precedent. He added that if the legislators thought differently he would, having honestly admitted his error in signing the resolve, be content with their decision. Adams was clearly attempting to force the members of the General Court to rescind their resolution by placing them on the wrong side of a basic-rights issue. He failed to move them.[34]

As governor Adams also tried to convince the legislators to follow the principle of equality when it came to serving in the militia. Over the years Massachusetts legislators had crafted laws exempting large numbers of men from serving in the state militia. The exemptions, as such exceptions normally do, favored the wealthier and more prominent. In January 1797 Governor Adams tried to call the members of the General Court back to first principles. He urged them to eliminate those parts of the militia statutes that created what he labeled invidious exemptions. Adams maintained that the obligation of militia service "should equally apply" to all able-bodied citizens. The legislators did not share his ardor for the equality that would accompany universal militia service. They did not recast the militia laws.[35]

In addition to continuing his lifelong goal of protecting the people's essential rights, as governor, Adams continued his quest to promote virtue. As he grew older and contemplated facing God's final judgment, Governor Adams alluded ever-more frequently to the importance of religion and the possible intervention of God in public affairs. He often pointed out that the state constitution said public officials should promote piety, religion, and morality because these virtues were essential to maintaining free republican government.[36] But, as he had since the days before independence was declared, Adams continued to single out education as the linchpin to attaining a virtuous republican society.

The four addresses Adams gave as governor when opening the General Court sessions in January were, in essence, state of the state messages. In these address Adams stressed education's vital role and reiterated ideas and even language he had employed in the early 1780s when he headed Boston's education committee. Throughout his years as governor Adams kept accentuating the importance of a public education that emphasized piety, religion, and morality and that would lead children "to the knowledge and love of those true Republican principles upon which our civil institutions are founded." The importance Adams placed on education was demonstrated in his crucial first address as acting governor. That presentation focused on the nature of government, and the only other subject he discussed was, as he put it, the great and important issue of the education of our children and youth. He suggested that a virtuous education would emphasize piety, benevolence, and love of country as it enlarged the youth's mental powers. While he did not advocate a specific curriculum, he did maintain that children should receive instruction in government. Adams touted the tangible benefits such an education would produce. It would prevent crimes. It would prompt youths to search for truth in everything they reflected on. Educated people would not only be better able both to detect errors in government policy and the structure of government but also to point out how to correct them. Implying that his audience already shared his enthusiasm, Adams noted he need not press the subject further because the legislators would naturally be inclined to promote education and because the Massachusetts constitution directed them to do so.

Given his repeated appeals about implementing the constitution's call for cherishing education, the returning members of the General Court probably smiled knowingly when, in his last state of the state address in January 1797, Adams revisited the topic. He remarked that he had frequently reminded the legislators of the great importance of encouraging education from town schools through the university. And he proceeded to do it yet again. Education should do more than promote "the pursuit of useful science." It should also serve a moral purpose by instilling in children "a strong sense of the duties they owe to their God, their instructors, and each other."[37]

Samuel Adams wanted to ensure that the public-education system would be based on the essential principles of liberty and equality. His concern for equality even caused him to question the value of academies, privately run institutions that typically prepared youths for university studies. The 1790s marked a great period of academy founding in Massachusetts, and Adams's constant reminders to the General Court about its constitutional duty to promote education probably helped fuel that development. The General Court typically provided a land grant to those who wanted to establish an academy. Adams might have been expected to applaud the rise of academies; instead, he viewed them skeptically. He told the General Court that the dramatic expansion of academies could injure the town grammar schools, which provided education to rich and poor on an equal basis. The problem with the academies, said Adams, was that in general only the wealthier could attend. If the wealthy focused their attention and influence on developing such schools, support for the town schools might diminish. If that happened, useful learning and a sense of social cohesion "may cease to be so equally and universally disseminated." As a group, Massachusetts's legislators did not share Adams's assessment. They responded to his pleas by preparing a lengthy report on academies. It did not, however, emphasize the need for a fully integrated and egalitarian system of public education at the secondary level; rather, the legislators' main concern was ensuring that academies would be established throughout the state and receive support in the form of land grants. Despite his efforts, it would take decades for Massachusetts to create the system of free, universal education Adams deemed so essential to preserving republicanism. Still, by the time he left public office Boston and Massachusetts had, in no small part through his efforts, tremendously expanded the educational opportunities available to all of the Commonwealth's children.[38]

Governor Adams's efforts to help Massachusetts build a virtuous republican society were generally noncontroversial even if the General Court did not always share his enthusiasm for promoting egalitarianism. And based on the 1795 election results Adams seemed firmly entrenched in the governors' office. As the 1790s progressed, however, Massachusetts was becoming a bastion of Federalist Party strength. Given their sense of increasing power and the fact that in January 1796 Adams had spoken out against the very controversial and still unratified commercial treaty with Britain, Federalists decided to wage a vigorous campaign to unseat him. The fact that 1796 would also be a presidential election year likely also figured into the Federalists' decision.

The 1796 gubernatorial campaign began in the fall of 1795. In September Federalists denounced Adams for not calling out the military to halt what they portrayed as extraordinarily dangerous crowd actions in Boston; Republicans dismissed the accusations about rampaging crowds as ridiculous exaggerations. Although the claim that Governor Adams had helped import Jacobin horrors into Massachusetts did not gain traction, it was not forgotten when the election season opened in the spring of 1796.[39] Once again the Federalist press offered up invective against Adams. Old charges were recycled and often amplified. Critics dredged up his failures as a tax collector and claimed that Adams *never* was a friend to John Hancock and that he supposedly opposed *both* the United States Constitution and President Washington. Adams's harsh attitude toward Shays's rebels was highlighted. Yet, despite the seeming incongruity, voters also heard that Adams supported riotous American Jacobins. In addition, Federalists accused the governor of being too friendly toward revolutionary France, especially when the vital interests of the two nations clashed. Opponents lambasted

Adams for supposedly overstepping his bounds when he used his position as governor to denounce the immensely unpopular commercial treaty John Jay had negotiated with Great Britain. The Federalists also resurrected and intensified their arguments about Adams's age. Now in his mid-seventies, Adams was routinely described as too old and infirm to function as governor. One critic even asserted that Adams had entered his "dotage." Some writers suggested it would be a kindness to let the worn-out governor retire to a well-earned life of leisure. Adams was also charged with believing he had a right to be governor forever; the people of Massachusetts were told they had done more than enough for this tired old man. In addition to pummeling Governor Adams, Federalists put forward a more credible gubernatorial candidate who did not carry the sort of negative baggage that had made Judge Cushing such an easy target in 1794. The Federalist's rather reluctant standard-bearer, Increase Sumner, did not take an active part in the War for Independence, but he was a well-respected lawyer and state judge and committed Federalist.[40]

For their part, Adams supporters revisited themes that worked so well in previous elections and also systematically countered what one writer called the Federalists' "scandalous lies." It was repeatedly claimed that Adams still exhibited great physical vigor. He deserved to be reelected because he was "the American Cato" and "*the father of the America Revolution.*" Federalists were portrayed as "the enemies of Republicanism" and as "the aristocratic party." These "enemies to the liberties of America" hated both Adams and Hancock precisely because these two friends had firmly championed republicanism.[41]

When the ballots were counted, although Adams actually improved his showing in Boston, the numbers were generally similar to the 1794 totals. Bostonians cast 1,614 ballots for Adams in 1796; Increase Sumner garnered 848 votes. In the state as a whole, Adams got 15,195 votes to Sumner's 10,184. Just over a thousand votes were cast for other candidates. Given these results, even with the increasing division of the people into competing political parties, Adams likely could have continued to occupy the governor's chair past the end of his term in 1797. But in the spring of 1796 he was approaching his seventy-fourth birthday, and that made Samuel contemplate retiring to private life. Events soon turned his thoughts into conviction.[42]

In September 1796 President Washington said he would retire. That announcement convinced Samuel that he too should finally leave public office. In January 1797 he informed the General Court that he would not allow his name to be put forth as a candidate for governor. He displayed the sense of humor he was noted for in personal life by wryly alluding to the repeated attacks on his age. "The infirmities of age," he observed, "render me an unfit person in my own eyes, and very probably in the opinion of others, to continue in this station." He noted that he had served Massachusetts "in various stations to the best of my ability, and I hope with general approbation." Having grown old in the service of Massachusetts, Adams voiced his sense of duty by adding that, "when released from the burdens of my public station, I shall not forget my country.—Her welfare and happiness, her peace and prosperity, her liberty and independence will always have a great share in the best wishes of my heart."[43]

EPILOGUE:
"THE PATRIARCH OF LIBERTY"

Samuel Adams always enjoyed children and in retirement spent many hours with his three grandchildren, his posterity. He also loved reminiscing about the Revolutionary days. Perhaps he thought occasionally of how, years before, his cousin John had his son John Quincy, then age eighteen, carry a letter to Samuel. John's letter reminded Samuel that when John Quincy was but a child Samuel had taken him onto the Boston Common "to see with detestation the British troops, and with pleasure the Boston militia." John indicated the lessons had not been lost. John Quincy, his father said, thinks of peace and civil life and wanted to pursue the law. Samuel had responded, "That *Child* whom I led by the Hand with a particular Design, I find is now become a promising youth." "If I was instrumental at that Time of enkindling the Sparks of Patriotism in his tender Heart," Samuel added, "it will add to my Consolation in the latest Hour."[1]

As Samuel enjoyed his posterity and reminisced about the Revolution, he and Elizabeth no longer had money worries. The 1788 bequest of Samuel Jr. had given them financial security, and wise investments in land increased their wealth. By the mid-1790s the Adamses could accurately be called rich. Wealth did not change Samuel and Elizabeth's plain style of living. He exhibited the simple republican frugality for which he had long been famous. He still dressed plainly in the style of the Revolutionary era. The Adamses did not keep a carriage. Their house in Winter Street, which they purchased in 1782 because the occupying British forces had trashed their home, suggested that in some ways plain living could blend into indifference. The family's two-story frame home was decidedly weather-beaten. Only old-timers could attest to its once having been yellow. As the century turned, Samuel got his earthly affairs in order. In late December 1799 he wrote his last will, a will that revealed his love and respect for Elizabeth, his dearest Betsy. He made Elizabeth and her brother, who was his daughter Hannah's husband, his executors. In 1802 the last vestiges of the old family Purchase Street estate were sold.[2]

Samuel always considered his cousin John a friend and in 1797 wrote to President Adams as "Your Old and unvaried Friend." John responded in kind. Nevertheless, Samuel was pleased when John lost the bitterly contested election of 1800 because Thomas Jefferson replaced him. Jefferson offered a revealing tribute to the man he praised as the one person who might be called the helmsman of the American Revolution. When he took office on March 4, 1801, the new president delivered a justifiably famous inaugural address that invited all Americans of whatever political party to celebrate what united them: a commitment to the same fundamental political values, above all a commitment to majority rule and the rule of law under the Constitution. But he also added that all Americans "will bear in mind this sacred principle, that though the will of the majority is in all cases to prevail, that will, to be rightful, must be reasonable; that the minority possess their equal rights, which equal laws must protect, and to violate would be oppression." Later in March Jefferson wrote to Samuel and said "I addressed a letter to you, my very dear and & antient friend, on the 4th. of March: not indeed to you by name, but through the medium of some of my fellow citizens, whom occasion called on me to address." Jefferson extended his extraordinary compliment by adding, "in meditating the matter of that address, I often asked myself, is this exactly in the spirit of the patriarch of liberty, Samuel Adams? is it as he would express it? will he approve of it?" Jefferson phrased the ideal of majority rule tempered by reasonable consideration of minority rights more elegantly than Samuel Adams had, but, as Jefferson suggested, Adams had articulated and lived by those ideals. Samuel approved.

President Jefferson, who profoundly respected Adams from their early days together in the Continental Congress onward, added that he had received reports of Samuel being "avoided, insulted, frowned on." Jefferson observed that all he could think of when he received those reports was "'Father, forgive them, for they know not what they do.'" The new president stressed that he counted on receiving Adams's wise counsel. Samuel responded with thanks but added, "it is not in my power dear friend to give you council." Still, "though an Old Man cannot advise you, he can give you his Blessing."[3]

Even though Adams had retired from politics, the Jeffersonian Republicans, as they were now known, found ways to have him defend what he called "the principles of Democratic Republicanism." In 1802 Boston publishers who had long supported Adams and Jefferson printed a series of four letters Samuel and John Adams had exchanged a dozen years before. John initiated a philosophical discussion by asking, "is the millennium commencing?" In his two lengthy responses, Samuel offered commentary that, when matched with the words and deeds of his long public life, shows how consistently he strove to protect constitutional rights and promote liberty for posterity. Samuel maintained that "the love of liberty is interwoven in the soul of man, and can never be totally extinguished." To protect their liberty, the people needed a republican form of government that possessed "a mixture of powers to check the human passions" and stop them from rushing to extremes. When John suggested that in a republic "the People have an essential share in the sovereignty," Samuel gently but firmly chided him by asking, "Is not the *whole* sovereignty, my Friend, essentially in the people?" For Samuel, constitutions became magnificent if the people had created them and if the constitutions gave the people the power, through frequent elections, to retain or replace their public servants.[4]

Although he glorified America's republican constitutions, Samuel Adams believed that even the best manmade constitution would contain defects and so something more was necessary to preserve good republican government. That something was, he emphasized in his exchange with John, a virtuous education. Samuel proclaimed that "to renovate the age" leaders must realize "the importance of educating their *little boys*, and *girls*." Education must be universal; it should draw the rich and the poor together and make no distinction among them. He wanted all children to learn the importance of "the fear, and love of the Deity, and universal Philanthropy" as well as love of country and "the art of self government, without which they can never act a wise part in the government of societies, great, or small." Samuel again lauded Massachusetts's ancestors for having founded an educational system "by which means wisdom, knowledge and virtue have been generally diffused among the body of the people." It had enabled the people "to form and establish a civil constitution, calculated for the preservation of their rights and liberties."[5]

Samuel Adams's last-known letter revealed how he continued to see morality as essential to America and how, at the same time, he defended religious liberty. In the fall of 1802 he wrote to another old American revolutionary, Thomas Paine. While praising him for his great work in bringing about the decision for American independence, Adams chastised Paine for reportedly having undertaken a defense of infidelity. The people of New England, Adams insisted, would never turn their backs on God. Samuel also maintained, however, that "we ought to think ourselves happy

320   *Epilogue*

in the enjoyment of opinion, without the danger of persecution by civil or ecclesiastical law." And speaking of the need for honesty and civility in public life, he stressed that "neither religion nor liberty can long subsist in the tumult of altercation, and amidst the noise and violence of faction." Those words reflected Adams's anger about President Jefferson being "calumniated for his liberal sentiments" and being libeled "without the least shadow of proof."[6] Samuel could retire from public office, but he could never fully retire from politics.

As 1802 turned into 1803, friends noticed that Adams, now eighty, was growing weaker. He ventured out of doors less and less often. What he had called the latest hour came on Sunday, October 2, 1803. The next edition of Boston's *Independent Chronicle*, the city's leading Jeffersonian Republican paper, carried a black bordered announcement: "SAMUEL ADAMS Is Dead!" The editors lamented the loss of "the consistent and inflexible Patriot and Republican" who was "our *political parent*." The man they called "the Father of the American Revolution" had been, they proclaimed, "the undeviating friend of civil and religious liberty." A week later the editors filled their front page and much of the second with a biographical tribute written by James Sullivan, an old friend and often political ally. Saying he had produced only a newspaper sketch of Adams, Sullivan maintained that "to give his history at length, would be to give an history of the American revolution."[7]

The praise Jeffersonian Republicans lavished upon Samuel Adams sounds excessive. Yet the Reverend William Bentley of Salem, a man who had recently had very harsh things to say about Adams, expressed remarkably similar thoughts in his diary just one day after Adams died. Observing that Adams's "religion & manner were from our ancestors" and that he "was a puritan in his manners always," Rev. Bentley asserted that "no man contributed more towards our revolution." Adams achieved great popular influence due to "his inflexibility & undaunted courage." He "persevered through life in his Republican principles without any conformity to parties, influence or times." And Adams's politics, said Bentley, rested on his beliefs that "rulers should have little, the people much," and that rulers should be judged by "the good they do, & the difference among the people only from personal virtue. No entailments, not privileges. An open world for genius & industry."[8]

As tributes to Samuel Adams poured forth, the United States House of Representatives voted unanimously to wear crepe on their left arms for thirty days "in testimony of the National Gratitude and reverence towards the memory of that undaunted & illustrious patriot." Jeffersonian Republicans took umbrage when nine United States senators refused to wear crepe in honor of Adams and Edmund Pendleton, another notable revolutionary who had also recently died. One of the nine was John Quincy Adams, the now-grown child Samuel had taken to the Boston Common to scorn the redcoats and salute the local militia. Even more galling to those who venerated Adams, when a "very honorary" resolution for him was introduced into the Massachusetts House of Representatives, it was "whittled down . . . from its original form" by Federalists. It seemed that even in death Samuel Adams could not escape the growing noise and violence of party politics.[9]

The partisan political wrangling extended to Adams's funeral. For comparison it is worth considering what happened when John Hancock, who was then the governor of Massachusetts, died almost exactly one decade earlier in October 1793. Hancock's body lay in state for eight days before an elaborate parade of military personnel, dignitaries, and others accompanied him to his interment. Of course, contemporaries knew that Hancock loved pomp and that Samuel Adams despised it. As the last hour approached, Samuel told his family he did not want any parade or showy public displays and that his coffin should be plain. Given his stature, it would hardly have been surprising if Samuel's request for a simple funeral were overridden. But when he did die, none of the leading Massachusetts officials on hand, all members of the Federalist Party, planned on having Adams lie in state or even arranging the kind of state funeral traditionally given to major Massachusetts dignitaries. In fact, when he inquired about funeral preparations on the day after Adams died, James Sullivan was informed that the normal military escort could not be arranged. Sullivan, a well-respected and notable political personage in his own right, wanted a proper military escort or none at all. As he recounted it, things changed quickly and dramatically when he suggested that Adams's funeral might merely consist of "the bier of Samuel Adams, followed only by his widow, supported by two '75 men, who had never forsaken their old principles." Sullivan remarked that, being afraid of this suggestion, the officials suddenly found it in their power quickly to arrange a state funeral complete with the accustomed military escort. That state funeral occurred on October 6, just four days after Adams died.[10]

Although born to a life of promise, Samuel Adams was in his forties before it seemed that promise might be fulfilled. It happened when he was called on to champion American rights. Samuel ran what he called his political race for almost half a century, and, having once emerged as a leader in the movement that led to American independence, he stood in the political glare from the mid-1760s until the dawn of the nineteenth century. Adams was arguably America's first professional and first modern politician. He made politics his lifelong occupation, and he pioneered ways of drawing the people into the political process. His call for installing a gallery in the Massachusetts House, his leadership of mass meetings, his regular use of newspapers to distribute political commentary, his development and use of committees of correspondence, and his personal interaction with an extraordinary number of ordinary people all helped transform the political process. As a politician, as a public figure, he can fairly be faulted for shoddy tax collecting, for winking at his own plural office-holding, and perhaps for how he mishandled the 1783 letter from the Massachusetts congressmen who wanted to blackmail Congress. Still, as his harshest critics typically admitted, even if backhandedly, he was a remarkably upright man who was motivated neither by a desire to enrich himself nor by a desire for popularity. As Samuel himself emphasized, legions of people, including many lost to history or known only as amorphous members of crowds or mass meetings, contributed to the movement to independence. Nevertheless, more than any other American, Samuel Adams did merit the titles "the Father of the American Revolution" and helmsman of the American Revolution.

Based on his own deep immersion in the history of defenders of freedom and his assertion that "the Man who nobly vindicates the Rights of his Country & Mankind shall stand foremost in the List of fame," Samuel Adams may have wanted posterity to honor him as a staunch defender of the rights of his country and of mankind. But he did not take pains to promote his own fame. He did not keep a diary or craft autobiographic musings. He even destroyed letters lest they harm others in the revolutionary movement. When his cousin John urged him in April of 1783 to compile and publish his writings, Samuel apparently did not even bother to respond, and he never undertook the task of compiling his writings. Even if he did hope to stand high on the list of the defenders of rights in America and the world, that was, in the end, not what really mattered to him. Writing to his cousin John in November of 1783, Samuel, who knew of John's ravenous desire to receive credit for his own impressive accomplishments in the great cause, urged his cousin to be reconciled to the fact that "the faithful Historian will do Justice to your Merits—Perhaps not till you are dead." Having added that "the leading Characters in this great Revolution will not be fairly marked in the present Age," Samuel stressed that "it will be well if the leading principles are remembered long."[11] That was quintessential Samuel Adams.

Samuel Adams not only articulated the leading principles of that "great Revolution," he embodied them in a lengthy political life that, as his contemporaries often emphasized, was notable for its philosophical consistency. He believed that everyone had duties to posterity, above all by promoting and protecting liberty. Reasonable people would, he argued, protect the rights of others lest their own rights be trampled. But, following John Locke as he so often did, Adams observed that humans were not always reasonable and so needed constitutions—republican constitutions—to protect their fundamental rights. Early in life he determined that a constitution that protected the people's liberty and provided them with the means to seek legal redress should be steadfastly, should be jealously safeguarded. Adams became an American revolutionary because he believed the British were trying to destroy the people's rights and the constitutions that protected those rights. And he always trumpeted the view that the people, the legitimate source of power, should keep a watchful eye on their public servants. In a republic, that meant the citizens should exercise their sacred trust of voting and vote not for self-interested reasons but for the public good and those who would promote the public good. Certainly if liberty were in peril, individuals had a duty to protect it and thus should put the interest of the community ahead of their own interests.[12]

Even as he proclaimed the importance of the citizenry keeping a watchful eye on their political servants, Samuel also stressed that the people should treat those servants with respect, and he insisted that the people must obey the laws. As he put it in 1784, "there is Decency & Respect due to Constitutional Authority." Anyone who weakened the power of government "lawfully exercised" must be considered "Enemies to our happy Revolution & the Common Liberty." Indeed, this American revolutionary argued that even unconstitutional laws should be opposed through legal means. He never wavered from a commitment to the rule of law. If the people had the constitutional means to obtain redress of grievances, they must, he insisted, not resort to violence. Open rebellion, as Locke had observed, was justified *only* if tyrants gave an injured people no alternative but to fight or be enslaved.[13]

Samuel Adams also analyzed what attributes the political servants in the newly established republic should possess. They should have knowledge and wisdom. They should display temperance, moderation, and perseverance. They should live a life of "true Republican Simplicity of Manners . . . for the Honor of the Supreme Being & Welfare of the Common Wealth." Certainly public servants should have "no ruling Passion but the Love of their Country," and they should be willing to give their country "the most arduous and important Services with the Hope for no other Reward in this Life than the Esteem of their virtuous Fellow Citizens." Above all, the people's political servants needed to understand and act on the principle that they had a duty to do everything possible for "promoting the Cause of Liberty & Virtue."[14]

As he helped nudge America toward independence, Adams added a consuming desire to build a virtuous society to his lifelong quest of protecting constitutional liberties. He did that because he believed that God intended people to live under a republican form of government and that, to preserve that government, the people as well as their political servants must be virtuous. Over the last two decades of his public career, as he labored to convince the people to embrace republican virtues, Samuel placed extraordinary faith in the ability of education to produce and protect a virtuous society. As he argued on more than one occasion, "no People will tamely surrender their Liberties, nor can any be easily subdued, when Knowledge is diffusd and Virtue is preservd." His words and deeds mark him as a true proponent of public education for all children, for posterity.[15]

Adams was convinced that education diffused throughout the population would do more than protect liberty. He believed an educated populace would be better equipped to achieve what he maintained was the promise of the Declaration of Independence. Building on the fact that every state had voted for the Declaration of Independence, Adams had boldly proclaimed that "the doctrine of Liberty and Equality is an article in the political creed of the United States." It followed that every citizen had a duty "to secure the blessings of equal liberty to the present and future generations."[16] In voicing and working for that ideal of equal liberty as well as in defending already established rights and calling for government rooted in the rule of law, Samuel Adams's words and deeds provide us, his posterity, with a veritable guide to responsible citizenship and public service in a republic. In this enduring way the helmsman of the America Revolution and "consistent republican" will forever remain a patriarch of liberty.

ABBREVIATIONS
AND SHORT TITLES

Adams, *Diary and Autobiography*	L. H. Butterfield, ed., *Diary and Autobiography of John Adams*, 4 vols. (Cambridge, MA: Harvard University Press, 1961)
ANB	John A. Garraty and March C. Carnes, eds., *American National Biography*, 24 vols. (New York: Oxford University Press, 1999)
CSM	Colonial Society of Massachusetts
DNB	*Oxford Dictionary of National Biography: In Association with the British Academy; from the Earliest Times to the Year 2000*, ed. H. C. G. Matthew and Brian Harrison. 60 vols. (Oxford and New York: Oxford University Press, 2004)
DHRC	Merrill Jensen, John P. Kaminski, et al., eds., *Documentary History of the Ratification of the Constitution*, 23 vols. (Madison: State Historical Society of Wisconsin, 1976–)
Evans [+ Number]	Documents listed by number in Charles Evans, Clifford K. Shipton, and Roger P. Bristol, eds., *American Bibliography*, 14 vols. (city and publisher vary, 1903–1959); Clifford K. Shipton and James E. Mooney, *National Index of American Imprints through 1800: The Short-Title Evans*, 2 vols. (Worcester, MA: American Antiquarian Society, 1969); Roger P. Bristol, *Supplement to Charles Evans' American Bibliography* (Charlottesville: University Press of Virginia, 1970)

Gage, *Correspondence*	Clarence E. Carter, comp. and ed., *The Correspondence of General Thomas Gage . . . 1763–1775*, 2 vols. (New Haven, CT: Yale University Press, 1931–1933)
Gipson, *British Empire*	Lawrence H. Gipson, *The British Empire before the American Revolution*, 15 vols. (Caldwell, ID; and New York: The Caxton Printers and Knopf, 1936–1970)
Hutchinson, *History*	Thomas Hutchinson, *The History of the Colony and Providence of Massachusetts-Bay*, ed. Lawrence S. Mayo, 3 vols. (Cambridge, MA: Harvard University Press, 1936)
JCC	Worthington C. Ford et al., eds., *Journals of the Continental Congress, 1774–1789*, 34 vols. (Washington, DC: Government Printing Office, 1904–1937)
JHRM	*Journals of the House of Representatives of Massachusetts* [for 1715–1779], 55 vols. (Boston: Massachusetts Historical Society, 1919–1990)
LDC	Paul H. Smith and Ronald M. Gephart, eds., *Letters of Delegates to Congress 1774–1789*, 26 vols. (Washington, DC: Library of Congress, 1976–2000)
MHS	Massachusetts Historical Society
NEQ	*The New England Quarterly*
Oliver, *Origin & Progress*	*Peter Oliver's Origin & Progress of the American Rebellion: A Tory View*, ed. Douglas Adair and John A. Schutz, rev. ed. (Stanford, CA: Stanford University Press, 1967)
Rowe, *Letters and Diary*	*Letters and Diary of John Rowe, Boston Merchant, 1759–1762, 1764–1779*, ed. Anne Rowe Cunningham (Boston: W. B. Blake, 1903)
SAP	Samuel Adams Papers (New York Public Library)
Warren-Adams Letters, 1	*Warren-Adams Letters: Being chiefly a correspondence among John Adams, Samuel Adams, and James Warren*, vol. 1, *1743–1777*. Collections, 72 (Boston: Massachusetts Historical Society, 1917)

Wells, *Life*	William V. Wells, *The Life and Public Services of Samuel Adams*, 3 vols. (Boston: Little, Brown, 1865)
WJA	Charles Francis Adams, ed., *The Works of John Adams, Second President of the United States: With a Life of the Author. . .* , 10 vols. (Boston: Little, Brown, 1850–1856)
WMQ	*The William & Mary Quarterly*, 3rd series
WSA	Harry A. Cushing, ed., *The Writings of Samuel Adams*, 4 vols. (New York: G. P. Putman's Sons, 1904–1908)

NOTES

PREFACE

1. Sayre as quoted in Wells, *Life*, 1: 375; Clymer to Josiah Quincy Jr., July 29, 1773, Josiah Quincy, *Memoir of the Life of Josiah Quincy Jun. of Massachusetts* (Boston: Cummings, Hilliard, & Company, 1825), 145; Warren to Adams, Nov. 2, 1780, *Warren-Adams Letters: Being chiefly a correspondence among John Adams, Samuel Adams, and James Warren, vol. 2 1778–1814*, MHS, *Collections* 73 (1925): 145; *ANB* s.v. "Clymer, George."

2. Oliver, *Origin & Progress*, 39; Quincy, *Memoir of the Life of Josiah Quincy*, 258; Margaret W. Willard, ed., *Letters on the American Revolution 1774–1776* (Boston: Houghton Mifflin, 1925), 35, 131.

3. Marquis de Chastellux, *Travels in North America in the Years 1780, 1781, and 1782*, trans. and ed. Howard C. Rice Jr., 2 vols. (Chapel Hill: University of North Carolina Press, 1963), 1: 142; Adams to William Tudor, Feb. 9, 1819, *WJA*, 10: 263–64; James Sullivan, "A Biographical Sketch," *Independent Chronicle*, Oct. 10, 1803. Here and elsewhere, if a newspaper is cited without mention of the place of publication, it was published in Boston.

4. Pauline Maier, *The Old Revolutionaries: Political Lives in the Age of Samuel Adams* (with a new introduction, New York: W. W. Norton 1990), 5–16; John K. Alexander, *Samuel Adams: America's Revolutionary Politician* (Lanham, MD: Rowman & Littlefield Publishers, 2002), 229–32; the best way to grasp the recent rise of interest in Adams is to visit www.amazon.com and enter *Samuel Adams* as the search term.

CHAPTER 1

1. Unless otherwise indicated, dates of family events were derived from entries in the Adams Bible published in the *New England Historical and Genealogical*

Register 8 (July 1854): 283–85 (as reprinted in Wells, *Life*, 3: 427–29). Once one gets beyond the Adams Bible, most of what can be known about Adams's early years comes from his great-grandson William V. Wells. He had the advantage of family accounts and a no-longer-available 1804 "Manuscript Memoir" of Adams produced by his daughter Hannah, who was born in January 1756. See Wells, *Life*, 1: 2, 138, 217n, 193n, 300n, 323n, 3: 21–22, 429, quotation 1: 217n; Samuel A. Drake, *Old Landmarks and Historic Personages of Boston* (Boston: Roberts Brothers, 1876), 309; Clifford K. Shipton et al., *Sibley's Harvard Graduates: Biographies of Those Who Attended Harvard University*, 18 vols. (Cambridge, MA: Harvard University Press, 1933–1975), 10: 420; Boston Street Laying-Out Department, *A Record of the Streets, Alleys, Places, Etc. in the City of Boston* (Boston: City of Boston Printing Dept., 1910), 379; Record Commissioners of the City of Boston, *A Report [–the Fourteenth–] of the Record Commissioners of the City of Boston, Containing the Boston Town Records from 1742 to 1757* (Boston: Rockwell and Churchill, 1885), 46, 48, 51–52, 76, 116, 191, 347 (hereafter *BTR*, 14); "[Map of] The Town of Boston in New England by John Bonner 1722" (Boston: Francis Dewing, 1722; Evans 2318); *Boston News-Letter*, Aug. 10, 1758; Carl Bridenbaugh, *Cities in the Wilderness: The First Century of Urban Life in America, 1625–1742*, rev. ed. (New York: Oxford University Press, 1971), 143n1.

2. Record Commissioners of the City of Boston, *A Report [–the Eighth–] of the Record Commissioners of the City of Boston, Containing Boston Town Records from 1700 to 1728* (Boston: Rockwell and Churchill, 1883), 114 (hereafter *BTR*, 8); Wells, *Life*, 1: 3–4; Bonner map of 1722. If given in New Style, Adams's birth date becomes September 27, 1722. Unfortunately, online sources, even reputable ones, often adopt the New Style date without explanation. See, e.g., http://bioguide. congress.gov/scripts/biodisplay.pl?index=A000045 (accessed September 23, 2010).

3. Quotations, Wells, *Life*, 1: 2, 4; history of children based on Adams Bible entries given in ibid., 3: 427–28. While the evidence is less than clear, it appears the infant-mortality rate in the Adams family was higher than the norm in Massachusetts and in Boston. See Philip J. Greven Jr., *Four Generations: Population, Land, and Family in Colonial Andover, Massachusetts* (Ithaca, NY: Cornell University Press, 1970), 188–97; see also John B. Blake, *Public Health in the Town of Boston, 1630–1822* (Cambridge, MA: Harvard University Press, 1959), 106–7, 247–48, 250, 255.

4. By 1728, if not sooner, the senior Adams also owned a wharf. Although later versions of the Bonner map—such as that reproduced as figure 1.1—label Adams's wharf, the original 1722 Bonner map shows a wharf in the same location but does not indicate to whom it belonged. William Burgis's 1728 "Plan of Boston" does indicate Adams's ownership of the wharf. See the maps reproduced in Walter M. Whitehill, *Boston: A Topographical History*, 2nd ed. (Cambridge, MA: Harvard University Press, 1969), 23, 25; and see also Wells, *Life*, 1: 2. Shipton (*Sibley's Harvard Graduates*, 10: 420) does not document his claim that the senior Adams owned slaves. The senior Adams is described as "maltster, owner of wharf, warehouse, and

land" in John A. Schutz, *Legislators of the Massachusetts General Court, 1691–1780: A Biographical Dictionary* (Boston: Northeastern University Press, 1997), 147.

5. On the senior Adams's offices and on a constable's duties, see *BTR*, 8: 70, 128–29, 162, 170, 181, 186, 193, 202, 216; and see also Record Commissioners of the City of Boston, *A Report [–the Twelfth–] of the Record Commissioners of the City of Boston, Containing the Boston Town Records from 1729 to 1742* (Boston: Rockwell and Churchill, 1885), 3 (hereafter *BTR*, 12); on tithingman duties, see Samuel Freeman, *The Town Officer*, 5th ed. (Boston: Thomas & Andrews, 1802), 150–53.

6. William Gordon, *The History of the Rise, Progress, and Establishment, of the Independence of the United Sates of America*, 4 vols. (London: Charles Dilly, 1788), 1: 365. Gordon's source for his comments on the caucus may well have been Samuel Adams. The two discussed politics so often that Adams, in a 1781 letter to Horatio Gates, remarked that Gordon "is well acquainted with the Internal State of this Common Wealth—He knows my Mind, & will communicate to you, more than I can now do for Want of Leisure" (*WSA*, 4: 264). See also G. B. Warden, "The Caucus and Democracy in Colonial Boston," *NEQ* 43 (March 1970): 19–45; and Aland and Katherine Day, "Another Look at the Boston 'Caucus,'" *Journal of American Studies* 5 (April 1971): 19–42. Studying the office of tax collector, Catherine S. Menand—who did not utilize some of the contemporary evidence given here and in discussions of the caucus that appear later in this work—questions the very existence of a powerful caucus. While the caucus did not exert the kind of total control John Adams and its opponents attributed to it, Menand's suggestion that the caucus might most realistically be see as "an informal gathering of local political leaders" is not convincing. See her "Things That Were Caesar's: Tax Collecting in Eighteenth-Century Boston," *Massachusetts Historical Review* 1 (1999): 62–63, quotation 63.

7. Because the British government typically followed the practice of letting the colonies pay the salaries of most colonial officials, the Massachusetts Charter of 1691 gave the colony's legislature the power to determine and pay the salary of the royal governor as well as the salaries of other royally appointed officials such as judges. That system saved the Crown money in the short run, but in the long run it gave colonial legislators the power of the purse, an advantage they used to pursue their own, not necessarily Britain's, interests. On the general system and for relevant Massachusetts examples, see Leonard W. Labaree, *Royal Government in America: A Study of the British Colonial System before 1783* (New Haven, CT: Yale University Press, 1930), 312–72.

8. Schutz (*Legislators*, 146) indicates the senior Adams became a Justice of the Peace in 1732. On the post's importance, see Russell K. Osgood, "John Clark, Esq., Justice of the Peace, 1667–1728," in ed. Daniel R. Coquillette, *Law in Colonial Massachusetts 1630–1800*, CSM, *Publications* 62 (Boston, 1984), 107–51; on Marcus Porcius Cato s.v. http://encyclopedia.jrank.org.

9. This description of course work is based on the assumption that the curriculum described in 1712 by Nathaniel Williams, master of the Boston Latin School

when Samuel entered, remained largely unchanged through the early 1730s. Given how the curriculum evolved, that is highly likely. See Pauline Holmes, *A Tercentenary History of the Boston Public Latin School 1635–1935* (Cambridge, MA: Harvard University Press, 1935), 96–98, 145, 256–62, 302; and see also Alexander J. Ingles, *The Rise of the High School in Massachusetts* (New York: Teachers College of Columbia University, 1911), 2–3.

10. Wells, *Life*, 1: 6; Marquis de Chastellux, *Travels in North America in the Years 1780, 1781, and 1782*, trans. and ed. Howard C. Rice Jr., 2 vols. (Chapel Hill: University of North Carolina Press, 1963), 1: 163; *LDC*, 16: 523.

11. Of the twenty-three students in Samuel's class, four were fourteen years of age. Another four were fifteen; eight were sixteen; the rest were between the ages of seventeen and twenty-one. See Wells, *Life*, 1: 6 and Shipton, *Sibley's Harvard Graduates*, 10: 418–19, 420.

12. Three members of the class died very young. Analysis based on information from Shipton, *Sibley's Harvard Graduates*, 10: 418–540 passim, 553.

13. *Harvard College Records*, 2 vols., CSM, *Publications*, 15–16, (1925), 1: 144; Samuel E. Morison, *Three Centuries of Harvard, 1636–1936* (Cambridge, MA: Harvard University Press, 1936), 60, 73–75, 78, 83, 112–13, quotation 78; Wells, *Life*, 1: 5; Shipton, *Sibley's Harvard Graduates*, 10: 418, 421, quotation 421.

14. On Wigglesworth, see Shipton, *Sibley's Harvard Graduates*, 5: 552–53.

15. Quotation, Wells, *Life*, 1: 6. See also *WJA*, 10: 263.

16. Shipton (*Sibley's Harvard Graduates*, 10: 421n3) corrected John C. Miller's inaccurate assertions that Samuel resided at Harvard from 1740 to 1743 and, due to his family's financial difficulties, waited tables. See Miller's *Sam Adams: Pioneer in Propaganda* (Boston: Little, Brown, 1936), 5.

17. Wells, *Life*, 1: xiii, 11–12. Confusion and debate abound as to whether Adams managed a malt house or was a brewer and for how long he followed either profession. Wells (*Life*, 1: 13, quotation 24) said the younger Adams first managed the family malt house and in 1748 "succeeded to his father's business of a brewer"; however, Wells did not say when Samuel left the business. On the other hand, as noted above, Schutz (*Legislators*, 147) described the senior Adams as "maltster, owner of wharf, warehouse, and land," not as a brewer. Various modern authors proclaim the younger Adams was a maltster *or* a brewer. Compare, e.g., Shipton, *Sibley's Harvard Graduates*, 10: 420, 422; and Ira Stoll, *Samuel Adams: A Life* (New York: Free Press, 2008), 275n16. The younger Adams could have been, for some period, both a maltster and a brewer. Still, as indicated, when the Adams family property was described in a legal notice for a public sale in 1758, the sheriff listed a malt house but no brewery. Moreover, contemporaries typically described the younger Adams as a maltster, not a brewer. In any case, Adams apparently did not continue in either capacity once he became politically prominent in the mid-1760s. Schutz (*Legislators*, 148) lists Samuel's occupation merely as "officeholder." See also Oliver, *Origin & Progress*, 39; Verner W. Crane, ed., *Benjamin Franklin's Letters to*

the Press 1758–1775 (Chapel Hill: University of North Carolina Press, 1950), 211; "J," *Salem Gazette,* June 30, 1815.

18. Max Savelle and Darold D. Wax, *A History of Colonial America,* 3rd ed. (Hinsdale, IL: Dryden Press, 1973), 539–52; *BTR,* 12: 195, 222, 224–29; Andrew M. Davis, *Currency and Banking in the Province of Massachusetts-Bay,* 2 vols. (New York: Macmillan, 1900–1901), 1: 253–56, 436, 443, 2: 123–29, 131.

19. Davis, *Currency,* 2: 133; and *JHRM,* 43 (part II): 332–33.

20. Hutchinson, *History,* 2: 297–300, quotations 299, 300; and Davis, *Currency,* 2: 145.

21. Quotation, *WJA,* 4: 49; Hutchinson, *History,* 2: 298–304, 3: 108; Davis, *Currency,* 1: 406–12, 2: 137–67.

22. Writing in 1772, John Adams said Samuel had done this "for full 20 Years before" 1761. See Adams, *Diary and Autobiography,* 2: 55.

23. *WSA,* 4: 288.

24. Morison, *Three Centuries,* 34–35, 91, quotations 91.

25. *BTR,* 14: 110, 133, 157, 171.

26. Isaiah Thomas, *The History of Printing in America with a Biography of Printers & an Account of Newspapers,* Marcus A. McCorison, ed. (New York: Weathervane Books, 1970; originally published 1810), 254–56.

27. These essays were attributed to Adams by Wells (*Life,* 1: 16), who worked diligently to determine what Adams had authored. Cushing, editor of the *WSA,* did not challenge Wells's attribution; he merely said, incorrectly, that the essays "constitute no real part of his [Samuel Adams's] real life work" (*WSA,* 1: vi). John Lax and William Pencak, in their "Knowles Riot and the Crisis of the 1740s in Massachusetts" [in *Perspectives in American History* 10 (1976): 163–214], build a circumstantial case that Adams authored a November 1747 pamphlet that attacked the British practice of impressment. They then use that attribution to speculate further that Adams probably authored anti-impressment items published in the *Independent Advertiser.* Lax and Pencak even assert that the famous Knowles Riot of 1747 was "the immediate cause" of Adams's "formulation of an ideology of resistance, in which the natural rights of man were used for the first time in the province to justify mob activity" (ibid., 214). I find the case for Adams's authorship of the 1747 pamphlet unconvincing and question Lax and Pencak's depiction. Whoever wrote the pamphlet did oppose impressment, but the author also denounced the "indecent, illegal" riot and displayed a haughty attitude toward the lower orders that would have been out of character for Adams. The pamphlet author sniffed that "when it is consider'd, that the immediate Sufferers [of impressement], were People of the lowest Rank, (though I think full as useful as their Neighbours, who live at Ease upon the Produce of their Labour) it is not at all suprizing, that their Resentment grew up into Rage, and Madness." Indeed, the people "weakly imagin'd" their violence would bring redress, "which, every prudent thinking Man knew could not be done; and consequently, there could not be a prudent, thinking Man

among them." (See *An Address to the Inhabitants of the Province of the Massachusetts-Bay . . . By a Lover of his Country* [Boston: Rogers and Fowle, 1747; Evans 5900], 4.) And while it would be highly likely that Adams, like his father and Bostonians generally, opposed impressment, neither of the *Independent Advertiser* essays Wells attributed to Adams dealt with impressment. On the senior Adams's stance and the general opposition to impressment, see *BTR*, 14: 79–80, 84–86; and see Jesse Lemisch, "Jack Tar in the Streets: Merchant Seamen in the Politics of Revolutionary America," *WMQ* 25 (July 1968): 371–407, especially 383–95.

28. *Independent Advertiser*, Aug. 8, 1748.

29. Ibid., April 10, 1749.

30. *BTR*, 14: 28, 63, 78, 98; Schutz, *Legislators*, 147; Wells, *Life*, 1: 13–14, 24.

31. *Independent Advertiser*, March 14, 1748; and Wells, *Life*, 1: 24, 3: 425.

32. Wells, *Life*, 1: 24–25, 3: 428.

33. Ibid., 3: 428–29, quotation 429.

34. He was elected an assessor in 1753, a natural post to have held before becoming a tax collector. For the elections and how remuneration would be determined, see *BTR*, 14: 228, 286–87, 298; and see also Record Commissioners of the City of Boston, *A Report [–the Sixteenth–] of the Record Commissioners of the City of Boston, Containing the Boston Town Records, 1758 to 1769* (Boston: Rockwell and Churchill, 1886), 8, 15, 21, 36, 45, 51, 67, 81, 107 (hereafter *BTR*, 16).

35. "Samuel Adams," *Boston Gazette*, Aug. 14, 1758.

36. "Samuel Adams," ibid., Feb. 23 and March 1, 1756.

37. Sherriff's sale announcements, *Boston News-Letter*, Aug. 10, 1758; and "Samuel Adams," *Boston Gazette*, Aug. 14, 1758.

38. *Boston Gazette*, Aug. 21, 1758. I attribute this to Adams on the basis of argument, style, and the timing of its appearance; Miller (*Sam Adams*, 24) also attributes this to Adams.

39. Sherriff's sale announcements and "Samuel Adams," *Boston News-Letter*, Aug. 17 and 24, 1758.

40. Sherriff's sale announcements, ibid., Sept. 21 and 28, 1758.

41. Hutchinson, *History*, 3: 211–12.

42. *WSA*, 2: 206; and Stephen T. Riley and Edward W. Hanson, eds., *The Papers of Robert Treat Paine*, 3 vols., MHS, *Collections*, 87–89, (1992–2005), 3: 78.

43. Although there is no evidence Adams faced additional threats of a forced sale due to land-bank problems, the issue remained alive well into the 1760s. See, e.g., *JHRM*, 43 (part II): 333–35, 417, 421; 44: 36, 83, 136–37, 138, 140, 147–48, 149, 154, 156, 162–63.

44. John Adams made this comment in 1819. See *WJA*, 10: 364; and *WSA*, 2: 165.

45. Quotation, supplement to *Boston Gazette*, May 5, 1760; see also "The Committee of Tradesmen," ibid., May 12, 1760. In 1763, an anticaucus author maintained that, although the caucus did not keep written records, the members spoke much of the "antiquity" of the organization. See "Impartial Account" by "E. J." in *Boston Evening-Post*, March 21, 1763 (hereafter *BEP*).

46. *BEP*, Feb. 14, 1763; "J.," *BEP*, March 14, 1763; dialogue between Tom and Robin, *BEP*, March 21, 1763; "E. J.," *BEP*, March 21, 1763.

47. Adams, *Diary and Autobiography*, 1: 238, 239n1, 239n4, quotations 1: 238. In 1763, a member of the caucus ("W. D—s," *BEP*, March 21, 1763) claimed the caucus was not concerned "with Offices of little Consequence." See also Hutchinson, *History*, 3: 120–21; and G. B. Warden, *Boston 1689–1776* (Boston: Little, Brown, 1970), 141.

48. "E. J.," *BEP*, March 21, 1763; and compare to Hutchinson, *History*, 3: 120–22.

49. Elbridge H. Goss, *The Life of Colonel Paul Revere*, 2 vols. (Boston: Howard W. Spurr, 1891), 1: 115–17 and 2: 635–44, which give what purports to be minutes of the North End Caucus for March 23, 1772, to May 9, 1774.

50. Wells, *Life*, 1: 36; and Oliver, *Origin & Progress*, 41.

51. Warden, *Boston*, 128–32, 141; and *BTR*, 16: 51, 58.

52. *BTR*, 16: 74, 84–85, 90–93, 98–99, 101–2, 110, 150–51; and Gary B Nash, *The Urban Crucible: Social Change, Political Consciousness, and the Origins of the American Revolution* (Cambridge, MA: Harvard University Press, 1979), 244–47, 253–54, 257.

53. Adams, *Diary and Autobiography*, 1: 271.

54. The possibility that he served as a clerk is based on an announcement signed by a Samuel Adams serving as the clerk for the proprietors developing a property called Phillips-town and also on a later Adams petition claiming, via his father's estate, portions of land granted to members of the Phillips family. See *Boston Weekly Advertiser*, Aug. 17 and 21 and Sept. 11, 1758; see also "To the Hon. The Justices of the Supreme Judicial Court," *Independent Chronicle*, June 25, 1789.

55. Wells, *Life*, 1: 53. Mark Puls offers analysis of what he claims were conversations and personal reactions that supposedly took place during the courtship of Samuel and Elizabeth. But Puls offers no documentation to support his depictions. See Puls's *Samuel Adams: Father of the American Revolution* (New York: Palgrave Macmillan, 2006), 27, 28–29, 31.

56. L. H. Butterfield et al., eds., *Adams Family Correspondence*, 9 vols. (Cambridge, MA: Harvard University Press, 1963–), 1: 54.

57. Adams, *Diary and Autobiography*, 1: 271; Wells, *Life*, 3: 355; for Samuel Adams's own description of his tax-collecting methods through 1764, which showed a concern for a taxpayer's circumstances and ability to pay, see *WSA*, 1: 319–20.

58. The testimony of a longtime political opponent who hated Samuel is most instructive on this point. See Hutchinson, *History*, 3: 212.

59. John K. Alexander, "Reflections on Political Deference in Early America: Let's Meet at the Graveside," *Early American Studies* 3 (Fall 2005): 390; and Bernard Bailyn, *The Ordeal of Thomas Hutchinson* (Cambridge, MA: Harvard University Press, 1974), 1–8.

60. Oliver, *Origin & Progress*, 39, 41; Wells, *Life*, 1: 201–202; Hutchinson, *History*, 3: 211; Adams, *Diary and Autobiography*, 1: 271; John Elliot, *A Biographical*

Dictionary (Boston: Edward Oliver, 1809), 7. Although several important revolutionaries were Freemasons, Adams was not. See Steven C. Bullock, *Revolutionary Brotherhood: Freemasonry and the Transformation of the American Social Order, 1730–1840* (Chapel Hill: University of North Carolina Press, 1996).

61. For a good general overview of these changes and the place of the colonies in the structure of the British Empire, see Lawrence H. Gipson, *The Coming of the Revolution, 1763–1775* (New York: Harper & Row, 1954).

62. The precise wording of William Pitt's 1766 utterance was "The Americans are the sons, not the bastards of England." See Edmund S. Morgan, ed., *Prologue to Revolution: Sources and Documents on the Stamp Act Crisis* (Chapel Hill: University of North Carolina Press, 1959), 136.

63. See, for example, Morgan, *Prologue*, 17–23, 62–69, 97–103, 134–41.

64. Morgan, *Prologue*, 4–5, 137–38; and John L. Bullion, *A Great and Necessary Measure: George Grenville and the Genesis of the Stamp Act, 1763–1765* (Columbia: University of Missouri Press, 1982), especially 116, 154.

CHAPTER 2

1. Robert F. Seybolt, *The Town Officials of Colonial Boston, 1634–1775* (Cambridge, MA: Harvard University Press, 1939), 292, 295, 299, 303, 308, 314; and Record Commissioners of the City of Boston, *A Report [–the Sixteenth–] of the Record Commissioners of the City of Boston, Containing the Boston Town Records from 1758 to 1769* (Boston: Rockwell and Churchill, 1886), 33, 36–37, quotation 37 (hereafter *BTR*, 16).

2. Adams, *Diary and Autobiography*, 1: 235n3.

3. *WSA*, 1: 1, 7; and Wells, *Life*, 1: 46.

4. *WSA*, 1: 1–2, quotations 2.

5. *WSA*, 1: 4–5, 6; and compare to similar arguments on trade from British sources in Edmund S. Morgan, ed., *Prologue to Revolution: Sources and Documents on the Stamp Act Crisis* (Chapel Hill: University of North Carolina Press, 1959), 129–32, 140.

6. *WSA*, 1: 1–2, 4–5, quotations 2, 5.

7. Quotation, *WSA*, 1: 3; Leonard W. Labaree, *Royal Government in America: A Study of the British Colonial System before 1783* (New Haven, CT: Yale University Press, 1930), 373–419; Oliver, *Origin & Progress*, 107–111.

8. *WSA*, 1: 5–6, quotation 6.

9. *BTR*, 16: 116, 122; Wells, *Life*, 1: 45–46n; *WJA*, 10: 294.

10. Bernard Bailyn, ed., *Pamphlets of the American Revolution 1750–1776*, 1 vol. (Cambridge, MA: Harvard University Press, 1965–), 1: 410–17, quotations 412; and Hutchinson, *History*, 3: 65–69.

11. Bailyn, *Pamphlets*, 1: 409, and 418–82 for a reprinting of the publication. See also *JHRM*, 41: 72–77; and Adams, *Diary and Autobiography*, 1: 299, 310.

12. Bailyn, *Pamphlets*, 1: 460–61, 479–80; and compare to *JHRM*, 41: 75–76. For the general British attitude toward such ideas, see, for example, Morgan, *Prologue*, 131–32, 137–38.

13. *WSA*, 1: 4–5.

14. Bailyn, *Pamphlets*, 1: 476.

15. Ibid., 1: 447.

16. Ellen E. Brennan, "James Otis: Recreant and Patriot," *NEQ* 12 (Dec. 1939): 691–725; and John J. Waters Jr., *The Otis Family in Provincial and Revolutionary Massachusetts* (Chapel Hill: University of North Carolina Press, 1968), 152–61, 176–79.

17. Adams, *Diary and Autobiography*, 1: 271; Hutchinson, *History*, 3: 96–97; Oliver, *Origin & Progress*, 39, 41.

18. Adams, *Diary and Autobiography*, 1: 271; and Hutchinson, *History*, 3: 96, 212, quotations 96, 212; and see also ibid., 296–97n.

19. As quoted in Wells, *Life*, 1: 203.

20. Adams, *Diary and Autobiography*, 1: 271; Hutchinson, *History*, 3: 70, 86n, 96–97, 105–6, 131, 243–44; Brennan, "James Otis"; Waters Jr., *Otis Family*, 153–54, 175–77.

21. *JHRM*, 41: 77; and Edmund S. and Helen M. Morgan, *The Stamp Act Crisis: Prologue to Revolution*, rev. ed. (Chapel Hill: University of North Carolina Press, 1995), 107.

22. Arthur M. Schlesinger, *The Colonial Merchants and the American Revolution* (New York: Columbia University, 1918), 63–65, quotation 64.

23. *JHRM*, 42: viii–ix, 108–9, quotation 109.

24. Morgan, *Prologue*, 44–45, 47–48.

25. For an early example of Adams accentuating the importance of precedent, see *WSA*, 1:10. Only one colonial legislature openly called for illegal defiance of the Stamp Act before it was scheduled to go into effect; the Rhode Island Assembly took that stance in September 1765. For the actions of the Rhode Island and other colonial legislatures, see Morgan, *Prologue*, 47–48, 50–62. On the type of person who served in colonial legislators, see Bruce C. Daniels, ed., *Power and Status: Officeholding in Colonial America* (Middletown, CT: Wesleyan University Press, 1986).

26. Schlesinger, *Colonial Merchants*, 63–68, 74–76; and Morgan, *Stamp Act*, 127–29.

27. Alfred F. Young, *Liberty Tree: Ordinary People and the American Revolution* (New York: New York University Press, 2006), 297, 327–28; and Dirk Hoerder, *Crowd Action in Revolutionary Massachusetts, 1765–1780* (New York: Academic Press, 1977), 97–101, quotation 97.

28. Hoerder, *Crowd Action*, 92–102.

29. Morgan, *Prologue*, 108–9, quotations passim; Hoerder, *Crowd Action*, 102–10, quotation 109; Morgan, *Stamp Act*, 132–34.

30. Miller, *Sam Adams*, 65.

31. Edward Channing and Archibald C. Coolidge, eds., *The Barrington-Bernard Correspondence and Illustrative Matter 1760–1770* (Cambridge, MA: Harvard

University Press, 1912), 167–68 (hereafter *Barrington-Bernard Correspondence*); Hutchinson, *History*, 3: 98; Oliver, *Origin & Progress*, 65, 41, 39; Hutchinson as quoted in James K. Hosmer, *Samuel Adams* (Boston: Houghton, Mufflin, 1885), 132–33.

32. See especially Miller, *Sam Adams*, 53, 61–70; and Hiller B. Zobel, *The Boston Massacre* (New York: W. W. Norton, 1970), 27–33, 47, 61, 70, 81, 112. For basic weaknesses in both the Miller and Zobel volumes, see Bernard Bailyn, *The Ordeal of Thomas Hutchinson* (Cambridge, MA: Harvard University Press, 1974), 7–8n11. Aspects of Zobel's analysis have been, and justifiably so, severely criticized. See Jesse Lemisch, "Radical Plot in Boston (1770): A Study in the Use of Evidence," *Harvard Law Review* 84 (Dec. 1970): 485–504; and Pauline Maier, "Revolutionary Violence and the Relevance of History," *Journal of Interdisciplinary History* 2 (Summer 1971): 119–35.

33. Gary B. Nash, *The Urban Crucible: Social Change, Political Consciousness, and the Origins of the American Revolution* (Cambridge, MA: Harvard University Press, 1979), 246–57; Schlesinger, *Colonial Merchants*, 54–58; *BTR*, 16: 103–4, 117–18; Rowe, *Letters and Diary*, 74–75.

34. *BTR*, 16: 134, 143–44, 150; Hoerder, *Crowd Action*, 96; George P. Anderson, "Ebenezer Mackintosh: Stamp Act Rioter and Patriot," CSM, *Transactions*, 1924–1926 (1927), 15–64; Robert J. Brink, "'Immorality brought to Light': An Overview of Massachusetts Colonial Court Records," in *Law in Colonial Massachusetts 1630–1800*, CSM, *Publications*, 62 (1984), 492–93, quotation 492.

35. Jesse Lemisch, "Jack Tar in the Streets: Merchant Seamen in the Politics of Revolutionary America," *WMQ* 25 (July 1968): 371–407; and John K. Alexander, *Render Them Submissive: Responses to Poverty in Philadelphia, 1760–1800* (Amherst: University of Massachusetts Press, 1980), 7–8.

36. *WSA*, 1: 56–61, 2: 201, quotations 2: 201, 1: 60; *BTR*, 16: 152; *Boston Gazette*, September 2, 1765; "Boston," *Massachusetts Gazette*, Nov. 7, 1765; Anderson, "Ebenezer Mackintosh," 32–39.

37. Quotations, *WSA*, 1: 21, 59–60; and see also 3: 83–84.

38. Hoerder, *Crowd Action*, 108–18; Lemisch, "Jack Tar," 396–98; Morgan, *Stamp Act*, 150–64.

39. On other colonies, see Jesse Lemisch, "New York's Petitions and Resolves of December 1765: Liberals vs. Radicals," *New-York Historical Society Quarterly* 49 (Oct. 1965): 313–26; and Edmund S. Morgan, "Colonial Ideals of Parliamentary Power, 1764–1766," *WMQ* 5 (July 1948): 311–41; and corresponding letters to the editor in *WMQ* 6 (Jan. 1949): 162–70.

40. "London," *Boston Evening Post*, Sept. 9, 1765; Margaret M. Spector, *The America Department of the British Government, 1768–1782* (New York: Columbia University Press, 1940), 11–12; *DNB* s.v. "Conway, Henry Seymour"; *WSA*, 1: 12–13; *BTR*, 16: 157; Morgan, *Prologue*, 29–35, Barré quotation 32.

41. *WSA*, 1: 7–12; and *BTR*, 16: 155–56, quotations 155.

42. *BTR*, 16: 157–58; and *JHRM*, 42: 129.

43. Adams, *Diary and Autobiography*, 1: 299, 310, 341; Oliver, *Origin & Progress*, 35–37, 39–41, 83–84; Waters, *Otis Family*, 153–54, 161, 176–79.

44. Morgan, "Colonial Ideas," 318–19, 325; Hutchinson, *History*, 3: 81–83, 96–97, 98, quotations 97, 98; Bernard as quoted in Miller, *Sam Adams*, 61, 95.

45. *JHRM*, 42: 118–23, 124, 129–38. For Adams's authorship, see Wells, *Life*, 1: 13n1, and note that, while he was not a member of the House when the original committee was created to respond to Bernard's address, when the response was formally presented Adams's name headed the list of presenters.

46. Adams, *Diary and Autobiography*, 1: 271, 300; *WJA*, 10: 367; Hutchinson, *History*, 3: 96–97, 212, 296–97n.

47. *JHRM*, 42: 131–38, quotations 132, 134, 136, 137.

48. These points were made in separate petitions sent to the king, the House of Lords, and the House of Commons. New Hampshire declined to attend. Virginia, which had spearheaded active legislative resistance to the act, along with North Carolina and Georgia, did not send delegations because their governors refused to allow the assemblies to convene. See Morgan, *Prologue*, 45, 62–69, quotations 62, 63.

49. *JHRM*, 42: 151–53, quotation 151; Adams, *Diary and Autobiography*, 1: 301n4 and Hopkins quotation 300; Hutchinson, *History*, 3: 94–97; Bailyn, *Pamphlets*, 500–505.

50. Morgan, *Stamp Act Crisis*, 127–38,165–73; Hutchinson, *History*, 3: 98; Anderson, "Ebenezer Mackintosh," 42; Hoerder, *Crowd Action*, 117–24.

51. Robert Z. Finkelstein, "Merchant, Revolutionary, and Statesman: A Reappraisal of the Life and Public Services of John Hancock, 1737–1793," Ph.D. diss., University of Massachusetts, 1981, 105–6, 125–31; *WJA*, 10: 280; Hoerder, *Crowd Action*, 117; Oliver, *Origin & Progress*, 39–41.

52. Schlesinger, *Colonial Merchants*, 78–81; Hutchinson, *History*, 3: 99–100; Morgan, *Stamp Act Crisis*, 136–43; Lemisch, "Jack Tar," 397–98; Hoerder, *Crowd Action*, 123.

53. Morgan, *Stamp Act Crisis*, 143–45; and Adams, *Diary and Autobiography*, 1: 265.

54. *BTR*, 16: 159; Wells, *Life*, 1: 84; Adams, *Diary and Autobiography*, 1: 265n1, 265–70.

55. *BTR*, 16: 160; and Morgan, *Stamp Act Crisis*, 143–49.

56. Philip Davidson, *Propaganda and the American Revolution* (Chapel Hill: University of North Carolina Press, 1941), 70–73; and *WSA*, 1: 110–11.

57. *WSA*, 1: 26–71 passim, quotation 42.

58. *WSA*, 1: 39–48, quotations 45.

59. *WSA*, 1: 30; for the British position, see, e.g., Morgan, *Prologue*, 19, 21, 22, 29–34; see also John L. Bullion, *A Great and Necessary Measure: George Grenville and the Genesis of the Stamp Act, 1763–1765* (Columbia: University of Missouri Press, 1982), 114–15, 136–44.

60. See, e.g., *WSA*, 1: 30–31, 38–39, 46–48, 53–56, 66–70, quotation 67.

61. Morgan, *Prologue*, 29, 127–28; Adams, *Diary and Autobiography*, 1: 287, 294; Morgan, *Stamp Act Crisis*, 273–79; *BTR*, 16: 175–76.

62. Wells, *Life*, 1: 114–15; Clarence S. Brigham, *Paul Revere's Engravings*, 2nd ed. rev. (New York: Atheneum, 1969), 26–29; Morgan, *Stamp Act Crisis*, 295.

63. Morgan, *Prologue*, 155–56, quotation 155.

64. Ibid., 29–32, 134–41, quotation 136.

65. Morgan, *Stamp Act Crisis*, 295–300.

66. Waters, *Otis Family*, 160–63; Wells, *Life*, 1: 119; *BTR*, 16: vii–x, 177.

67. Hutchinson, *History*, 3: 107–8, 110; Wells, *Life*, 1: 120–22; *WJA*, 4: 62–64; *JHRM*, 43 (part I): x–xi, 5–13, quotation 12.

68. *JHRM*, 43 (part II), 231–34, quotation 233; Hutchinson, *History*, 3: 127–29; *WSA*, 1: 114–30; John K. Alexander, "Reflections on Political Deference in Early America: Let's Meet at the Graveside," *Early American Studies* 3 (Fall 2005): 390.

69. Hutchinson, *History*, 3: 113.

70. Wells, *Life*, 1–120; and *JHRM*, 50: 218.

71. Wells, *Life*, 1: 36, 201–2, "Publican" quotation 36; and Oliver, *Origin & Progress*, 41.

CHAPTER 3

1. Oliver, *Origin & Progress*, 33, 35–37; Hutchinson, *History*, 3: 213–14; John J. Waters Jr., *The Otis Family in Provincial and Revolutionary Massachusetts* (Chapel Hill: University of North Carolina Press, 1968), 118–21, 133, 179–80; Adams, *Diary and Autobiography*, 1: 306–7.

2. Peter O. Hutchinson, ed., *The Diary and Letters of His Excellency Thomas Hutchinson, Esq.*, 2 vols. (London: S. Low, Marston, Searle & Rivington, 1883–1886), 1: 53–54, quotation 54; Oliver, *Origin & Progress*, passim but especially 30, 35, 41, 42, 65; *WSA*, 1: 114–30; Malcolm Freiberg, "Thomas Hutchinson and the Province Currency," *NEQ* 30 (June 1957): 190–208.

3. *WSA*, 1: 108–11, quotations 109–10, 109.

4. *JHRM*, 43 (part I): 35, 74; ibid., 43 (part II): 224, 406; "A. B.," *Boston Gazette*, Feb. 17, 1766; Hutchinson, *History*, 3: 296–97n.

5. Wells, *Life*, 1: 80, 129–30; *JHRM*, 42: 167, 43 (part I): 9, 27, 66, 106, 138, 180, 182, 190, 206, 207, 208, 212–13, 214, 216–17. The agent's name is sometimes rendered as *Dennis* and as *DeBert* or *Debert*.

6. As quoted in Wells, *Life*, 1: 196, and see also 195. In January 1768, about six months before Adams made these comments, the House did at least temporarily try to limit his freedom to release letters. See *JHRM*, 44: 116. On newspapers reprinting political items, see, e.g., David A. Copeland, *Debating the Issues in Colonial Newspapers: Primary Documents on Events of the Period* (Westport, CT: Greenwood Press, 2000), xi–xii; and John K. Alexander, *The Selling of the Constitutional Convention of 1787: A History of News Coverage* (Madison, WI: Madison House, 1990), 5–7.

7. *WSA*, 1: 108–11, 112–13, quotations 110, 111.

8. *WSA*, 1: 109.

9. Bernard Bailyn, *The Ideological Origins of the American Revolution* (Cambridge, MA: Harvard University Press, 1967), 232–46; and Douglas R. Egerton, *Death of Liberty: African Americans and Revolutionary America* (New York: Oxford University Press, 2009), 44–49, 51, 55, 57.

10. Wells, *Life*, 1: 138, 2: 20–21, 3: 337.

11. Record Commissioners of the City of Boston, *A Report [–the Sixteenth–] of the Record Commissioners of the City of Boston, Containing the Boston Town Records from 1758 to 1769* (Boston: Rockwell and Churchill, 1886), 182–84, 200, quotations 183, 200 (hereafter *BTR*, 16); *JHRM*, 43 (part I): 110; ibid., 43 (part II): 387, 390, 393, 408, 409–10, 411, 420, quotation 393; W. E. Burghardt Du Bois, *The Suppression of the African Slave-Trade to the United States of America 1638–1870* (New York: Russel & Russel, 1896), 221, 222; *WSA*, 3: 78; George H. Moore, *Notes on the History of Slavery in Massachusetts* (New York: D. Appleton, 1866), 130–40.

12. Basing her argument above all on what appeared in the press—and ignoring the actions of the town meeting—Patricia Bradley argues that, except for opposing the slave trade, Adams actually strove to thwart antislavery activity at least through the early 1770s. Bradley's unconvincing analysis, which depicts Adams exerting extraordinary control over publishers and other authors as well as crowds, and which also ignores the evidence of the status of Surry (whom Bradley inexplicitly calls "Sully"), is presented in her *Slavery, Propaganda and the American Revolution* (Jackson: University Press of Mississippi, 1998), quotation 6.

13. *JHRM*, 43 (part I), 29–33, 209–11, 213, 221, quotation 30; Hutchinson, *History* 3: 113–15; Massachusetts General Court, *The Following Bill* (Boston: Green and Russell, 1766; Evans 10382), 1–4, quotation 2; *ANB* s.v. "Hawley, Joseph"; E. Francis Brown, *Joseph Hawley: Colonial Radical* (New York: AMS Press, 1966), 105–10; Colin Nicolson, *The "Infamous Govener": Francis Bernard and the Origins of the American Revolution* (Boston: Northeastern University Press, 2001), 147–48.

14. Wells, *Life*, 1: 131; *WSA*, 1: 108–13, 132–33, quotation 133; Hutchinson, *History* 3: 122–23; *JHRM*, 43 (part II): 229, 230, 238, 242–44.

15. Hutchinson, *History* 3: 118–19; Adams, *Diary and Autobiography*, 1: 324–25; *WSA*, 1: 114–30.

16. Rowe, *Letters and Diary*, 125–26, 139, 172, quotation 126; and Adams, *Diary and Autobiography*, 1: 341.

17. MHS, *The Harbottle Dorr Collection of Annotated Massachusetts Newspapers 1765–1776*, 1: 636; and on Dorr's ardor for the American cause, see, e.g., 2: 3 (hereafter Dorr Collection).

18. Cushing as quoted in Waters Jr., *Otis Family*, 165–66; Adams, *Diary and Autobiography*, 1: 313; Nicolson, *The "Infamous Govener*," 72, 143–44, 151–52.

19. Peter D. G. Thomas, *The Townshend Duties Crisis: The Second Phase of the American Revolution 1767–1773* (Oxford: Oxford University Press, 1987), 9, 23–25, 33; Robert J. Chaffin, "The Townshend Acts of 1767," *WMQ* 27 (Jan. 1970):

90–121; Ian R. Christie and Benjamin W. Labaree, *Empire or Independence, 1760–1776: A British-American Dialogue on the Coming of the American Revolution* (New York: W. W. Norton, 1976), 102–4.

20. Thomas C. Barrow, *Trade and Empire: The British Customs Service in Colonial America, 1660–1775* (Cambridge, MA: Harvard University Press, 1967), 216–24; and Oliver, *Origin & Progress*, 42, 56.

21. Thomas, *Townshend Duties Crisis*, 76; *BTR*, 16: 221–24; Hutchinson, *History*, 3: 132–33.

22. Franklin to William Franklin, Dec. 29, 1767, in Leonard W. Labaree et al., eds., *The Papers of Benjamin Franklin*, 39 vols. (New Haven, CT: Yale University Press, 1959–), 14: 349; same to same, Jan. 9, 1768, ibid., 15: 15; London *Gazetteer*, Jan. 5, 1768, as quoted in John C. Miller, *Origins of the American Revolution*, rev. ed. (Stanford, CA: Stanford University Press, 1959), 231.

23. Thomas, *Townshend Duties Crisis*, 77; Christie and Labaree, *Empire or Independence*, 115; Hutchinson, *History*, 3:145.

24. Memoirs of the Historical Society of Pennsylvania, 14, Paul L. Ford, ed., *The Writings of John Dickinson, Vol. 1, Political Writings 1764–1774* (1895), 277–406, especially 356.

25. Quoted in Gipson, *British Empire*, 11: 149.

26. Although not officially approved until January 13, the letter is dated January 12 both in official publications and in *WSA*. See *JHRM*, 44: 89, 93, 99, 102, 107, 108, 109, 241–50, quotations 89, 243, 249, 245; see also *WSA*, 1: 134–52.

27. *JHRM*, 44: 121–22, 217–19, quotations 218.

28. *JHRM*, 44: 129, 135, 148; Edward Channing and Archibald C. Coolidge, eds., *The Barrington-Bernard Correspondence and Illustrative Matter 1760–1770* (Cambridge, MA: Harvard University Press, 1912), 145–46, quotations 146 (hereafter *Barrington-Bernard Correspondence*); *WSA*, 1:225–26.

29. *JHRM*, 44: 147, 250–51, quotations 251; and Thomas, *Townshend Crisis*, 4.

30. *WSA*, 1: 225–26, quotations 226; and *JHRM*, 44: 148, 157, 45: 91–92. On authorship, see Gipson, *British Empire*, 11: 149n; Christie and Labaree, *Empire or Independence*, 113; Wells, *Life*, 1: 172–74n.

31. *JHRM*, 44: 236–39, quotations 237, 238.

32. *WSA*, 1: 135, 152–53n2. The full title indicates the compound nature of the 1768 publication: *The True Sentiments of America Contained in a Collection of Letters Sent from the House of Representatives of the Province of Massachusetts Bay to Several Persons of High Rank in This Kingdom. Together with Certain Papers Relating to a Supposed Libel on the Governor of That Province and a Dissertation on the Canon and Feudal Law* (London: J. Almon, 1768). On this work, see Justin Winsor, ed., *Narrative and Critical History of America*, 8 vols. (Boston: Houghton, Mifflin, 1884–1889), 6: 41–43, 83n2.

33. *JHRM*, 44: 164, 171, 176–78, 188, 250–51, quotations, 164; *Barrington-Bernard Correspondence*, 146, 149–50; *Boston Gazette*, 7 March 1768.

34. "Friday the 18th" and "M.Y.," *Boston Gazette*, March 21, 1768; *WSA*, 1: 201–12, quotations passim; Dorr Collection, 2: 67, 77, 82, quotation 67.

35. *BTR*, 16: 199, 200–203, 216–17, 218–19, 241, 242, 243, 271–72; *JHRM*, 45: 182, 196; Rowe, *Letters and Diary*, 157; *WSA*, 1: 199–200, 319–22, quotation 200; Record Commissioners of the City of Boston, *A Report [–the Eighteenth–] of the Record Commissioners of the City of Boston, Containing the Boston Town Records from 1770 through 1777* (Boston: Rockwell and Churchill, 1887), 69; Andrew H. Ward, "Notes on Ante-Revolutionary Currency and Politics," *New England Historical and Genealogical Register* 14 (July 1860): 262; Catherine S. Menand, "The Things That Were Caesar's: Tax Collecting in Eighteenth-Century Boston," *Massachusetts Historical Review* 1 (1999): 66.

36. *BTR*, 16: 245; Oliver, *Origin & Progress*, 39–40; Wells,. *Life*, 1: 183–84, Bernard quotation 183; *Barrington-Bernard Correspondence*, 145–46.

37. Gage, *Correspondence*, 2: 449–50, quotations 450; Thomas, *Townshend Duties Crisis*, 81; *JHRM*, 45: 68–69, 70–71, 72–73, 75–76, 85, 86–87, 88.

38. *JHRM*, 45: 89–91, quotations 92, 93; and compare to Locke's *Second Treatise of Government*, §123, §124, §222.

39. *JHRM*, 45: 94, 95–96, 98, 115, quotations 95–96; and *Barrington-Bernard Correspondence*, 163.

40. Oliver, *Origin & Progress*, 39, 41; Adams, *Diary and Autobiography*, 1: 271; Wells, *Life*, 1: 217.

41. Hutchinson, *History*, 3: 143; *WSA*, 1: 188n, 2: 212–22; Christie and Labaree, *Empire or Independence*, 113–15; Thomas, *Townshend Duties Crisis*, 83–85.

42. November 5 description and quotation, John P. Reid, *In a Rebellious Spirit: The Argument of Facts, the Liberty Riot, and the Coming of the American Revolution* (University Park: Pennsylvania State University Press, 1979), 6; *WSA*, 1: 216–17, quotation 216; Oliver Dickerson, *The Navigation Acts and the American Revolution* (Philadelphia: University of Pennsylvania Press, 1951), 208–65.

43. Reid, *In a Rebellious Spirit*, 87–88, 90–94, 116, 119, which should be compared with Hiller B. Zobel, *The Boston Massacre* (New York: W. W. Norton, 1970), 68–77; Jesse Lemisch, "Jack Tar in the Streets: Merchant Seamen in the Politics of Revolutionary America," *WMQ* 25 (July 1968): 385–95; Dirk Hoerder, *Crowd Action in Revolutionary Massachusetts, 1765–1780* (New York: Academic Press, 1977), 164–70; Thomas C. Barrow, *Trade and Empire: The British Customs Service in Colonial America, 1660–1775* (Cambridge, MA: Harvard University Press, 1967), 236–40; Anne Hulton, *Letters of a Loyalist Lady: Being the Letters of Anne Hulton, Sister of Henry Hulton, Commissioner of Customs at Boston, 1767–1776* (Cambridge, MA: Harvard University Press, 1927), 15.

44. *WSA*, 1: 236–40, 245; Reid, *In a Rebellious Spirit*, 96; *BTR*, 16: 253–57, quotation 254.

45. *WJA*, 10: 364; John Cary, *Joseph Warren: Physician, Politician, Patriot* (Urbana: University of Illinois Press, 1961), 37–40, 76–78; *BTR*, 16, 255–56, 257–59.

46. *BTR*, 16: 256–57; Zobel, *Boston Massacre*, 79; *Barrington-Bernard Correspondence*, 160–61, quotation 160.

47. Hutchinson, *History*, 3: 145–46; and Arthur M. Schlesinger, *The Colonial Merchants and the American Revolution* (New York: Columbia University, 1918), 119–21.

48. *Barrington-Bernard Correspondence*, 161–63, 165, 167–70, quotation 168; *WSA*, 1: 213–19; *Letters to the Ministry from Governor Bernard, General Gage, and Commodore Hood* (Boston: Edes and Gill, 1769; Evans 11176), 32–46, 85–86, 101–2, quotation 41.

49. John Shy, *Toward Lexington: The Role of the British Army in the Coming of the American Revolution* (Princeton, NJ: Princeton University Press, 1965), 295–96; Hutchinson, *History*, 3: 146–47; *Letters to the Ministry*, 35–41, quotation 40; Gage, *Correspondence*, 2: 68–69, 72–74, quotations 68.

50. *WSA*, 1: 236–40, quotations 236, 238, 240.

51. Rowe, *Letters and Diary*, 172; Hutchinson, *History*, 3: 146; "Boston," *Boston Gazette*, Aug. 22, 1768; Pauline Maier, *From Resistance to Revolution: Colonial Radicals and the Development of American Opposition to Britain, 1765–1776* (New York: Knopf, 1972), 162–69, 180–83, 198–200; Pauline Maier, "John Wilkes and American Disillusionment with Britain," *WMQ* 20 (July 1963): 373–95; George P. Anderson, "Pascal Paoli, an Inspiration to the Sons of Liberty," in CSM, *Transactions* 1924–1926 (1927), 180–210. Since August 14 was a Sunday, the celebrations occurred on Monday.

52. Hutchinson, *History*, 3: 145–46; and Schlesinger, *Colonial Merchants*, 91–93, 96–97, 104–6, 112–17, 126–28.

53. Wells, *Life*, 1: 209–11.

54. Nicolson, *The "Infamous Govener,"* 177; Wells, *Life*, 1: 212–13; *Barrington-Bernard Correspondence*, 280–83; *BTR*, 16: 259–61.

55. *BTR*, 16: 261–64, quotations 261, 263; and N. Neville Williams, *The Eighteenth-Century Constitution 1688–1815: Documents and Commentary* (Cambridge: Cambridge University Press, 1960), 1–4, 18–20.

56. *WSA*, 1: 241–47, quotation 247; Hutchinson, *History*, 3: 148–49, 151–53; *Letters to the Ministry*, 65–66, 69, quotation 69.

57. Hutchinson, *History*, 3: 152n; depiction of ships based on Paul Revere's engraving reproduced as figure 4.1 and *Massachusetts Gazette*, Oct. 6, 1768. See also Rowe, *Letters and Diary*, 175; and Oliver M. Dickerson, comp., *Boston under Military Rule (1768–1769) as Revealed in a Journal of the Times* (Boston: Chapman & Grimes, 1936), 2.

CHAPTER 4

1. Oliver M. Dickerson, comp., *Boston under Military Rule (1768–1769) as Revealed in a Journal of the Times* (Boston: Chapman & Grimes,1936), 2–3, 21

(hereafter Dickerson, "A Journal of the Times"); Rowe, *Letters and Diary*, 175–76, 179; Gary B. Nash, *The Urban Crucible: Social Change, Political Consciousness, and the Origins of the American Revolution* (Cambridge, MA: Harvard University Press, 1979), 194, 313; John Shy, *Toward Lexington: The Role of the British Army in the Coming of the American Revolution* (Princeton, NJ: Princeton University Press, 1965), 303; *Boston Chronicle*, Oct. 3, 1768; Carl Bridenbaugh, *Cities in Revolt: Urban Life in America 1743–1776*, rev. ed. (New York: Oxford University Press, 1971), 216.

2. Oliver, *Origin & Progress*, 148; William Gordon, *The History of the Rise, Progress, and Establishment, of the Independence of the United Sates of America*, 4 vols. (London: Charles Dilly, 1788), 1: 347; George W. Corner, ed. *The Autobiography of Benjamin Rush* (Princeton, NJ: Princeton University Press, 1948), 139; *WJA*, 9: 596–97; Peter O. Hutchinson, ed., *The Diary and Letters of His Excellency Thomas Hutchinson, Esq.*, 2 vols. (London: S. Low, Marston, Searle & Rivington, 1883–1886), 1: 167; Hutchinson, *History*, 3: 96–97; James Sullivan, "Biographical Sketch," *Independent Chronicle*, Oct. 10, 1803.

3. *WSA*, 1: 290.

4. *WSA*, 1: 249–54, 255–59, 264–68, 269–78, 306–9, 316–19, quotations 276, 318, 252, 253. Having advanced the argument that raising a stranding army in peacetime violated England's Bill of Rights, Adams had to retreat to the position that Parliament could authorize such a deployment but that doing so was wrong since Americans were not represented in Parliament. Compare to *WSA*, 1: 257–58 and 269–72, 272–74.

5. *WSA*, 1: 248–49, 249–51; Shy, *Toward Lexington*, 304–305; Dickerson, "A Journal of the Times," 1–2, 3, 7–9, 11–12, 13; *Letters to the Ministry from Governor Bernard, General Gage, and Commodore Hood* . . . (Boston: Edes and Gill, 1769; Evans 11176 and reprinted in *JHRM*, 46: 197–279); "Copies of Letters from Governor Bernard, &c, to the Earl of Hillsborough" (Boston: Edes and Gill, 1769; Evans 11179), 1–7, quotation 2; Rowe, *Letters and Diary*, 175–76, 177, 178; *Massachusetts Gazette*, Oct. 6 and Nov. 3, 1768; *Boston News-Letter*, Oct. 13, 1768; Gage, *Correspondence*, 2: 200–205, quotation 204; Nathaniel B. Shurtleff, *A Topographical and Historical Description of Boston*, 3rd ed. (Boston: Rockwell and Churchill, 1891), 472–73.

6. *WSA*, 1: 256; and Shy, *Toward Lexington*, 305–10, 317.

7. Dickerson, "A Journal of the Times," vii–xii, 2, quotations viii, 2; MHS, *The Harbottle Dorr Collection of Annotated Massachusetts Newspapers 1765–1776*, 2: 3 (hereafter Dorr Collection); Philip Davidson, *Propaganda and the American Revolution* (Chapel Hill: University of North Carolina Press, 1941), 236–37; Arthur M. Schlesinger, *Prelude to Independence: The Newspaper War on Britain 1764–1776* (New York: Knopf, 1958), 313.

8. The authorship of the "Journal" is clouded in mystery. Writing four months after the series began, Bernard said the authors were "Adams and his associates," at least one of whom had to be a member of the Council. Harbottle Dorr, like Bernard a contemporary, said the "Journal" entries "were done" by William Cooper,

the town clerk. That wording suggests that Cooper might have been the compiler rather than the sole author. While he did not cite Dorr, Richard Frothingham was probably relying on Dorr's comment when, in 1862, he said that "the Patriots, mainly William Cooper, the town-clerk, prepared a chronicle." Reviewing the bits of evidence then available but not knowing about Dorr's direct statement, Dickerson, who compiled the modern reprinting of the "Journal," emphasized that it had to have been produced by more than one person. In 1937, Arthur M. Schlesinger agreed with Dickerson's analysis while also suggesting that Samuel Adams was an important author. In his long-standard 1936 biography of Adams, a work Davidson did not cite, John C. Miller spoke of Adams "and his fellow journalists" but implied that Samuel was the principal author. In 1941, without giving specific documentation, Davidson asserted that the "Journal" was "written in large part by Samuel Adams, Samuel Cooper, perhaps [Benjamin] Edes, and one or two others of the Boston radicals." In 1958, Schlesinger, while rightly discounting John Adams as one of the authors, again stressed that the "Journal" had more than one author. In 1970, Hiller B. Zobel, like Miller, referred to Samuel Adams and other authors but then wrote as if the "Journal" was essentially an Adams production. It is worth noting that an entire Adams essay attacking Bernard was incorporated into the "Journal." The collective evidence suggests that Adams was a key member of a group of writers who produced the "Journal" and that William Cooper might well have served as something of a general editor as well as an author. On authorship, see Dorr Collection, 2: 323; Frothingham, "The Sam Adams Regiments in the Town of Boston," *Atlantic Monthly* 10 (August, 1862): 195–96; Dickerson, "A Journal of the Times," ix–x, Bernard quotation x; Arthur M. Schlesinger review of *Boston under Military Rule* in *NEQ* 10 (June 1937): 386–87; John C. Miller, *Sam Adams: Pioneer in Propaganda* (Boston: Little Brown, 1936), 174–77, quotation 174; Davidson, *Propaganda*, 236–37, quotation 236; Schlesinger, *Prelude*, 312; Hiller Zobel, *The Boston Massacre* (New York: W. W. Norton, 1970), 109–10. For the incorporated Adams essay, compare his "A Tory," *Boston Gazette*, May 1, 1769, and the May 9 entry (Dickerson, "Journal of the Times," 96–97).

9. Dickerson, "A Journal of the Times," passim and quotation 16.

10. Ibid., passim but especially 82–83 and quotations 55, 83; and Gipson, *British Empire*, 11: 234–39.

11. *WSA*, 1: 238–40.

12. For Adams's many essays published in the *Boston Gazette* between December 5, 1768, and February 13, 1769, see *WSA*, 1: 259–315; for the "Candidus" essays, see 254, 259–64, 268–69, 278–81, 291–97, 309–16. For the specifics given in the text, see 261–64, 296–97, 310–12, 314.

13. Arthur M. Schlesinger, *The Colonial Merchants and the American Revolution* (New York: Columbia University, 1918), 120–22, 124–32.

14. Record Commissioners of the City of Boston, *A Report [–the Sixteenth–] of the Record Commissioners of the City of Boston, Containing the Boston Town Records from 1758 to 1769* (Boston: Rockwell and Churchill, 1886), 274 (hereafter *BTR*, 16);

WSA, 1: 332–36; Francis G. Walett, "Governor Bernard's Undoing: An Earlier Hutchinson Letters Affair," *NEQ* 38 (June 1965): 217–26.

15. *WSA*, 1: 336–38, quotation 337.

16. Leonard W. Labaree et al., eds., *The Papers of Benjamin Franklin*, 39 vols. (New Haven, CT: Yale University Press, 1959–), 16: 129–30n6; *WSA*, 1: 339–40, quotation 340; Dickerson, "Journal of the Times," 96–97.

17. *WSA*, 1: 340–42, quotations 341, 341–42; and compare to *BTR*, 16: 278.

18. *BTR*, 16: 278; and *JHRM*, 45: 119–23.

19. Alan Bradford, ed., *Speeches of the Governors of Massachusetts 1765–1775 . . .* (Boston: Russell and Gardner, 1818), 166–71.

20. Bradford, *Speeches of the Governors*, 171–75, quotations 172, 175.

21. Adams, *Diary and Autobiography*, 2: 177.

22. Hutchinson, *History*, 3: 171; and *WSA*, 1: 349–54. The similarity of the 1768 and 1769 petitions suggests Adams was the major, if not the only, author.

23. Bradford, *Speeches of the Governors*, 176–80.

24. Hutchinson, *History*, 3: 168, 358–60; and *JHRM*, 45: 168–72.

25. Bradford, *Speeches of the Governors*, 183–88, quotation 188.

26. Dickerson, "A Journal of the Times," 123–27; Rowe, *Letters and Diary*, 190, 191, quotation 190; Hutchinson, *History*, 3: 182; Cooper as quoted in Shy, *Toward Lexington*, 313; Adams, *Diary and Autobiography*, 1: 341–42; *Boston Gazette*, July 31, Aug. 7 and 21, 1769, quotations Aug. 21 and 7.

27. *WSA*, 1: 378–80, quotations 379, 380.

28. Thomas C. Barrow, *Trade and Empire: The British Customs Service in Colonial America, 1660–1775* (Cambridge, MA: Harvard University Press, 1967), 214; Hutchinson, *History*, 3: 145, 181–82, quotations 181; Schlesinger, *Colonial Merchants*, 131–32.

29. William Tudor, *The Life of James Otis of Massachusetts* (Boston: Wells and Lilly, 1823), 361–63; Wells, *Life*, 1: 274; *WSA*, 1: 380–86; John J. Waters Jr., *The Otis Family in Provincial and Revolutionary Massachusetts* (Chapel Hill: University of North Carolina Press, 1968), 176–83; Hutchinson, *History*, 3: 145; Oliver, *Origin & Progress*, 41.

30. *WSA*, 1: 386–95, quotation 391.

31. *BTR*, 16: 297–98, quotations 297, 298; and *WSA*, 1: 380.

32. Schlesinger, *Colonial Merchants*, 131–32; *WSA*, 1: 396–445, quotations 396, 441; Wells, *Life*, 1: 282–83, 285–86n.

33. Shy, *Toward Lexington*, 311–17; Zobel, *Boston Massacre*, 136–44, 152–60, Rogers quotation 146; *WSA*, 1: 380.

34. Hutchinson as quoted in Wells, *Life*, 1: 292.

35. Wells, *Life*, 1: 292, 294–95, Hutchinson quotation 292; and *WSA*, 2: 1–4.

36. *WSA*, 2: 64–65; SAP, "Minutes of the Meeting of the Merchants 1770 January 23"; Schlesinger, *Colonial Merchants*, 174–75.

37. *WSA*, 2: 4–7, quotations 7.

38. Dirk Hoerder, *Crowd Action in Revolutionary Massachusetts, 1765–1780* (New York: Academic Press, 1977), 216–19; broadside "The Merchants, and all Others . . . January 16, 1770" (Boston: n.p., 1770; Evans 11575); Rowe, *Letters and Diary*, 196; *Boston Gazette*, Jan. 29, 1770; broadside "At a Meeting of the Merchants & Traders . . . 23d January 1770" (Boston: n.p., 1770; Evans 11576).

39. *Boston Gazette*, Feb. 12 and 19, 1770. On the role of Boston women in the coming of the revolution, see Alfred F. Young, *Liberty Tree: Ordinary People and the American Revolution* (New York: New York University Press, 2006), 100–143.

40. The name was sometimes given as *Snyder* or *Seider*. See *Boston Evening-Post*, Feb. 26, 1770; *Massachusetts Gazette*, March 1, 1770; *Boston Chronicle*, Feb. 22 and 25, 1770; *WSA*, 2: 60; Zobel, *Boston Massacre*, 174–75; Oliver, *Origin & Progress*, 84; Hutchinson, *History*, 3: 193–94; Wells, *Life*, 1: 304; "Boston," Feb. 19 and 26 and March 1 in *Boston Gazette*.

41. Quotations: "Boston" and "A Mourner," Feb. 26 and March 5 in *Boston Gazette*; Rowe, *Letters and Diary*, 197; Adams, *Diary and Autobiography*, 1: 350. See also Hutchinson, *History*, 3: 193–94; and Zobel, *Boston Massacre*, 178–79.

42. G. B. Warden, *Boston, 1689–1776* (Boston: Little, Brown, 1970), 226; Rowe, *Letters and Diary*, 196, 197; Shy, *Toward Lexington*, 307, 308–9; Jesse Lemisch, *Jack Tar vs. John Bull: The Role of New York's Seamen in Precipitating the Revolution* (New York: Garland Publishing, 1998), 125, 141–42.

43. Zobel, *Boston Massacre*, 181–84, quotation 182; and James Murray to Elizabeth Smith, March 12, 1770, in Nina M. Tiffany and Susan Lesley, eds. *Letters of James Murray, Loyalist* (Boston: Privately Printed, 1901), 162, 163.

44. Hutchinson, *History*, 3: 194–97; Hoerder, *Crowd Action*, 223–32; Zobel, *Boston Massacre*, 184–205; Frederic Kidder, *History of the Boston Massacre, March 5, 1770* (Albany, NY: Munsell, 1870), for objects thrown see 73–74, 93, 95, 205, 216, and for crowd quotations see 12, 204, 203, 205, 275; Record Commissioners of the City of Boston, *A Report [–the Eighteenth–] of the Record Commissioners of the City of Boston, Containing the Boston Town Records from 1770 through 1777* (Boston: Rockwell and Churchill, 1887), 1 (hereafter *BTR*, 18).

45. L. Kinvin Worth and Hiller B. Zobel, eds., *Legal Papers of John Adams*, 3 vols. (Cambridge, MA: Harvard University Press, 1965), 3: 266; Hoerder, *Crowd Action*, 230; Zobel, *Boston Massacre*, 182, 199; Kidder, *History*, 287.

46. Hutchinson, *History*, 3: 197–98; and *BTR*, 18: 1, 2–3, quotation 2.

47. *BTR*, 18: 2–3; Hutchinson as quoted in *WSA*, 1: 326; Adams as quoted in George Bancroft, *History of the United States, from the Discovery of the American Continent*, 10 vols. (Boston: Little, Brown, 1834–74), 6: 344; Oliver, *Origin & Progress*, 90; Tiffany and Lesley, *Letters of James Murray,* 164.

48. Dalrymple quotation from "An Anecdote," *Independent Chronicle*, March 31, 1794; Hutchinson, *History*, 3: 197–99, quotation 199; *Warren–Adams Letters*, 1: 9; Shy, *Toward Lexington*, 318; *WJA*, 10: 253; Frothingham, "The Sam Adams Regiments," 701.

49. *BTR*, 18: 3–4, 8–9, 10, 14–15, 16.

50. The town meetings occurred on March 6, 12, 13, 16, 22, 26 with the March 12 meeting being the regular meeting to elect local officials. See *BTR*, 18: 1–21.

51. *BTR*, 18: 14; Rowe, *Letters and Diary*, 199; *A Short Narrative of the Horrid Massacre in Boston, Perpetrated in the Evening of the Fifth Day of March, 1770* (Boston: Edes and Gill, 1770; Evans 11580).

52. *BTR*, 18: 15; Hutchinson, *History*, 3: 205, 207, 235; Worth and Zobel, *Legal Papers of John Adams*, 3: 3, 3–4n5, 12, quotation 12.

53. Wells, *Life*, 1: 328–30; and Worth and Zobel, *Legal Papers of John Adams*, 3: 3–4, 6–8, 11, 24n85.

54. *BTR*, 18: 12–13, 16, 20, quotations 12, 16.

55. *BTR*, 18: quotations 12, 20.

56. Bernard Bailyn, *The Ordeal of Thomas Hutchinson* (Cambridge, MA: Harvard University Press, 1974), 162; *JHRM*, 46: xii, 90, 91, 92, 93, quotation 91; James H. Stark, *The Loyalists of Massachusetts and the Other Side of the American Revolution* (Boston: James H. Stark, 1910), 326. For a detailed analysis of this controversy, see Donald C. Lord and Robert M. Calhoon, "The Removal of the Massachusetts General Court from Boston, 1769–1772," *Journal of American History* 55 (March 1969): 735–55.

57. *JHRM*, 46: 97–98.

58. *JHRM*, 46: 139, 145, 178, quotation 139; and Hutchinson, *History*, 3: 212.

59. *JHRM*, 46: 178–81, quotations 178.

60. *JHRM*, 46: 194–96.

61. *BTR*, 18: 21, 33; and Hutchinson, *History*, 3: 210–11.

62. Hutchinson, *History*, 3: 210, 212, 214; and Wells, *Life*, 1: 352, quoting Hutchinson letters of August 3 and 5, 1770.

63. *JHRM*, 47: 6–8, 12–13, 15–16, 17–22, 54–55, 62, quotations 20, 21; and Lord and Calhoon, "The Removal," 741–42.

64. *JHRM*, 47: 63, 78; *WSA*, 2: 19–35, quotations 22, 26; Hutchinson quoted in Wells, *Life*, 1: 347.

65. *WSA*, 2: 35–46, quotation 41; and on Verres s.v. "Gaius Verres" in http://encyclopedia.jrank.org.

66. Wells, *Life*, 1, 355–57, Hutchinson quotation 357.

67. James Warren and John Adams later added their names to the nays list. *JHRM*, 47: 89, 90–91, 97–98.

68. *JHRM*, 47: 94–95, 97, 99–101, 111, 112–13, 126–27, 128, 134–36,145–47, 149–50, 159–63, 169, 170–74, 179–82, 183–84, quotations 172, 182.

69. *JHRM*, 47: 113, 123, 124, 139.

70. Peter D. G. Thomas, *Townshend Duties Crisis: The Second Phase of the American Revolution 1767–1773* (Oxford: Oxford University Press, 1987), 171–76.

71. Schlesinger, *Colonial Merchants*, 224–33; and *WSA*, 2: 65, 58.

72. *WSA*, 2: 46–56, quotation 55.

73. *JHRM*, 47: 164.

74. *WSA*, 2: 56–61, quotations 57, 58; and John Alden, *Stephen Sayre: American Revolutionary Adventurer* (Baton Rouge: Louisiana State University Press, 1983), 8–10, 29, 32, 36–37, 42–43.

75. *WSA*, 2: 64–65, quotations 65.

76. *WSA*, 2: 65; and compare to Locke's *Second Treatise of Government*, §168.

77. Hutchinson, *History*, 3: 190; and compare to Gordon, *History*, 1: 347.

78. *WSA*, 1: 446–47, quotation 447.

CHAPTER 5

1. *LDC*, 1: 571; and *Warren-Adams Letters*, 1: 24.

2. Edmund S. Morgan and Helen M. Morgan, *The Birth of the Republic 1763–89*, 3rd ed. (Chicago: University of Chicago Press, 1992), 50–51; John Alden, *Stephen Sayre: American Revolutionary Adventurer* (Baton Rouge: Louisiana State University Press, 1983), 8–10, 29, 32, 36–37, 42–43; Wells, *Life*, 1: 375–76, Sayre quotation 375; *WSA*, 3: 18, 22; R. H. Lee, *Life of Arthur Lee, LL. D.*, 2 vols. (Boston: Wells and Lilly, 1829), 1: 222, 249, quotation 222.

3. *WSA*, 2, 150–51.

4. *WSA*, 2: 62–63, 70–77; L. Kinvin Worth and Hiller B. Zobel, eds., *Legal Papers of John Adams*, 3 vols. (Cambridge, MA: Harvard University Press, 1965), 3: 22, 312–14; Hutchinson, *History*, 3: 235–37.

5. *WSA*, 2: 77–100, 102–34, 135–62; Adams also referred to his three "Vindex" essays published in December 1769 (*WSA*, 1: 264–68, 269–78) that warned of the dangers posed by standing armies.

6. *WSA*, 2, 83–84, 89–90, 91, 142–44.

7. Quotations, *WSA*, 2: 92, 115, 81, and on the supposed conspiracy to assassinate, a point Adams made repeatedly, see, e.g., 87–88, 97–98, 113, 124–25.

8. *WSA*, 2: 79, 88–89, 118–21, quotations 89, 79.

9. Catherine B. Mayo, ed., "Additions to Thomas Hutchinson's 'History of Massachusetts Bay,'" *American Antiquarian Society Proceedings* 59, part 1 (April, 1949): 33–34 (hereafter Hutchinson, *History* Additions); Hutchinson, *History*, 3: 237, 239; Bernard Bailyn, *The Ordeal of Thomas Hutchinson* (Cambridge, MA: Harvard University Press, 1974), 169.

10. *WSA*, 2: 149, 150–51; and *Warren-Adams Letters*, 1: 20.

11. *WSA*, 2, 148–53, 163, 164, quotations 149, 150, 163.

12. *Warren-Adams Letters*, 1: 8–10, quotations 9.

13. *Boston Gazette*, March 11, 1771.

14. Record Commissioners of the City of Boston, *A Report [–the Eighteenth–] of the Record Commissioners of the City of Boston, Containing the Boston Town Records from 1770 through 1777* (Boston: Rockwell and Churchill, 1887), 47, 48, 52, quotations 48 (hereafter *BTR*, 18); James Lovell, *An Oration* . . . (Boston: Edes and Gill, 1771; Evans 12099); Hutchinson, *History*, 3: 241. Subsequent orations were to be delivered on the actual anniversary date, March 5.

15. *JHRM*, 47: 185–92, 222; and *WSA*, 2: 165.

16. *WSA*, 2: 164–67, quotations 165; and *JHRM*, 47: 242, 245–46, 252–53.

17. Adams, *Diary and Autobiography*, 2: 6–7, 10–11, 38–39, quotations 7, 10, 11.

18. As quoted in Wells, *Life*, 1: 393.

19. Hutchinson, *History*, 3: 243–44, quotations 244; Adams, *Diary and Autobiography*, 2: 20; John J. Waters Jr., *The Otis Family in Provincial and Revolutionary Massachusetts* (Chapel Hill: University of North Carolina Press, 1968), 178–80; Robert Z. Finkelstein, "Merchant, Revolutionary, and Statesman: A Re-appraisal of the Life and Public Services of John Hancock, 1737–1793," Ph.D. diss., University of Massachusetts, 1981, 226–27.

20. Oliver, *Origin & Progress*, 40–41; Hutchinson, *History*, 3: 248–49; Finkelstein, "Merchant, Revolutionary, and Statesman," 226–32.

21. *WSA*, 2; 172–75, quotations 174; *JHRM*, viii–ix, 48, 11, 62–64, quotations 62, 64; Hutchinson, *History*, 3: 249.

22. Wells, *Life*, 1: 120, 271–72, 337, 3: 154–55, 331, 428–29; the clerk's annual salary was not raised to £100 until 1774, just before Adams finished his service in that post (*JHRM*, 50: 218); Clifford K. Shipton et al., *Sibley's Harvard Graduates*, 18 vols. to date (Cambridge, MA: Harvard University Press, 1933–), 17: 334. Unfortunately, the Samuel Adams entry from the detailed 1771 tax records is one of the many entries that has not survived. See Bettye Hobbs Pruitt, ed., *The Massachusetts Tax Valuation List of 1771* (Boston: G. K. Hall, 1978), ix–xvi, 777.

23. Hutchinson quotations from Wells, *Life*, 2: 194; and from Hutchinson, *The Diary and Letters*, 1: 167.

24. Hutchinson as quoted in George Bancroft, *History of the United States, from the Discovery of the American Continent*, 10 vols. (Boston: Little, Brown, 1834–74), 6: 406; *WSA*, 2: 198–204, 230–31, 204–30, 237–45, 246–56, 297–306, quotations 298–99, 228 (and compare §155 of Locke's *Second Treatise of Government*); for Adams's early-summer attacks, see *WSA*, 2: 176–77, 186–88, 198–204.

25. *WSA*, 2: 246–50, quotations 246–47, 248. Hutchinson's salary was £1,500 sterling per year, which in Massachusetts currency of the day would have been about £2,000. See Bailyn, *Ordeal of Thomas Hutchinson*, 259; and John J. McCusker, *Money and Exchange in Europe and America, 1600–1775: A Handbook* (Chapel Hill: University of North Carolina Press, 1978), 142.

26. Quotations, *WSA*, 2: 245; and for additional emphasis on Locke, see especially 209–10, 224.

27. Quotations, *WSA*, 2: 221, 222, 213, 220; see also ibid., 234.

28. Quotations, *WSA*, 2: 249, 250, 251, 252, 256, 255, 251.

29. *WSA*, 2: 246–56, quotations passim; and Hutchinson as quoted in Wells, *Life*, 1, 438.

30. *WSA*, 2: 256–64, quotations 257; and compare to Hutchinson, *History*, 1: 272–73. See also "Valerius, surnamed Publicola (Or Puplicola)," at http://encyclopedia.jrank.org.

31. *WSA*, 2: 257–62, quotations passim.

32. See "A Proclamation for a Public Thanksgiving" (Boston: Richard Draper, 1771; Evans 12119). Contrast that with "A Proclamation for a Public Thanksgiving" (Boston: Richard Draper, 1770; Evans 11729); *WSA*, 2: 268–74, 274–76; and Hutchinson, *History*, 3: 249–59, quotations 249, 250.

33. Adams did not call this a series; the use of *series* is based on the fact that Adams emphasized political philosophy in these essays. The series, which included "Valerius Poplicola" (Oct. 28), "Cotton Mather" (Nov. 25), and the "Candidus" essays published between December 2, 1771, and January 27, 1772, are reprinted in *WSA*, 2: 256–64, 276–96, 297–306, 313–26.

34. Quotations, *WSA*, 2: 306, 326, 259, 278, 280, 286.

35. Hutchinson as quoted in Wells, *Life*, 1: 427; and in *WSA*, 2: especially 259–60, and quotations 262, 289.

36. Adams's next essay appeared in the *Boston Gazette* on April 20, and he did not produce another until October 5, 1772. See *WSA*, 2: 329–31, 332–37.

37. "In the evening," *Boston Gazette*, March 9, 1772; *Orations Delivered at the Request of the Inhabitants of the Town of Boston, to Commemorate the Evening of the Fifth of March, 1770 . . .* (Boston: Peter Edes, 1785; Evans 18997); Rowe, *Letters and Diary*, 225, 239–40, 264, 290.

38. Hutchinson, *History*, 3: 250–51; *JHRM*, 48: 119–32; Wells, *Life*, 1: 465–69, Hutchinson quotation 469.

39. *WSA*, 2: 329–31, quotation 330–31.

40. *WSA*, 2: 329–31; *BTR*, 18: 78; Hutchinson, *History*, 3: 255–56; Oliver as quoted in Finkelstein, "Merchant, Revolutionary, and Statesman," 234.

41. *WSA*, 2: 281–87, quotation 285.

42. *WSA*, 2:164 and Hutchinson, *History*, 3: 252.

43. Merrill Jensen, *The Articles of Confederation: An Interpretation of the Social-Constitutional History of the American Revolution, 1774–1781*, with additional prefaces (Madison: University of Wisconsin Press, 1970), 16–53, especially 41–47.

44. Hutchinson, *History*, 3: 256; Finkelstein, "Merchant, Revolutionary, and Statesman," 249–50; *JHRM*, 49: 8–9, 11–12, 15, 19, 21–22, 23, 29, 52.

45. Hutchinson, *History* Additions, 48; *JHRM*, 49: 90, 91, 102–3, 103–8, quotations 106, 104, 107, 104; Hutchinson, *History*, 3: 257.

46. *JHRM*, 49: 113, 120, 121, 127–32, 135, quotations 113, 121; Hutchinson, *History*, 3: 256–59, quotations 257; Leonard W. Labaree et al., eds., *The Papers of Benjamin Franklin*, 39 vols. (New Haven, CT: Yale University Press, 1959–), 19: 208–9 (hereafter Franklin, *Papers*); Adams to James Warren, July 17, 1772, as quoted in Wells, *Life*, 1: 481.

47. Richard D. Brown, *Revolutionary Politics in Massachusetts: The Boston Committee of Correspondence and the Towns, 1772–1774* (Cambridge, MA: Harvard University Press, 1970), 49–50, 52–53; *Warren-Adams Letters,* 1: 14–15; Hutchinson, *History*, 3: 259–60; Oliver, *Origin & Progress*, 107–11, quotation 107.

48. Brown, *Revolutionary Politics*, 52–53; and *WSA*, 2: 332–57, quotations 336, 334, 337.

49. Carl Bridenbaugh, *Mitre and Sceptre: Transatlantic Faiths, Ideas, Personalities, and Politics 1689–1775* (New York: Oxford University Press, 1962), 42, 96–97, 202–4, 231, 285–86, 326–27, 332; and Brown, *Revolutionary Politics*, vii–ix, 43–54. Thus John Adams's claim—first advanced in 1774 and most famously in a 1780 letter to Thomas Digges—that Samuel Adams invented the committee-of-correspondence system is tenable only when referring to the creation of a locally based system to link the communities of a single large governmental unit such as Massachusetts. See *WJA*, 4: 94–95; *John Adams to Thomas Digges, March 14, 1780, Papers of John Adams*, ed. Robert J. Taylor et al., 10 vols. (Cambridge, MA: Harvard University Press, 1977–), 9: 43–44.

50. Brown, *Revolutionary Politics*, 54–55; Hutchinson, *History*, 3: 259–60; *ANB* s.v. "Gerry, Elbridge"; *WSA*, 2: 337–39, 339–40, quotations 339, 340.

51. *WSA*, 2: 340–42, quotation 341; and *BTR*, 18: 88–90.

52. *WSA*, 2: 340–42, quotations, 341–42 passim.

53. *BTR*, 18: 90–92; and *WSA*, 2: 341.

54. *WSA*, 2: 346; *BTR*, 18: 92 93, quotation 93; Cooper as reprinted in Franklin, *Papers*, 20: 111–12, quotation 112; Hutchinson, *History* Additions, 51; Hutchinson, *History*, 3: 259–64.

55. Finkelstein, "Merchant, Revolutionary, and Statesman," 243–45; and Brown, *Revolutionary Politics*, 46–48, 59–61.

56. Brown, *Revolutionary Politics*, 62; *WSA*, 2: 346–50, quotations 346, 347, 350; *Warren-Adams Letters*, 1: 11–15, quotation 14.

57. Wells, *Life*, 1: 499–501; Brown, *Revolutionary Politics*, 70n27; *WSA*, 2: 350–74, 374n1, quotations 354, 369, 371; Bailyn, *Ordeal of Thomas Hutchinson*, 206.

58. *BTR*, 18: 93–94 for actions and 95–108 for the official text; *The Votes and Proceedings* . . . (Boston, 1772; Evans 12332), Brown, *Revolutionary Politics*, 80; *WSA*, 2: 379–80 quotation 379.

59. Gipson, *British Empire*, 12: 24–35; and *WSA*, 2: 389–92, 395–401, 427–28, quotation 401.

60. Adams, *Diary and Autobiography*, 2: 74; Brown, *Revolutionary Politics*, 124–31; *WSA*, 2: 392–95, 426.

61. Brown, *Revolutionary Politics*, 58–59, 65–66, Hutchinson quotation 65–66; and *WSA*, 2: 379–80, 382.

62. Henry H. Edes, "Memoir of Dr. Thomas Young, 1731–1777," CSM, *Transactions*, 1906–1907 (1910): 2–50; *WSA*, 2: 374–79, quotations 375, 376, 377, 376; Wells, *Life*, 2: 238–39n. Edes reprints the Davis item (18–21); for the Davis quotations, see 19, 18, 19, 20.

63. *WJA*, 10: 262–63; Mercy Otis Warren, *History of the Rise, Progress and Termination of the American Revolution interspersed with Biographical, Political and Moral Observations*, ed. Lester H. Cohen, 2 vols. (Indianapolis: Liberty Classics, 1989; originally published in 1805), 1: 116; James Sullivan, "Biographical Sketch," *Independent Chronicle*, Oct. 10, 1803; Wells, *Life*, 2: 422; Ira Stoll, *Samuel Adams: A Life* (New York: Free Press, 2008), 92, and see also 305n37, which undercuts Stoll's unconvincing exaggeration of the importance of religion in Adams's political efforts.

64. Brown, *Revolutionary Politics*, 68, 85, 99–100, Hutchinson quotations 68, 85; Adams, *Diary and Autobiography*, 2: 74–79, 3: 297–98; Finkelstein, "Merchant, Revolutionary, and Statesman," 245–50; *JHRM*, 49: 228.

65. *Warren-Adams Letters*, 1: 14; Richard Frothingham, *Life and Times of Joseph Warren* (Boston: Little, Brown, 1865), 221–22; Hutchinson, *History*, 3: 264–67; *WSA*, 3: 18–19.

66. Hutchinson, *History*, 3: 266–67; and Alan Bradford, ed., *Speeches of the Governors of Massachusetts 1765–1775* . . . (Boston: Russell and Gardner, 1818), quotations 336, 339, 337, 338, 340.

67. On authorship, see Hutchinson, *History*, 3: 269; Bancroft, *History*, 6: 448–49; Wells, *Life*, 2: 31–41n1; Frothingham, *Life and Times*, 223–24; *WJA*, 2: 310–13; E. Francis Brown, *Joseph Hawley: Colonial Radical* (New York: AMS Press, 1966), 124.

68. Bradford, *Speeches of the Governors*, 351–65, quotations 353, 355, 356, 364, 363, 364.

69. Ibid., 342–45, 368–96; Hutchinson, *History*, 3: 270–75, quotation 275; *JHRM*, 49: 298; Brown, *Revolutionary Politics*, 92–94.

70. *JHRM*, 49: 202, 206, 208, 210, 224, 228, 242, 243, 245, 247, 248, 255, 258, 260–61, 265, 280–82, 286, quotations 224, 282, 260; Franklin, *Papers*, 20: 125n4; Oliver, *Origin & Progress*, 107–11.

71. *JHRM*, 49: 290, 293–99, quotation 290; *The Speeches of His Excellency Governor Hutchinson, to the General Assembly of the Massachusetts-Bay* (Boston: Edes and Gill, 1773; Evans 12856); *WSA*, 3: 38; Frothingham, *Life and Times*, 223, 224n; Bernard Bailyn, *Ordeal of Thomas Hutchinson*, 218–20.

72. *BTR*, 18: 118, 120–25, quotations 120, 122, 124; March 30, 1773, broadside "By Direction of the Committee of Correspondence" (Evans 12688); *WSA*, 3: 3–12.

73. Committee of correspondence broadside of April 9, 1773 (Evans 12689); *WSA*, 3: 20; *BTR*, 18: 132–36.

74. *WSA*, 3: 18, 50; *Warren-Adams Letters*, 1: 245; Franklin, *Papers*, 20: 112 for Cooper quotation.

75. *WSA*, 3: 22; and Brown, *Revolutionary Politics*, 95, 101–5, 113–14, 122–23.

76. *WSA*, 3: 25–2, 32–33, quotations 26, 25, 26, 32–33; on imagery, compare "the Colonies are all embarked in the same bottom" (*WSA*, 3: 25) with his 1764 instructions statement that "His Majestys other Northern American Colonys are embarked with us in this most important Bottom" (*WSA*, 1: 5–6).

77. *BTR*, 18: 129.

78. *BTR*, 18: 132–36.

79. *BTR*, 18: 129, 131–34, quotations 129; and *WSA*, 3: 37–38, quotation 38.

80. Hutchinson, *History*, 3: 284; and *JHRM*, 50: 8–10.

81. *JHRM*, 50: 11–14, quotation 12; and Gipson, *British Empire*, 12: 34–38.

82. *WSA*, 3:122–25, quotation 123.

83. Franklin, *Papers*, 19: xxxii, 399–413; Bailyn, *Ordeal of Thomas Hutchinson*, 233–42; *WSA*, 3: 39–40.

84. *WSA*, 3: 39–40, 40–41; *JHRM*, 50: 26–27, 28, 29, 30, 40–41, 42, 43, 44, 58–61, quotations 27, 28; Hutchinson, *History*, 3: 286–88, quotation 288n.

85. Committee of Correspondence broadside of June 22, 1773 (Evans 12690); and Hutchinson, *History*, 3: 286–94.

86. Hutchinson, *History*, 3: 294; Bailyn, *Ordeal of Thomas Hutchinson*, 242–44, quotation 243; *Copies of Letters Sent to Great-Britain* (Boston, 1773; Evans 12818).

87. *JRHM*, 50: 75; *WSA*, 3: 44–45, 45–48, quotations 45, 46; and Richard Henry Lee, ed., *Life of Arthur Lee*, 2 vols. (Boston: Wells and Lilly, 1829), 1: 226.

88. Hutchinson, *History*, 3: 296–97n, quotations passim.

89. *JHRM*, 50: 98–99.

CHAPTER 6

1. Peter D. G. Thomas, *Townshend Duties Crisis: The Second Phase of the American Revolution 1767–1773* (Oxford: Oxford University Press, 1987), 245–57; Benjamin W. Labaree, *The Boston Tea Party* (New York: Oxford University Press, 1964), 12–13, 32, 50–51, 58–62, 74–76, 89–90, 258–59; Gipson, *British Empire*, 12: 12–17

2. Gipson, *British Empire*, 12: 75–76; *Pennsylvania Gazette*, Oct. 20, 1773; Francis S. Drake, ed., *Tea Leaves: Being a Collection of Letters and Documents Relating to the Shipment of Tea to the American Colonies in the Year 1773, by the East India Company* (Boston: A. O. Crane, 1884), xi–xii; Arthur M. Schlesinger, *The Colonial Merchants and the American Revolution* (New York: Columbia University, 1918), 279–81; Charles S. Olton, *Artisans for Independence: Philadelphia Mechanics and the American Revolution* (Syracuse, NY: Syracuse University Press, 1975), 49–63.

3. *WSA*, 3: 62–67, quotations 64.

4. Labaree, *Boston Tea Party*, 104–5.

5. "Proceedings of the North End Caucus," in Elbridge H. Goss, *The Life of Colonel Paul Revere*, 2 vols. (Boston: Howard W. Spurr Publisher, 1891), 2: 641–43, quotations 641, 642, 643; broadside of November 3, 1773 (Evans 12691); statement of Clarke as reprinted in James H. Stark, *The Loyalists of Massachusetts and the Other Side of the American Revolution* (Boston: James H. Stark, 1910), 406–7, quotations 406, 407; Labaree, *Boston Tea Party*, 142.

6. Record Commissioners of the City of Boston, *A Report [–the Eighteenth–] of the Record Commissioners of the City of Boston, Containing the Boston Town Records from 1770 through 1777* (Boston: Rockwell and Churchill, 1887), 141–44 passim (hereafter *BTR*, 18).

7. *BTR*, 18: 141–46, quotations 143, 146; and Labaree, *Boston Tea Party*, 50–52.

8. *BTR*, 18: 146–48; and Hutchinson, *History*, 3: 305–6, quotations 305, 306.

9. Richard D. Brown, *Revolutionary Politics in Massachusetts: The Boston Committee of Correspondence and the Towns, 1772–1774* (Cambridge, MA: Harvard University Press, 1970), 151, 158–59; and broadside of November 23, 1773 (Evans 12693).

10. Labaree, *Boston Tea Party*, 118–20; Adams as quoted in Brown, *Revolutionary Politics*, 161; broadside of November 29, 1774 (Evans 12774).

11. L. F. S. Upton, "Proceedings of Ye Body Respecting the Tea," *WMQ* 22 (April 1965): 287–300, quotations 290, 291; John Locke, *The Second Treatise of Government*, §168; Hutchinson, *History*, 3: 309.

12. Hutchinson, *History*, 3: 309–10, quotation 309; and Upton, "Proceedings," 292–96, quotations 293, 294, 296.

13. Hutchinson, *History*, 3: 304–5, 309–11, quotations 304, 310–11 passim; Hutchinson as quoted in Richard Frothingham, "Tea-Party Anniversary," MHS, *Proceedings*, 1873–1875 (1885), 170; Upton, "Proceedings," 300.

14. Labaree, *Boston Tea Party*, 95–103, 124–32, 146–47; Hutchinson quoted in Drake, *Tea Leaves*, lv; Hutchinson, *History*, 3: 311–13; Wells, *Life*, 2:118–19.

15. Attendance and shouted quotations, Labaree, *Boston Tea Party*, 138, 141; *WSA*, 3: 73–77, quotations 76; Upton, "Proceedings," 297–98; report on December 14 and 16 meetings, supplement to *Boston Gazette*, Dec. 27, 1773; Alfred F. Young, *The Shoemaker and the Tea Party: Memory and the American Revolution* (Boston: Beacon Press, 1999), 42–45; Wells, *Life*, 2: 124–25, 127.

16. Goss, *Life of Colonel Paul Revere*, 1: 128–32; and *Warren-Adams Letters*, 1: 20–21, quotation 21.

17. See, e.g., *WSA*, 3: 54, 104–5.

18. *JHRM*, 50: 145–48, 149– 51, 153–54, quotation 146; and Hutchinson, *History*, 3: 316–22.

19. *JHRM*, 50: 232–36; and Wells, *Life*, 2: 135–37.

20. Hutchinson, *History*, 3: 324–25; Wells, *Life*, 2: 137; *JHRM*, 50: 241, 243.

21. *JHRM*, 50: 101–3, 104, 129–31, quotations 130, 131; and Wells, *Life*, 2: 131.

22. Ward L. Miner, *William Goddard, Newspaperman* (Durham, NC: Duke University Press, 1962), 118–31; *Warren-Adams Letters,* 1: 24–25, 92–94, quotation 25; *WSA*, 3: 80–82, 85–92, quotations 81, 89.

23. *WSA*, 3: 18–25, 104–5, quotations 19, 105; *Orations Delivered at the Request of the Inhabitants of the Town of Boston* (Boston: Peter Edes, 1785; Evans 18997), 53–54; Robert Z. Finkelstein, "Merchant, Revolutionary, and Statesman: A Reappraisal of the Life and Public Services of John Hancock, 1737–1793," Ph.D. diss., University of Massachusetts, 1981, 452n72; John Cary, *Joseph Warren: Physician, Politician, Patriot* (Urbana: University of Illinois Press, 1961), 136.

24. *Warren-Adams Letters*, 1: 19–21, quotation 20; and *WSA*, 3: 71–73, 73–78, 78–80, 82–84, 92–94, quotations 93, 72, 83.

25. *WSA*, 3: 85–92, quotations 89, 90, 89; and Charles H. McIlwain, *The American Revolution: A Constitutional Interpretation* (New York: Macmillan, 1924), 91–95, 107–9n1, 110–15, 123n1, 144, 150.

26. Avon J. Murphy, "The Royal American Magazine," in Edward E. Chielens, ed., *American Literary Magazines: The Eighteenth and Nineteenth Centuries* (New York: Greenwood Press, 1986), 343–48.

27. *WSA*, 3: 57; and *Warren-Adams Letters*, 1: 24.

28. Wells, *Life*, 2:143n.

29. Peter D. G. Thomas, *Tea Party to Independence: The Third Phase of the American Revolution 1773–1776* (Oxford: Oxford University Press, 1991), 29–38, 51–52, quotation 30; David O. Murdoch, ed., *Rebellion in America: A Contemporary British Viewpoint, 1765–1783* (Santa Barbara, CA: Clio Press, 1979), 121–22, 160–62, quotations 121–22; Labaree, *Boston Tea Party*, 183–86; David Ammerman, *In the Common Cause: American Response to the Coercive Acts of 1774* (Charlottesville: University Press of Virginia, 1974), 5–6. The Murdoch volume provides facsimile reprintings of sections of the *Annual Register* that dealt with American issues.

30. "The Bostonians in Distress" (London: Printed for R. Sayer and J. Bennett, November 19, 1774). Despite the November 1774 publication date, it is not clear when the engraving was created. Still, while the engraver could not have been aware of the most recent developments in the colonies, he would have known about the arrival of troops in Boston in June and of the passage of additional Coercive Acts. As figure 6.3 reveals, one would need a sharp copy of the engraving to be able to read the language drawn from Psalm 107.

31. "Boston," *Boston Gazette*, May 16, 1775; Ammerman, *In the Common Cause*, 5; Labaree, *Boston Tea Party*, 219; BTR, 18: 166; Brown, *Revolutionary Politics*, 185–86, Bowler quotation 186.

32. *WSA*, 3: 106–7, 107–9, 109–11, quotations 106, 107; and broadside of May 12, 1774 (Evans 42562).

33. *BTR*, 18: 172–74, quotations 174; and Goss, *Life of Colonel Paul Revere*, 1: 143–44.

34. *WSA*, 3: 122–25, 125–27, 127–29, quotations 129, 126, 123, 124, 126, 124.

35. *BTR*, 18: 175–76, quotations 176.

36. *JHRM*, 50: 15; and *WSA*, 3: 122–25, 125–27.

37. Wells, *Life*, 1: 54; and *WSA*, 3: 127–29, quotations 128, 127, 128; and see also *WSA*, 2: 163.

38. Labaree, *Boston Tea Party*, 224; Gadsden to Adams, June 5 and 14, 1774, Richard Walsh, ed., *The Writings of Christopher Gadsden, 1746–1805* (Columbia: University of South Carolina Press, 1966), 94–99, quotations 97; Julian P. Boyd et al., eds., *The Papers of Thomas Jefferson*, 36 vols. (Princeton, NJ: Princeton University Press, 1950–), 1: 105–7, quotations 105, 106; George Bancroft, *History of the United States, from the Discovery of the American Continent*, 10 vols. (Boston: Little, Brown, 1834–74), 7: 56–58, Norfolk quotations 58; *Boston Gazette*, June 13, 1774; William Duane, ed., *Extracts from the Diary of Christopher Marshall . . .* (Albany, NY: Joel Munsell, 1877), 6; *Pennsylvania Packet*, June 6, 1774. Marshall did not discuss the fact that the Society of Friends, the Quakers, had issued an official statement saying that, while Quakers also supported the Bostonians, the shutting of businesses went against Quaker religious principles. See Philadelphia *Pennsylvania Packet*, June 1 and 6, 1774.

39. Rowe, *Letters and Diary*, 273–74; *Boston Gazette*, June 6, 1774; Murdoch, *Rebellion in America*, 162–63, quotation 163.

40. *WSA*, 3:136–39, quotations passim.

41. Arthur M. Schlesinger, *The Colonial Merchants and the American Revolution* (New York: Columbia University, 1918), 318–21, quotation 319n1; Cary, *Joseph Warren*, 140–46; *BTR*, 18: 176–78, quotations 176, 178; Albert Matthews, "The Solemn League and Covenant, 1774," CSM, *Transactions*, 1915–1916 (1917), 103–22. On the ever-increasing inclusive nature of the boycott movement in the colonies and not just in Massachusetts, see T. H. Breen, *The Marketplace of Revolution: How Consumer Politics Shaped American Independence* (New York: Oxford University Press, 2004).

42. *WSA*, 3: 138; and Rowe, *Letters and Diary*, 273–74.

43. Ammerman, *In the Common Cause*, 5–10, 12–17, Shippen quotation 15.

44. Stephen T. Riley and Edward W. Hanson, eds., *The Papers of Robert Treat Paine*, 3 vols., MHS, *Collections*, 87–89 (1992–2005), 2: 544–46, quotations passim. Compare to Wells, *Life*, 2: 174–78.

45. Gage, *Correspondence*, 1: 357; *JHRM*, 50: 264–65, 287–90, quotations 288, 290; Riley and Hanson, *Papers of Robert Treat Paine*, 3: 546; Gordon E. Kershaw, *James Bowdoin: Patriot and Man of the Enlightenment* (East Syracuse, NY: Salina Press, 1976), 80.

46. Hawley to John Adams, July 25, 1774, *WJA*, 9: 342–46, quotation 345; Wells, *Life*, 2: 190–96, quotation 193; Elizabeth E. Dana, ed., *The British in Boston: Being the Diary of Lieutenant John Barker of the King's Own Regiment from November 15, 1774, to May 31, 1776* (Cambridge, MA: Harvard University Press, 1924), 23; John Shy, *Toward Lexington: The Role of the British Army in the Coming of the American Revolution* (Princeton, NJ: Princeton University Press, 1965), 411–13.

47. *WSA*, 3: 133–34, 136–39, 139–40, 141–44, quotations 140, and compare to 134, 136, 139, 144.

48. *BTR*, 18: 173, 175, 178, 184–85, 186; and *WSA*, 3: 141–53 passim.

49. Wells, *Life*, 2: 207–10, Andrews quotation 209.

50. Cary, *Joseph Warren*, 147–51; and Bancroft, *History*, 7: 108–9.

CHAPTER 7

1. Wells, *Life*, 2: 209, 213–17; *WSA*, 1: 5, 2: 334, 359, quotation 334; Adams, *Diary and Autobiography*, 2: 114–22; Merrill Jensen, *The Articles of Confederation: An Interpretation of the Social-Constitutional History of the American Revolution, 1774–1781*, with additional prefaces (Madison: University of Wisconsin Press, 1970), 33–35; Arthur M. Schlesinger, *The Colonial Merchants and the American Revolution* (New York: Columbia University, 1918), 393–99.

2. Richard Frothingham, *Life and Times of Joseph Warren* (Boston: Little, Brown, 1865), 375–76, quotations 376; and *WSA*, 2: 156–57, 3: 206, quotations 2: 157, 3: 206.

3. *Journal of the Proceedings of the Congress, Held at Philadelphia, September 5, 1774* (Philadelphia: William and Thomas Bradford, 1774; Evans 13737); *The Petition . . . to the King* (Philadelphia: William and Thomas Bradford, 1774; Evans 13738); Joseph Galloway, *Historical and Political Reflections on the Rise and Progress of the American Rebellion* (London: G. Wilkie, 1780), 63–67, quotations 66, 64.

4. William Gordon, *The History of the Rise, Progress, and Establishment, of the Independence of the United Sates of America*, 4 vols. (London: Charles Dilly, 1788), 1: 347; Charles H. Metzger, *The Quebec Act: A Primary Cause of the American Revolution* (New York: The United States Catholic Historical Society, 1936); Woody Holton, *Forced Founders: Indians, Debtors, Slaves, and the Making of the American Revolution in Virginia* (Chapel Hill: University of North Carolina Press, 1999), 32–38, 208–9, Lee quotation 36.

5. Galloway to William Franklin, Sept. 5, 1774, *LDC*, 1: 27; and Deane's Sept. 3 diary entry, ibid., 19; Edmund C. Burnett, *The Continental Congress* (New York: Macmillan, 1941), 33–34.

6. Galloway to William Franklin, Sept. 5, 1774, *LDC*, 1: 27; Adams, *Diary and Autobiography*, 2: 115; Burnett, *Continental Congress*, 33–34.

7. *WSA*, 3: 157–59, quotation 158; and *LDC*, 1: 31–32, 55, 60, 74–75, quotations 60, 74.

8. *LDC*, 1: 55.

9. Galloway, *Historical and Political Reflections*, 67, 68; and *JCC*, 1: 31–39, 39–40, 41, 43, 43–53, quotations 33, 35. Galloway's depiction of "continual expresses" is supported by the pattern of Adams's correspondence. See *LDC*, 1: 72n1.

10. Galloway, *Historical and Political Reflections*, 68, 70–82; *JCC*, 1: 43–53; Burnett, *Continental Congress*, 47–50.

11. *JCC*, 1: 63–73; and Charles H. McIlwain, *The American Revolution: A Constitutional Interpretation* (New York: Macmillan, 1924), 114–15, 152, 191.

12. *JCC*, 1: 75–81, quotations 76, 79, 80; Thomas Balch, ed., *The Examination of Joseph Galloway, Esq. by a Committee of the House of Commons* (Philadelphia: Seventy-Six Society, 1855), 55, 52; Willi Paul Adams, *The First American Constitutions: Republican Ideology and the Making of the State Constitutions in the Revolutionary Era*, expanded ed. (Lanham, MD: Rowman & Littlefield, 2001), 315–27.

13. *JCC*, 1: 81–101, 104–5, 115–22; and Gage, *Correspondence*, 1: 384.

14. Julian P. Boyd et al., eds., *The Papers of Thomas Jefferson*, 36 vols. (Princeton, NJ: Princeton University Press, 1950–), 1: 141–43, quotation 142.

15. Galloway, *Historical and Political Reflections*, 67.

16. Josiah Quincy, *Memoir of the Life of Josiah Quincy Jun. of Massachusetts* (Boston: Cummings, Hilliard, 1825), 258; and Balch, *Examination of Joseph Galloway*, 7n.

17. SAP, Elizabeth Adams to Samuel Adams, Sept. 12, 1774.

18. Wells, *Life*, 2: 247; *BTR*, 18: 190–96; Cary, *Joseph Warren*, 164–67; *The Journals of Each Provincial Congress of Massachusetts in 1774 and 1775, and of the Committee of Safety* . . . (Boston: Dutton and Wentworth, 1838), 19, 23, 29, 32–34, 38–40, 41, 41, 42, 47–48, 50, quotations 47, 50; "By the Governor" proclamation of November 10, 1774 (Boston: M. Draper, 1774; Evans 13414).

19. *WSA*, 3: 162–63.

20. *Journals of Each Provincial Congress*, 49, 51, 55, 56–59, 62–67, 69, 70–71; *JCC*, 1: 122; Wells, *Life*, 2: 274–75; Richard D. Brown, *Revolutionary Politics in Massachusetts: The Boston Committee of Correspondence and the Towns, 1772–1774* (Cambridge, MA: Harvard University Press, 1970), 224.

21. *BTR*, 18: 176, 177, 178, 205–12; and *WSA*, 3: 174–79, 181–82, 189–94, 200–205, quotation 174.

22. *WSA*, 3: 194–98, quotations 195, 196; and Wells, *Life*, 2: 278–81.

23. *BTR*, 18: 214–16; and *WSA*, 3: 199–200, 206.

24. Thomas Bolton, *An Oration Delivered March Fifteenth 1775* . . . (Boston, 1775; Evans 13840), quotations 1, 2–3 passim.

25. *WSA*, 3: 179–80, 182–88, quotation 182; Cary, *Joseph Warren*, 211–13; Wells, *Life*, 2: 274–77.

26. *Journal of Each Provincial Congress*, 116, 118–20; *WSA*, 3: 211–13, quotations 212, 213; Wells, *Life*, 2: 281–84; Colin G. Calloway, *The American Revolution in Indian Country: Crisis and Diversity in Native American Communities* (Cambridge: Cambridge University Press, 1995), 1–25.

27. *Journal of Each Provincial Congress*, 135–39, 143–44.

28. Wells, *Life*, 2: 288–92; Peter O. Hutchinson, ed., *The Diary and Letters of His Excellency Thomas Hutchinson, Esq.*, 2 vols. (London: S. Low, Marston, Searle & Rivington, 1883–1886), 1: 302 for Dartmouth quotation; Murdoch, *Rebellion in America*, 172–74; George III quoted in Cary, *Joseph Warren*, 159; Gage, *Correspondence*, 1: 396–97, 2: 179–83, 673–74, quotation 183; John R. Alden, *General Gage in America: Being Principally a History of His Role in the American Revolution* (Baton Rouge: Louisiana State University Press, 1948), 237–45; Elizabeth E. Dana, ed., *The British in Boston: Being the Diary of Lieutenant John Barker of the King's Own Regiment from November 15, 1774 to May 31, 1776* (Cambridge, MA: Harvard University Press, 1924), 31–37; Gordon, *History*, 1: 479.

29. *LDC*, 1: 361–62, quotation 362; *WSA*, 3: 220, 222, 239, 256; *Warren-Adams Letters*, 1: 54–56, 124–25, 132–34, quotations 132, 125.

30. *LDC*, 1: 362; and WSA, 3: 239, 256.

31. *LDC*, 26: xvi; *WSA*, 3: 226; *Warren-Adams Letters*, 1: 109–11.

32. "By his Excellency," June 12, 1774, broadside proclamation (Boston: n.p., 1774; Evans; 14184); *WSA*, 3: 214, 215–16, 217–18, 220–21, 221–23, 227–29, 239–40, 270–71 (but for the correct date, see *LDC*, 1: 421–22), quotations 220, 221, 214, 220, 270; *Warren-Adams Letters*, 1: 89–90, quotation 90. Adams was not saying his son had been imprisoned; he was saying Boston itself had become a prison.

33. *WSA*, 3: 214–18, 220–23, 227–29, 239–40, 266–68, quotations 266, 217, 221, 214, 216, 218, 239, 218, 217, 222; *Warren-Adams Letters*, 1: 203–4; Elizabeth Adams "Obituary," *Independent Chronicle*, May 5, 1808; Linda K. Kerber, *Women of the Republic: Intellect and Ideology in Revolutionary America*, with an added preface (New York: W. W. Norton, 1986).

34. *Warren-Adams Letters*, 1: 279; and *WJA*, 10: 264.

35. Peter Force, ed., *American Archives . . .* , 9 vols. (Washington, DC: M. St. Clair Clarke and Peter Force, 1837–53), series 4, 2: 507; and John Ferling, *Almost a Miracle: The American Victory in the War of Independence* (New York: Oxford University Press, 2007), 38–39.

36. *JCC*, 2: 52–53, 64, 67, 98–99, 102, 3: 114–15, 193–94, 265–66, 306–7, 416, 420, 488–89, quotation 3: 488; *WSA*, 3: 248; *LDC*, 2: 506–508, quotation 507; *Warren-Adams Letters*, 1: 69–70, quotation 70; Jefferson as quoted in Henry S. Randall, *The Life of Thomas Jefferson*, 3 vols. (New York: Derby & Jackson, 1858), 1: 182.

37. *Warren-Adams Letters*, 1: 54–56, 140–42, quotations 141, 55.

38. *LDC*, 2: 506–8, 3: 602n, quotations 3: 602n, 2: 507; *Warren-Adams Letters*, 1: 54–56, 69–70, quotation 69; *WSA*, 3: 273–77, 277–81, 281–85, 303–5, 337–38, quotation 281.

39. *WSA*, 3: 281–85, 294–95, 296–99, quotations 283.

40. *JCC*, 2: 83–84, quotation 83.

41. *JCC*, 3: 298, 319, 326–27, quotation 319.

42. *JCC*, 2, 344, 403–4 and *Warren-Adams Letters*, 1: 169–73, quotations 170, 171.

43. *Warren-Adams Letters*, 1: 191–92, quotation 191; and *WSA*, 3: 253–54, 281–85, quotation 284.

44. *JCC*, 3: 54, 63–64n1; John K. Alexander, "'A Year . . . Famed in the Annals of History': Philadelphia in 1776," in *Philadelphia 1776–2076: A Three Hundred Year View*, Dennis Clark, ed. (Port Washington, NY: Kennikat Press, 1975), 19–20, George III quotations 20; *WSA*, 3: 257–58, 261–66, quotations 257; Eric Foner, *Tom Paine and Revolutionary America* (New York: Oxford University Press, 1976), 71–87.

45. *LDC*, 3: 63–64n1, 138–39n1; *WSA*, 3: 258–61, quotations 260; Wells, *Life*, 2: 357–59; Burnett, *Continental Congress*, 129–31. Adams's assertion that Franklin supported this plan is not supported by any source I have unearthed.

46. *WSA*, 261–66, quotations 264, 265, 266, 263.

47. *Warren-Adams Letters*, 1: 224–25, quotation 225; *WSA*, 3: 273–76, 277–81, 281–85, 285–88, quotations 281, 284–85; Pauline Maier, *American Scripture: Making the Declaration of Independence* (New York: Knopf, 1977), especially 47–96.

48. *Warren-Adams Letters*, 1: 244–45, 255–56, quotations 245, 256.

49. *JCC*, 5: 425–26, 427, 428–29, 433–34, 506–7, 510–15, quotation 507.

50. The men's strikingly similar phrasing suggests that this story was likely a staple of loyalist conversation in Philadelphia. Still, while he did not suggest his

cousin openly boasted of this once independence was declared, John Adams, as noted, made the same point about Samuel having striven to convince talented young men of the importance of protecting American rights against British encroachments. See Galloway, *Historical and Political Reflections*, 109–10, quotations 109, 110; Edward H. Tatum Jr., ed., *The American Journal of Ambrose Serle, Secretary to Lord North, 1776–1778* (San Marino, CA: The Huntington Library, 1940), 167; *WJA*, 10: 364. Given such views, it seemed only natural, as the title page of this London publication boldly proclaimed, that "An Oration Delivered at the state-House in Philadelphia to A very numerous Audience" on August 1, 1776, was "By SAMUEL ADAMS." The author wrote in Adams's style; the rhetorical close trumpeting the writer's desire "that these *American States* may never *cease to be free and independent*" certainly expressed his thoughts. The work was translated into French and German. The oration, however, was a fabrication. The person who created it in England put Adams's name on it to give it credibility, which it did in spite of the obvious problem that the supposed August 1, 1776, oration was written as if independence had not yet been declared. See Wells, *Life*, 2: 439–40; the document itself is reprinted in ibid., 3: 405–22, quotations 405, 422.

51. SAP, Samuel Adams Wells transcription of John's April 29, 1774, comment attached to a copy of the July 18, 1694, will of Joseph Adams.

52. Mercy Otis Warren, *History of the Rise, Progress and Termination of the American Revolution . . .*, ed. Lester H. Cohen, 2 vols. (Indianapolis: Liberty Classics, 1989; originally published Boston, 1805), 1: 116.

53. Margherita A. Hamm appears to have been the first author to claim that Patrick Henry said "the good that was to come from these Congresses was owing to the work of Adams." But she did not provide a source for the quotation; thus, while other of Hamm's undocumented quotations are accurate, her quotation of Henry cannot be accepted at face value. See Hamm's *Builders of the Republic: Some Great Americans Who Have Aided in the Making of the Nation* (New York: James Pott & Company, 1902), 136.

54. George W. Corner, ed., *The Autobiography of Benjamin Rush . . .* (Princeton, NJ: Princeton University Press, 1948), 139–40, quotations 140, 139; *LDC*, 26: xxxvii; Adams, *Diary and Autobiography*, 2: 182; *ANB*, s.v. "Houston, John"; Wells, *Life*, 2: 413; James C. Ballagh, ed., *The Letters of Richard Henry Lee*, 2 vols. (New York: Macmillan, 1911–14), 2: 197.

55. John Adams made these observations in 1818. See *WJA*, 10: 365.

56. Jefferson to Samuel Adams Wells, May 12, 1819, in Andrew A. Lipscomb and Albert E. Bergh, eds., *The Writings of Thomas Jefferson: Monticello Edition*, 20 vols. (Washington, D.C.: The Thomas Jefferson Memorial Association, 1904–05), 15: 191–202, quotations 201; Jefferson to Benjamin Waterhouse, Jan. 31, 1819, in Paul L. Ford, ed., *The Writings of Thomas Jefferson*, 10 vols. (New York: G. P. Putnam's Sons, 1892–99), 10: 123–24, quotation 124; "Memorandum of Mr. Jefferson's Conversations" in December 1824, *The Writings and Speeches of Daniel Web-*

ster, 18 vols. (Boston: Little, Brown, 1903), 17: 364–73, quotation 370; Jefferson as quoted in Randall, *Life of Thomas Jefferson*, 1: 182. See also *LDC*, 13: 167–69.

CHAPTER 8

1. *WSA*, 4: 88–90, 227–30, 260–62, 268–71, quotations 269, 90.

2. *JCC*, 4: 114–15, 194, 5: 419; 6: 915, 985, 1039, 1041, 7: 32, 11: 537; *Independency the Object of the Congress in America* (London: John, Francis, and Charles Rivington, 1776), 15; Frank More, *The Diary of the Revolution: A Centennial Volume* (Hartford, CT: J. B. Burr, 1876), 670; Jefferson to Samuel Adams Wells, May 12, 1819, in Andrew A. Lipscomb and Albert E. Bergh, eds., *The Writings of Thomas Jefferson: Monticello Edition*, 20 vols. (Washington, DC: The Thomas Jefferson Memorial Association, 1904–1905), 15: 191–202, quotation 201; and Jefferson as quoted in Henry S. Randall, *The Life of Thomas Jefferson*, 3 vols. (New York: Derby & Jackson, 1858), 1: 182.

3. *WSA*, 3: 229–32, 250–54, 310–11, 4: 218, quotations 3: 310, 4: 218; and *JCC*, 5: 762–63.

4. *WSA*, 3: 321–27, quotations 323, 327; Howard H. Peckham, *The War for American Independence: A Military History* (Chicago: University of Chicago Press, 1958), 41–51, Washington quotation 51; Mary Beth Norton, *Liberty's Daughters: The Revolutionary Experience of American Women, 1750–1800*, with added preface (Ithaca, NY: Cornell University Press, 1996), 202–4.

5. *Pennsylvania Journal*, Dec. 19, 1776; and *JCC*, 6: 1041–46, quotation 1043.

6. Peckham, *War for American Independence*, 51–57; and *WSA*, 3: 370–72, 376–79, 382–84, 386–88, quotations 370, 387.

7. *WSA*, 3: 373–74, quotations 374.

8. *JCC*, 2: 109–10; *WSA*, 3: 387–88; H. James Henderson, *Party Politics in the Continental Congress* (New York: McGraw-Hill, 1974), 112–14; John Ferling, *Almost A Miracle: The American Victory in the War of Independence* (New York: Oxford University Press, 2007), 80–83, 217–19.

9. St. Clair as quoted in Ferling, *Almost A Miracle*, 220; Charles Deane, ed., "Extracts from Dr. Belknap's Note-books," MHS, *Proceedings*, 1875–1876 (1876), 95–96; *JCC*, 8: 585, 596; *WSA*, 3: 389–92, quotation 392; Bernard Knollenberg, *Washington and the Revolution: A Reappraisal—Gates, Conway, and the Continental Congress* (New York: Macmillan, 1940), 12–20, Clinton quotation 20.

10. *LDC*, 7: 405; *JCC*, 8: 603–4; *WSA*, 3: 386–88, quotation 388.

11. Knollenberg, *Washington and the Revolution*, 18–20; Henderson, *Party Politics*, 118–20; Douglas S. Freeman, *George Washington: A Biography—Leader of the Revolution* (New York: Charles Scribner's Sons, 1951), 581–611, Washington quotation 609; *LDC*, 8: 330n1, 570–73, quotation 571; Ferling, *Almost A Miracle*, 282–84, 437–38, 571, quotation 571; John Ferling, *The Ascent of George Washington: The*

Hidden Political Genius of an American Icon (New York: Oxford University Press, 2009), 140–64. Of the authors cited, Knollenberg and Henderson, like Ferling, undercut the argument that a Conway Cabal existed; Freeman says it existed but is circumspect about members of Congress being involved. The most strident, and unconvincing, assertion not only that the Conway Cabal existed but that it centered on actions of Massachusetts delegates to the Congress appears in John C. Fitzpatrick, *George Washington Himself: A Common-Sense Biography Written from His Manuscripts* (Indianapolis: Bobbs-Merrill, 1933), 333–51. The Conway Cabal thesis is directly challenged in "Rush and Washington," *Letters of Benjamin Rush*, ed. L. H. Butterfield, 2 vols. (Princeton, NJ: Princeton University Press, 1951), 2: 1197–1208. For a claim by someone who knew him that Samuel was part of a Conway Cabal, see William Gordon, *The History of the Rise, Progress, and Establishment, of the Independence of the United Sates of America*, 4 vols. (London: Charles Dilly, 1788), 3: 54–60. When he read Gordon's comment, Samuel flatly denied the charge and said he supposed Gordon's inaccurate depiction stemmed from a misunderstanding of comments Adams had made about trying to get General Schuyler cashiered. (See Deane, "Extracts from Dr. Belknap's Note-books," 95–96.) Edmund C. Burnett, who is especially important because he edited the original *Letters of Members of the Continental Congress* published between 1921 and 1936, said the Conway Cabal existed. See his *Continental Congress* (New York: Macmillan Company, 1941), 267–70, 279–97. However, the editors of the modern *LDC*, who finished their labors in 2000, offered a different and, when considered in the light of the relevant evidence, more convincing interpretation. The editors, who typically use the term *so-called* when referring to the Conway Cabal, conclude that a very few revolutionaries, not including Samuel Adams, would have liked to see Washington replaced. However, "there does not appear to have been any serious effort to replace Washington as commander in chief." See, *LDC*, 8: xxvii, 314–15n5, 330–31n1, 549n5, 657n5, 9: 359n1, 744n4, quotation 8: 330n1. The same interpretation is advanced in the useful brief analysis offered in Jonathan G. Rosie, *The Politics of Command in the American Revolution* (Syracuse, NY: Syracuse University Press, 1975), 188–202.

12. *LDC*, 9: 743, 744n4; *WSA*, 4: 1–5, 21–24, 61–62, 83, 139–40, 244–48, quotations 140, 1–3 passim, 22, 61; on Count Daun, s.v "Daun (Dhaun), Leopold Josef, Count Von (1705–1766)," at hhtp://encyclopedia.jrank.org.

13. Wells, *Life*, 3: 78; *LDC*, 6: 637–38, quotation 637; *WSA*, 4: 175–79, 217–18, 221–23, quotations 177, 221.

14. *WSA*, 4: 191–96, quotations 193, 192.

15. Marquis de Chastellux, *Travels in North America in the Years 1780, 1781, and 1782*, trans. and ed. Howard C. Rice Jr., 2 vols. (Chapel Hill: University of North Carolina Press, 1963), 1: 142.

16. Adams was so well known for doing this, and, moreover, his reputation was such that when John Almon—who had extensive American contacts and who published the well-respected English publication *The Remembrancer, or, Impartial Repository of Public Events*—speculated on the authorship of an important June 1778

item signed "An American," he attributed it to Adams. So too did William Wells and Cushing, the editor of *WSA*. The sentiments expressed in that "An American" letter closely matched those of Adams, but he did not author it or any of the subsequent three letters in the series. They were crafted by Gouverneur Morris, a fellow member of Congress. See Wells, *Life*, 3: 16–26; *WSA*, 4: 25–38; *LDC*, 10: 154–62; *DNB* s.v. "Almon, John."

17. *WSA*, 3: 373–74, 4: 1–5, 188–91, 268–71, quotations 3: 374, 4: 5, 191, 269.

18. *WSA*, 1: 322–25, 400–405, 410–11, quotations 323, 400, 410.

19. *WSA*, 3: 359–60, 361–62, 4: 12–14, 61–62, 75–77, 275–76, quotations 4: 77, 3: 361; Peckham, *War for American Independence*, 199–200; Robert M. Calhoon, *The Loyalists in Revolutionary America* (New York: Harcourt Brace Jovanovich, 1965), especially 479–83, 504–5.

20. *JCC*, 3: 459–60, 4: 17–22, 6: 915, 7: 291, quotations 3: 460, 4: 20, 6: 915, 7: 291.

21. Claude H. Van Tyne, *The Loyalists in the American Revolution* (New York: Macmillan, 1902), 237–40, 318–19; *WSA*, 3: 360–62, 379 81, quotations 361; James H. Stark, *The Loyalists of Massachusetts and the Other Side of the American Revolution* (Boston: James H. Stark, 1910), 55, 137–40, 141–44.

22. *JCC*, 5: 431, 433, 546–57, quotations 546, 552; and Merrill Jensen, *The Articles of Confederation: An Interpretation of the Social-Constitutional History of the American Revolution, 1774–1781*, with additional prefaces (Madison: University of Wisconsin Press, 1970), 126–39.

23. *WSA*, 3: 298, 379–81, quotations 298, 380; *JCC*, 9: 907–35, quotation 908; Jensen, *Articles of Confederation*, 140–60.

24. *LDC*, 26: xvii; *WSA*, 4: 6–8, 11, quotation 6; Record Commissioners of the City of Boston, *A Report [–the Eighteenth–] of the Record Commissioners of the City of Boston, Containing the Boston Town Records from 1770 through 1777* (Boston: Rockwell and Churchill, 1887), 294, 295, 298, quotation 298.

25. *WSA*, 4: 41; and Jensen, *Articles of Confederation*, 235–38.

26. *WSA*, 4: 19–21, 121–22; Wells, *Life*, 3: 74–79; Barbara Clark Smith, "Food Rioters and the American Revolution," *WMQ* 51 (Jan. 1994): 3–38.

27. *WSA*, 3: 365–66, 4: 6–8, 19–21, quotations 4: 20, 3: 365, 4: 19, 4: 6.

28. *WSA*, 3: 227–29, 4: 9–10, 45–48, 225–27, 227–29, 253–55, quotations 3: 228, 4: 255, 10, 46, 226.

29. John Adams quoting Samuel Adams, Jared Sparks, ed., *The Diplomatic Correspondence of the American Revolution*, 12 vols. (Boston: Hale and Gray & Bowen, 1829–30), 4: 257; *WSA*, 3: 275–77; William C. Stinchcombe, *The American Revolution and the French Alliance* (Syracuse, NY: Syracuse University Press, 1969), 7–13.

30. *JCC*, 6: 1039, 11: 688, 751–57; *WSA*, 3: 337–38, 4:1–5, 21–24, 45–48, 58–65, 68–72, 79–81, quotations 4: 3, 48; Adams to James Warren, July 15, 1778, *LDC*, 10: 280–81, quotation 280; description of the ceremonies in B. J. Lossing, *The Pictorial Field-Book of the Revolution; or, Illustrations, by Pen and Pencil, of the History, Biography, Scenery, Relics, and Traditions of the War for Independence*, 2 vols. (New York: Harper Brothers, 1851–1852), 2: 856n.

31. Adams to Warren, June 1, 1778, *LDC*, 10–11, quotation 10; *WSA*, 4: 21–24, 45–48, 58–65, 68–72, 79–81, 287–91, quotation 62; Ferling, *Almost A Miracle*, 523–39, 541–42, 546–47, Lord North quotation 541.

32. *WSA*, 4: 281–82, 287–91, quotations 289, 281.

33. *WSA*, 3: 235, 4: 148–50, 176–79, 260–62, 271–72, quotations 4: 261, 177, 149; *JCC*, 6: 1055–56; Mary A. Giunta et al., eds., *The Emerging Nation: A Documentary History of the Foreign Relations of the United States under the Articles of Confederation, 1780–1789*, 3 vols. (Washington, DC: National Historical Publications and Records Commission, 1996), 1: 103.

34. *JCC*, 13: 239–44, 14: 956–62, quotations 13: 241; Giunta, *Emerging Nation*, 1: 189 *LDC*, 26: xvii.

35. Charles W. Akers, *The Divine Politician: Samuel Cooper and the American Revolution in Boston* (Boston: Northeastern University Press, 1982), 275–303, 355, de Valnais quotations 280, 279, 298; and Giunta, *Emerging Nation*, 1: 189.

36. *LDC*, 2: 73–74, 153–54, 253–54, 417, 3: 82–83, 215, 266, 291, 313–15, 320–23, 11: 312–20, 393n3, 13: 312–20, 348–49, quotations 3: 320; *JCC*, 8: 721, 9: 946–47, 11: 799–801, 802, 14: 928–30, quotation 14: 930; Julian P. Boyd, "Silas Deane: Death by a Kindly Teacher of Treason?" *WMQ* 26 (April, July, and Oct. 1959): 165–87, 319–42, 515–50; E. James Ferguson, *The Power of the Purse: A History of American Public Finance, 1776–1790* (Chapel Hill: University of North Carolina Press, 1961), 70–105; Louis W. Potts, *Arthur Lee: A Virtuous Revolutionary* (Baton Rouge: Louisiana State University Press, 1981), especially 145–46, 157–63, 179–218. A useful narrative of the Deane-Lee controversy appears in Henderson, *Party Politics*, 187–217.

37. Henderson, *Party Politics*, 192–99; *LDC*, 26: xii; and Lovell to Adams, July 8, 1779, *LDC*, 13: 167–69, quotation 167. For discussion of the authorship of the essay and for the quotations taken from that essay, see *LDC*, 13: 168–69n2. Lowell responded by saying the author of the essay was a member of the nefarious "inveterate Party" that he, Adams, and other virtuous men were seeking to thwart. See *LDC*, 13: 190 and also 363. It is worth noting that Langworthy's depiction matches well with the analyses John Adams, Thomas Jefferson, and Joseph Galloway offered about the methods Adams used to exert great influence in the first and second congresses.

38. *LDC*, 11: 395–97, quotations 396; and *WSA*, 3: 228, 4: 113–15, 115–18, 118–20, 126–28, quotations 3: 228, 4: 115, 120.

39. The dating of "America Triumphant" is based on the fact that the publishers of *Weatherwise's Town and Country Almanack, for . . . 1782*, which used the political cartoon as a frontispiece, dated their comments to readers September 26, 1781 (Boston: Nathaniel Coverly and Robert Hodge, 1781; Evans 17354).

40. *WSA*, 4: 56–57, 132, 137, 139, 141, 178, 180, 225–27, 227–28, 249, 254–55, 259, 260, quotation 226; *LDC*, 16: 139; Wells, *Life*, 3: 154–55.

41. *WSA*, 3: 293, 348, 362–64, 372–73, 399, 403, 408–9, 4: 56–57, 65–66, 131, 209–10, 219–20, quotations 4: 56, 65, 209, 210n1.

42. *WSA*, 4: 223–25, quotations 223, 224.

43. *WSA*, 3: 348–50, 403–4, quotations 348, 349, 404; on traditional attitudes toward women and the influence of the American Revolution on such attitudes, see Norton, *Liberty's Daughters*; Linda K. Kerber, *Women of the Republic: Intellect and Ideology in Revolutionary America*, with an added preface (New York: W. W. Norton, 1986); Nancy F. Cott, *The Bonds of Womanhood: "Women's Sphere" in New England, 1780–1835*, 2nd ed. (New Haven, CT: Yale University Press, 1997); Rosemarie Zagarri, *Revolutionary Backlash: Women and Politics in the Early American Republic* (Philadelphia: University of Pennsylvania Press, 2007).

44. *WSA*, 3: 318–20, 355–56, 362–64, 367–70, 403–4, 4: 24–25, 41, 65–66, 77–78, 95–98, quotations 3: 319, 404; and *LDC*, 6: 186n5.

45. *WSA*, 4: 95–98, 128–31, quotations 97, 131 129. Adams did not, however, resign the post. See Wells, *Life*, 3: 69, 79.

46. *WSA*, 4: 244–48, 258–60, quotations 245, 259.

47. *LDC*, 17: xx, 58n2, 220; *JCC*, 20: 450, 628; *WSA*, 4: 223n1, 258–59; Record Commissioners of the City of Boston, *A Volume of Records [–the Thirtieth–] relating to the Early History of Boston, Containing Boston Marriages From 1752 to 1809* (Boston: Municipal Printing Office, 1903), 419, 448.

48. Wells, *Life*, 3: 101, 137–38, 153; *WSA*, 4: 93–95; Record Commissioners of the City of Boston, *A Report [–the Twenty-sixth–] of the Record Commissioners of the City of Boston, Containing the Boston Town Records from 1778 to 1783* (Boston: Rockwell and Churchill, 1895), 196, 200 (hereafter *BTR*, 26).

49. *WSA*, 4: 260–62, 262–63, 263–64, 265–67, 270–71, 279–80, quotations 261, 263; *BTR*, 26: 219; *LDC*, 18: xviii, 19: 26–28; Wells, *Life*, 3: 152–53; *ANB*, s.v. "McKean, Thomas."

50. Giunta, *Emerging Nation*, 1: 185–90, 273–78, 283–84, quotations 273, 275, 284.

51. Ibid., 1: 313–16, quotations 313–14 passim; and Samuel F. Bemis, *The Diplomacy of the American Revolution*, rev. ed. (Bloomington: Indiana University Press, 1957), 232–36, 238, 241–42, 261, quotation 261. While he provides only superficial coverage of the post-1776 efforts to preserve the fisheries, Christopher P. Magra explains why New Englanders considered them so important. See Magra's *The Fisherman's Cause: Atlantic Commerce and Maritime Dimensions of the American Revolution* (Cambridge: Cambridge University Press, 2009).

52. *WSA*, 3: 243–46, 408–9, 4: 284–85, quotations 3: 409, 4: 285; and Bemis, *Diplomacy*, 254, 259.

CHAPTER 9

1. *Warren-Adams Letters*, 1: 191–92, quotation 192, and *WSA*, 3: 346–48, quotations 347–48 passim.

2. *JCC*, 2: 83–84; *Warren-Adams Letters*, 1: 169–73; *WSA*, 3: 243–46, quotations 246, 245.

3. *WSA*, 3: 229–30, 242–43, 244–45, 246–48, quotation 247; and *LDC*, 2: 373–74.

4. *Warren-Adams Letters*, 1: 171.

5. See, e.g., *WSA*, 3: 237–38, 244, 245–46, 246–48, 4: 211–14.

6. *WSA*, 3: 229–32, 246–48, 250–54, quotations 250, 251.

7. *WSA*, 3: 243–46, quotations 245, 244.

8. *WSA*, 3: 229–32, 232–38, quotations 231, 237; and Ellen E. Brennan, *Plural Office-Holding in Massachusetts, 1760–1780: Its Relation to the "Separation" of Departments of Government* (Chapel Hill: University of North Carolina Press, 1945), especially 27–35.

9. Wells, *Life*, 2: 51–52, 313–14, 332–33; and *WSA*, 3: 229–32, 4: 68, 227–30, quotations 3: 231, 236.

10. *WSA*, 3: 229–32, 232–38, 243–46, 4: 24–25, quotations 3: 236, 235, 4: 25.

11. *WSA*, 3: 229–32, 232–38, quotations 231, 235, 236, 237.

12. *WSA*, 3: 250–51, 4: 16–17, quotation 3: 251.

13. *WSA*, 3: 285–88, quotations 285, 286.

14. Wells, *Life*, 2: 17–18, 333n, 3: 136–37; *WSA*, 3: 325–26, 411–12, 4: 223–25, 236–39, quotations 3: 326, 4: 225, 238, 412; George W. Corner, ed., *The Autobiography of Benjamin Rush* (Princeton, NJ: Princeton University Press, 1948), 139–40, quotations passim.

15. *WSA*, 4: 236–39, quotations 237, 236, 238, and see also, e.g., 188–91.

16. *WSA*, 2: 374–79; and *WJA*, 10: 262–63.

17. Robert Z. Finkelstein, "Merchant, Revolutionary, and Statesman: A Reappraisal of the Life and Public Services of John Hancock, 1737–1793" (Ph.D. diss., University of Massachusetts, 1981), 290–91, 295, 301–3, 306–20, 323–29, quotation 328; *Warren-Adams Letters*, 1: 377–79; *WSA*, 3: 416–17.

18. *Warren-Adams Letters: Being chiefly a correspondence among John Adams, Samuel Adams, and James Warren*, vol. 2 *1778–1814*, MHS, *Collections*, 73, (1925), 9–10, 11–14, 27–29 (hereafter *Warren-Adams Letters*, 2); *WSA*, 4: 19–21, 45–48, 49–50, 52–54, 63–65, quotations 49, 65; *LDC*, 26: xviii.

19. *WSA*, 4: 67–68, 92–93, quotations 67, 68.

20. *WSA*, 4: 123–25, quotation 124–25.

21. *Warren-Adams Letters*, 2: 9–10, 11–14, 21–29; and *WSA*, 4: 95–98, 139–42, quotations 140, 97.

22. *WSA*, 3: 305, 311–13; Oscar Handlin and Mary Handlin, eds., *The Popular Sources of Political Authority: Documents on the Massachusetts Constitution of 1780* (Cambridge, MA: Harvard University Press, 1966), 18–23, 171–73; Robert J. Taylor, ed., *Massachusetts, Colony to Commonwealth: Documents on the Formation of Its Constitution, 1775–1780* (Chapel Hill: University of North Carolina Press, 1961), 13–15, 36–37, 48–49, 90–92, 112; Ronald M. Peters Jr., *The Massachusetts*

Constitution of 1780: A Social Compact (Amherst: University of Massachusetts Press, 1978), 18–20.

23. *LDC*, 13: 71n1; Taylor, *Massachusetts, Colony to Commonwealth*, 116–17; Peters Jr., *Massachusetts Constitution*, 20–22; Record Commissioners of the City of Boston, *A Report [–the Twenty-sixth–] of the Record Commissioners of the City of Boston, Containing the Boston Town Records from 1778 to 1783* (Boston: Rockwell and Churchill, 1895), 83–84 (hereafter *BTR*, 26).

24. Adams, *Diary and Autobiography*, 2: 400–401n1, 414n1, 3: 324, 359, 4: 210, quotation 2: 400n1; Peters Jr., *Massachusetts Constitution*, 13–14, 23–26; *Journal of the Convention for Framing a Constitution of Government for the State of Massachusetts Bay, from the Commencement of Their First Session, September 1, 1779, to the Close of Their Last Session, June 16, 1780* (Boston: Dutton and Wentworth, 1832), 23–24, quotations 24; *WJA*, 4: 215–18, 220–30; Wells, *Life*, 3: 80–87n1.

25. *Journal of the Convention*, 216–21, quotation 216; and *WSA*, 4: 182–83.

26. *Journal of the Convention*, 222–27, quotations 222, 225.

27. Ibid., 228–49; Wells, *Life*, 3: 83n; *WJA*, 4: 231–32n1.

28. *WJA*, 4: 221–24n1, 245, quotations 221, 222n; Samuel Elliot Morison, "The Struggle over the Adoption of the Constitution of Massachusetts, 1780," MHS, *Proceedings*, 1916–1917 (1917), 369–81; *WSA*, 4: 52; *Journal of the Convention*, 218.

29. *Journal of the Convention*, 213–14, quotations 214; and *BTR*, 26: 127. For Adams's linkage of the diffusion of knowledge and virtue among the people, see, e.g., *WSA*, 3: 237, 4: 124–25, 236.

30. *Journal of the Convention*, 186–87; and *WSA*, 4: 236, 252.

31. Marquis de Chastellux, *Travels in North America in the Years 1780, 1781, and 1782*, trans. and ed. Howard C. Rice Jr., 2 vols. (Chapel Hill: University of North Carolina Press, 1963); 1: 142, 160–64, quotation 161; Robert J. Taylor, *Western Massachusetts in the Revolution* (Providence, RI: Brown University Press, 1954), 142–43; Elisha P. Douglass, *Rebels and Democrats: The Struggle for Equal Political Rights and Majority Rule during the American Revolution* (Chapel Hill: University of North Carolina Press, 1955), 208–13.

32. Chastellux, *Travels*, 1: 160–63, quotation 162; Morison, "Struggle," 396–401; Andrew C. McLaughlin, "American History and American Democracy," *American Historical Review* 20 (Jan. 1915): 255–76, quotations 265.

33. Chastellux, *Travels*, 1: 160–63, quotations 162, 163; Douglass, *Rebels and Democrats*, 6–9, 317–26; Willi Paul Adams, *The First American Constitutions: Republican Ideology and the Making of the State Constitutions in the Revolutionary Era*, expanded ed., (Lanham, MD: Rowman & Littlefield, 2001), 315–27.

34. Chastellux, *Travels*, 1: 163.

35. Ibid., 162; *WSA*, 4: 306; *Journal of the Convention*, 216–18, quotation 217.

36. *WSA*, 4: 199–200, 203, 205–6, 219–20, 227–30, 233, quotations 199, 229, 200.

37. *WSA*, 4: 207– 9, 211–12, 245–46, quotation 211. On Massachusetts political groupings in this period, see Van Beck Hall, *Politics Without Parties: Massachusetts, 1780–1791* (Pittsburgh: University of Pittsburgh Press, 1972); and Jackson T. Main, *Political Parties before the Constitution* (Chapel Hill: University of North Carolina Press, 1973), 83–119.

38. *WSA*, 4: 212–14, 219–20, 221–23, 225–27, 227–30, 236–38, 241–42, 242–44, 244–48, quotations 229, 230.

39. *WSA*, 3: 237–38; and Brennan, *Plural Office-Holding*, 110–19.

40. *WSA*, 4: 221–23, 225–27, 227–30, 410, quotations 228, 221; and Wells, *Life*, 3: 116, 357, 381.

41. *WSA*, 4: 137–38, 225–27, quotations 226, 137–38.

42. *WSA*, 4: 212–14, 250–53, 255–58, quotations 214, 213.

43. *WSA*, 4: 250–53, quotations passim.

44. *BTR*, 26: 193; and Hall, *Politics Without Parties*, 133–34.

45. *WSA*, 4: 255–58, quotations 256, 258, 257–58.

46. Charles Warren, "Samuel Adams and the Sans Souci Club in 1785," MHS, *Proceedings*, 1926–1927 (1927), 319–20; and *WSA*, 4: 236–39.

47. *BTR*, 26: 220, 234–35, 310, 313–14; and *WSA*, 4: 270.

48. Record Commissioners of the City of Boston, *A Volume [–the Thirty-first–] of the Records Relating to the Early History of Boston, Containing Boston Town Records from 1784 to 1796* (Boston: Municipal Printing Office, 1903), 16–22, 35–36, 41, 46, quotations 16, 17 (hereafter *BTR*, 31).

49. *WSA*, 4: 315–16, quotations 315, 316; "A Proclamation . . . June 8, 1785" (Boston: Adams and Nourse, 1785; Evans 19085); Jacqueline B. Carr, *After the Siege: A Social History of Boston, 1775–1800* (Boston: Northeastern University Press, 2005), 197–200, 205, 207–8, 218–21.

50. *Acts and Laws . . . of Massachusetts* [May 27–June 25, 1789] (Boston: Adams and Nourse, 1789; Evans 21945), 18–21, quotations 19.

51. *BTR*, 31: 205–6, 206–7, 208–10, 211, quotations 206, 210, 211; Wells, *Life*, 1: 4; Joel Perlmann and Dennis Shirley, "When Did New England Women Acquire Literacy?" *WMQ* 48 (Jan. 1991): 50–67.

52. Jon C. Teaford, *The Municipal Revolution in America: Origins of Modern Urban Government, 1650–1825* (Chicago: University of Chicago Press, 1975), 35–44, 67–68, 69–71; John K. Alexander, *Render Them Submissive: Responses to Poverty in Philadelphia, 1760–1800* (Amherst: University of Massachusetts Press, 1980), 42–46, 72–73, 198n62, 203n34; *WSA*, 4: 303–6, quotations 306.

53. *BTR*, 31: 25, 40–41, 42, quotations 42; Boston Town Meeting, *Two Plans for forming the Town of Boston into an Incorporated City* (Boston: n.p., 1784; Evans 18375); reports of meetings and "Extract of a letter," *Massachusetts Centinel*, May 15, June 5, July 10, 1784; Josiah Quincy, *A Municipal History of the Town and City of Boston . . .* (Boston: C. C. Little and J. Brown, 1852), 23–26.

54. *BTR*, 31: 45–48; and *Massachusetts Centinel*, Dec. 18, 1784.

55. "PLAN proposed," *Boston Gazette*, Feb. 7, 1785; "*A Friend to Truth and good Order*," *Independent Chronicle*, Feb. 10, 1785; *BTR*, 31: 49, 51, 68, 88.

56. According to the *Centinel*, the town meeting was asked to consider "'Whether Boston shall continue the humble name of *town*, or aspire to the honorary and dignified appellation of CITY.'" See the Oct. 22, 1785, broadside "Notification" (Evans 18937); see also *Massachusetts Centinel*, Oct. 26, 1785.

57. *BTR*, 31: 88–94 passim, 96; reports on town meeting, *Massachusetts Centinel*, Oct. 26 and 29, 1785; reports on town meetings, *American Recorder*, Dec. 13 and 20, 1785; Quincy, *A Municipal History*, 32–33, 40–41.

58. *WSA*, 4: 365; and Samuel Adams death notice, *Independent Chronicle*, Oct. 3, 1803.

CHAPTER 10

1. Jacques Pierre Brissot de Warville, *New Travels in the United States of America* (London: J. S. Jordan, 1792), 117.

2. *WSA*, 4. 287–91, quotations 288, 289, and Record Commissioners of the City of Boston, *A Report [—the Twenty-sixth—] of the Record Commissioners of the City of Boston, Containing the Boston Town Records from 1778 to 1783* (Boston: Rockwell and Churchill, 1895), 310, 312–14, quotations 314 (hereafter *BTR*, 26).

3. Thomas A. Bailey, *A Diplomatic History of the American People*, 8th ed. (New York: Appleton-Century Crofts, 1969), 54–58; *WSA*, 4: 308–12, quotation 312; David E. Mass, "The Massachusetts Loyalists and the Problem of Amnesty, 1775–1790," in Robert C. Calhoon, Timonthy M. Barnes, and George A. Rawlyk, eds. *Loyalists and Community in North America* (Westport, CT: Greenwood Press, 1994), 65–74.

4. Edgar E. Hume, ed., *General Washington's Correspondence concerning the Society of the Cincinnati* (Baltimore: Johns Hopkins Press, 1941), xi–xviii, xxiii–xxv, 1–8, 152–64, quotations 2, 5; *WSA*, 4: 293–97, 298–303, quotations 296, 301, 302; Van Beck Hall, *Politics Without Parties: Massachusetts, 1780–1791* (Pittsburgh: University of Pittsburgh Press, 1972), 157–58.

5. SAP, Adams to Gerry, Sept. 19, 1785.

6. SAP, Adams to Christopher Gadsden, Nov. 29, 1784; and *WSA*, 4: 277–80, 285–87, 323–26, quotations 279, 286–87.

7. *JCC*, 18: 958–59.

8. Jackson Turner Main, *The Antifederalists: Critics of the Constitution, 1781–1788* (Chapel Hill: University of North Carolina Press, 1961), 106–10; *JCC*, 18: 958–59, 25: 578–87, 606–13; SAP, Adams to "a Gentleman in Connecticut," Sept. 9, 1783 (recipient identification based on *WSA*, 4: 303); SAP, Noah Webster to Adams, March 24, 1784; *WSA*, 4: 303–6.

9. *LDC*, 17: 31n4; and *WSA*, 3: 344, 4: 272–74, 285–87, quotations 273, 287.

10. James Trecothick, *The Life of Elbridge Gerry*, 2 vols. (Boston: Wells and Lilly, 1828–29), 1: 411–15; *WSA*, 4: 272–74, 285–87, 292–93, 308–12, quotations 311, 292, 293; SAP, Adams to Richard Henry Lee, Sept. 23, 1783.

11. *WSA*, 4: 293–97; SAP, Adams to Gerry, Sept. 19, 1785; *DHRC*, 7: xxxii–xxxv; *Boston Magazine* (July 1785): 275–76; *Boston Magazine* (June 1786): 318.

12. Robert J. Taylor, *Western Massachusetts in the Revolution* (Providence, RI: Brown University Press, 1954), 103–27, quotation 112.

13. *WSA*, 4: 287–91, 303–6, quotations 305.

14. Taylor, *Western Massachusetts*, 128–34, 136–39, 143–49; Sept. 2, 1786, broadside, "A Proclamation" (Boston: Adams and Nourse, 1786; Evans 19789); Record Commissioners of the City of Boston, *A Volume [–the Thirty-first–] of the Records Relating to the Early History of Boston, Containing Boston Town Records from 1784 to 1796* (Boston: Municipal Printing Office, 1903), 124–32 (hereafter *BTR*, 31); Thomas C. Avery, *Life of James Sullivan: With Selections from His Writings*, 2 vols. (Boston: Phillips, Sampson and Company, 1859), 1: 195.

15. Sept. 13, 1786, broadside, "A Proclamation"(Boston: Adams and Nourse, 1786; Evans 19788); Taylor, *Western Massachusetts*, 150–53; "An Address from the General Court" (Boston: Adams and Nourse, 1786; Evans 19781), quotation 25.

16. Taylor, *Western Massachusetts*, 158–61; and David P. Szatmary, *Shays' Rebellion: The Making of an Agrarian Insurrection* (Amherst: University of Massachusetts Press, 1980), 101–8. Szatmary erred when he claimed Samuel Adams was among the political leaders who "speculated in continental and state securities." That assertion is based on a misreading of material from the work of Van Beck Hall who documents that it was Samuel's son who received "large sums of interest" based on the securities he held. See Szatmary, *Shays' Rebellion*, quotation 11 and corresponding 141n46; and compare to Van Beck Hall, *Politics Without Parties: Massachusetts, 1780–1791* (Pittsburgh: University of Pittsburgh Press, 1972), 44n47.

17. This often-cited quotation comes from Wells (*Life*, 3: 246), who, despite normally being careful about documentation, does got give a source for the statement, and I have not found any contemporary source for it. And, given Adams's 1782 response to crowd actions and his support for pardoning protestors, the quoted statement's suggestion that *any* challenge to a law should equal death seems questionable. Still, while the exact wording may not be from Adams, he did embrace its general sentiments at least as it applied to a massive armed rebellion against a republican government. See ibid., 392.

18. Robert A. Feer, *Shays's Rebellion* (New York: Garland Publishing, 1988), 415–28.

19. Marcus Cunliffe, *George Washington: Man and Monument* (London: Collins, 1959), 114–19; Main, *Antifederalists*, 207–9, 249; *DHRC*, 1: 185–90.

20. *DHRC*, 5: 506–7, 627–28, 628–34, 656–57, quotation 506; and Helen R. Pinkney, *Christopher Gore: Federalist of Massachusetts, 1758–1827* (Waltham, MA: Gore Place Society, 1969), 23–24.

21. *WSA*, 4: 323–26, quotations 324, 325; Main, *Antifederalists*, xi–xiii; *WSA*, 4: 325.

22. *DHRC*, 5: 627–28; and Pinkney, *Christopher Gore*, 3–4, 10–14, 23–24.

23. *DHRC*, 5: 752, 753, 6: 1335, 7: 1572, quotations 6: 1335, 5: 752.

24. *DHRC*, 6: 1175–81, 1526–27; and *BTR*, 26: 125–26, 128.

25. *DHRC*, 6: 1182, 1183n2, 1334–36; *BTR*, 26: 125–26; Record Commissioners of the City of Boston, *A Report [–the Eighteenth–] of the Record Commissioners of the City of Boston, Containing the Boston Town Records from 1770 through 1777* (Boston: Rockwell and Churchill, 1887), 211.

26. *DHRC*, 6: 1346, 1358.

27. Main, *Antifederalists*, 227, 239; *DHRC*, 7: 1553–54; James C. Ballagh, ed., *The Letters of Richard Henry Lee*, 2 vols. (New York: Macmillan, 1911 14), 2: 447.

28. *DHRC*, 6: 1116–21, 1378–79, 7: 1546, 1560, 1570–71, 1571–72, 1157–73, 1579–80, quotation 7: 1572.

29. *DHRC*, 6: 1118–19, 1381–87, 1394–96, 1402n14, 7: 1558, quotations 6: 1381, 1395.

30. *DHRC*, 6: 1452–54, 1490, quotation 1453; and Samuel B. Harding, *The Contest over the Ratification of the Federal Constitution on the State of Massachusetts* (Cambridge, MA: Harvard University Press, 1896), 95–99.

31. *DHRC*, 6: 1461–67, 1476–78, 1491; and see also *LDC*, 25: 93.

32. *DHRC*, 6: 1248–49; Wells, *Life*, 3: 255; Forrest McDonald, *We the People: The Economic Origins of the Constitution* (Chicago: University of Chicago Press, 1958), 184 85n82, 200.

33. Trecothick, *Life of Elbridge Gerry*, 2: 85–86, quotation 86; "April Meeting," March 10, and "A correspondent," March 31, 1789, in *Herald of Freedom*; Brissot de Warville, *New Travels*, 117–19, quotations 117–118 passim.

34. *WSA*, 4: 241–42; newspaper quotations: "Belisarius," *Boston Gazette*, Dec. 13, 1788; "Common Sense" and "A Correspondent," *Independent Chronicle* Dec. 18, 1788; "An Elector," *Boston Gazette*, Dec. 15, 1788. See also from 1788: "A.B.," Dec. 15 and "A Bostonian," Dec. 18 in *Herald of Freedom*; "A Friend to Union" and "a Caucus," *Massachusetts Centinel*, Dec. 17; "Civis," "The Independent Electors," "An Old Whig," and "A Bostonian," *Independent Chronicle*, Dec. 18.

35. Quotations: "Constitutionalist," Dec. 13, and "Mentor," Dec. 17, 1788, in *Massachusetts Centinel*; "Marcus," *Herald of Freedom*, Dec. 18, 1788. See also: "An Elector" and "From Correspondents," *Massachusetts Centinel*, Dec. 17, 1788; "A Real Mechanic," *Herald of Freedom*, Dec. 18, 1788.

36. *BTR*, 31: 183; and "Suffolk District," *Independent Chronicle*, Dec. 25, 1788.

37. Quotations: "An American," *Massachusetts Centinel*, Dec. 24, 1788; "Bostoniensis," *Boston Gazette*, Dec. 29, 1788; "Candidus" and "We are authorized," *Massachusetts Centinel*, Dec. 31, 1788. See also "A correspondent," *Herald of Freedom*, Dec. 22, 1788, and "An American," *Massachusetts Centinel*, Dec. 24, 1788.

38. Main, *The Antifederalists*, 266–71; Orin G. Libby, *The Geographical Distribution of the Vote of the Thirteen States on the Federal Constitution, 1787–8* (Madison:

University of Wisconsin, 1894); Staughton Lynd, "The Mechanics in New York Politics, 1774–1788," *Labor History* 5 (Fall 1964): 241–46.

39. "The elections," Dec. 20, 1788, "An American," Dec. 24, 1788, and April 8, 1789, in *Massachusetts Centinel*; *Independent Chronicle*, April 9, 1789; Brissot de Warville, *New Travels*, 118–19; *WSA*, 4: 332, 354n1; for Adams's honorary degree, see http://www.commencement.harvard.edu/background/hon_deg.html.

40. *WSA*, 4: 326–27, 329–38, quotations 334, 327, 331.

41. *DHRC*, 6: 1453–54n1; Jacob E. Cooke, ed., *The Federalist* (Middletown, CT: Wesleyan University Press, 1961), 521–30, 575–87, quotation 524, 526; John C. Miller, *The Federalist Era 1789–1801* (New York: Harper & Row, 1960), 55–60.

CHAPTER 11

1. Quotation from "Gratitude," *Salem Gazette*, April 1, 1794; "A Federalist," *Independent Chronicle*, April 6, 1795; Adams death notice, *Independent Chronicle*, Oct. 3, 1803. See also *WSA*, 4: 365.

2. Quotations from "A Republican," *Independent Chronicle*, March 17, 1794; "Republican Federalist List," *Independent Chronicle* Extra, April 1, 1796; and "Annual Election," *Independent Chronicle*, April 7, 1796. See also Joseph Charles, *The Origins of the American Party System* (New York: Harper & Row, 1961; originally published 1956); John C. Miller, *The Federalist Era 1789–1801* (New York: Harper & Row, 1960), 99–125; Stanley Elkins and Eric McKitrick, *The Age of Federalism* (New York: Oxford University Press, 1993), 257–302; Anson E. Morse, *The Federalist Party in Massachusetts to the Year 1800* (Princeton, NJ: The University Press, 1909), 64–65.

3. Rogers M. Smith, "Constructing American National Identity: Strategies of the Federalists" in Doron Ben-Atar and Barbara B. Oberg, eds., *Federalists Reconsidered* (Charlottesville: University Press of Virginia, 1998), 19–20, 27–28, 28–29; Matthew Seccombe, "From Revolution to Republic: The Later Political Career of Samuel Adams, 1774–1803," Ph.D. diss., Yale University, 1978, 292–95; "Speech of His Excellency . . ." (Boston: Adams & Larkin, 1793; Evans 25790); *Resolves of the General Court of the Commonwealth of Massachusetts . . . Twenty-Ninth Day of May . . . 1793* (27 September, 1793), (Boston: Adams & Larkin, 1793; Evans 25785), 28; SAP, Hancock to Adams, Aug. 31, 1793, and Adams to Hancock, Sept. 3, 1793, along with Adams circular letter, Oct. 9, 1793; James H. Stark, *The Loyalists of Massachusetts and the Other Side of the American Revolution* (Boston: James H. Stark, 1910), 138, 288; Philip B. Kurland and Ralph Lerner, eds., *The Founders' Constitution*, 5 vols. (Chicago: University of Chicago Press, 1987), 5: 407–29.

4. Morse, *Federalist Party*, 67–71, 215; John H. Stewart, *A Documentary Survey of the French Revolution* (New York: Macmillian, 1951), 112–15, 167–69, 181–82, 195–98, 224–25, 229–30; Alexander DeConde, *Entangling Alliance: Politics &*

Diplomacy under George Washington (Durham, NC: Duke University Press, 1958), 173–80; Charles D. Hazen, *Contemporary Opinion of the French Revolution* (Baltimore: Johns Hopkins Press, 1897), 139–45, 150–51, 152–53, 164–74.

5. Morse, *Federalist Party*, 70–71; DeConde, *Entangling Alliance*, 180–81; Philip S. Foner, *The Democratic-Republican Societies, 1790–1800: A Documentary Sourcebook of Constitutions, Addresses, Resolutions, and Toasts* (Westport, CT: Greenwood Press, 1976), 7, 255–72; Hazen, *Contemporary Opinion*, 188–89.

6. DeConde, *Entangling Alliance*, 185–90, 206–34, 283–310; Morse, *Federalist Party*, 72–73; Charles M. Thomas, *American Neutrality in 1793: A Study in Cabinet Government* (New York: Columbia University Press, 1931), 212–20; Harold C. Syrett, ed., *The Papers of Alexander Hamilton*, 26 vols. (New York: Columbia University Press, 1961–1987), 15: 314–16.

7. Gore to Rufus King, Aug. 1, 4, 8, 1793, in Charles R. King, ed., *The Life and Correspondence of Rufus King*, 6 vols. (New York: G. P. Putnam's Sons, 1894–1900), 1: 487–88, 490–92, 493–94.

8. SAP, Dannery to Adams, Nov. 25, 1793, and Adams to Dannery, Nov. 27, 1793; Syrett, *Papers of Alexander Hamilton*, 15: 383–84n.11.

9. Because *WSA* contains Adams's speech (4: 353–60) but not the General Court's response, the material cited here comes from *Resolves of the General Court of the Commonwealth of Massachusetts . . . the Twenty-ninth Day of May, Anno Domini, 1793; and from thence . . .* (to 15 January 1794) (Boston: Adams and Larkin, 1794; Evans 27289), 33–35, quotations passim.

10. *WSA*, 4: 361–63, quotations 361, 362 passim; and Morse, *Federalist Party*, 126–27.

11. Because all of the newspaper items cited here and elsewhere concerning this election appeared in 1794, the citations will not include the year of publication. Quotations: "Candour," March 5, and "An Elector," April 5, in *Columbian Centinel*; "Veritas," *Independent Chronicle*, March 13; "Rights of Man," *Columbian Centinel*, March 22. See also Morse, *Federalist Party*, 140–43; and "Veritas," *Columbian Centinel*, March 22. For rare public statements declaring a person would not serve if elected, see "A Card," April 2, 1794, and "Francis Dana," Feb. 1, 1797, in *Columbian Centinel*.

12. Although he said "entre nous" that he had, in fact "declined" the invitation to be a candidate for governor, Cushing never made a public statement to that effect. Quotations from Cushing to Increase Sumner, Feb. 24, 1794, reprinted in W. H. Sumner, "Memoir of Governor Increase Sumner," *New England Historical and Genealogical Register* 8 (April 1854): 117–18.

13. Quotation from report of meeting, *Columbian Centinel*, March 29; and see also in *Columbian Centinel* the following: "Truth," March 8; "An Elector," March 15; "For the Centinel," March 26; "Harmony," April 2; "A True Republican," "An Inhabitant of the Town of Hingham," and "Civis," April 5. In the *Independent Chronicle* see "An Enemy to Electioneering," March 27.

14. "Union" and "Song," March 1, and "Trimsharp," March 12, in *Columbian Centinel*. See also "Old Times," *Independent Chronicle*, April 7.

15. "Queries," *American Apollo*, March 20; and *Columbian Centinel*, March 19 and 26.

16. "An Elector," *Salem Gazette*, March 25; "Querist" and "An Independent Republican," *Columbian Centinel*, April 2; "Communications," *Independent Chronicle*, April 3.

17. "Querist" and "Civis," *Columbian Centinel*, April 5.

18. Quotations found in the following: "State Suability," *Salem Gazette*, March 18; "Consistency," March 6, and "Extract," March 31, in *Independent Chronicle*. See also the following in the *Independent Chronicle*: "State Union," March 17; "Suability of the States Considered," March 20; "A. B.," March 31; "An Elector," March 31. In the *Columbian Centinel* see the following: "Honorius," March 22; and "A Citizen," March 29. And finally see Morse, *Federalist Party*, 143–44; and *DAB* s.v. "Cushing, William."

19. Quotation from "An Elector," *Columbian Centinel*, April 5. See also "Whisper," *Independent Chronicle*, April 3; and "A Citizen," *Columbian Centinel*, March 29.

20. Quotations are from the following: *Columbian Centinel*, April 2; "An Elector," March 31, and "An Independent Farmer," 6 March in *Independent Chronicle*. See also *Independent Chronicle*: "Boston Massacre," March 6; "State Union," March 17; "A real Republican," March 20; "For the Chronicle," March 27; "An Anecdote," March 31; "A plain Countryman," April 3; "Gratitude," *Salem Gazette*, April 1, which was reprinted in the *Chronicle*, April 3.

21. "A Voter," March 6, and "For the Chronicle," March 27, in *Independent Chronicle*.

22. "An Inhabitant of the Town of Hingham" and "We are assured," *Columbian Centinel*, March 5; "Town-Meeting," *Independent Chronicle*, April 7.

23. "Extract of a letter," March 14, and "General Election," April 9, in *Independent Chronicle*; and Morse, *Federalist Party*, 143.

24. *WSA*, 4: 363–65, quotations 364–65 passim.

25. Syrett, *Papers of Alexander Hamilton*, 16: 130–34, 210n3; and *WSA*, 4: 366–67, quotations 367.

26. *WSA*, 4: 368–69, quotations 369.

27. "Proclamation For a Day of Public Thanksgiving," issued Oct. 15, 1794 (Boston: Adams and Larkin, 1795; Evans 27280); Morse, *Federalist Party*, 126–31, 156–57; Ellis Sandoz, ed., *Political Sermons of the America Revolution* (Indianapolis: Liberty Press, 1991), 1217–34, quotation 1218. While editor Sandoz provides the text of Osgood's sermon and accurately depicts the reverend, he errs (p. 1218) in suggesting the issue was linked to a proclamation issued by President Washington in 1789.

28. Sandoz, *Political Sermons*, 1218; Morse, *Federalist Party*, 126, 129–30; Miller, *Federalist Era*, 155–59, Jefferson quotation 159; *WSA*, 4: 373.

29. Quotation from "A Friend," *Independent Chronicle*, April 3, 1795. In Boston, ten men received votes for governor in 1795. Vote totals calculated from Record Commissioners of the City of Boston, *A Volume [–the Thirty-first–] of the Records Relating to the Early History of Boston, Containing Boston Town Records from 1784 to 1796* (Boston: Municipal Printing Office, 1903), 392 (hereafter *BTR*, 31).

30. *WSA*, 4: 375–82, quotations 376, 377, 379, 382.

31. *WSA*, 4: 355, 365, 384.

32. *WSA*, 4: 388, 392, 394.

33. *WSA*, 4: 388, 387, 365.

34. *WSA*, 4: 397, 398–99, quotations 397, 399.

35. *WSA*, 4: 402–3, quotation 403; and *An Act for Regulating and Governing the Militia of the Commonwealth of Massachusetts* (Boston: I. Thomas and E. T. Andrews, 1794; Evans 27276), 6–7 (§2, §3).

36. See, e.g., *WSA*, 4: 359–60, 373, 377–78, 386, 393.

37. *WSA*, 4: 359–60, 371, 386–87, 401–2, quotations 371, 401; for additional Adams pronouncements to the General Court on the importance of expanded educational opportunities, see also 377, 378–79.

38. *WSA*, 4: 378–79, quotation 379; *Resolves of the General Court of the Commonwealth of Massachusetts . . . Begun . . . on Wednesday, the twenty-fifth Day of January, Anno Domini, 1797* (Boston: Young & Minns, 1797; Evans 32449), 65–67; Alexander J. Ingles, *The Rise of the High School in Massachusetts* (New York: Teachers College of Columbia University, 1911), 9–23, 149–53; George H. Martin, *The Evolution of the Massachusetts Public School System* (New York: D. Appleton, 1923), 118–22, 127–30.

39. "To his excellency Sam. Adams, &c." and "Political Catechism," Sept. 14, "'Moses Wallach," Sept. 17, in 1795 *Federal Orrery*; "A Picture," Sept. 16, "As insinuations," "A.B," and "Truth," Sept. 19, "Brief History" and "M. Wallach," Sept. 26, in 1795 *Columbian Centinel*; "Communications," *Independent Chronicle*, Sept. 14 and 17, 1795; Wells, *Life*, 3: 351.

40. Quotation from "Communications," *Columbian Centinel*, March 5, 1796. In the 1796 *Centinel*, see also: "A Farmer," March 5, "A Real Farmer," March 9, "One of the Grand Jury," March 12, "Harmony," March 23, 26, and 30, "A Farmer," March 30, "Truth" and "Communications," April 2; "Annual Election," *Independent Chronicle*, April 7, 1796; Elkins and McKitrick, *Age of Federalism*, 415–36; Morse, *Federalist Party*, 159–61; *BTR*, 31: 406–9; *DAB* s.v. "Sumner, Increase."

41. Quotations: "Extract," March 31, "Electioneering," March 7, "Hancock," March 21, "Sidney," March 3, 1796, in the *Independent Chronicle*; and "Truth" and "no Secophant," *Postscript* to *Independent Chronicle*, April 1, 1796. See also in the 1796 *Chronicle*: "For the Chronicle," Feb. 29, "Electioneering," "Another of the Grand Jury," and "A Countryman," March 14; "An Observer," "An Elector," and "A Farmer," March 17; "R.Y.," March 22; "Common Sense" and "From a Correspondent," March 24 and 28; "No Sycophant," March 28; "Communications,"

March 31; "The Voice of the People," April 1; "From a Correspondent," April 4; "A Customer," April 6; "Annual Election," April 7.

42. Quotation from "Truth," *Postscript* to *Independent Chronicle*, April 1, 1796; see also *Independent Chronicle*, "From a Correspondent," "The Voice of the People," and "no Secophant," April 1, 1796; *BTR*, 31: 392, 427; Morse, *Federalist Party*, 143, 161. Adams did fail in his effort to win election as a presidential elector for Thomas Jefferson in 1796, but then the other chief candidate for president was Samuel's cousin John, a native son of Massachusetts. See Elkins and McKitrick, *Age of Federalism*, 519.

43. Miller, *Federalist Era*, 196; and *WSA*, 4: 403–4, quotation 404.

EPILOGUE

1. James Sullivan, "A Biographical Sketch," *Independent Chronicle*, Oct. 10, 1803; Record Commissioners of the City of Boston, *A Report [–the Twenty-fourth–] of the Record Commissioners of the City of Boston, Containing Boston Births from A.D. 1700 to A.D. 1800* (Boston: Rockwell and Churchill, 1894), 333, 337, 339; Wells, *Life*, 3: 337, 366–67, 373–74; *WJA*, 9: 532; *WSA*, 4: 320–22, quotations 322.

2. Wells, *Life*, 3: 289–90, 331–37, 379–91; Forrest McDonald, *We the People: The Economic Origins of the Constitution* (Chicago: University of Chicago Press, 1958), 184–85n82, 200; Van Beck Hall, *Politics Without Parties: Massachusetts, 1780–1791* (Pittsburgh: University of Pittsburgh Press, 1972), 44n47; SAP, David Sewall to Samuel Adams, April 24, 1792.

3. *WSA*, 4: 408, 408–11, quotations 408, 410; SAP, John Adams to Samuel Adams, May 11, 1797; Julian P. Boyd et al. eds., *The Papers of Thomas Jefferson*, 36 vols. (Princeton, NJ: Princeton University Press, 1950–), 33: viii, 148–52, 213–14, 487–88, quotations 149, 487.

4. *WSA*, 4: 411; and *Four Letters: Being an Interesting Correspondence between Those Eminently Distinguished Characters, John Adams, Late President of the United States; and Samuel Adams, Late Governor of Massachusetts, on the Important Subject of Government* (Boston: Printed for Adams & Rhoades, 1802), quotations 6, 8, 26, 12, 22.

5. *Four Letters*, quotations 10, 25. Some of Adams's spellings and capitalizations were altered in the 1802 reprinting. See *WSA*, 4: 340–53.

6. *WSA*, 4: 412–13, quotations passim.

7. Wells, *Life*, 3: 373–74. Samuel Adams death notice, Oct. 3, and Sullivan, "A Biographical Sketch," Oct. 10, in 1803, *Independent Chronicle*; *ANB* s.v. "Sullivan, James."

8. William Bentley, *The Diary of William Bentley, D.D.: Pastor of the East Church Salem, Massachusetts*, ed. authority of the Essex Institute, 4 vols. (Salem, MA: The Essex Institute, 1905–14), 3: 49.

9. John Quincy Adams led the opposition to wearing crepe for the two men he described as "illustrious patriots." The issue, as he explained it, had nothing to

do with politics but with how the Senate's time should be used. See Charles F. Adams, ed., *Memoirs of John Quincy Adams, Comprising Portions of His Diary from 1795 to 1848*, 12 vols. (Philadelphia: J. B. Lippincott, 1874), 17: 268–69, quotation 269; "Mourning for Samuel Adams," Oct. 31, and "Ægis," Nov. 21, 1803, in *Independent Chronicle*; Thomas C. Amory, *Life of James Sullivan: with Selections from his Writings*, 2 vols. (Boston: Phillips, Sampson, and Company, 1859), 2: 110–11, quotation 111.

10. Wells, *Life*, 3: 374–77; Samuel A. Drake, *Old Landmarks and Historic Personages of Boston* (Boston: Roberts Brothers, 1876), 296–97; Robert Z. Finkelstein, "Merchant, Revolutionary, and Statesman: A Re-appraisal of the Life and Public Services of John Hancock, 1737–1793," Ph.D. diss., University of Massachusetts, 1981, 387–88; "Order of Procession," Oct. 14, and "Funeral Procession," Oct. 17, 1793, *Independent Chronicle*; Amory, *Life of James Sullivan*, 2: 110–11 quotations 111.

11. Adams quotations, *WSA*, 2: 163, 4: 290; and John to Abigail Adams, March 28, 1783, L. H. Butterfield et al., eds., *Adams Family Correspondence*, 9 vols. (Cambridge, MA: Harvard University Press, 1963–), 5: 107–12, and corresponding 112n10 where the editors note that John Adams also wrote directly to Samuel and presented the same general arguments he had written to Abigail. The editors further note that John, in yet a third letter on the subject, also asked William Lee to approach Samuel about compiling and publishing his writings and suggested that by doing so Samuel might document his central place in the American Revolution.

12. Quotation *WSA*, 3: 365.

13. Quotation *WSA*, 4: 305.

14. Quotations *WSA*, 4: 230, 226.

15. Quotation *WSA*, 3: 237.

16. Quotations *WSA*, 4: 357, 365.

BIBLIOGRAPHY

BIBLIOGRAPHIES AND SOURCE GUIDES

Brigham, Clarence S. *History and Bibliography of American Newspapers, 1690–1820.* 2 vols. Worcester, MA: American Antiquarian Society, 1947.

Bristol, Roger P. *Index to Supplement to Charles Evans' American Bibliography.* Charlottesville: University Press of Virginia, 1971.

———. *Supplement to Charles Evans' American Bibliography.* Charlottesville: University Press of Virginia, 1970.

Evans, Charles, Clifford K. Shipton, and Roger P. Bristol, eds. *American Bibliography: A Chronological Dictionary of All Books, Pamphlets and Periodical Publications Printed in the United States of America from the Genesis of Printing in 1639 Down to and Including the Year 1820.* 14 vols. New York: Peter Smith, 1941–1967; originally published 1903–1959.

Shipton, Clifford K., and James E. Mooney. *National Index of American Imprints through 1800: The Short-Title Evans.* 2 vols. Worcester, MA: American Antiquarian Society, 1969.

PRIMARY SOURCES (EXCLUDING NEWSPAPERS, MAGAZINES, AND BROADSIDES)

Adams, Abigail, John Adams, et al. *Adams Family Correspondence.* Ed. L. H. Butterfield et al. 9 vols. Cambridge, MA: Harvard University Press, 1963– .

Adams, John. *Diary and Autobiography of John Adams.* Ed. L. H. Butterfield. 4 vols. Cambridge, MA: Harvard University Press, 1961.

———. *Legal Papers of John Adams.* Ed. L. Kinvin Worth and Hiller B. Zobel. 3 vols. Cambridge, MA: Harvard University Press, 1965.

———. *Papers of John Adams*. Ed. Robert J. Taylor et al. 10 vols. Cambridge, MA: Harvard University Press, 1977– .

———. *The Works of John Adams, Second President of the United States: With a Life of the Author*. . . . Ed. Charles Francis Adams. 10 vols. Boston: Little, Brown, 1850–1856.

Adams, John, and Samuel Adams. *Four Letters: Being an Interesting Correspondence between Those Eminently Distinguished Characters, John Adams, Late President of the United States; and Samuel Adams, Late Governor of Massachusetts, on the Important Subject of Government*. Boston: Printed for Adams & Rhoades, 1802.

Adams, John, Samuel Adams, and James Warren. *Warren-Adams Letters: Being chiefly a correspondence among John Adams, Samuel Adams, and James Warren, vol. 1, 1743–1777*. Collections 72. Boston: Massachusetts Historical Society, 1917.

———. *Warren-Adams Letters: Being chiefly a correspondence among John Adams, Samuel Adams, and James Warren, vol. 2, 1778–1814*. Collections 73. Boston: Massachusetts Historical Society, 1925.

Adams, John Quincy. *Memoirs of John Quincy Adams, Comprising Portions of His Diary from 1795 to 1848*. Ed. Charles F. Adams. 12 vols. Philadelphia: J. B. Lippincott, 1874.

Adams, Samuel. *The Writings of Samuel Adams*. Ed. Harry A. Cushing. 4 vols. New York: G. P. Putman's Sons, 1904–1908.

Adams, Samuel, et al. *Samuel Adams Papers*. New York Public Library.

An Address to the Inhabitants of the Province of the Massachusetts-Bay in New England: More Especially, to the Inhabitants of Boston; By a Lover of His Country. Boston: Rogers and Fowle, 1747. (Evans 5900.)

Bailyn, Bernard, ed. *Pamphlets of the American Revolution 1750–1776*. 1 vol. Cambridge, MA: Harvard University Press, 1965– .

Barker, John. *The British in Boston: Being the Diary of Lieutenant John Barker of the King's Own Regiment from November 15, 1774, to May 31, 1776*. Ed. Elizabeth E. Dana. Cambridge, MA: Harvard University Press, 1924.

Barrington, Viscount, and Francis Bernard. *The Barrington-Bernard Correspondence and Illustrative Matter 1760–1770*. Ed. Edward Channing and Archibald C. Coolidge. Cambridge, MA: Harvard University Press, 1912.

Bentley, William, *The Diary of William Bentley, D.D.: Pastor of the East Church Salem, Massachusetts*. Ed. authority of the Essex Institute. 4 vols. Salem, MA: 1905–1914.

Bernard, Francis, et al. *Copies of Letters from Governor Bernard, &c, to the Earl of Hillsborough*. Boston: Edes and Gill, 1769. (Evans 11179.)

Bernard, Francis, Thomas Gage, and Samuel Hood. *Letters to the Ministry from Governor Bernard, General Gage, and Commodore Hood*. . . . Boston: Edes and Gill, 1769. (Evans 11176.)

Bolton, Thomas. *An Oration Delivered March Fifteenth 1775*. . . . Boston: n.p., 1775. (Evans 13840.)

Bonner, John. "[Map of] The Town of Boston in New England by John Bonner 1722." Boston: Francis Dewing, 1722. (Evans 2318.)

Boston Street Laying-Out Department. *A Record of the Streets, Alleys, Places, Etc. in the City of Boston*. Boston: City of Boston Printing Dept., 1910.

Boston Town Meeting. *Copies of Letters Sent to Great-Britain, by His Excellency Thomas Hutchinson, the Hon. Andrew Oliver, and Several Other Persons Born and Raised among Us*. Boston: Edes and Gill, 1773. (Evans 12818.)

———. *Two Plans for Forming the Town of Boston into an Incorporated City*. Boston: 1784. (Evans 18375.)

Bradford, Alan, ed. *Speeches of the Governors of Massachusetts 1765–1775: The Answers of the House of Representatives Thereto with Their Resolutions and Addresses for That Period; And Other Public Papers. . . .* Boston: Russell and Gardner, 1818.

Brissot de Warville, Jacques Pierre *New Travels in the United States of America*. London: J. S. Jordan, 1792.

Burnett, Edmund C., ed. *Letters of Members of the Continental Congress*. 8 vols. Washington, DC: Carnegie Institution of Washington, 1921–1936.

Chastellux, Marquis de. *Travels in North America in the Years 1780, 1781, and 1782*. Trans. and ed. Howard C. Rice Jr. 2 vols. Chapel Hill: University of North Carolina Press, 1963.

Commonwealth of Massachusetts. *An Act for Regulating and Governing the Militia of the Commonwealth of Massachusetts*. Boston: I. Thomas and E. T. Andrews, 1794. (Evans 27276.)

———. *An Address from the General Court, to the People of the Commonwealth of Massachusetts*. Boston: Adams and Nourse, 1786. (Evans 19781.)

———. *The Perpetual Laws of the Commonwealth of Massachusetts: From the Establishment of Its Constitution, in the Year 1780, to the End of the Year 1800; With the Constitutions of the United States of America and of the Commonwealth, Prefixed; To Which Is Added, an Appendix, Containing Acts and Clauses of Acts, from Laws of the Late Colony, Province and State of Massachusetts, Which Either Are Unrevised or Respect the Title of Real Estate*. Boston: I. Thomas and E. T. Andrews, 1801.

———. *Resolves of the General Court of the Commonwealth of Massachusetts . . . the Twenty-ninth Day of May, Anno Domini, 1793; and from thence . . . [to 15 January 1794]*. Boston: Adams and Larkin, 1794. (Evans 27289.)

———. *Resolves of the General Court of the Common-wealth of Massachusetts: Together with the Messages, &c. of His Excellency the Governor, to the Said Court: Begun and Held at Boston, in the County of Suffolk, on Wednesday, the twenty-Fifth Day of January, Anno Domini, 1797*. Boston: Young & Minns, 1797. (Evans 32449.)

Continental Congress. *Journal of the Proceedings of the Congress, Held at Philadelphia, September 5, 1774*. Philadelphia: William and Thomas Bradford, 1774. (Evans 13737.)

Cooke, Jacob E., ed. *The Federalist*. Middletown, CT: Wesleyan University Press, 1961.

Deane, Charles, ed. "Extracts from Dr. Belknap's Note-books." 92–98 in *Proceedings of the Massachusetts Historical Society 1875–1876*. Boston: Massachusetts Historical Society, 1876.

Dickerson, Oliver M., compiler. *Boston under Military Rule (1768–1769) as Revealed in A Journal of the Times*. Boston: Chapman & Grimes, 1936.

Dickinson, John. *The Writings of John Dickinson: Vol. 1, Political Writings, 1764–1774*. Ed. Paul L. Ford. Historical Society of Pennsylvania, *Memoirs*. Vol. 16. Philadelphia, 1895.

Dorr, Harbottle. *The Harbottle Dorr Collection of Annotated Massachusetts Newspapers 1765–1776*. Boston: Massachusetts Historical Society.

Drake, Francis S., ed.. *Tea Leaves: Being a Collection of Letters and Documents Relating to the Shipment of Tea to the American Colonies in the Year 1773, by the East India Company*. Boston: A. O. Crane, 1884.

Duane, William, ed., *Extracts from the Diary of Christopher Marshall* . . . Albany, NY: Joel Munsell, 1877.

Edes, Peter, ed. *Orations Delivered at the Request of the Inhabitants of the Town of Boston, to Commemorate the Evening of the Fifth of March, 1770*. . . . Boston: Peter Edes, 1785. (Evans 18997.)

Foner, Philip S., ed. *The Democratic-Republican Societies, 1790–1800: A Documentary Sourcebook of Constitutions, Addresses, Resolutions, and Toasts*. Westport, CT: Greenwood Press, 1976.

Force, Peter, ed. *American Archives: Consisting of a Collection of Authentick Records, State Papers, Debates, and Letters and Other Notices of Publick Affairs, the Whole Forming a Documentary History of the Origin and Progress of the North American Colonies; Of the Causes and Accomplishment of the American Revolution; And of the Constitution of Government for the United States, to the Final Ratification Thereof. In Six Series*. . . . 9 vols. Washington, DC: M. St. Clair Clarke and Peter Force, 1837–1853.

Ford, Worthington C., et al., eds. *Journals of the Continental Congress, 1774–1789*. 34 vols. Washington, DC: Government Printing Office, 1904–1937.

Franklin, Benjamin. *The Papers of Benjamin Franklin*. Ed. Leonard W. Labaree et al. 39 vols. New Haven, CT: Yale University Press, 1959– .

———. *Benjamin Franklin's Letters to the Press, 1758–1775*. Collected and ed. Verner W. Crane. Chapel Hill: University of North Carolina Press, 1950.

Gadsden, Christopher. *The Writings of Christopher Gadsden, 1746–1805*. Ed. Richard Walsh. Columbia: University of South Carolina Press, 1966.

Gage, Thomas, et al. *The Correspondence of General Thomas Gage* . . . *1763–1775*. Compiled and ed. Clarence E. Carter. 2 vols. New Haven, CT: Yale University Press, 1931–1933.

Galloway, Joseph. *The Examination of Joseph Galloway, Esq. by a Committee of the House of Commons*. Ed. Thomas Balch. Philadelphia: Seventy-Six Society, 1855.

———. *Historical and Political Reflections on the Rise and Progress of the American Rebellion*. London: G. Wilkie, 1780.

Giunta, Mary A., et al., eds. *The Emerging Nation: A Documentary History of the Foreign Relations of the United States under the Articles of Confederation, 1780–1789.* 3 vols. Washington, DC: National Historical Publications and Records Commission, 1996.

Handlin, Oscar, and Mary Handlin, eds. *The Popular Sources of Political Authority: Documents on the Massachusetts Constitution of 1780.* Cambridge, MA: Harvard University Press, 1966.

Harvard College Records. 2 vols. CSM, *Publications*, 15–16. Boston: Colonial Society of Massachusetts, 1925.

Hulton, Anne. *Letters of a Loyalist Lady: Being the Letters of Anne Hulton, Sister of Henry Hulton, Commissioner of Customs at Boston, 1767–1776.* Cambridge, MA: Harvard University Press, 1927.

Hutchinson, Thomas. *The History of the Colony and Providence of Massachusetts-Bay.* Ed. Lawrence S. Mayo. 3 vols. Cambridge, MA: Harvard University Press, 1936.

———. "Additions to Thomas Hutchinson's *History of Massachusetts Bay.*" In ed. Catherine B. Mayo, *American Antiquarian Society Proceedings* 59, part 1 (April, 1949): 11–74.

———. *The Diary and Letters of His Excellency Thomas Hutchinson, Esq.* Ed. Peter O. Hutchinson. 2 vols. London: S. Low, Marston, Searle & Rivington, 1883–1886.

Independency the Object of the Congress in America. London: John, Francis, and Charles Rivington, 1776.

Jefferson, Thomas. *The Papers of Thomas Jefferson.* Ed. Julian P. Boyd et al. 36 vols. Princeton, NJ: Princeton University Press, 1950– .

———. *The Writings of Thomas Jefferson.* Ed. Paul L. Ford. 10 vols. New York: G. P. Putnam's Sons, 1892–1899.

———. *The Writings of Thomas Jefferson: Monticello Edition.* Ed. Andrew A. Lipscomb and Albert E. Bergh. 20 vols. Washington, D.C.: The Thomas Jefferson Memorial Association, 1904–1905.

Jensen, Merrill, John P. Kaminski, et al., eds. *Documentary History of the Ratification of the Constitution.* 20 vols. Madison: State Historical Society of Wisconsin, 1976– .

Journal of the Convention for Framing a Constitution of Government for the State of Massachusetts Bay, from the Commencement of Their First Session, September 1, 1779, to the Close of Their Last Session, June 16, 1780. Boston: Dutton and Wentworth, 1832.

The Journals of Each Provincial Congress of Massachusetts in 1774 and 1775, and of the Committee of Safety . . . and other Documents, Illustrative of the Early History of the American Revolution. Boston: Dutton and Wentworth, 1838.

Journals of the House of Representatives of Massachusetts [for 1715–1779]. 55 vols. Boston: Massachusetts Historical Society, 1919–1990.

King, Rufus, et al. *The Life and Correspondence of Rufus King.* Ed. Charles R. King. 6 vols. New York: G. P. Putnam's Sons, 1894–1900.

Lee, R. H. *The Letters of Richard Henry Lee.* Ed. James C. Ballagh. 2 vols. New York: Macmillan, 1911–1914.

———. *Life of Arthur Lee, LL. D.* 2 vols. Boston: Wells and Lilly, 1829.

Letters on the American Revolution 1774–1776. Ed. Margaret W. Willard. Boston: Houghton Mifflin, 1925.

Locke, John. *Two Treatises of Government*. Ed. Peter Laslett. Revised ed. Cambridge: Cambridge University Press, 1970; originally published 1690.

Lovell, James. *An Oration Delivered April 2d, 1771*. Boston: Edes and Gill, 1771. (Evans 12099.)

Massachusetts General Court. *The Following Bill, Now Pending in the House of Representatives, Is Published by Their Order, for the Consideration of the Several Towns in This Province: A Bill Intituled, An Act for Granting Compensation to the Suffers, and of Free and General Pardon, Indemnity and Oblivion to the Offenders in the Late Times*. Boston: Green and Russell, 1766. (Evans 10382.)

More, Frank. *The Diary of the Revolution: A Centennial Volume*. Hartford, CT: J. B. Burr, 1876.

Morgan, Edmund S., ed. *Prologue to Revolution: Sources and Documents on the Stamp Act Crisis*. Chapel Hill: University of North Carolina Press, 1959.

Murdoch, David O., ed. *Rebellion in America: A Contemporary British Viewpoint, 1765–1783*. Santa Barbara, CA: Clio Books, 1979.

Murray, James. *Letters of James Murray, Loyalist*. Ed. Nina M. Tiffany and Susan Lesley. Boston: Privately printed, 1901.

Oliver, Peter. *Peter Oliver's Origin & Progress of the American Rebellion: A Tory View*. Ed. Douglas Adair and John A. Schutz. Rev. ed. Stanford, CA: Stanford University Press, 1967.

Paine, Robert Treat. *The Papers of Robert Treat Paine*. Ed. Stephen T. Riley and Edward W. Hanson. 3 vols. *Collections* 87–89. Boston: Massachusetts Historical Society, 1992–2005.

Pruitt, Bettye Hobbs, ed. *The Massachusetts Tax Valuation List of 1771*. Boston: G. K. Hall, 1978.

Record Commissioners of the City of Boston. *A Report [–the Eighteenth–] of the Record Commissioners of the City of Boston, Containing the Boston Town Records from 1770 through 1777*. Boston: Rockwell and Churchill, 1887.

———. *A Report [–the Eighth–] of the Record Commissioners of the City of Boston, Containing Boston Town Records from 1700 to 1728*. Boston: Rockwell and Churchill, 1883.

———. *A Report [–the Fourteenth–] of the Record Commissioners of the City of Boston, Containing the Boston Town Records from 1742 to 1757*. Boston: Rockwell and Churchill, 1885.

———. *A Report [–the Sixteenth–] of the Record Commissioners of the City of Boston, Containing the Boston Town Records from 1758 to 1769*. Boston: Rockwell and Churchill, 1886.

———. *A Report [–the Twelfth–] of the Record Commissioners of the City of Boston, Containing the Boston Town Records from 1729 to 1742*. Boston: Rockwell and Churchill, City Printers, 1885.

———. *A Report [–the Twenty-Fourth–] of the Record Commissioners of the City of Boston, Containing Boston Births from A.D. 1700 to A.D. 1800*. Boston: Rockwell and Churchill, 1894.

———. *A Report [–the Twenty-Sixth–] of the Record Commissioners of the City of Boston, Containing the Boston Town Records from 1778 to 1783*. Boston: Rockwell and Churchill, 1895.

———. *A Volume of Records [–the Thirtieth–] Relating to the Early History of Boston, Containing Boston Marriages from 1752 to 1809*. Boston: Municipal Printing Office, 1903.

———. *A Volume [–the Thirty-First–] of the Records Relating to the Early History of Boston, Containing Boston Town Records from 1784 to 1796*. Boston: Municipal Printing Office, 1903.

Rowe, John. *Letters and Diary of John Rowe, Boston Merchant, 1759–1762, 1764–1779*. Ed. Anne Rowe Cunningham. Boston: W. B. Clarke, 1903.

Rush, Benjamin. *The Autobiography of Benjamin Rush: His "Travels through Life," Together with His* Commonplace Book *for 1789–1813*. Ed. George W. Corner. Princeton, NJ: Princeton University Press, 1948.

———. *Letters of Benjamin Rush*. Ed. L. H. Butterfield. 2 vols. Princeton, NJ: Princeton University Press, 1951.

Serle, Ambrose. *The American Journal of Ambrose Serle, Secretary to Lord North, 1776–1778*. Ed. Edward H. Tatum Jr. San Marino, CA: The Huntington Library, 1940.

Smith, Paul H., and Ronald M. Gephart, eds. *Letters of Delegates to Congress, 1774–1789*. 26 vols. Washington, DC: Library of Congress, 1976–2000.

Sparks, Jared, ed. *The Diplomatic Correspondence of the American Revolution*. 12 vols. Boston: Hale and Gray & Bowen, 1829–1830.

Taylor, Robert J., ed. *Massachusetts, Colony to Commonwealth: Documents on the Formation of Its Constitution, 1775–1780*. Chapel Hill: University of North Carolina Press, 1961.

Town of Boston. *The Votes and Proceedings of the Freeholders and Other Inhabitants of the Town of Boston, in Town Meeting Assembled, According to Law*. Boston: Edes and Gill, 1772. (Evans 12332.)

The True Sentiments of America Contained in a Collection of Letters Sent from the House of Representatives of the Province of Massachusetts Bay to Several Persons of High Rank in This Kingdom: Together with Certain Papers Relating to a Supposed Libel on the Governor of That Province and a Dissertation on the Canon and Feudal Law. London: J. Almon, 1768.

Upton, L. F. S. "Proceedings of Ye Body Respecting the Tea." *William & Mary Quarterly* 22 (April 1965): 287–300.

Washington, George. *General Washington's Correspondence concerning the Society of the Cincinnati*. Ed. Edgar E. Hume. Baltimore: Johns Hopkins Press, 1941.

Weatherwise's Town and Country Almanack, for the Year of our Lord, 1782. Boston: Nathaniel Coverly and Robert Hodge, 1781.

Webster, Daniel. *The Writings and Speeches of Daniel Webster*. 18 vol. Boston: Little, Brown, 1903.

NEWSPAPERS AND MAGAZINES

American Apollo (Boston)
American Recorder (Charlestown, MA)
Boston Chronicle
Boston Evening-Post
Boston Gazette
Boston Magazine
Boston News-Letter
Boston Post-Boy
Boston Weekly Advertiser
Columbian Centinel (Boston)
Federal Orrery (Boston)
Herald of Freedom (Boston)
Independent Advertiser (Boston)
Independent Chronicle (Boston)
Independent Ledger (Boston)
Massachusetts Centinel (Boston)
Massachusetts Gazette (Boston)
Pennsylvania Journal (Philadelphia)
Pennsylvania Gazette (Philadelphia)
Salem Gazette

BROADSIDES (LISTED CHRONOLOGICALLY)

"The Merchants, and all others . . . are desired to meet at *Faneuil*-Hall To-Morrow . . . Boston, January 16, 1770 ." (Evans 11575.)

"At a Meeting of the Merchants & Traders . . . on the 23d January 1770." [Boston, 1770.] (Evans 11576.)

"By the Honorable Thomas Hutchinson . . . A Proclamation For a Public Thanksgiving . . . Given . . . the Thirtieth Day of October, 1770. . . . " Boston: Richard Draper, 1770. (Evans 11729.)

"By the Governor: A Proclamation for a Public Thanksgiving. . . . Given . . . the Twenty-third Day of October, 1771. . . . " Boston: Richard Draper, 1771. (Evans 12119.)

"Boston, March 30th, 1773. By Direction of the Committee of Correspondence for the Town of Boston, I now transmit to you an attached Copy of the Proceedings of said Town on the 8th Instant. . . ." Boston: Isaiah Thomas, 1773. (Evans 12688.)

"Boston, April 9, 1773. Sir, The Committee of Correspondence of this Town have received the following Intelligence. . . ." [Boston, 1773.] (Evans 12689.)

"Boston, June 22d, 1773. Sir, The Committee of Correspondence of the Town of *Boston* . . . again address you with a very important Discovery. . . ." [Boston, 1773.] (Evans 12690.)

"To the freemen of this and neighbouring towns: Gentlemen !–You re desired to meet at the Liberty-tree this day . . . Boston, 3 Nov. 1773. . . ." [Boston: Edes and Gill, 1773.] (Evans 12691.)

"In Consequence of a Conference . . . November 23, 1773." [Boston, 1773.] (Evans 12693.)

"FRIENDS! brethern! countrymen! That worst of all plagues, the detestable tea . . . . Boston, Nov. 29, 1773." [Boston: Edes and Gill, 1773.] (Evans 12774.)

"Boston, May 12, 1774. Gentlemen, By the latest advices from London we learn that an Act has been passed by the British Parliament for blocking up the Harbour of Boston. . . ." [Boston, 1774.] (Evans 42562.)

"By the Governor. A Proclamation. Whereas a Number of Persons unlawfully assembled at *Cambridge* . . . calling themselves a Provincial Congress . . . [10 November] 1774 . . . ." Boston: M. Draper, 1774. (Evans 13414.)

"By his Excellency the Honorable Thomas Gage . . . A Proclamation. Whereas the infatuated multitudes . . . have at length proceeded to avowed rebellion . . . [12 June] 1775. . . . " [Boston, 1775.] (Evans, 14184.)

"Commonwealth of Massachusetts. By his Excellency James Bowdoin . . . A Proclamation, For the Encouragement of Piety, Virtue, Education and Manners, and for the Suppression of Vice . . . Given . . . the eighth Day of June, A. B. 1785. . . ." [Boston, 1785.] (Evans 19085.)

"Notification . . . to meet at Faneuil Hall on Wednesday 26th Octob. inst. at Ten o'clock. . . Boston, Octob. 22, 1785." [Boston, 1785.] (Evans 18937.)

"Commonwealth of Massachusetts. By his Excellency James Bowdoin . . . A Proclamation. Whereas information has been given to the Supreme Executive Council of this Commonwealth, that . . a large course of people . . . assembled at the Court-House in Northampton, many of whom were armed . . . Encouragement of Piety, Virtue, Education and Manners, and for the Suppression of Vice . . . Given . . . this second day of September [1786]. . . ." Boston: Adams and Nourse, 1786. (Evans 19789.)

"Commonwealth of Massachusetts. By his Excellency James Bowdoin . . . A Proclamation, Whereas . . . it appears highly expedient that the General Court should be convened on an earlier day . . . Given . . . this thirteenth day of September [1786]. . . ." Boston: Adams and Nourse, 1786. (Evans 19788.)

"Proclamation For a Day of Public Thanksgiving," issued Oct. 15, 1794. Boston: Adams and Larkin, 1795. (Evans 27280.)

SECONDARY SOURCES

Adams, Willi Paul. *The First American Constitutions: Republican Ideology and the Making of the State Constitutions in the Revolutionary Era.* Expanded ed. Lanham, MD: Rowman & Littlefield, 2001.

Akers, Charles W. *The Divine Politician: Samuel Cooper and the American Revolution in Boston*. Boston: Northeastern University Press, 1982.

Alden, John R. *General Gage in America: Being Principally a History of His Role in the American Revolution*. Baton Rouge: Louisiana State University Press, 1948.

———. *Stephen Sayer: American Revolutionary Adventurer*. Baton Rouge: Louisiana State University Press, 1983.

Alexander, John K. "'A Year . . . Famed in the Annals of History': Philadelphia in 1776." In pp. 5–39, ed. Dennis Clark, *Philadelphia 1776–2076: A Three Hundred Year View*. Port Washington, NY: Kennikat Press, 1975.

———. "Reflections on Political Deference in Early America: Let's Meet at the Graveside." *Early American Studies* 3 (Fall 2005): 383–401.

———. *Render Them Submissive: Responses to Poverty in Philadelphia, 1760–1800*. Amherst: University of Massachusetts Press, 1980.

Alexander, John K. *Samuel Adams: America's Revolutionary Politician*. Lanham, MD: Rowman & Littlefield Publishers, 2002.

———. *The Selling of the Constitutional Convention of 1787: A History of News Coverage*. Madison: Madison House, 1990.

Ammerman, David. *In the Common Cause: American Response to the Coercive Acts of 1774*. Charlottesville: University Press of Virginia, 1974.

Amory, Thomas C. *Life of James Sullivan: With Selections from His Writings*. 2 vols. Boston: Phillips, Sampson, and Company, 1859.

Anderson, George P. "Ebenezer Mackintosh: Stamp Act Rioter and Patriot." In pp. 15–64, *Transactions*, 1924–1926. Boston: Colonial Society of Massachusetts, 1927.

———. "Pascal Paoli, an Inspiration to the Sons of Liberty." In pp. 180–210, *Transactions* 1924–1926. Boston: Colonial Society of Massachusetts, 1927.

Avery, Thomas C. *Life of James Sullivan: with Selections from his Writings*. 2 vols. Boston: Phillips, Sampson and Company, 1859.

Bailyn, Bernard. *The Ideological Origins of the American Revolution*. Cambridge, MA: Harvard University Press, 1967.

———. *The Ordeal of Thomas Hutchinson*. Cambridge, MA: Harvard University Press, 1974.

Bailey, Thomas A. *A Diplomatic History of the American People*. 8th ed. New York: Appleton-Century Crofts, 1969.

Bancroft, George. *History of the United States, from the Discovery of the American Continent*. 10 vols. Boston: Little, Brown, 1834–1874.

Barrow, Thomas C. *Trade and Empire: The British Customs Service in Colonial America, 1660–1775*. Cambridge, MA: Harvard University Press, 1967.

Beach, Stewart. *Samuel Adams: The Fateful Years, 1764–1776*. New York: Dodd, Mean & Company, 1965.

Bemis, Samuel F. *The Diplomacy of the American Revolution*. Rev. ed. Bloomington: Indiana University Press, 1957.

Blake, John B. *Public Health in the Town of Boston, 1630–1822.* Cambridge, MA: Harvard University Press, 1959.

Boyd, Julian P. "Silas Deane: Death by a Kindly Teacher of Treason?" *William and Mary Quarterly* 26 (April, July, and October 1959): 165–87, 319–42, 515–50.

Bradley, Patricia. *Slavery, Propaganda and the American Revolution.* Jackson: University Press of Mississippi, 1998.

Breen, T. H. *The Marketplace of Revolution: How Consumer Politics Shaped American Independence.* New York: Oxford University Press, 2004.

Brennan, Ellen E. "James Otis: Recreant and Patriot." *New England Quarterly* 12 (Dec. 1939): 691–725.

———. *Plural Office-Holding in Massachusetts, 1760–1780: Its Relation to the "Separation" of Departments of Government.* Chapel Hill: University of North Carolina Press, 1945.

Bridenbaugh, Carl. *Cities in Revolt: Urban Life in America, 1743–1776.* Rev. ed. New York: Oxford University Press, 1971.

———. *Cities in the Wilderness: The First Century of Urban Life in America, 1625–1742,* rev. ed. New York: Oxford University Press, 1971.

———. *Mitre and Sceptre: Transatlantic Faiths, Ideas, Personalities, and Politics 1689–1775.* New York: Oxford University Press, 1962.

Brigham, Clarence S. *Paul Revere's Engravings.* 2nd ed. rev. New York: Atheneum, 1969.

Brink, Robert J. "'Immorality brought to Light': An Overview of Massachusetts Colonial Court Records." *Law in Colonial Massachusetts, 1630–1800.* In pp. 471–97, *Publications* 62. Boston: Colonial Society of Massachusetts, 1984.

Brown, E. Francis. *Joseph Hawley: Colonial Radical.* New York: AMS Press, 1966.

Brown, Richard D. *Revolutionary Politics in Massachusetts: The Boston Committee of Correspondence and the Towns, 1772–1774.* Cambridge, MA: Harvard University Press, 1970.

Bullion, John L. *A Great and Necessary Measure: George Grenville and the Genesis of the Stamp Act, 1763–1765.* Columbia: University of Missouri Press, 1982.

Bullock, Steven C. *Revolutionary Brotherhood: Freemasonry and the Transformation of the American Social Order, 1730–1840.* Chapel Hill: University of North Carolina Press, 1996.

Burnett, Edmund C. *The Continental Congress.* New York: Macmillan, 1941.

Butterfield, L. H. "Rush and Washington." In ed. L. H. Butterfield, *Letters of Benjamin Rush,* 2 vols. Princeton, NJ: Princeton University Press, 1951. Vol. 2: 1197–1208.

Calhoon, Robert M. *The Loyalists in Revolutionary America.* New York: Harcourt Brace Jovanovich, 1965.

Calloway, Colin G. *The American Revolution in Indian Country: Crisis and Diversity in Native American Communities.* New York: Cambridge University Press, 1995.

Carr, Jacqueline B. *After the Siege: A Social History of Boston, 1775–1800.* Boston, MA: Northeastern University Press, 2005.

Cary, John. *Joseph Warren: Physician, Politician, Patriot.* Urbana: University of Illinois Press, 1961.

Chaffin, Robert J. "The Townshend Acts of 1767." *William & Mary Quarterly* 27 (January 1970): 90–121.

Charles, Joseph. *The Origins of the American Party System.* New York: Harper & Row, 1961.

Christie, Ian R., and Benjamin W. Labaree. *Empire or Independence, 1760–1776: A British-American Dialogue on the Coming of the American Revolution.* New York: W. W. Norton, 1976.

Copeland, David A. *Debating the Issues in Colonial Newspapers: Primary Documents on Events of the Period.* Westport, CT: Greenwood Press, 2000.

Cott, Nancy F. *The Bonds of Womanhood: "Women's Sphere" in New England, 1780–1835.* 2nd ed. New Haven, CT: Yale University Press, 1997.

Cunliffe, Marcus. *George Washington: Man and Monument.* London: Collins, 1959.

Daniels, Bruce C., ed. *Power and Status: Officeholding in Colonial America.* Middletown, CT: Wesleyan University Press, 1986.

Davidson, Philip. *Propaganda and the American Revolution.* Chapel Hill: University of North Carolina Press, 1941.

Davis, Andrew M. *Currency and Banking in the Province of Massachusetts-Bay.* 2 vols. New York: Macmillan, 1900–1901.

Day, Aland, and Katherine Day. "Another Look at the Boston 'Causus.'" *Journal of American Studies* 5 (April 1971): 19–42.

DeConde, Alexander. *Entangling Alliance: Politics & Diplomacy under George Washington.* Durham, NC: Duke University Press, 1958.

Dickerson, Oliver M. *The Navigation Acts and the American Revolution.* Philadelphia: University of Pennsylvania Press, 1951.

Douglass, Elisha P. *Rebels and Democrats: The Struggle for Equal Political Rights and Majority Rule during the American Revolution.* Chapel Hill: University of North Carolina Press, 1955.

Drake, Samuel A. *Old Landmarks and Historic Personages of Boston.* Boston: Roberts Brothers, 1876.

Du Bois, W. E. Burghardt. *The Suppression of the African Slave-Trade to the United States of America, 1638–1870.* New York: Russel & Russel, 1896.

Edes, Henry H. "Memoir of Dr. Thomas Young, 1731–1777." In pp. 2–50, *Transactions 1906–1907.* Boston: Colonial Society of Massachusetts, 1910.

Egerton, Douglas R. *Death of Liberty: African Americans and Revolutionary America.* New York: Oxford University Press, 2009.

Elkins, Stanley, and Eric McKitrick. *The Age of Federalism.* New York: Oxford University Press, 1993.

Elliot, John. *A Biographical Dictionary: Containing a Brief Account of the First Settlers, and Other Eminent Characters among the Magistrates, Ministers, Literary and Worthy Men, in New-England.* Boston: Edward Oliver, 1809.

Feer, Robert A. *Shays's Rebellion.* New York: Garland Publishing, 1988.

Ferguson, E. James. *The Power of the Purse: A History of American Public Finance, 1776–1790.* Chapel Hill: University of North Carolina Press, 1961.

Ferling, John. *Almost A Miracle: The American Victory in the War of Independence.* New York: Oxford University Press, 2007.

———. *The Ascent of George Washington: The Hidden Political Genius of an American Icon.* New York: Oxford University Press, 2009.

Finkelstein, Robert Z. "Merchant, Revolutionary, and Statesman: A Re-appraisal of the Life and Public Services of John Hancock, 1737–1793." Ph.D. diss., University of Massachusetts, 1981.

Fitzpatrick, John C. *George Washington Himself: A Common-Sense Biography Written from His Manuscripts.* Indianapolis: Bobbs-Merrill, 1933.

Foner, Eric. *Tom Paine and Revolutionary America.* New York: Oxford University Press, 1976.

Fowler, William M. Jr. *Samuel Adams: Radical Puritan.* New York: Longman, 1997.

Freeman, Douglas S. *George Washington: A Biography; Leader of the Revolution.* New York: Charles Scribner's Sons, 1951.

Freeman, Samuel. *The Town Officer.* 5th ed. Boston: Thomas & Andrews, 1802.

Freiberg, Malcolm. "Thomas Hutchinson and the Province Currency." *New England Quarterly* 30 (June 1957): 190–208.

Frothingham, Richard. *Life and Times of Joseph Warren.* Boston: Little, Brown, 1865.

———. "Tea-Party Anniversary." In pp. 156–82, *Proceedings* 1873–1875. Boston: Massachusetts Historical Society, 1885.

———. "The Sam Adams Regiments in the Town of Boston." *Atlantic Monthly* 9 (June 1862): 701–20; 10 (August 1862): 179–203; 12 (November 1863): 595–616.

Gipson, Lawrence H. *The British Empire before the American Revolution.* 15 vols. Caldwell, ID; and New York: The Caxton Printers and Knopf, 1936–1970.

———. *The Coming of the Revolution, 1763–1775.* New York: Harper & Row, 1954.

Gordon, William. *The History of the Rise, Progress, and Establishment, of the Independence of the United Sates of America.* 4 vols. London: Charles Dilly, 1788.

Goss, Elbridge H. *The Life of Colonel Paul Revere.* 2 vols. Boston: Howard W. Spurr Publisher, 1891.

Greven, Jr., Philip J. *Four Generations: Population, Land, and Family in Colonial Andover, Massachusetts.* Ithaca, NY: Cornell University Press, 1970.

Hall, Van Beck. *Politics Without Parties: Massachusetts, 1780–1791.* Pittsburgh: University of Pittsburgh Press, 1972.

Hamm, Margherita A. *Builders of the Republic: Some Great Americans Who Have Aided in the Making of the Nation.* New York: James Pott & Company, 1902.

Harding, Samuel B. *The Contest over the Ratification of the Federal Constitution on the State of Massachusetts.* Cambridge, MA: Harvard University Press, 1896.

Harlow, Ralph V. *Samuel Adams: Promoter of the American Revolution; A Study in Psychology and Politics.* New York: Henry Holt and Company, 1923.

Hazen, Charles D. *Contemporary Opinion of the French Revolution.* Baltimore: Johns Hopkins Press, 1897.

Henderson, H. James. *Party Politics in the Continental Congress.* New York: McGraw-Hill, 1974.

Hoerder, Dirk. *Crowd Action in Revolutionary Massachusetts, 1765–1780.* New York: Academic Press, 1977.

Holmes, Pauline. *A Tercentenary History of the Boston Public Latin School, 1635–1935.* Cambridge, MA: Harvard University Press, 1935.

Holton, Woody. *Forced Founders: Indians, Debtors, Slaves, and the Making of the American Revolution in Virginia.* Chapel Hill: University of North Carolina Press, 1999.

Hosmer, James K. *Samuel Adams.* Boston: Houghton, Mufflin, 1885.

———. *Samuel Adams, The Man of the Town-Meeting.* Baltimore: Johns Hopkins University, 1884.

Ingles, Alexander J. *The Rise of the High School in Massachusetts.* New York: Teachers College of Columbia University, 1911.

Jensen, Merrill. *The Articles of Confederation: An Interpretation of the Social-Constitutional History of the American Revolution, 1774–1781.* With additional prefaces. Madison: University of Wisconsin Press, 1970.

Kerber, Linda K. *Women of the Republic: Intellect and Ideology in Revolutionary America.* With added preface. New York: W. W. Norton, 1986.

Kershaw, Gordon E. *James Bowdoin: Patriot and Man of the Enlightenment.* East Syracuse, NY: Salina Press, 1976.

Kidder, Frederic. *History of the Boston Massacre, March 5, 1770.* Albany: Munsell, 1870.

Knollenberg, Bernard. *Washington and the Revolution: A Reappraisal; Gates, Conway, and the Continental Congress.* New York: Macmillan, 1940.

Kurland, Philip B., and Ralph Lerner, eds. *The Founders' Constitution.* 5 vols. Chicago: University of Chicago Press, 1987.

Labaree, Benjamin W. *The Boston Tea Party.* New York: Oxford University Press, 1964.

Labaree, Leonard W. *Royal Government in America: A Study of the British Colonial System before 1783.* New Haven, CT: Yale University Press, 1930.

Lax, John, and William Pencak. "The Knowles Riot and the Crisis of the 1740s in Massachusetts." *Perspectives in American History* 10 (1976): 163–214.

Lee, Richard Henry. *Life of Arthur Lee, LL. D, Joint Commissioner of the United States to the Court of France, and Sole Commissioner to the Courts of Spain and Prussia, during the Revolutionary War: With His Political and Literary Correspondence and His Papers on Diplomatic and Political Subjects, and the Affairs of the United States during the Same Period.* 2 vols. Boston: Wells and Lilly, 1829.

Lemisch, Jesse. "Jack Tar in the Streets: Merchant Seamen in the Politics of Revolutionary America." *William & Mary Quarterly* 25 (July 1968): 371–407.

———. *Jack Tar vs. John Bull: The Role of New York's Seamen in Precipitating the Revolution.* New York: Garland Publishing, 1998.

———. "New York's Petitions and Resolves of December 1765: Liberals vs. Radicals." *New-York Historical Society Quarterly* 49 (October 1965): 313–26.

———. "Radical Plot in Boston (1770): A Study in the Use of Evidence." *Harvard Law Review* 84 (Dec. 1970): 485–504.

Libby, Orin G. *The Geographical Distribution of the Vote of the Thirteen States on the Federal Constitution, 1787–8*. Madison: University of Wisconsin, 1894.

Lord, Donald C., and Robert M. Calhoon. "The Removal of the Massachusetts General Court from Boston, 1769-1772." *Journal of American History* 55 (March 1969): 735–55.

Lossing, B. J. *The Pictorial Field-Book of the Revolution: Or, Illustrations, by Pen and Pencil, of the History, Biography, Scenery, Relics, and Traditions of the War for Independence*. 2 vols. New York: Harper Brothers, 1851–1852.

Lynd, Staughton. "The Mechanics in New York Politics, 1774–1788." *Labor History* 5 (Fall 1964): 225–46.

Magra, Christopher. *The Fisherman's Cause: Atlantic Commerce and Maritime Dimensions of the American Revolution*. Cambridge: Cambridge University Press, 2009.

Maier, Pauline. *American Scripture: Making the Declaration of Independence*. New York: Knopf, 1977.

———. *From Resistance to Revolution: Colonial Radicals and the Development of American Opposition to Britain, 1765–1776*. New York: Knopf, 1972.

———. "John Wilkes and American Disillusionment with Britain." *William & Mary Quarterly* 20 (July 1963): 373–95.

———. *The Old Revolutionaries: Political Lives in the Age of Samuel Adams*. New York: W. W. Norton 1990.

———. "Revolutionary Violence and the Relevance of History." *Journal of Interdisciplinary History* 2 (Summer 1971): 119–35.

Main, Jackson T. *The Antifederalists: Critics of the Constitution, 1781–1788*. Chapel Hill: University of North Carolina Press, 1961.

———. *Political Parties before the Constitution*. Chapel Hill: University of North Carolina Press, 1973.

Martin, George H. *The Evolution of the Massachusetts Public School System*. New York: D. Appleton, 1923.

Mass, David E. "The Massachusetts Loyalists and the Problem of Amnesty, 1775–1790." In pp. 65–74, ed. Robert C. Calhoon, Timothy M. Barnes, and George A. Rawlyk, *Loyalists and Community in North America*. Westport, CT: Greenwood Press, 1994.

Matthews, Albert. "The Solemn League and Covenant, 1774." In pp. 103–22, *Transactions* 1915–1916. Boston: Colonial Society of Massachusetts, 1917.

McCusker, John J. *Money and Exchange in Europe and America, 1600–1775: A Handbook*. Chapel Hill: University of North Carolina Press, 1978.

McDonald, Forrest. *We the People: The Economic Origins of the Constitution*. Chicago: University of Chicago Press, 1958.

McIlwain, Charles H. *The American Revolution: A Constitutional Interpretation*. New York: Macmillan, 1924.

McLaughlin, Andrew C. "American History and American Democracy." *American Historical Review* 20 (Jan. 1915): 255–76.

Menand, Catherine S. "The Things That Were Caesar's: Tax Collecting in Eighteenth-Century Boston." *Massachusetts Historical Review* 1 (1999): 49–77.

Metzger, Charles H. *The Quebec Act: A Primary Cause of the American Revolution.* New York: The United States Catholic Historical Society, 1936.

Miller, John C. *The Federalist Era, 1789–1801.* New York: Harper & Row, 1960.

———. *Origins of the American Revolution.* Rev. ed. Stanford, CA: Stanford University Press, 1959.

———. *Sam Adams: Pioneer in Propaganda.* Boston: Little, Brown, 1936.

Miner, Ward L. *William Goddard, Newspaperman.* Durham, NC: Duke University Press, 1962.

Moore, George H. *Notes on the History of Slavery in Massachusetts.* New York: D. Appleton, 1866.

Morgan, Edmund S. *The Birth of the Republic, 1763–89.* 3rd ed. Chicago: University of Chicago Press, 1992.

———. "Colonial Ideals of Parliamentary Power, 1764–1766." *William & Mary Quarterly* 5 (July 1948): 311–41.

Morgan, Edmund S., and Helen M. Morgan. *The Stamp Act Crisis: Prologue to Revolution.* Rev. ed. Chapel Hill: University of North Carolina Press, 1995.

Morison, Samuel E. *Three Centuries of Harvard, 1636–1936.* Cambridge, MA: Harvard University Press, 1936.

———. "The Struggle over the Adoption of the Constitution of Massachusetts, 1780." In pp. 369–81, *Proceedings 1916–1917.* Boston: Massachusetts Historical Society, 1917.

Morse, Anson E. *The Federalist Party in Massachusetts to the Year 1800.* Princeton, NJ: The University Press, 1909.

Murphy, Avon J. "The Royal American Magazine." In pp. 343–48, ed. Edward E. Chielens, *American Literary Magazines: The Eighteenth and Nineteenth Centuries.* New York: Greenwood Press, 1986.

Nash, Gary B. *The Urban Crucible: Social Change, Political Consciousness, and the Origins of the American Revolution.* Cambridge, MA: Harvard University Press, 1979.

Nicolson, Colin. *The "Infamous Govener": Francis Bernard and the Origins of the American Revolution.* Boston: Northeastern University Press, 2001.

Norton, Mary Beth. *Liberty's Daughters: The Revolutionary Experience of American Women, 1750–1800.* With added preface. Ithaca, NY: Cornell University Press, 1996.

Olton, Charles S. *Artisans for Independence: Philadelphia Mechanics and the American Revolution.* Syracuse, NY: Syracuse University Press, 1975.

Osgood, Russell K. "John Clark, Esq., Justice of the Peace, 1667–1728." In pp. 107–51, ed. Daniel R. Coquillette, *Law in Colonial Massachusetts, 1630–1800, CSM, Publications,* 62. Boston: Colonial Society of Massachusetts, 1984.

Peckham, Howard H. *The War for American Independence: A Military History.* Chicago: University of Chicago Press, 1958.

Perlmann, Joel, and Dennis Shirley. "When Did New England Women Acquire Literacy?" *William & Mary Quarterly* 48 (Jan. 1991): 50–67.

Peters, Jr., Ronald M. *The Massachusetts Constitution of 1780: A Social Compact.* Amherst: University of Massachusetts Press, 1978.

Pinkney, Helen R. *Christopher Gore: Federalist of Massachusetts, 1758–1827.* Waltham, MA: Gore Place Society, 1969.

Potts, Louis W. *Arthur Lee: A Virtuous Revolutionary.* Baton Rouge: Louisiana State University Press, 1981.

Puls, Mark. *Samuel Adams: Father of the American Revolution.* New York: Palgrave Macmillan, 2006.

Quincy, Josiah. *Memoir of the Life of Josiah Quincy Jun. of Massachusetts.* Boston: Cummings, Hilliard, 1825.

———. *A Municipal History of the Town and City of Boston, during Two Centuries: From September 17, 1630, to September 17, 1830.* Boston: C. C. Little and J. Brown, 1852.

Randall, Henry S. *The Life of Thomas Jefferson.* 3 vols. New York: Derby & Jackson, 1858.

Reid, John P. *In a Rebellious Spirit: The Argument of Facts, the Liberty Riot, and the Coming of the American Revolution.* University Park: Pennsylvania State University Press, 1979.

Rosie, Jonathan G. *The Politics of Command in the American Revolution.* Syracuse, NY: Syracuse University Press, 1975.

Sandoz, Ellis, ed. *Political Sermons of the America Revolution.* Indianapolis: Liberty Press, 1991.

Savelle, Max, and Darold D. Wax. *A History of Colonial America.* 3rd ed. Hinsdale, IL: Dryden Press, 1973.

Schlesinger, Arthur M. Review of *Boston under Military Rule. New England Quarterly* 10 (June 1937): 386–87.

———. *The Colonial Merchants and the American Revolution.* New York: Columbia University, 1918.

———. *Prelude to Independence: The Newspaper War on Britain, 1764–1776.* New York: Knopf, 1958.

Schutz, John A. *Legislators of the Massachusetts General Court, 1691–1780: A Biographical Dictionary.* Boston: Northeastern University Press, 1997.

Seccombe, Matthew. "From Revolution to Republic: The Later Political Career of Samuel Adams, 1774–1803." Ph.D. diss., Yale University, 1978.

Seybolt, Robert F. *The Town Officials of Colonial Boston, 1634–1775.* Cambridge, MA: Harvard University Press, 1939.

Shipton, Clifford K., et al. *Sibley's Harvard Graduates: Biographies of Those Who Attended Harvard University.* 18 vols. Cambridge, MA: Harvard University Press, 1933–1975.

Shurtleff, Nathaniel B. *A Topographical and Historical Description of Boston.* 3rd ed. Boston: Rockwell and Churchill, 1891.

Shy, John. *Toward Lexington: The Role of the British Army in the Coming of the American Revolution.* Princeton, NJ: Princeton University Press, 1965.

Smith, Barbara Clark. "Food Rioters and the American Revolution." *William & Mary Quarterly* 51 (January 1994): 3–38.

Smith, Rogers M. "Constructing American National Identity: Strategies of the Federalists." In pp. 19–40, ed. Doron Ben-Atar and Barbara B. Oberg, *Federalists Reconsidered.* Charlottesville: University Press of Virginia, 1998.

Spector, Margaret M. *The America Department of the British Government, 1768–1782.* New York: Columbia University Press, 1940.

Stark, James H. *The Loyalists of Massachusetts and the Other Side of the American Revolution.* Boston: James H. Stark, 1910.

Stewart, John H. *A Documentary Survey of the French Revolution.* New York: Macmillan, 1951.

Stinchcombe, William C. *The American Revolution and the French Alliance.* Syracuse, NY: Syracuse University Press, 1969.

Stoll, Ira. *Samuel Adams: A Life.* New York: Free Press, 2008.

Sullivan, James. "A Biographical Sketch." *Independent Chronicle* (10 October 1803).

Syrett, Harold C., ed. *The Papers of Alexander Hamilton.* 26 vols. New York: Columbia University Press, 1961–1987.

Szatmary, David P. *Shays' Rebellion: The Making of an Agrarian Insurrection.* Amherst: University of Massachusetts Press, 1980.

Taylor, Robert J. *Western Massachusetts in the Revolution.* Providence: Brown University Press, 1954.

Teaford, Jon C. *The Municipal Revolution in America: Origins of Modern Urban Government, 1650–1825.* Chicago: University of Chicago Press, 1975.

Thomas, Charles M. *American Neutrality in 1793: A Study in Cabinet Government.* New York: Columbia University Press, 1931.

Thomas, Isaiah. *The History of Printing in America with a Biography of Printers & an Account of Newspapers.* Ed. Marcus A. McCorison. New York: Weathervane Books, 1970; originally published 1810.

Thomas, Peter D. G. *Tea Party to Independence: The Third Phase of the American Revolution, 1773–1776.* Oxford: Oxford University Press, 1991.

———. *The Townshend Duties Crisis: The Second Phase of the American Revolution, 1767–1773.* Oxford: Oxford University Press, 1987.

Trecothick, James. *The Life of Elbridge Gerry.* 2 vols. Boston: Wells and Lilly, 1828–1829.

Tudor, William. *The Life of James Otis of Massachusetts: Containing Also, Notices of Some Contemporary Characters and Events, from 1760 to 1775.* Boston: Wells and Lilly, 1823.

Van Tyne, Claude H. *The Loyalists in the American Revolution.* New York: Macmillan, 1902.

Walett, Francis G. "Governor Bernard's Undoing: An Earlier Hutchinson Letters Affair." *New England Quarterly* 38 (June 1965): 217–26.

Ward, Andrew H. "Notes on Ante-Revolutionary Currency and Politics." *New England Historical and Genealogical Register* 14 (July 1860): 261–64.

Warden, G. B. *Boston, 1689–1776*. Boston: Little, Brown, 1970.

———. "The Caucus and Democracy in Colonial Boston." *New England Quarterly* 43 (March 1970): 19–45.

Warren, Charles. "Samuel Adams and the Sans Souci Club in 1785." In pp. 318–44, *Proceedings* 1926–1927. Boston: Massachusetts Historical Society, 1927.

Warren, Mercy Otis. *History of the Rise, Progress and Termination of the American Revolution Interspersed with Biographical, Political and Moral Observations*. Ed. Lester H. Cohen. 2 vols. Indianapolis: Liberty Classics, 1989. Originally published 1805.

Waters, John J., Jr. *The Otis Family in Provincial and Revolutionary Massachusetts*. Chapel Hill: University of North Carolina Press, 1968.

Wells, William V. *The Life and Public Services of Samuel Adams*. 3 vols. Boston: Little, Brown, 1865.

Whitehill, Walter M. *Boston: A Topographical History*. 2nd ed. Cambridge, MA: Harvard University Press, 1969

Williams, N. Neville, comp. and ed. *The Eighteen-Century Constitution, 1688–1815: Documents and Commentary*. Cambridge: Cambridge University Press, 1960.

Winsor, Justin, ed. *Narrative and Critical History of America*. 8 vols. Boston: Houghton, Mifflin, 1884–1889.

Young, Alfred F. *Liberty Tree: Ordinary People and the American Revolution*. New York: New York University Press, 2006.

———. *The Shoemaker and the Tea Party: Memory and the American Revolution*. Boston: Beacon Press, 1999.

Zagarri, Rosemarie. *Revolutionary Backlash: Women and Politics in the Early American Republic*. Philadelphia: University of Pennsylvania Press, 2007.

Zobel, Hiller B. *The Boston Massacre*. New York: W. W. Norton, 1970.

WEB SITES

A list of some Harvard honorary degrees is found at http://www.commencement.harvard.edu/background/hon_deg.html.

The Biographical Dictionary of the United States Congress is found at http://bioguide.congress.gov/scripts/biodisplay.pl?index=A000045.

The Eleventh Edition of the Encyclopedia Britannica is found at http://encyclopedia.jrank.org.

INDEX

Within entries: Samuel Adams is abbreviated SA; Massachusetts is abbreviated MA.

ABOUT THE AUTHOR

John K. Alexander is professor of history and distinguished teaching professor at the University of Cincinnati. An associate editor of *American National Biography* (1999), he is also the author of *Render Them Submissive: Responses to Poverty in Philadelphia, 1760–1800* (1980), *The Selling of the Constitutional Convention of 1787: A History of News Coverage* (1990), and *Samuel Adams: America's Revolutionary Politician* (2002).